# VAN COU VER ISM

The experience of Vancouver is one
of urban life on the water.

To Gabor —

Enjoy this
fascinating story
of our city's
journey.

Larry

Beasley

# VAN
# COU
# VER
# ISM

**LARRY
BEASLEY**

WITH A
PROLOGUE BY
FRANCES BULA

on
point
PRESS

27 26 25 24 23 22 21 20 19   5 4 3 2 1

Printed in Canada on paper that is processed chlorine- and acid-free, with vegetable-based inks.

Cataloguing data is available from Library and Archives Canada.

978-0-7748-9031-1 (paperback)
978-0-7748-9032-8 (PDF)

Canadä

UBC Press gratefully acknowledges the financial support for our publishing program of the Government of Canada (through the Canada Book Fund), the Canada Council for the Arts, and the British Columbia Arts Council. We also acknowledge support from Furthermore, a program of the J.M. Kaplan Fund.

Printed and bound in Canada by Friesens
Text design: Jessica Sullivan
Set in GothicNo13, Alright, and Guardian
  by Artegraphica Design Co. Ltd.
Copy editor: Deborah Kerr
Proofreader: Judith Earnshaw
Indexer: Cheryl Lemmens

UBC Press
The University of British Columbia
2029 West Mall
Vancouver, BC V6T 1Z2
www.ubcpress.ca

*To all the men and women of Vancouver who*

*gave their hearts and souls, their energy and*

*creativity, to the reinvention of our beloved*

*city – all are colleagues, all are friends, all*

*are personal inspirations to me.*

# CONTENTS

# PREFACE

**VANCOUVER IS A PLACE.** If you are reading this book, you probably know that Vancouver is a delightful city on the west coast of Canada, just north of the American border. There it sits in magnificent geographic splendour – part of "super, natural British Columbia" – presenting itself with pride and distinction, and offering, hopefully, a touch of Canadian hospitality to all who visit.

*Vancouverism is an idea.* It carries the name of this place because it is an idea about this place – about how to reinvent Vancouver from a perfectly typical mid-twentieth-century North American city of little relevance outside its home province to a vanguard city of world stature and world importance. Among urbanists, the concept of Vancouverism has become well known, maybe not ubiquitous but certainly popular, as shorthand for the type of contemporary city building that integrates strategies for livability, sustainability, and competitiveness with gracious beauty. Contrary to what some might say, Vancouverism is not a simple idea. Indeed, it will take all the pages in this book to tell you about it. Nor was bringing it into being a simple task. I know, because I was at the centre of the action for the duration. In fact, it took hundreds of creative and courageous people over a generation to make it real. It is my honour to tell their story.

The phenomenon of Vancouverism is also one with deep precedents, resulting from a fascinating unfolding of events that prompted a group of reformers to wrest local government from the old-timers, thus setting us off on our adventure. I am not a historian, so my good friend and colleague, the distinguished journalist Frances Bula, sets the stage for *Vancouverism* in her prologue to this book.

For a city as beautiful as Vancouver, it is perhaps fitting that this chronicle be a visual one as much as a tale told in words. To that end, I have gathered a collection of my own photographs to accompany the text. They offer a vivid tableau of the city as well as an illustrative guide to Vancouverism in action. A few essential images by others round out the mix. Of course, one visit to Vancouver will be worth all my pictures put together, so with this book I proffer a standing invitation for you to come see what we have achieved.

Read this account and visit this place, and you will find a song in your heart. I hope you enjoy it. For that, ultimately, is what this story is really all about – it is about a song to be delicately insinuated into every heart.

**LARRY BEASLEY**
**VANCOUVER, AUGUST 2018**

Modern Vancouver has found the sweet spot between intensity, livability, and sustainability.

# PROLOGUE

**P.1** Vancouver feels like a settled if modest town in 1912, as this view of Coal Harbour illustrates.

FRANCES BULA

# THE BEGINNINGS

**NOTHING ABOUT VANCOUVER** in its early decades gave any hint that this city, of all the new settlements created on the American and Canadian territory of the North American continent, would embrace a style of urbanism that differed so completely from the rest.

It was an unlikely candidate at the start, being part of the last wave of city building on the continent. Places like New York and Montreal, founded in the 1600s, had incorporated European city-building patterns. Even midwestern cities, such as Chicago or Winnipeg, developed central neighbourhoods that were populated with housing forms from an older, denser style of urban organization. But Vancouver was a city of the North American west. Its white settlers didn't arrive until almost three hundred years after the first eastern cities were built. When they did show up, they created cities that were shaped – or rather, allowed to spread out endlessly – by what was seen as infinite open space around them.

The puzzle then is how Vancouver came to be the North American city that most embraced an idea of urban living that was so at odds with its origins. How did this one-time cottagers' paradise turn into a city whose forest of slender, glassy towers is marvelled at, admired, examined, emulated – and also sometimes criticized – by many in the region and around the globe? How did it go from valuing the right of every man (yes, man) to have his own small castle in a garden to one where people were willing to trade individual gardens for a fifteenth-storey apartment that was surrounded by lavish, but shared, public spaces: seawalls, parks, community centres, playgrounds? How did it manage to break away from the lockhold of the vaunted American Dream – the single-family house in a neighbourhood of same – to one where its downtown has more than 100,000 people living in a variety of neighbourhoods that have one thing in common: they are almost completely made up of apartment buildings?

In the pages that follow, Larry Beasley tells this story in all its complexity. He argues that what became known as Vancouverism is not just about the shaping of buildings. He and other city historians make a convincing case that the approach to neighbourhood building that emerged in the late 1980s and early 1990s was a far more nuanced phenomenon, both in its origins and in the scope of what Vancouverism encompasses.

As a journalist who watched this unfold and as a long-time Vancouverite, I didn't initially understand it. I simply took it for granted that the former industrial land around the downtown peninsula would be developed as new residential neighbourhoods. This seemed the obvious, even pre-ordained solution, especially since the city's dense West End had been transformed from a problem child in the 1960s (too dense, too crime-ridden, too traffic-congested) to a highly desirable and even family-friendly place by the late 1980s. Later, as I learned more about how other cities were changing – or not – as they moved through the post-industrial era, and as I covered the resistance to even the mildest forms of densification elsewhere in the region (townhouses, in one notable example), I began to understand how unusual Vancouver's path was when it came to developing these new downtown areas.

My recent research has confirmed for me the unique path of Vancouver's development – a path that began long before its post–Expo 86 building boom or before anyone even thought of the word "Vancouverism." It became clear to me that the city's dramatic changes sprang from a distinctive blend of circumstances that went back decades. Those circumstances ensured that Vancouver, in spite of some similarities to Seattle, Portland, San Francisco, and Los Angeles, or to Calgary, Edmonton, Regina, and Winnipeg, ultimately developed in a quite different way from these other western cities.

The Vancouverism that emerged at the end of the twentieth century is the result of the intersection of several factors, which I'll detail later. Pure geography is one. The downtown core sits on a peninsula that is bordered by ocean waters and the mountains, with the bonus of the city's largest park at its tip. This drove an economic equation that favoured more density in the residential areas of downtown. Geography also influenced the form of Vancouver apartments. The views that were so spectacular and attractive produced a public and architectural predilection for buildings that were tall and thin, rather than low and blocky (the standard 1920s apartment in North America everywhere) or tall and wide (like Toronto's concrete buildings of the 1950s on). Second, Vancouver's colonial connections resulted in a British-style approach to planning, where planners and their scientific schemes for city development were a powerful force. Besides actually hiring a long line of planners from England, Vancouver politicians, inheriting British attitudes to city governance, also gave them far more leeway than American bureaucrats enjoyed. And, though citizens occasionally rebelled against the plans of bureaucrats, the residual faith in good government was strong enough that the later move toward new residential neighbourhoods downtown, densification, and Vancouverism sparked little negative public commentary, political squabbling, or business backlash in its heyday. In fact, as I often tell journalism or planning classes, what was striking during the 1990s and 2000s in Vancouver was the remarkable degree of consensus among planners, politicians, developers, and the public about the arrival of Vancouverism. A few critics noted that the new developments had a disturbing suburban aesthetic. There was an early dust-up about condos being marketed in Hong Kong before being put on sale in Vancouver, with fears that the city would be loaded with empty investment condos. But those were small blips in what was generally viewed as the addition of an interesting new element to the city. It's certainly a world away from the divisiveness, anger, and suspicion that now permeates the city when it comes to housing and development as a combination of stressors has broken down the consensus.

## EARLY DAYS: UTOPIAN DREAM VERSUS HARDSCRABBLE REALITY

Vancouver began this way. Many early white settlers viewed it as an almost utopian future city of single-family houses, free from the crowded apartment buildings and tenements of the Old World. Even duplexes were uncommon. It was the anti-Liverpool, the anti-Montreal. A 1928 study showed that 72 percent of Vancouver houses were detached, single-family homes. In what was then the separate municipality of South Vancouver (now the easterly part of town), the figure stood at 75 percent.[1]

"The opportunity of owning a home in the city distinguished Vancouver from its east Canadian counterparts," wrote Deryck Holdsworth in a 1986 article that vividly described the early life and housing dreams of the people who flooded into the city (see Figure P.1). "Although there were shacks and cabins congested near the sawmills and the railroad round-house, Vancouver has no close counterpart to St. Henri in Montreal or to the back-to-back housing that was still being built in Britain," Holdsworth noted. "What was only a dream in such older cities seemed a reality in the 'fresh' new city on the Pacific."[2]

Of course, that vision was always a little distorted. The boosters put on their blinders to avoid seeing the parts of Vancouver that didn't fit the single-family dream. It was true that workers who had stable employment often managed to buy a small house, something that might not have been possible in an eastern city. But many others didn't have stable jobs or, for one reason or another, they ended up on the bottom rungs of the employment, housing, and social ladders. They lived in rented apartments, tenements, self-built hovels – or nothing at all.

Historian Jill Wade paints this alternative picture in her book *Houses for All*. As she points out, in 1911 Vancouver, "between one-quarter and one-third of suburban wage earners rented accommodation, and between 10 and 15 percent of the population lived in crowded, substandard housing in Chinatown and in the immigrant quarters of the east end."[3] The shores of Burrard Inlet and False Creek were lined with shacks.

Apartments became even more popular as the 1920s wore on, and renters began to dominate the demographic makeup of the city. The West End, in particular, became characterized by dense living and an unusually high proportion of tenants.

### THE WEST END: A PRECURSOR

For more than half a century, urban historians have been mesmerized by the post–Second World War era and the enormous popularity of suburban living. But the reality is that Canadian and American cities also saw another kind of urban transformation throughout the early twentieth century: the development of dense apartment zones in and near central cores.

Many of us have images of happy suburban families in their single-family homes burned into our memory banks, the result of literally thousands of articles, books, pictures, and public talks that emphasize the dominance of the single-family house in North American cities. But that doesn't tell the whole story.

A tremendously energetic boom in apartment building occurred in North America before the Second World War, one that few writers have documented with the same thoroughness as the urban researchers who wrote about the suburbs. As a result, many of us who think we know the history of cities and urban development have a misleading view of the relative proportions or popularity of housing types. Seattle, for example, only two hundred kilometres south of Vancouver, experienced a sustained wave of apartment building from 1900 to the start of the Second World War. Eventually, blocks and blocks of apartments covered Capitol Hill and some of the lower parts of the Queen Anne district – two areas close to the downtown business core.

As Diana James documents in her book *Shared Walls: Seattle Apartment Buildings, 1900–1939,* boomtowns such as Seattle saw big influxes of working people who came to make their fortune – or at least get jobs in construction.[4] At first, they lived in hotels, boarding houses, and lodging houses. Soon that wasn't enough, so these boomtowns started to include apartments. Blocks of flats often sat next to single-family homes, duplexes, lodging houses, or shops. In many cities, zoning did not really come into play until the end of the 1920s. Nor did agencies such as the National Housing Association in the United States, which lobbied aggressively to ban multi-family housing as a danger to sacred middle-class values and lifestyles, really pick up speed until the 1920s. As a result, the apartments in these burgeoning towns weren't segregated into separate zones away from single-family residences. That made them even more appealing to people who aspired to a middle-class life and, eventually, a detached house but who hadn't yet reached the necessary income level.

In Vancouver, the West End was the prime apartment zone from fairly early on. As Beasley emphasizes, this area, in its several iterations over the years, has usually been the forerunner of alternatives to the single-home status quo. It is key to understanding the city's move toward Vancouverism, with its embrace of density and its focus on how to create livability amid that. A unique neighbourhood, the West End would eventually help foster a form of architecture and lifestyle that were not the norm in any other North American city. That form and lifestyle were the precursors to Vancouverism.

What was so special about the West End? First of all, to invoke the real estate mantra, it was location, location, location. The West End is immediately adjacent to the central business district, as many North American apartment zones were and are. But it also has a spectacular setting. Stanley Park – Vancouver's version of Central Park – lies just to the northwest, a lush forest blessed with pathways, wildlife, and ocean beaches. It is an oasis of tranquility and green in the heart of the city. The park's creation was also encouraged by the real estate developers of the 1880s. In those days, the West End was home to many rich families, and developers wanted to ensure that its property values remained high and that no polluting industry or low-income neighbourhoods sprang up nearby.

a West End Street. Vancouver B.C.

As well, the West End has water on another two sides: Burrard Inlet on the north and English Bay on the southwest. Looking north across that water, often dotted today with sailboats, kayaks, motorboats, and freighters, residents with a clear sightline also look up to the blue-green Coast Mountains that frame one edge of the city, beyond which extend other ranges endlessly into the distance.

In the beginning, the West End apartment district didn't seem that different from its equivalents in many other cities. In fact, it had started out as an enclave for the wealthy, with large mansions occupying many prime sites (see Figure P.2). The well-off remained there until the Canadian Pacific Railway began to develop a new subdivision, called Shaughnessy, in 1907. Well-heeled West End residents who wanted to get away from the increasing industrial pollution and the unnerving proximity to poor people migrated to Shaughnessy through the 1910s and 1920s. Others moved out to the North Shore and West Point Grey as bridges and better transportation made those areas more feasible for commuting.[5] These were early examples of the flight to the suburbs.

**P.2** The West End, on Vancouver's downtown peninsula, has been the crucible for early experimentation in housing forms. This view from around 1910 shows how it looked in its initial incarnation as a gracious neighbourhood of lovely mansions.

**P.3** As the first residents of the West End moved out, many homes were converted to rooming houses, but the area also saw infill of handsome buildings called mansion flats, an early type of middle-class apartment living. This 1912 photograph shows a mansion flat at the left, below the pyramidal roof of the old Hotel Vancouver.

The mansions were gradually converted into boarding houses, and empty lots were developed, as some had been earlier, into apartment buildings, some of them shabbier, others in the grand red-brick style that was popular in many North American towns (see Figure P.3). Like other cities, Vancouver installed tram lines to serve neighbourhoods close to the downtown. That helped accelerate denser development in the West End. And that, in turn, changed the demographics of the area. As rooming houses and apartments became the dominant forms of accommodation, the numbers of children began to drop, whereas those of young people (twenty-five to thirty-five) and older people (over fifty-five) expanded. The district became increasingly attractive to retirees, as well as singles and couples who worked downtown.

The West End's second big transformation took place during its exceptional period of apartment building after the Second World War (see Figure P.4). There was an enormous wave of development between 1955 and 1972, as 181 high-rises went up. By the end of that wave, which was terminated by a new council that put a lid on high-rise development in response to resident opposition, the West End was studded with a new kind of apartment tower – tall rectangles whose orientation favoured views of the mountains to the north, of Stanley Park, or of the ocean on both sides of the downtown peninsula. They weren't as needle-shaped as they would be by the end of the century. But some were point towers that were slim, with small floorplates, and a higher proportion of corner suites

**P.4** Another big transformation of the West End after the Second World War was the widespread development of tall towers so that residents could enjoy the beautiful views of the mountains and water. In this 1969 shot, we see them popping up within the established neighbourhood.

**P.5** Ultimately, the West End built out incrementally as a forest of towers, creating a unique neighbourhood for North America, with location, density, and amenities. Here the transformation is complete. ▶

than the usual apartment building. They were less intrusive on the skyline than "slab" apartment buildings that were often as wide or wider than they were tall. And most of the others not as slim as point towers were no longer big square or rectangular blocks. Instead, many had a lozenge-shaped footprint, oriented so that the narrow end was all that was visible to those looking across English Bay to the downtown. Observers would see what looked like a forest of slim towers in the tight cluster of West End buildings, reinforcing the image of Vancouver as a place that was not dominated by the heavy slab towers of other cities.

Of course, other North American downtowns built high-rises during the 1950s and 1960s, as the construction standstill of the war came to a close. But none rivalled the kind of development and density that characterized the West End. To this day, Seattle's Capitol Hill and Queen Anne neighbourhoods have retained their grand early-twentieth-century apartment buildings, but there are no towers to speak of. Portland's apartment district near downtown, around the Park blocks and west of there, is lined with majestic apartments that are now almost a hundred years old. But there are few towers.

One kind of tall tower that did briefly proliferate in American downtowns, which would eventually give high-rise living a dubious reputation, was that favoured by public-housing designers. In cities from Toronto to St. Louis to Chicago, new public-housing (or social-housing, in Canada) projects were built according to the utopian ideas of European architects. Their promoters believed that social problems could be eliminated by razing inner-city slums,

which usually consisted of rowhouses or tenement buildings, and erecting towers that sat in splendid isolation in the middle of parks.

Vancouver's West End, in contrast, became a forest of high-rises strictly
through the efforts of private landowners (see Figure P.5). In part, this was
because it was not "blighted," the term applied by local politicians and developers to areas where the poor lived. Instead, what landowners realized during the
post-war move to greater prosperity was that middle-class people were willing to
pay, and pay handsomely, for the privilege of living near an enormous park and
the central business district (and its thousands of jobs), with views of the mountains and ocean. A young urban-studies student, Ann McAfee, who eventually
became a co-director of planning for Vancouver, highlighted the transformation
in her 1962 master's thesis that studied apartment development in the West End
between 1955 and 1965.[6] She noted that the number of apartment dwellers sky-

rocketed from twenty-five thousand in 1961 to nearly fifty thousand in 1966, a huge change for such a short time. This relatively small area, a square mile, came to account for 40 percent of all apartments in Vancouver.[7]

Even more importantly, it was evident to McAfee and to apartment builders that, in addition to the expected low- and middle-income renters, a group of very well-off households wanted to live downtown and were willing to pay for prime spots. McAfee's analysis showed that people who worked in finance clustered next to Stanley Park and the beaches at English Bay. People in the service industries, on the other hand, were consigned to the interior of the peninsula or the somewhat grubby section near the port.

Other North American cities did see increases in downtown apartment living during the 1950s. Again, this trend is usually ignored by urban historians, who typically focus on the boom in suburban living. But some researchers did speculate that a certain category of people seemed to be rejecting suburbia in favour of downtown living. In New York and Toronto, they noted that middle-class families, usually without children, preferred the amenities of the central city.

As early as 1939, housing scholar Homer Hoyt, who developed the influential "sector model" that explained the way cities grow through development of particular specialist sectors, stated that upper-class households often saw having an expensive apartment near the business centre (something that reduced commuting time) as a prestige marker.[8] And Theodore Anderson, who specialized in the spatial analysis of cities, wrote that "in the late forties and early fifties it became fashionable to move to the suburbs ... Now, living in a luxury uptown apartment seems to be the thing to boast about."[9] Surveys of the 1950s and 1960s seemed to demonstrate that the return from suburbia was a reality. Basing his claim on a survey by *Fortune* magazine, noted urbanist W.H. Whyte commented, "There are definite signs of a small but significant move back from suburbia ... Of the returnees the largest single group are upper-income people whose children have married, and while such people have long been the best prospects for luxury apartment houses, there are indications that their numbers can increase much more than the real estate men expect."[10]

As it turned out, these statements may have had more to do with hype than with reality. Or they were truer for eastern cities than for Vancouver. McAfee, who did extensive surveys of West End residents, found little proof that they were refugees from the suburbs. She discovered that "most of the West End apartment dwellers [had] never lived outside the central city."[11] But they were early indicators of a new urban phenomenon: people who had not returned from the suburbs simply because they had never moved there in the first place.

Wherever these residents were coming from, their numbers were large enough that landowners soon discovered how to profit from the influx. They could make more money from their properties by tearing down existing buildings and constructing much taller ones with more units for this new, affluent group. This was one essential element in the West End's transformation.

But its exceptional turn toward density was more than just the result of a demographic or cultural shift. A certain attitude from city officials was also required to unleash the development. And before the civic policies could achieve liftoff, a particular pattern of landownership was necessary, as was a group of developers and architects who understood the new technologies available for high-rises and were willing to use them.

## PLANNERS AS CITY BUILDERS

A key piece in the puzzle of the West End's development was the recommendations and policy changes that came from planners and City bureaucrats. One of Vancouver's first planners was an Englishman named Thomas Mawson, who is little remembered. But Robert Walsh, an American architectural-studies professor who has intensively researched Vancouverism, complete with a seven-hundred-plus-page doctoral thesis, points out that Mawson brought an idea of what the city should feel like. This later became a principle of Vancouverism. For Mawson, who worked for the park board just prior to the First World War, when Vancouver was still a somewhat ramshackle city with heavy industry flanking its downtown, the beginning point of every plan was what it would feel like from the perspective of the average person who walked through it: an "experiential" approach. The word "experiential," which will appear later in this book to explain a fundamental principle that Vancouver planners relied on during the 1980s and 1990s, wasn't one that Mawson would have used. But he embodied that approach, calling for something he defined as "the lovable city."

As a result, his plans emphasized elements such as trees, parks (including a grand design for the land set aside for Stanley Park), and public plazas. He may have been the first to imagine a seawall, the seaside walkway that now extends around most of downtown Vancouver and False Creek.

Next came the man whom many see as the city's first real planner, the American Harland Bartholomew. He worked in Vancouver during two distinct periods:

the 1920s, which culminated in a 1928 master plan, and the late 1940s. The first is often referred to as the foundation for the careful distribution of parks and schools across the city – a move that helped create and entrench a neighbourhood feel everywhere – but his later work was just as important.

During the late 1940s, Bartholomew grappled with change – with the rise of the automobile and the move of industry out of downtown. He proposed two solutions that epitomize the contradictory nature of Vancouver planning. One was a "radical increase of the residential density of the West End" – which aimed to reduce the need for cars.[12] To achieve this, he suggested eliminating the six-storey height limit. He also recommended a spacing system so that the towers wouldn't be too close together – a principle that undergirds development in Vancouver today.

His second recommendation was for a freeway system that could shuttle cars more speedily into the central business district. Making some concession to the East Side residents who would be affected, he suggested that the freeway should follow the existing rail lines and then cross the industrial False Creek Flats, rather than snaking through Chinatown and Strathcona. Ultimately, of course, city hall backed the more high-impact route, long after Bartholomew had departed the scene.

Both of his recommendations were later pursued by Vancouver's administrators. One would succeed, one would fail. Both were undertaken by Gerald Sutton Brown, the first director of city planning and later city manager – a legendary, or infamous, figure, depending on one's point of view. He oversaw the city from 1965 to 1972, presiding over the West End redevelopment boom and the plans for a freeway through downtown. Originally from Lancashire, Sutton Brown demonstrated a couple of approaches to city planning that would become important in Vancouver. He believed that increasing density would solve some housing problems. And he believed in "self-contained, self-sufficient neighbourhoods, with an explicit intention of fostering a sense of community."[13] In other words, he saw planning as being about more than just buildings. However, he was not a believer in community engagement. Because of that, he was well aligned with the Non-Partisan Association (NPA), the dominant political party of the day. The NPA's technocratic approach to city government, which Sutton Brown exemplified, would ultimately lead to his downfall and that of the party he served.

Sutton Brown wouldn't have been such an important figure if he had gone to an American city instead of a Canadian one. In many sectors, Canada has zigzagged between its British heritage and the trends set by its American neighbour. In city management, Canadian towns were more inclined to the British approach, which favoured a strong bureaucracy. As a result, Vancouver city managers and planners developed more comprehensive approaches than their US counterparts and carried them out without being overly affected by the swings of here-today-gone-tomorrow politicians, as happened in the United States. They had a stronger hand with developers, when they chose. So, someone like Sutton Brown, fresh from Europe and its familiarity with new high-rise concrete construction and accustomed to being a benevolent planning dictator, could wield enormous influence.

One of Sutton Brown's early changes was to the West End, where he essentially did what Bartholomew had recommended by increasing allowable building heights with a new zoning by-law that included regulations to shape the taller buildings.

But zoning alone can't produce change. Sometimes a city changes its zoning, but local resistance to new projects is so intense that very few are approved. However, the ownership pattern of the West End meant that the likelihood of neighbourhood resistance was slim. Much of the property still belonged to those who had decamped to other parts of the city in earlier decades. Renter-advocacy groups were non-existent, and few residents owned their flats. In fact, it was almost impossible to do so. The idea that apartments could be owned via strata arrangements was still a couple of decades off. A few buildings were owned by residents through a cooperative mechanism, but the vast majority of the lodging houses and apartments belonged to a wide variety of local investors. As a group, these absentee landlords were more favourable to wholesale redevelopment than resident property owners would have been.

There were a few big players, such as Block Brothers Realty. Its research paved the way for the smaller landowners to follow. Block Brothers predicted that two big population bulges would be coming through Vancouver and that they would produce more renters in the groups who were most likely to opt for living in the West End. That made for an appealing scenario. As well, West End rents were higher than the Vancouver average.[14] Thus, the West End had the highest land values in the region.[15] But, with the density that was allowed, the apartments had the lowest land costs per dwelling unit.[16] Beasley notes that the resulting stock of apartment buildings was architecturally mundane and generally undistinguished. But developers aimed for the middle-income market, pinned their hopes on location, and enticed future renters with attractions such as views, recreation in Stanley Park, and convenience to the downtown.

There was another driver to the change in the West End: technology. Concrete construction was starting to emerge, particularly in Europe, as a way of escaping old models of building shape and height that had been dictated by the use of either wood or brick. Obviously, concrete buildings could go higher than either of those two and it was more fire resistant than wood. It allowed for something beyond squares and rectangles. And it meant that floor thickness could be reduced because the floor of one suite was the ceiling of another. All of these factors would be important as developers considered the cost-benefit ratio of going higher and trying to attract wealthier tenants.

But concrete-construction costs were two and a half to three times higher per square foot than those for wood construction. That extra cost is worthwhile only if the housing that it produces can be sold or rented at a high enough price to justify it. As well, concrete slab towers – buildings that were not just tall but as wide as a block in some cases – are cheaper than slim point towers. But developers can rent more units in point towers for a higher price because of the additional views. Again, the willingness of people to pay the higher price drove the shape. That favoured the erection of point towers in the West End, a place with views in every direction, in a way that didn't happen in, for example, Toronto or Montreal.

The point tower also developed because people rebelled against the slab towers that were common in other cities. One such building, Ocean Towers, the extremely wide apartment built in 1959 that stretches along Morton Avenue (near Beach Avenue) west of the high street, Denman, generated a robust backlash because it obstructed ocean views for blocks behind it. Planners changed the regulations to stymie that kind of design.

Finally, a fifth key element in the post-war transformation of the West End was the group of architects who designed its buildings. Sometimes European-trained, they created structures and streetscapes specifically for Vancouver's setting, coming up with forms, such as thin towers and even occasionally townhouses, and approaches to urban design that would repeat themselves several times as the city developed.

Looking at what occurred in the West End during the post-war boom, one could conclude that the ideas of Vancouverism percolated up from the ground, almost on their own, called forth by something about the city that kept leading people to certain ideas about how to shape its buildings and neighbourhoods.

Wilf Buttjes was one of the many architects who designed new-style towers for West End developers in the 1960s. He built one of the first clusters of high-rises, starting with the Silhouette next to Stanley Park in 1961 – a twenty-storey tower whose tapered edges gave it a slim, point-like appearance from certain angles. Buttjes, who had trained in Germany and was comfortable with concrete construction methods, had designed more than twenty towers in the West End by 1968. He was interviewed for the *Vancouver Sun* on what to do about the neighbourhood.[17] His suggestion? Put townhouses at the street level of the West End's interior blocks and then have a twenty-six-storey tower rise out of their midst – an approach that foreshadows a core feature of Vancouverism. And, like many who came after him, he argued that architects should not concentrate solely on buildings. They needed to design for people on the ground, with the aim of creating a pleasant environment at street level.

## TEAM, THE DEMISE OF THE FREEWAY, AND A NEW START

Given Vancouver's history of urban density through to the 1970s, one might naturally expect that the next generation of builders would emulate the model supplied by the West End. In fact, the opposite happened. Beasley argues that though the West End was a strong reference, it was cited as both an example to follow and one to shun. Throughout the 1960s and 1970s, it was perceived as a problem neighbourhood. A newspaper article from 1973 quotes councillors worrying aloud that False Creek South – the first former industrial neighbourhood in the central city that would get redeveloped in the 1970s – would become, horror of horrors, a new West End, which was seen as dirty, crowded, and traffic-congested. It was occupied by lower-income people, including sex workers who met their customers on the street. The customers added to the traffic problems. And many people saw the proliferation of towers not as a new urban utopia, but as a sign that developers were out of control. As a result, anti-development fever blossomed in the city.

In the late 1960s, many Vancouverites turned to a new political party called The Electors' Action Movement, almost always shortened to TEAM. Although TEAM is frequently portrayed as a progressive force that overthrew the technocrats at city hall, killed the freeway proposal, and returned the city to its citizens, the reality is more complicated. Under Mayor Art Phillips, TEAM did start laying the foundation for Vancouverism and brought in a revolutionary chief planner who oversaw the work. But it also incurred some changes that were antithetical to urban density.

What was TEAM? Vancouver had been dominated for decades by a centre-right party, the NPA, which had been launched in 1937 to counter what was seen as the menace of a potential socialist party. Dominated by businessmen, developers, and other subcategories of real estate boosters, the NPA ran Vancouver like a corporation, aiming for maximum efficiency. It supported the densification of the West End because property owners and developers wanted it to. Over the years, the NPA embraced various plans to build a freeway that would enable commuters to cut through eastern Vancouver and along the downtown waterfront to a third crossing of Burrard Inlet.

That freeway would have been a radical change. And its demise was a turning point for Vancouver because, as we'll see later, the realization that the city would never be bisected by a freeway galvanized politicians and planners to think about how to adapt. Ultimately, the death of the freeway led to the consensus view that if downtown office and shop workers couldn't have an easy commute from the suburbs, they would need to be provided with housing in the central city.

But that philosophy would be developed later. What came first was the fight over the freeway. In the early 1960s, Vancouver had a robust street grid and no actual freeway within its borders. A regional freeway skirted its eastern edge – the Trans-Canada Highway – but it narrowed to a regular road with congestion-producing traffic lights in its short Vancouver portion before continuing over the Second Narrows Bridge and cutting through the communities on the North Shore.

Neighbourhoods, which had accepted a lot of change under the long, benevolent dictatorship of the NPA and its bureaucrats, began to rebel. TEAM, formed in 1968, was both a result of that rebellion and a driver of it.

It wasn't just the prospect of a massive freeway running through the downtown that pushed the public into a revolt. It was also the fact that the freeway project was intertwined with a grand plan to remove some of the so-called slums of the east side, particularly in Chinatown and the neighbouring district of Strathcona. The idea of clearing out slums to improve urban centres is an old one, arising as cities were transformed during the Industrial Revolution into places that housed the millions of new residents whose agricultural way of life had disappeared and who had relocated to find work. One particularly powerful wave arrived in post-war North America, where slum removal was touted as benefitting the poor because they would move into modern social housing. It was also touted as benefitting the city itself because highways would be built through the former slums. Vancouver was late to this game, which started in the 1940s elsewhere, with its plans to eradicate what were seen as dangerous and troublesome neighbourhoods, such as Strathcona and Chinatown, and along the way, to construct a freeway that would propel commuters from North Vancouver and the eastern suburbs into downtown.

Like the West End, Strathcona and Chinatown were adjacent to the downtown business district, but they had never gentrified or densified. They were affected by extreme industrial pollution. Some parts had been classified as industrial by city planners, making it difficult for homeowners to get loans even for basic maintenance. As a result, the area was mostly occupied by older residential hotels, lodging houses, tenements, and single-family homes. Many ethnic groups concentrated there, including Chinese, Italian, and Portuguese, but it was also home to some poor whites of British descent. A 1950 report completed for the federal government by a Dr. Leonard Marsh supported urban renewal and condemned the area because "its housing is deplorable; its state of deterioration a menace."[18] He proposed tearing everything down and replacing it with low-rise apartments. By 1957, Sutton Brown, who became the city manager three years later, had submitted an urban-renewal plan to council. Block clearances started in 1959. By 1961, at least three thousand people had been displaced. The Chinese Benevolent Association and the Chinese Property Owners Association tried to mount an opposition, without success. Then they started to receive support from outside groups, one of which included future politicians Mike Harcourt and Darlene Marzari. By 1968, they had convinced Ottawa to stop funding urban renewal in Vancouver.

The anti-freeway struggle overlapped with the fight against urban renewal, but it started later. However, it became the larger battle that ultimately drew in many more people and toppled the NPA government. As Beasley emphasizes in his story, that event led to a new political culture and the beginnings of modern-day Vancouverism. One reason the freeway clash came so late was that plans remained secret for eight years, only finally being revealed in 1967. City council announced them without any public consultation. Running through Chinatown and Strathcona, the proposed route would skim along the waterfront until it reached a new third crossing.

Public opposition began to build, as did TEAM. The new party got two councillors elected in 1968, Art Phillips and a University of British Columbia geography professor named Walter Hardwick. In 1970, they were re-elected. Throughout those years, the TEAM representatives, along with a variety of community groups and another new political party, left-leaning, the Coalition of Progressive Electors, objected at length to the freeway scheme.

The federal, provincial, and city governments reached an agreement in late 1971 about funding and plans for the freeway, stirring debate to a fever-hot pitch. But the stake was driven through the heart of the project in early 1972, when two large public meetings brought out hundreds in opposition. The second meeting, on March 15, lasted six hours. On April 4, Ottawa announced that it would no longer fund any freeway construction. With that, the project essentially died. Eight months later, TEAM swept to power without even raising the issue during its election campaign. Nor did Art Phillips mention it in his January 1973 inaugural speech as mayor. In a perfunctory vote that February, with no debate and no associated report, council voted to rescind its support for the planned third crossing.

Some commentators claim that the opposition to the freeway was intimately linked to the planning for dense neighbourhoods. As Beasley notes, there was obviously a functional cause and effect, but that did not occupy the thoughts of people who were in the midst of the battle. They concentrated solely on abolishing the freeway. There were no utopian visions of urban density attached. As well, many politicians and groups who opposed the project were actually dubious about densification, which they saw as a developer-driven threat to neighbourhoods. As Robert Walsh suggests, "Having a downtown that contained high rises but no freeways was not the result of effective urban planning but rather the somewhat accidental by-product of two competing factions with competing ideologies that have been locked in opposition throughout much of the history of Vancouver."[19]

Other cities saw pro-resident, anti-developer civic parties gain traction during this era, and TEAM certainly embodied that philosophy. One of its first acts, under Mayor Art Phillips, was to review plans for the West End and change the zoning so that high-rise development came to a screeching halt. Plans for towers in Kitsilano, West Point Grey, Langara, and other areas disappeared because the TEAM council favoured the opinion of residents – that low-density, single-family neighbourhoods should be preserved as is.

But the TEAM politicians immediately recognized that Vancouver must somehow compensate for the absence of a road system that could efficiently deliver commuters from the suburbs to downtown. The obvious solution: create more housing close to downtown so that future employees could live within easy walking or transit distance of their jobs.

Those were the marching orders that Phillips and TEAM gave to Ray Spaxman, the new planning director whom they chose to carry out their wishes. As Beasley details, Spaxman would have a profound influence on Vancouver's drive to bring residents downtown. Originally from England, he had done planning work for a number of cities there, including Coventry, where he helped create one of the first pedestrian-only town centres. He was hired as a planner by the City of Toronto in 1966. "I came to America because that's where things were happening," he said.[20] The TEAM council that retained him in 1973 as head of planning believed that he knew how to connect with residents. He would be the anti–Sutton Brown. He was also seen as capable of effecting change, which Phillips and TEAM wanted badly.

In fact, Spaxman recalls that he was "fired just about every year" because the mayor felt that he wasn't working fast enough. However, he had a lot on his plate: a demoralized staff, residents who were skeptical of council's public engagement outreach, ad hoc development in the West End that had no coherent whole, and no processes at city hall to give residents or businesses more of a say in the way that development was done. An Urban Design Panel had been created but had no resources. The Development Permit Board was still to come.

As Beasley will tell you, Spaxman was also trying to integrate, not just new rules or boards, but a philosophy, something that was hard to codify but that he saw as key. He felt that decisions about buildings and area plans must emphasize "neighbourliness." Merely erecting a spectacular building wasn't enough. It had to harmonize with those around it. Planners needed to look at all the impacts. To achieve that, they had to talk to everyone extensively about what those impacts might be. As well, Spaxman showed a concern for sustainability and environmental issues, though no one applied those words to their planning work. But the idea was there.

That's what Spaxman brought with him as he worked to realize council's big goals, one of which was creating housing in the central city. The planners who worked during that era remember that this objective was constantly emphasized. As Ann McAfee recalls, "With the new council, they said 'If we're not going to have a freeway, we need to have places to live.'"[21] By then, she had been hired as a planner by the City of Vancouver. She, along with Larry Beasley, an American immigrant and a recent graduate from Simon Fraser University and the University of British Columbia planning school, were part of the new generation of planners that Spaxman brought in. McAfee was hired in 1974, Beasley in 1976. In time, they would take on an unusual arrangement at city hall, officially becoming co-directors of planning in 1994, though they had effectively assumed those roles earlier. Known for his urban design leadership, community planning background, and ability to negotiate with politicians and developers, Beasley handled the downtown and all development approvals. McAfee, whose

**P.6** False Creek South was Vancouver's earliest comprehensive redevelopment in the inner-city. It targeted families through deliberate low-scale design. The question was at what scale would the families no longer find it appealing.

strength was in long-range planning and policy development, was in charge of the residential areas outside the core and regional planning.

The two, along with many other new hires, watched as Spaxman steered the city through sometimes contradictory positions. Yes, housing in the central core. But, no disruption of neighbourhoods. Yes, density. But, not too much. Obviously, development would be done differently from then on. TEAM would curtail it in the West End and ensure that it never got a chance to disfigure other neighbourhoods.

### FALSE CREEK SOUTH: A NEW DIRECTION

During the 1970s, a moribund part of industrial Vancouver became the focus of residential development. Owned by the City, this big piece of property stretched along the south shore of False Creek and was thus known as False Creek South (see Figure P.6). The idea of transforming it into a residential neighbourhood wasn't completely new. Discussion had started under the previous regime, but many Vancouverites were dubious. The area was miserable and polluted, after decades of industrial use. "The private market said nobody's going to want to live downtown," recalls McAfee.[22]

But the TEAM council took the initial concept and ran with it – in its own way. Since council was wary of anything too urban, too dense, too much like the West End, False Creek South was planned at remarkably low densities, compared to later norms in Vancouver. It was designed to attract families, but no one was sure whether families would want to live there – another reason cited for keeping densities low and more like single-family neighbourhoods. At the time, in the early 1970s, families typically headed for the suburbs.

As it turned out, they loved the new area and moved in en masse. So did the mayor and his wife, Carole Taylor, who later became a city councillor. After that success, there was far less doubt that families would willingly move downtown, at least if the densities were modest. But it was clear that any development had to be designed to encourage them.

So that was where Vancouver stood in the mid-1980s, on the cusp of a world's fair designed to catch the attention of potential investors, particularly Asian ones. It was a city where acceptance of non-single-family living, of dense urban development, had waxed and waned, and where council policies had both facilitated and stymied it. It had created a unique neighbourhood, the West End, which was unlike anything else in a western city, with its dense but extremely livable community. The city's population had plunged during the 1970s as families left for the suburbs, but they were starting to come back. And it was about to begin a new era of unprecedented building.

That is Larry Beasley's story to be told in this book.

Vancouverism is the story of many hands
inventing the city in concert.

# PART 1

# WHAT IS

# VANCOUVERISM?

**1.1** Vancouverism is the way that one city, Vancouver, on the west coast of Canada, decided to transform itself to be attractive, competitive, and resilient for the future. The result, shown here along the north shore of False Creek downtown, will be your adventure to discover in the following pages.

# 1

# SETTING THE STAGE

**VANCOUVERISM – HOW COULD** the name of a town come to be identified with a whole way of building cities? Well, in fact, it is not a new movement, as popular lore suggests, but it is a unique way that one city – Vancouver, in Canada – reinvented itself (see Figure 1.1). It is a concept that this one city crafted from its own roots, from many sources, and from the creative thinking of its own people. As a result, modern Vancouver turned out differently from almost any other city of its time. It followed a trajectory that was actually counter-intuitive to the common wisdom of the day. I want to tell the story of this place and this people and this time. That is what this book is all about.

This book presents an insider's view. It describes the unfolding of events, the shaping of new ideas, their application on the ground, the continuing challenges, and what the city may aspire to in the future – all from the perspective of a person who lived the drama and holds an undiminished passion for the place. These events and ideas redefined the urban culture of what has become a pacesetter city in Canada and North America. Vancouver is now an exemplar for cities around the world, which are in their own quest to find new forms, meaning, relevance, competitive edge, and environmental peace. This book will not be a history, although I will offer a perspective on the precedents that became the foundation of Vancouverism. This will not be a policy guide, although I will describe the policy framework that composes Vancouverism. This will not be an evaluation, although I will offer commentary on, as well as a critique of, the various tenets and oversights of Vancouverism. This will not be an individual memoir, although I will chronicle my personal experiences in order to make the story come alive, as only an insider could do. After all is said and done, what I offer most of all is just a fascinating urban story, which I hope anyone might find interesting, of a city that faced the unknown, seized its destiny, and created the future it wanted.

Partly, this story will record what happened during the frenetic years when Vancouverism emerged, to separate truth from fiction, at least from the perspective of one person who was on the scene from the beginning to the end, and who feels that his own fictions may be closer to the truth than those of total outsiders. Partly, this story will describe a way of doing things in city building that other planners and citizens elsewhere may find useful, although I would be the last person to recommend that ideas be exported in whole to another place. I do not think that works. But good ideas can be retrofitted to a new setting, and cautions can certainly help others to avoid a bad idea that may look good at first glance.

The purpose of this opening chapter, following on from the historical essay by Frances Bula, is to outline the conceptual framework of Vancouverism – a definition, a geography, a time frame, a summary of its challenges and focus, and several of the key attitudes that give Vancouverism its own special flavour.

## THE CONCEPTUAL FRAMEWORK FOR VANCOUVERISM

No one knows for sure who first coined and used the word "Vancouverism." Some credit John Punter and his seminal work *The Vancouver Achievement* as ground zero.[1] Others say they first read it in the media, perhaps as a pejorative. Some say it was an architect's shorthand for the simple notion of a building composed of a thin apartment tower sitting on a podium of townhouses (see Figure 1.2). That is surely an iconic image of Vancouverism that is special to this city, which I will talk about later. But it is only part of the picture – not the whole picture. Perhaps the origin of the word matters less than what it has come to mean, both for the general strategies of modern city change and perhaps even more so for the people who worked on it and lived through the trials and tribulations of its invention.

In essence, Vancouverism is an ethos for how to think about a livable, sustainable city, a formula for how to craft that vision on the ground, a process for how to determine the specifics of the vision, and a model for how to replicate the components over and over again to become the very image of a place.

The ethos of Vancouverism embraces deliberate planning, with the local government in the driver's seat, for a result that meets not just developer business needs but also the dreams of all the people who share the space. We were proud

**1.2** The tall thin tower rising from a rowhouse podium extending along the street is the first vision most people have of Vancouverism. This story will illustrate that our mission has been so much richer. From this typical example on Beach Avenue downtown, we will unfold a picture of many dimensions.

of our declaration that "the City plans the city" – it is not determined solely by the development sector or special-interest groups or powerful individuals or companies. Policies and design solutions have been adopted through the hot drama of local democracy.

The formula for Vancouverism is all about livability and, more recently, sustainability, with hundreds of moving parts. It is a formula for how buildings, open spaces, movement, and character come together with services, facilities, and infrastructure to satisfy users – a physical design expression. It is a formula for how a society can be mixed up and diversified to yield unexpected benefits and pleasures – a social-policy expression. It is a formula for how land can be used more efficiently, with densification tied to high quality – an economic policy and design expression. More recently, it has become a formula for retrofitting an urban system to stop diminishing its natural setting – an environmental fix. And there are compatible mindsets behind this formula that I will come back to.

At its heart, the process of Vancouverism is inclusive. To pursue its objectives, it is necessary to cooperate; it is necessary to be multi-disciplinary; and it is necessary to embrace wide and incessant public engagement. Partnerships must form that are not typical in the municipal culture of North America – partnerships of capital and government and community power. Vancouverism seems to flounder when disputes and antagonisms overwhelm the discourse because the lowest common denominator that often results simply does not

deliver on what it promises to do. It is necessary not just to work with market forces but to bring attention and solutions to people, situations, and aspects that are not well handled by the market – and especially for victims of the ebb and flow of the market.

At any one time, the model of Vancouverism is complete for the needs of the moment, but it is also always inherently incomplete, so it must be applied with care. It articulates a comprehensive proposition, not one that covers only one or a few sides of a situation. It is always there to be used and, better yet, to be built upon. But it is a flexible, changeable, and adaptable model. It is in a state of continuous realization, formulated in round after round of invention and experimentation that have assembled a puzzle of elements into a coherent proposition that at any point in time has been useful but is always ready to be further embellished. It looks different and is applied differently in different circumstances. It originated in a struggle for urban rebirth, offering clarity in a time of confusion about how the city might be rearranged or fixed. Now, it

**1.3** Metro Vancouver sits on an alluvial plain of the mighty Fraser River, edged to the north by the mountains and Burrard Inlet and to the south by the US border.

**1.4** Here at the Bayshore Hotel, downtown, adjacent to Stanley Park, the magnificent mountain and water setting of Vancouver is dramatic. In the foreground is Coal Harbour Park, with its underground community centre hidden beneath the lawn.

struggles for environmental reconciliation and better human fulfillment, along with the increasingly elusive requirement for affordability. The learning curve of Vancouverites has been a pleasure to watch.

## THE GEOGRAPHY OF VANCOUVERISM

Our greater city-region sits within a break in the mountains caused by the vast expanse of Burrard Inlet and the alluvial delta of the Fraser River (see Figure 1.3). Urban development, agriculture, and green open spaces sprawl within this opening, blanketing the plain, extending up the valley, and edging along the mountainsides. It stretches south to the American border on the 49th parallel. It is the largest urban area in the province of British Columbia, anchoring the west coast of Canada as the nation's third-largest metropolis. The actual City of Vancouver, off-centre in the region in a westerly direction, is directly hemmed in by the inlet and the river. The historic downtown is even further squeezed on its own small peninsula, which is almost an island. A majestic backdrop of mountains and the close proximity of water are pervasive in anyone's experience of the place (see Figure 1.4). It is undoubtedly one of the world's most beautiful settings, although the weather has its ups and downs – rarely too cold or snowy, seldom very hot, usually warm and sunny one minute and cool and grey the next. The beauty of the setting beguiles you while the climate claims and abuses you in turns. The very fickleness of the place makes it your mistress –

an important truth to understand as you read this story. So let me pause to offer a lyrical description of what this place is like, so well expressed by the late Arthur Erickson, Canada's greatest modern architect and a dear personal friend of mine:

> What is it about Vancouver that keeps many of us inescapably under its spell? Is it because we succumb so heedlessly to the sheer beauty of its setting – to the haunting melancholy of a summer evening's light or to the spring air washed with sea salt and the sap of alder? Yet this perpetual game of the senses – taunting us each time as if to test our loyalty – helps us endure the repeated rejections when our ardour is cooled by the awaiting downpour. Then, when memory of the physical beauty and its previous seduction is dimmed by the long grey aftermath where form, colour, light and scent give way to leaden skies – suddenly at the depth of our despair, out of formlessness, shapes begin to appear. Light shines on them and an entrancing world appears once more to beguile us ... Deep down and undeniably we know that it is the sheer transcendence of sensual splendor that keeps us constant even though the epiphany depends upon the utter dreariness that precedes it.[2]

To put it simply, the geography creates an atmosphere that is challenging and magical, all at the same time.

But, pulling our feet back to the ground, I will turn to the various places in which the experiment and experience of Vancouverism has unfolded. Throughout this story, most of the action takes place in the many districts and sub-areas that comprise the actual City of Vancouver, particularly in the inner-city. Without a basic orientation, the geography can be quite confusing. So, let me pause to introduce the names and locations of the key spots that will become familiar as our story unfolds. Since a picture is worth a thousand words, maps are provided here as a ready ongoing reference.

The region, officially called Metro Vancouver but often referred to as the Lower Mainland or Greater Vancouver, includes some twenty on-shore municipalities (see Figure 1.5). Metro Vancouver has about 2.5 million people. The City of Vancouver, the pre-eminent local jurisdiction, nudges Canada's largest port on the north, which commands major stretches of Burrard Inlet. The city sits proudly on a lovely sweep of water called English Bay, extending northwesterly from this urban shore, which offers delightful civic beaches. The city embraces a glimmering recreational water basin at its heart known as False Creek. The city's

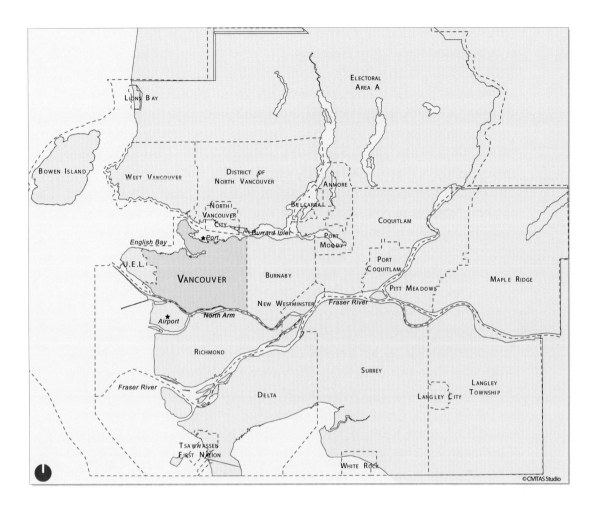

**1.5** This map shows Vancouver's regional context. Officially called Metro Vancouver, it is also known as the Lower Mainland or Greater Vancouver. Boundaries of the separate municipalities are shown. The city of Vancouver sits at the western edge of the region. Other cities include Burnaby, New Westminster, Richmond, Surrey, Delta, Coquitlam, Port Moody, North Vancouver, and West Vancouver. The port and airport are starred.

eastern edge is marked by a street called, not surprisingly, Boundary Road. About 650,000 people live in Vancouver.

The inner-city, or core city, is comprised of several features (see Figure 1.6). The downtown peninsula, which juts to the northwest, is rounded out by Stanley Park at its tip. Stretching east from the neck of this peninsula over to Clark Drive is the Downtown Eastside, and south of that is an area of one-time tidal flats, which is called, predictably, the False Creek Flats. Two water-oriented districts flank the southern edge of False Creek – what was first referred to as False Creek South but is now commonly called Southwest False Creek and the more recent Southeast False Creek, also known as the Athletes Village of the 2010 Winter Olympic Games (the moniker of "the Village" is sometimes added to or substituted for its name by those who wish to especially remember its famous initial mission). Outside the inner-city, the old streetcar neighbourhoods extend to the south and east, with Kitsilano to the southwest, Mount Pleasant to the southeast, and Grandview-Woodland to the east.

And, lastly, the downtown peninsula, the main stage for much of this tale, is comprised of several distinct districts and features (see Figure 1.7). At its heart is the official downtown, the traditional business centre of the city and region. This is bounded on the west by the residential West End, which extends to Stanley Park. To the east, the area generally called the Downtown Eastside contains a series of distinct sub-areas: Gastown (the original historic townsite), Chinatown (once the only legal precinct for Chinese immigrants, and also very historic), and Strathcona. The new development areas that dominate our story include the following: Coal Harbour (north waterfront of the peninsula) and the nearby upland district called Triangle West; False Creek North (south waterfront of the peninsula) and its upland districts of historic Yaletown and Downtown South; and False Creek East. A new area just coming together is Northeast False Creek, tucked between the historic districts and False Creek, at the foot of the downtown escarpment.

It all seems very complicated at the outset, but in fact, one of the many personalities of Vancouver that you will come to appreciate as you read this story is that it is enjoyed and understood in human-sized precincts. Each area has a name, a character, a history, and its own set of actors and myths.

### THE TIME FRAME OF VANCOUVERISM

My time frame for the emergence and flourishing of Vancouverism is specified here, but it is a tentative one intended to be taken with a grain of salt.

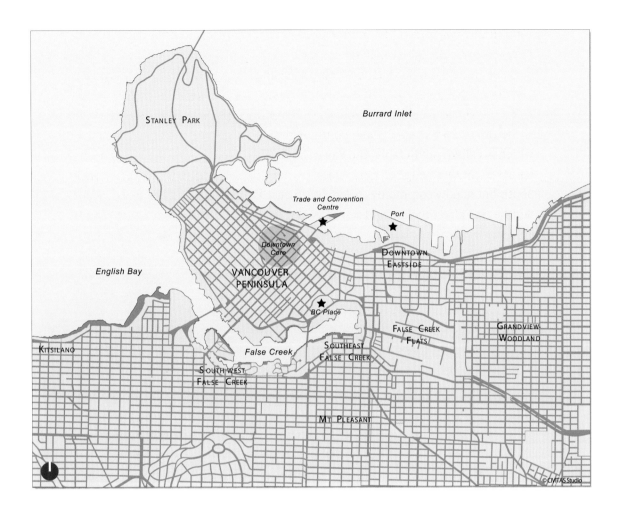

**1.6** This map shows Vancouver's inner-city, also referred to as the metropolitan core, with sub-areas marked for easy reference. Around the downtown peninsula, key locations include the Downtown Eastside, False Creek Flats, Southwest False Creek (also called False Creek South), Southeast False Creek (Athletes Village for the 2010 Olympics), Kitsilano, Mount Pleasant, and Grandview-Woodland.

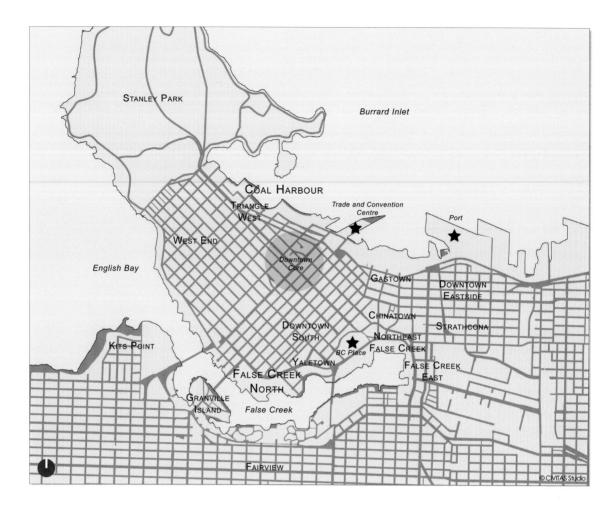

**1.7** This map zeroes in on Vancouver's downtown peninsula, again with specific sub-areas marked for easy reference. West of the downtown core are the West End and Stanley Park. East is the Downtown Eastside, which includes Gastown, Chinatown, and Strathcona. The biggest development areas are, to the north, Coal Harbour and Triangle West, and to the south, False Creek North (site of Expo 86), historic Yaletown, Downtown South, False Creek East, and Northeast False Creek. The port, BC Place, and the Vancouver Trade and Convention Centre are starred.

Vancouverism has integral precedents and later elaborations, which I will describe, but fixing it in time is nonetheless sensible. So, for the purposes of this story, I chose 1986–2006 as my time frame – a dynamic twenty-year period that began with the Expo 86 World's Fair and ended shortly before the Winter Olympic Games of 2010.

Taking a wide view, I will talk about three generations of activists and accomplishments. I use these descriptors not to suggest any kind of clubby, exclusive grouping but rather to clarify who did what before, during, and after the consolidation of Vancouverism.

### The precedent generation

What I have christened the "precedent generation" began with a benchmark moment – the sweeping city council victory of The Electors' Action Movement, usually called TEAM. Vancouver was taken over by a progressive movement of urban thinkers and activists that reformed everything and marshalled in modern thinking. I'll specify the years of this generation as 1972 to 1986. The politicians of TEAM secured one epochal direction that made everything I am going to talk about possible and maybe even inevitable. They made Vancouver a freeway-free zone. No direction in Vancouver's history has been more fundamental than that one – and no other direction has made it more necessary to figure out a completely different way to build the city as a result.

I arrived on the scene in 1976, fresh out of grad school, to dive into neighbourhood revitalization in my first planning roles. Almost immediately I was in the thick of things. There were many movers and shakers in this period, among them my constant and trusted companions-in-arms when I was a community planner, Councillors Marguerite Ford, May Brown, and Darlene Marzari, and the best mayor you could have on your side, Mike Harcourt. But the great hero of this generation was the chief planner whom the reformers selected to lead their wide agenda of change. His name was Ray Spaxman. He set up the initial systems, the perspectives, and the philosophy that resulted in Vancouverism. Among his many gifts to Vancouver were local area planning, a strong urban design direction, public participation, and a new way of managing development. Early on, in the 1970s, he created a fresh downtown plan and zoning that dramatically reshaped what the inner-city would become. This zoning was more flexible and offered much richer potential than in the past. It was very heavy on urban design considerations. It specified interesting mixes of uses. It offered new tools to garner public amenities. Spaxman's time was one of commercial growth in the inner-city, and he cut his teeth on that form of development, implementing his new plan, but he also rescued declining inner-city neighbourhoods. The West End was rezoned in the 1960s, well before Spaxman came along, but he did lead the planning for False Creek South. Both of these areas became influential precedents for Vancouverism. Indeed, you will read the details of Spaxman's accomplishments throughout these pages, because without these early achievements there would be no Vancouverism. Spaxman was a strong and inspiring leader, who will be a constant figure in this story – I would call him the "Father" of Vancouverism. During his tenure, most of the players in the next generation rose through the ranks, including myself, so we lived the precedents just as much as we later invented the full elaborations of Vancouverism.

### The Vancouverism generation

My generation consisted of the group of politicians, professionals, and citizens who were the thought leaders for Vancouverism between 1986 and 2006. Ray Spaxman retained his leadership role for a number of years, and after retiring from the City in 1989, he remained an active mentor to many who followed him. Then, in 1994, after some machinations and some personalities in between, I took the helm, along with my colleague Dr. Ann McAfee, as co-directors of planning, having been associate directors in the years before that. We were a unique planning leadership team in Canada for many years, and we bragged about our truly "gender-integrated" planning service. I smile in hindsight because our working relationship was a little like a marriage but with the jolting imperative that we could never publicly disagree. So, with our cadre of clever deputies, we had rich and fascinating debates within the privacy of city hall and a serene coherence out in public. In the scheme of things, though, we were quite compatible. Everything that either of us achieved was done with the involvement and support of the other – although we did have our comfortable division of labour. I concentrated on the inner-city, urban design, development approvals, and heritage. McAfee looked after long-range and general policy, neighbourhoods, and regional relations. We both covered different aspects of the transportation file with our engineering colleagues. During our generation, commercial growth floundered in Vancouver, so I spent most of my time, as you will see, in a quest to populate the inner-city with complete, new communities. McAfee completed the first overall city plan in living memory. These assignments gave a certain taste to the nectar of Vancouverism.

When I say "we" in this story, I will be talking about Ann McAfee and myself and our band of planning professionals, along with the other professionals in all the departments that make up the City, because we were always on the front lines together – often fighting a very hard fight. I will also be talking about our political masters, particularly those who sponsored the innovations. For me, close allies were Councillors Gordon Price and Jim Green, and Mayors Gordon Campbell, Philip Owen, and Larry Campbell. They were intelligent leaders, who often showed courage in their embrace of what we suggested. But the "we" will also include the developers and private design professionals who were constant collaborators, as well as the citizens who threw their hats into the ring to take part in what we were doing. Of course, we were all led by the chief of the City – known humbly as the city manager. Our generation was very lucky to have extraordinary, even brilliant, leaders in Ken Dobell and then Judy Rogers, who built on the legacy of the genius who preceded them, Fritz Bowers (I mean that seriously, he was a Mensa). For clarity, if the word "City" is capitalized in this narrative, I am referring to the local government, the City of Vancouver; if "city" is not capitalized, I am referring to the place. My recollection is that there were about two hundred key people, from every walk of life, who brought Vancouverism together. Make no mistake. No single person can claim to be the inventor of Vancouverism. It was a group effort – a generational effort.

However, sometimes, when I say "we," I will also just be referring to all the citizens of Vancouver at that time. I feel a heartfelt spiritual kinship with the whole city that I just cannot edit out of my language when I am talking about these times and events.

*The following generation*

What I will call the "following generation" refers to the people to whom we handed on the baton as we left the field – from around 2006 to the present day. Of course, they did not stand still. They evolved the propositions of Vancouverism, added their own special features, and carried on the traditions and philosophy that, with all the ups and downs, remain vital to this day and portend even more fascinating moves in the future.

Brent Toderian, who became chief planner in 2006, after McAfee and I left, was another strong, articulate leader and spokesperson for the new urbanism that we had espoused. One of his biggest challenges was an idea known as "eco-density." This concept for sustainable community change through densification was tabled by Mayor Sam Sullivan and thrust into Toderian's hands to articulate and establish. In and of itself, this effort is a book-length story, with all the drama one might never expect in the world of civic bureaucracy and politics.

Another prominent figure of these years is Sadhu Johnston. A primary force for the following generation, he ultimately became city manager, but here I refer to his earlier role as the key leader of the green agenda that is probably his generation's defining contribution so far. As deputy city manager, he put a lot of sustainability ideas and aspirations into a comprehensive policy that is now starting to reshape the city as profoundly as Vancouverism did in our day – it's a whole new story that transcends Vancouverism as my generation knew it.

Our omissions were this generation's opportunities, and so the beat goes on. I allude to the achievements of the following generation here, but mostly I feel that these people should tell their own tale, for which I wait in anticipation.

## THE ESSENTIAL CHALLENGES OF VANCOUVERISM

The primary focus of my generation and the practice of Vancouverism started with one central concern – the journey to work. During the 1980s, Ted Droettboom, Spaxman's planning deputy at the time, began to worry about the trip to work. With its river branches, inlet, topography, and other barriers, the Vancouver region is complicated, and moving across it can be difficult. Droettboom knew that fitting out the region for primarily automobile movement would be prohibitively expensive. Even public transit, which the regional plan had already identified as the best alternative, was very expensive to implement. Of course, freeways were off the list. So Droettboom suggested that people should live closer to their work, which led to the idea that Vancouver's downtown, where most jobs were traditionally located, needed a huge new resident population.

At about the same time, Vancouver experienced a significant economic downturn, with the globalization of the resource sector, and it needed a new economic model, especially for the inner-city. It had lived off the proceeds of lumber and mining, but that was over. Many people started talking about a new economy based upon tourism, the service sector, and the ideas industries, driven by people who lived downtown. After all, the story went, the best place to visit is a good place to live. All those residents would make big demands for services. Smart, creative people would want to live and work in the action of the city, not isolated out in the grey zones.

When we looked from that potential to what we saw on the ground, no one could deny that the core city was in a malaise. As in other cities, typical households were escaping to the suburbs. The business core was stalled. A plethora of vacant and under-utilized land, especially huge obsolete railyards, dominated the downtown peninsula. The only bright spot was the West End, but for most people, even this was problematic, with issues of traffic, prostitution, and what many saw as overcrowding.

So the defining challenges of Vancouverism became two-fold.

The first challenge was the inner-city and its revitalization. This is not a suburban story or a regional story. The generation after ours has offered suburban elaborations and is starting to realize the exciting potential of regional town centres, conceived long before our story began but never truly pulled together until recently. But those are not the stories of Vancouverism. All of those initiatives came later. Ours was a searing focus on the heart of the city.

The second challenge was to set off the necessary revitalization by fostering major population growth – people in residence by the thousands. This became known as the "living first" strategy. But this was not easy. We had to conceptualize a lifestyle at high density, in multiple-living configurations, with an intensive mix of uses and people – all very unpopular at the time. Changing that attitude was the hardest nut to crack for our generation. It was a tough slog to convince people en masse to live in a way that differed from what they grew up with.

Throughout this story, I return again and again to these prime challenges – what might be called the subject matter of our generation. They gave Vancouverism its personality, its strengths, and even its weaknesses.

To meet these challenges, we undertook three overarching planning initiatives that had to be coordinated on an ongoing basis. Every aspect of Vancouverism has been acted out through these initiatives or spun off from them. The first came together right after Expo 86, and I was privileged to lead it. It consisted of the megaproject planning programs and the associated area planning programs for the nearby upland districts. From 1990, in short order, around 200 hectares (nearly 500 acres) of the downtown peninsula were under active area planning – it was a big program of change. The under-developed megaproject sites consisted mostly of obsolete, dead railyards and their ancillary uses, all of which had become redundant as the railway companies decamped to more efficient locations on the urban fringe. False Creek North (including Granville Slopes), which encompassed the Expo 86 site, provided over 77 hectares (more than 190 acres) of new development area (see Figure 1.8). Coal Harbour (see Figure 1.9) offered almost 17 hectares (over 40 acres). And the east end of False Creek gave us close to 4 hectares (almost 10 acres). The development of these sites set off market action upland from them on adjacent under-utilized properties that were peppered within built areas – I have already mentioned Downtown South, historic Yaletown, and Triangle West – so several hundred further hectares were added to the mix. The megaprojects were ready to take whatever development we needed in our generation, and they gave us our taste for comprehensive planning. Needless to say, these were the perfect sandboxes for planners and citizens within which to build our castles.

The second planning initiative was about getting on top of how the new development areas would fit with the rest of the core city. This involved creating a new plan for the core city, which I also managed. In 1987, anticipating what lay ahead, we realized that we needed a contemporary policy context for the big area planning efforts, but we also saw an opportunity to fundamentally rethink and reinvent the inner-city. A new plan – the Central Area Plan – was the right way to achieve that.[3] It identified a constellation of districts around the historic downtown, converted over 650,000 square metres (over 7 million square feet) of excess downtown office commercial-use designations into residential- and mixed-use designations, allocated various preferred mix-use combinations to the districts, extended bonusing so that preferred uses would be incentivized even in less central locations, and designated the preferred uses to be accommodated in the newly developing areas. The plan was approved in 1991. This gave us our new vision.

In 1992, it was agreed that we also needed a new city-wide policy plan. So, an inspired planning program was initiated, through Mayor Gordon Campbell, under the management of Ann McAfee, to reconceive the entire city. The result, called CityPlan and adopted in 1995,[4] confirmed widely agreed-upon directions for the city's next twenty years. It outlined the principles to strengthen neighbourhood centres, define neighbourhood character, and better target community-based services, which could then be followed up later in detailed area planning. It posited moves to improve the environment and reduce reliance on the car. It outlined directions for more variety and affordability of housing, for diversification of parks and public places, and for the ongoing involvement of people in planning processes. This confirmed the broader overview and that our area-based principles for the inner-city were supportive of the way the city as a whole community wanted to go for the future.

**1.8** Megaprojects were the crucible for Vancouverism. This early model of False Creek North conveys their scale. New development is shown from end to end of this model.

**1.9** Vancouver's megaprojects redeveloped large obsolete rail and industrial sites in the inner-city. They were transformative, so massive that they changed the character and image of the whole city. Here is an early model of Coal Harbour. The proposed new development glows.

## A DIFFERENT WAY OF SEEING THE CITY

In retrospect, I realize that two imperatives determined our way of looking at the city. I also realize that they were not typical of planning practice in either Vancouver or most other cities at the time. Thankfully, they did eventually emerge as strong movements of a contemporary urbanism and have since been embraced by most urban cognoscenti. In any event, they coloured everything we did and how we did it, so I will introduce them here to help explain what followed.

The first, and earliest by many years, was a focus on quality of living. When we started the local planning to increase the population of the inner-city, we had one thing in mind – how to create a living situation that would really touch the hearts of people (see Figure 1.10). I have already alluded to what we were up against in terms of attitudes toward density. Densification was an idea that most people loved to hate. Mixed-use was feared. Multiple living was the booby prize for those who just did not succeed in society. And frankly, who could blame people for these attitudes? Although the city boasted a few gracious old buildings from early in the twentieth century, and though the West End appealed to a certain demographic, most of Vancouver's high-density residential structures were not very good. In fact, they were awful. They were stock buildings that represented a lowest common denominator of development. They were designed with little thought for the needs of residents and certainly no thought to making the living situation stylish. The suburban alternative – expansive, lushly landscaped, flexible, private, quiet, and socially superior – was a much

more compelling choice. What we as planners hoped to do bluntly contradicted what consumers seemed to want.

This consumer challenge, grounded in the marketplace, was not comfortable turf for most planners. As public officials, we were trained in and accustomed to a government perspective, brokering the demands of citizens related to public interests and public resources. But ask us to think about consumers, and we were effectively blinkered. Some planners even resented the idea – some still do. Fortunately, the people we started to engage with through our public discussions opened our eyes to a suite of new concerns and positive features for living that planners tended not to think about. And because we had artists draw up what we were hearing, these concerns and ideas became very tangible. The developers, who typically dismissed multiple-family consumers as a group with

**1.10** Vancouverism is driven by the quest for an exemplary quality of life in all its details. This view of Southeast False Creek, a later megaproject that grew out of the 2010 Olympics, shows the attention to extensive features for great livability.

**1.11** The second overarching imperative of Vancouverism is a concern for sustainability. This artificial addition to the water's edge, called Habitat Island, connected to Southeast False Creek, is a nature preserve. To compensate for the water lost due to its construction, part of the larger site was excavated to create a new water area.

few choices searching for the cheapest options, were also jarred out of their long-time complacency.

So, we all started dealing with a new agenda – things such as scale and sequencing of spaces, quality of materials and light, impacts mitigation, interface conditions, special features, landscape, and beauty. The list became increasingly elaborated, as I'll detail in Chapter 7. We joined ever more enlightened developers in an effort to broker people's preferred experience. The point is that we began not only to deal with the public agenda, engaging with people as citizens and members of the body politic, but also with the market agenda, working with people as consumers, as participants in trends that were often more influential than all the public policies put together. Ultimately, we coined a descriptor for this. We realized we were doing "experiential planning," and the result was "experiential urbanism." This was all about tapping into consumer preferences and then designing living solutions that not only worked within the limits of high-density multiple housing, meeting public requirements, but also met or exceeded people's wants and expectations – touching the emotional side, not just the functional side, and conjuring dreams, not just efficiencies.

The second imperative was a concern about the compatibility of the city with its natural setting – a focus on sustainability (see Figure 1.11). This arose years later in our thinking as planners. After all, the concept of sustainability, proffered by the UN Brundtland Commission in 1987,[5] took time to percolate down to our part of the world. We started the sustainability quest, which has been carried forward aggressively since our departure. But this reflected a deep vein in Vancouver's local culture perhaps best symbolized by Greenpeace, the environmental action organization founded in our city, and inspired by the philosophy of sensitivity to nature expressed so well and so long by David Suzuki, the articulate environmental spokesman and a Canadian treasure, also from Vancouver. No one could say that either Suzuki or Greenpeace had an active role in the story of Vancouverism – they did not – but they did help to set the tone, through the attitudes of the thousands of people who were profoundly influenced by their thinking and by their example.

In fact, what sent us in the direction of what became later known as sustainability may have been more a drive of intuition, with a little dose of practicality in the efficient use of scarce space, rather than an explicit intention. Our region has a hemmed-in footprint. So there was an early realization that we needed to use land at least slightly more intensively than other cities who were free to sprawl as far as the eye could see. It was also common thinking at that time that any forward-looking planning should try to focus development and take the pressure off the urban edge. Most of us easily embraced this basic planning perspective. It was obvious.

Initially, it was the common wisdom of the people at the grassroots level that pushed hardest on the environmental perspective. We are an outdoor-oriented community. We brag that we love to swim in the morning and ski in the afternoon on the same day. Outdoor recreation is widely popular, and the appeal of nature unspoiled by the human touch rates very high in the collective emotions. So, there were always lots of people who urged us to keep off the forested fringes, clean up the water and air, and get "with it" in repairing the damage done over a century of human exploitation of our gloriously beautiful but also delicate home base. As we learned more and more about the devastation that our species was inflicting on the environment, not only locally but also globally, and as a worldwide ethos started to gel about how to avoid all this damage, Vancouverites were right at the front of the line in demanding that we get our act together – and we planners were right beside them.

Every year, sustainability became an increasingly pervasive imperative, which took us into interesting and, for planners, unfamiliar areas of creative inquiry. We started with a comfortable discussion of alternative land use and transportation, which we had been trained to understand. Then we moved to less comfortable considerations of social engineering and ultimately to the furthermost questions of low-impact utilities, materials sourcing, and economic balancing, which were completely new subjects for most of us.

Seeing the city differently than others – and embracing this vision earlier than most – allowed us to transform the city in a different way. We could tap into a preferred user experience while also taking custodianship for the environment, thus enabling us to reconcile a responsible public interest with a natural flow of market forces. So, as Vancouverism repaired the ills of our past, it also made people happier, engendering a virtuous circle of cause and effect that will probably continue to play out against all odds. Well, perhaps not absolutely, as we shall see, but certainly giving our city pretty good odds.

## THE UNFOLDING OF OUR STORY

This chapter has provided a conceptual framework for Vancouverism, a take on the over-riding inquisitiveness of the people who made it happen and some basic definitions for the rest of this book. Chapters 2 and 3 will continue to elaborate this overview.

Contrary to popular perceptions, Canada is very different from its neighbour to the south. It is also unique as a country. Particularly for non-Canadians, this must be understood up front in order to understand what occurred during the gestation of Vancouverism. Chapter 2 summarizes the components of Canadian culture that fostered Vancouverism. It also discusses a certain Canadian view of the world and the implications of that view, the form of local and regional government, and the hierarchy of responsibilities in the governance system. It emphasizes several unique features of Vancouver that set the pace of our thinking. This chapter also describes the regional picture of Metro Vancouver to highlight vital and determining regional policies that supported the Vancouver-based urban strategy. It places Vancouver and its downtown within regional patterns that offered significant metropolitan opportunities.

In our generation, many people would have said that our attitude and approach to almost all the questions of city change and management were downright bizarre. In hindsight, it must be admitted that we did have a counter-intuitive view of the world. Chapter 3 summarizes the almost opposite-from-normal mindsets through which we looked at the issues we were attacking. It outlines the logic that compelled us to move away not only from the status quo of our city but also from the status quo of thinking about cities that we had been taught. This will clarify why Vancouverites were more inclined sooner than people in

other cities to entertain intense inner-city living, even though the trend toward suburban life was as strong here as anywhere else.

Planning and urban design during the years of Vancouverism were principles-based endeavours. We capitalized on opportunities if they presented themselves, and we had our ad hoc moments, but we generally acted from principles, and the results echoed those principles. Our story moves into the substantive side of Vancouverism by presenting six key urban principles, chapter by chapter.

*Principle 1: The neighbourhood is the prime increment for change*

Neighbourhoods are an overwhelming reality of Vancouver, so it is not surprising that the neighbourhood unit became the basic building block for contemporary

**1.12** A starting principle of Vancouverism saw the neighbourhood as the basic module for planning and urban design. This photo shows one of the centres of a new neighbourhood, Downtown South, which offers the kinds of retail and supports that are needed at hand by residents every day.

**1.13** Providing many choices for how to move around, and thereby making the private car only one among many options, and not the priority, was another principle of Vancouverism. Here we see three options, walking, cycling and transit, in False Creek East, to balance the preference for cars.

planning (see Figure 1.12). Chapter 4 explores this concept and describes its component features. It explains the local history and formulation of a place-based policy nexus, covering the form and scale of the neighbourhood template, the standards for community and commercial infrastructure, the diversity of neighbourhood types, and the ways and means for engendering character.

### Principle 2: The city should provide balanced transportation choices with the main motive being to tame the car

At the time, our approach to transportation was perhaps the most unusual of all the substantive ideas that dominated our thinking and it became one of the most distinctive aspects of Vancouverism. Chapter 5 tells the story of how we accommodated the car without prioritizing it. It also surveys the alternative strategy to diversify transportation choices (see Figure 1.13). It talks about the agenda for transit, cycling, and walking and also shows that the Vancouver transportation story is not yet the regional norm – cars are still a big part of Metro Vancouver suburbs.

### Principle 3: Diversity is essential

One thing that gave Vancouverism its one-off personality during its formative years was the insistence on inclusiveness at its very heart. It is ironic that this central aspiration that we worked so hard to accomplish has been more recently high-jacked by consumer response to all our other success so that, today, from housing costs alone, Vancouver is increasingly seen as exclusive rather than inclusive. The odyssey from what we wanted the city to be to what it became is fascinating if disheartening. Chapter 6 covers both land-use mix and housing mix, which resulted in people of very different income groups and household types living in close proximity, reversing the rigid separations of the past (see Figure 1.14). It talks about the shift from single-use buildings to mixed-use and looks at policy and other factors that engender a mix and make mixed-use viable.

Then, the chapter moves to the two key dimensions of social mix in housing that are typical in Vancouverism. First, it outlines roots, policies, practices, and outcomes for economic mix. It celebrates the historic focus on low-income housing, but it also laments the parallel decline of affordability for middle-income people. It exposes the unpredicted senior government shifts and complacency that resulted in some security for low-income residents and great choices for high-income residents but fewer and fewer options for the huge majority in the middle – particularly those wanting to purchase a first home.

Second, the chapter outlines roots, policies, practices, and outcomes for household mix. It discusses the strategy that we employed to draw families with children to live in high-density multiple housing. This became a successful and compelling result of Vancouverism as a transformative force. It is also one of the features of ongoing relevance for other inner-cities that continue to lose their families with children.

### Principle 4: The city must be created by direct physical design

A city must be designed. It cannot result from just the accident of colliding interests or even a conceptual policy formulation. Chapter 7 examines what most people usually have in mind when they think about Vancouverism – the unique urban design elements that make Vancouver look and feel significantly different from other modern North American urban places (see Figure 1.15). The chapter surveys the practices and results in shaping both the public and the private realms of the city. Regarding the public realm, it covers strategies handled in ways seen in few other cities, including networks integration, streetscape and park design, views and weather protection, landscape continuity, public art, and overall mood and character.

Regarding the private realm, it surveys the strong agenda for built form within and serving an urban setting. It looks at the iconic tower-podium building

**1.14** Social diversity is another principle of Vancouverism. That means making a place for everyone and everyone having fun, as these residents are doing in George Wainborn Park in False Creek North.

**1.15** A key principle of Vancouverism is that the city should be created through direct physical design, merging the design prowess of the public and private sectors. This has produced urban delights that go well beyond functionality or market interest. This fountain in George Wainborn Park is a surprising pleasure for all who come upon it.

**1.16** The principle of environmental sustainability became an increasingly vital part of Vancouverism through the years. This electric vehicle charging station in Southeast False Creek was unique when it was installed.

**1.17** Collaboration and dialogue constituted the prime principle for all the processes of Vancouverism. Here city hall staffers, with the developer, talk to citizens about East Fraser Lands, a megaproject outside the inner-city. They all had to find an accord before the project could go forward – which they did.

configuration, the emergence of courtyards, hidden parking, detailed features for neighbourliness, active use of roofs, and interface between buildings and the street. It also discusses tools and practices for heritage conservation and restoration.

### Principle 5: Environmental responsibility is paramount

Every city, including Vancouver, is degrading its environment. In our generation, as we began to better understand this, we started taking action to reset the balance. This knowledge grew into a principle. While we thought globally, we started acting locally. At first, as I alluded to earlier, we took small steps, but then we ventured into more impactful reforms. We have a long way to go, but at least the ignorance and complacency of the past are behind us. Chapter 8 looks at the evolution of understanding, experimentation, practices, and results of sustainability in the repertoire of Vancouverism. It begins with the initial, almost spiritual, fascination with environmentalism and moves to the early efforts for a more environmentally compatible structure of the city, particularly as realized in the inner-city megaprojects. Next, it looks at the very explicit program to achieve a targeted sustainability performance in Southeast False Creek as a showpiece for the 2010 Winter Olympics (see Figure 1.16), and it gives a glimpse of the current green-city agenda that transcends Vancouverism.

### Principle 6: Vancouverism is a practice of collaboration

From the inventive process, through detailed design, and then in operationalizing the conclusions, optimal results can be achieved when people in government, the private sector, non-profit community organizations, and individual citizens work together (see Figure 1.17). Chapter 9 dissects this into its component parts. This is the "how to" chapter. It discusses governance and management arrangements.

After touching on the basics of urban land economics, the chapter explains the unique discretionary zoning regime of the city to motivate joint venturing between the private and public sectors and to garner public goods from private development. Then it describes the transactional process through which this is acted out – an almost unprecedented level of negotiations between everyone to reconcile and balance interests. The chapter also describes the art and methods of public engagement. It covers the hierarchical policy framework used in Vancouver, planning in iterations from the general to the specific. It discusses

**1.18** Vancouver has often been referred to as "lotus land" in reference to our languid climate and the lifestyle that was said to go with it. The vibrant, creative city of today puts paid to all that nonsense.

the techniques for financing growth, including community amenity contributions, development cost charges, and cost-recovered planning teams. It describes the organizational arrangements that make Vancouverism work.

In closing the story for my generation, I look to the future and to the work that remains to be done in realizing the great dream of Vancouverism. The current paradigm has vulnerabilities, such as affordability of housing and ongoing difficulties with transportation, which require a smart new response. There is the current excitement in the city to further and diversify an aggressive program for sustainability to secure environmental compatibility. Several key progressive urban design moves in other cities have not yet entered the Vancouver repertoire. I suggest directions for bringing Vancouverism to the suburbs. And I list the lessons from Vancouverism that might be relevant elsewhere.

Vancouver has often been dubbed the "land of the lotus-eaters," or "lotus land" for short, riffing Alfred, Lord Tennyson's melancholy poem (see Figure 1.18). While the rest of the nation scraped and worked, it was said that we lived off the bounty of our landscape, far away from the centre of the action. It was also said that we were languid and complacent, playing more than we worked. It was said too that ours was "a setting in search of a city." The story that unfolds over these pages should quash all that nonsense. It introduces a vanguard of creative and hard-working people who led the way to a better type of modern city and found phenomenal community wealth in the process. The story is one of taking risks, innovating, and keeping our noses to the grindstone to change the trajectory of our city. In telling it, I hope to debunk a silly myth and show you a clever, energetic people.

To begin, let's turn to the socio-political context of Vancouverism.

**2.1** As is evident here, we look like Americans, but our culture and attitudes differ markedly from those of our cousins to the south and people elsewhere in the world. This creates our own set of dynamics for city building. Vancouverism is a truly Canadian expression, but its themes are relevant everywhere.

# 2

# A UNIQUE CONTEXT FOR URBAN INNOVATION

**WE LOOK LIKE** Americans and we sound like Americans and so we are often mistaken for Americans (see Figure 2.1). Many Canadians wear a little Maple Leaf pin to differentiate themselves when they travel abroad – it makes one chuckle. But looks can deceive. In fact, as my compatriot readers will well know, Canadians are quite different people. Modern Canadian culture is unique and distinct from those of our founding Indigenous, British, and French ancestors, and from that of our giant neighbour to the south. It evolved in its own fashion, partly as an amalgam for mutual coexistence, partly as a tolerant mosaic of hundreds of immigrant ways of living, and partly, especially during the past few decades, as a deliberate contrast to the American way. At a more subtle level, our special path may have had something to do with the vastness of our territory, the glory but also the terror of its nature, and the way we had to come together during our formative years to cope with the overwhelming impacts of our setting. Whatever the reasons, the story of our uniqueness is a grand tale unto itself and could fill a whole book of trends, directions, and indicators. Far be it for me to take on that task – I am simply not competent to do so. But a few aspects have to do with making cities, and these I know about because I lived them from day to day over many years. So, I will survey them in this chapter – at least my view of these aspects – because any reader, especially from beyond our borders, who wishes to understand the emergence of Vancouverism will need to have sensitivity not just to the personalities, policies, and practices but also to the socio-political context. For Canadians, even the contrasts between provinces can be significant, so for those who live outside British Columbia, I hope this overview will also be enlightening.

Let me start with general attitudes. In my experience, Canadians accept one another more spontaneously than other peoples do, and they embrace newcomers with little judgment. The oft repeated joke about Canadians is that we are the most polite people on the planet and perhaps the most accommodating to differing views and ways. As with the Dutch, this may be grounded more in pragmatism than in a deep-seated philosophy, but the reasons don't matter. As an immigrant from the United States, I felt from my first years in government that Canadians take a more collective view of living, community, and government than do our southern neighbours, which creates a fertile platform for action in the design and building of cities. Many people claim that Canada resembles the Nordic countries in its social contract. Our communalized health care system is a vivid indicator of this. Perhaps a more superficial but nonetheless telling one is that we are less litigious than our American friends – well, except for Ontario development fights, because of the strange legal distortions of what was long called the Ontario Municipal Board. In British Columbia and in most of the provinces of Canada, the contrast is remarkable. In all my years as a public official, I was never in court once to explain an action or defend a public policy – and I endured very few of what are called "exams for discovery," which are the preparations for litigation. Generally speaking, Canadians just seem to make more room for each other, so we live and let live, and we accommodate and compromise when we have to – so there is less need for the courts.

## ATTITUDES ABOUT GOVERNMENT

I can also testify from experience that, on the whole, Canadians still believe in the efficacy and mission of government. Although they may sometimes doubt the intentions of individual officials, they look positively to government for both resources and leadership. In the end, their trust enables government to move forward with confidence and determination. Their faith allows government to take progressive action and test ideas with enough time and rope to prove results. Most government officials are respected, which allows them to exercise real leadership in their communities. And because they generally enjoy high status in our society, the public service can take its pick of the brightest and best. In Canada, you just don't hear the comment that someone went into government because he or she could not succeed in the private sector – that is just not relevant to us. These are certainly the attitudes that I have always felt as a planner and urban designer working in Vancouver and in this country. This certainly contrasts with what I have felt during assignments in other countries. So, when my colleagues and I discovered or invented our ideas for building the new Vancouver, we were listened to, and we and our political masters had the clout to carry these ideas ahead. Of course, it was not easy. We had our battles, our defeats, and our setbacks. But we also had a more generous audience than professionals like us encounter in many countries.

However, in bringing forward new propositions, my colleagues and I felt that it was essential to convene a wide discussion so that people could learn about them, judge them, and embrace them on their own terms, not just because we felt they were good ideas. Contrary to what some might think, working in a setting of political and social trust makes you more responsible to reach out for consensus and support, rather than simply taking off on your own and hoping for the best. Thus, public engagement lies at the heart of Vancouverism, as will be obvious throughout this book.

Another aspect of respected government has been the opportunity for collaboration between the private and public sectors as we were putting together the formula and reality of Vancouverism. A complex city depends upon such collaboration because neither side can deliver the full result that people expect. In addition, the practical potential for this collaboration is fostered when there is a balance of power between the public and private sectors. I discuss the dimensions of this collaboration in Chapter 9, but my point here is that the general attitude of Canadians about government has nurtured a healthy collaboration among interests. Canadians' natural belief in and support for government makes for strong government, which can thus persuade the private sector to collaborate and accommodate, no matter how powerful the private forces may be. Peers respect peers – that's how it felt to me as we negotiated the solutions for innovative development and conferred the rights for that development. If negotiations are played out correctly among equals, a lot of finesse can come out of this dynamic, as a delicate balance is achieved between public and private interests.

## A HIERARCHY OF GOVERNMENTS

Although the tolerance and even support for government in Canada have generally been positive for city building, the institutional and organizational arrangements seem to neither particularly assist nor detract from it, except to make our cites quite self-reliant as compared to the norm in other countries. Nonetheless, it is helpful to understand these arrangements. Let me offer an overview.

Most readers will know that the government of English Canada was shaped by the British parliamentary system.[1] In Ottawa and the provinces, the party that controls the majority of seats in Parliament's House of Commons or in the provincial legislatures forms the government. Seats are allocated to geographically defined electoral districts called ridings,[2] and most laws are adopted by a simple democratic principle of majority rules. Most governments have a four-year mandate but can fall if they lose the confidence of the majority of members. An election is then held to find a new majority. This tends to encourage responsive government.

The Canadian Constitution, repatriated from Great Britain only in 1982, defines the rights and limits of federal and provincial authority. Key to our story is that cities are the responsibility of the provincial government and are created and managed through its legislation. We say that cities are the "creatures" of the provinces. As a result, they are more at arm's length from the federal government than in, say, the United States, and depend less on it for funding. In the late 1990s, it was estimated that for every dollar of senior government spending in a Canadian city, about eight dollars would have been spent by senior governments in an American city.[3] These proportions have probably remained relatively steady over the years. Except for a few years very long ago when we enjoyed a momentary ministry of urban affairs, Canada has seldom had a federal agenda for cities (though I will talk about several important exceptions). Federal programs and funding for cities are generally channelled through the provincial governments. Between provinces, there is no consistency of civic governance or funding. The national government typically does not play a dominant role in Canadian civic life, although occasionally it doles out some money for urgent infrastructure through its provincial partners. The result of all this is that cities have constrained local resources, which prompts them to be clever about where and how to acquire the resources they need. Necessity is the mother of invention, to quote a hackneyed phrase, which will become evident for Vancouver as our story unfolds.

Most Canadian cities are governed by one overarching provincial law that defines municipal powers and limits in each province. A few, usually older preeminent cities and several resort communities, have a charter, a special law that applies solely to them. Vancouver has one of these. This can be very useful for an innovative civic agenda because the Province can often be convinced to give a charter city the right to try something new, for good or ill, without at the same time extending that right to all cities and towns. Charter cities can experiment with new ways of doing things, and if these prove viable and beneficial, the same opportunity can be opened to other places. If an idea proves counterproductive or difficult, then it goes no further. Unique urban solutions can be enabled without setting off unexpected deformations of the same idea. In no uncertain terms, I would say that the Vancouver Charter has allowed for all kinds of experimentation resulting in innovation. Examples include Vancouver having its own building code, shaping a very agile development-permissions system, implementing a special infrastructure tax on redevelopment in the situation of urban infill, not just for new greenfield development, and even stopping the demolition of the small old hotels that house many low-income people.

## SPECIAL FEATURES OF LOCAL VANCOUVER GOVERNANCE

Various civic governance imperatives came out of the structure of the layers of government in the Canadian political culture, but some of the most important features that engendered Vancouverism are what might simply be called accidents of history, which influenced how the city and the region would be governed. Three such features come to mind.

### A constellation of local governments

First, the Vancouver region has not experienced the municipal amalgamation that befell the biggest Canadian cities, Toronto and Montreal, and even smaller regions such as Halifax. The Lower Mainland, as the overall metropolitan region of Vancouver is often called, remains a patchwork of twenty on-shore municipalities (there is also one additional island municipality and several special-purpose jurisdictions), with Vancouver at its centre. Each municipality exercises all the independent authorities of local government, which allows it to tailor its policies and procedures to suit itself. The biggest benefit for Vancouver, which has a more urban trajectory than the outriding municipalities and serves consumers with more urban tastes, is that it has not been politically overwhelmed or constrained by its suburbs. Toronto, by contrast, has been subject to severe suburban checks on its urban growth ideas, such as accommodating residential intensification, offering social supports, and shaping places through deliberate public design. Because no mega-amalgamations occurred in Vancouver, we were not compelled to negotiate between urban and suburban agendas, with the trade-offs that would inevitably have been required. We enjoyed both the political support of city council and the consumer support of urban citizens for the most advanced, intense, diverse, and complex urban structures that we could invent or import.

The downside of foregoing amalgamation is that the regional systems and perspectives that allow large complex urban regions to thrive could have been left to languish while the separate municipalities either squabbled among themselves or became complacent. The Lower Mainland avoided that fate by adopting a very simple governance solution. Its many local jurisdictions are augmented by one overarching metropolitan government that is a federation of the civic governments. Elected officials from each municipality are locally appointed to its board of directors, which is responsible for regional decision making. This federation was originally called the Greater Vancouver Regional District (GVRD); in recent years, the name has been nicely shortened to Metro Vancouver. This overarching but limited government only has authority over those few but vital functions that stretch across the whole region. Its core responsibilities are drinking water, waste-water treatment, and solid-waste management. It also regulates air quality, does high-level planning for urban growth, manages a regional parks system, and provides some affordable housing. It is enhanced by a regional-level transportation authority called TransLink, which handles transit and regional roads; TransLink also facilitates cycling and walking infrastructure, as well as goods movement. In addition, regional land use is controlled in part by a provincial farmland authority, the Agricultural Land Reserve (ALR), which protects useable farmland from urban development. Interestingly, as a result of the ALR, Metro Vancouver contains a higher proportion of farmland within its boundaries than any other major North American city-region – something that residents value but that has required local governments to be particularly efficient about land use. So, the Lower Mainland enjoys a special balance – local authorities preside over matters that are best met with unique and diverse solutions at the local level, whereas regional and higher authorities deal with metropolitan-wide functions and concerns. This very handy division of labour layers responsibilities and has very little overlap or duplication.

The implication of this regional system for Vancouverism has been a freedom to focus local government attention on a fine level of detail – not just as policy but also through very specific design and ongoing management of the new ideas for living with intensity and diversity – without the kind of distractions that take a lot of air time when a single decision-making body must cover all the bases. This reminds me of the system in Australia, where many core cities, with their historically constrained boundaries, have a very geographically focused authority but can attend in wonderful detail to the qualities of the place for which they are responsible. I think that is why big Australian cities are so refined in their public realm and culture. But our system is better, because the balance of the region, outside the old core, is not left to a totally separate state authority, as in Australia, and the local perspective in regional management is well represented through the federation.

## A city council elected at large

The second helpful characteristic of Vancouver municipal government is that councillors are not tasked with representing certain geographic areas, such as wards or districts. Instead, they are elected at large, and their job is to serve all citizens. City council is composed of the mayor and ten councillors, all elected through adult universal suffrage. Though individual councillors sometimes see themselves as speaking for a distinct area, often their personal home neighbourhood, their responsibility does not stop there. They must look after the interests of the whole city and all its residents. When I started out as a young planner, I felt that this system was wrong because no one councillor was right down there, face to face, at the level of individual citizens to fully understand and represent them. But then I spent many years watching area-based systems in action, and this changed my view 180 degrees. I have seen such parochialism, narrow-mindedness, and petty thinking in ward politics. I have seen general public interests trampled by local biases and political dynamics. I have seen the most vulgar kind of vote trading and political favours acted out between wards whose representatives ignored the overall public good. This made me realize that the city-wide at-large system is much more hospitable to positive, progressive urbanism because it forces elected officials to take the broader and longer view. To some degree, it also facilitates a more delicate division of labour between elected and appointed officials to ensure that the overall public interest is empowered and valued over any one particular private interest or even one particular public interest. I have learned that a holistic view is vital as cities become so complex and pluralistic. As those weaknesses in the ward system have become manifest in other cities as they matured, this has all been sidestepped in Vancouver because of its at-large system. On the whole, Vancouver has enjoyed talented and big-thinking councillors – what I call *real* civic leaders, with a sense of vision for the whole community. Its political and public inquiry into new ideas has been quite sophisticated. And major innovations have been sponsored, even when they would only seem to initially benefit one area or, conversely, would impact one area over others. Many of the ideas of Vancouverism would have bitten the dust without the overall responsibilities that characterize our political system and the broad perspective that it requires. This conclusion has certainly suited the size of city that Vancouver has been during the key years of Vancouverism. I realize that once a city gets too large, either through sheer growth or amalgamation, local interests can be trampled by an insensitive aloofness, so some form of local representation has to come back into play. To everything there is a season and a reason – if you're small, you must think big; if you're big, you must protect the small view. Perhaps, by chance rather than deliberately, Vancouver has so far achieved a balance that works well for city building.

### A strong bureaucracy

A final significant characteristic of Vancouver's local government is that the City is run under a "weak mayor" system, which is very much dominated by a highly professionalized bureaucracy. This is more typical in Canada than in many other countries, because of its English roots. However, Vancouver's system, even by Canadian standards, concentrates more power and authority in its bureaucracy than is the case elsewhere. Functionally, the mayor is just one member of council, though he or she chairs council and can make certain appointments to facilitate its business, such as membership in standing committees. Much of the mayor's power comes from personal clout rather than from authority that is conferred by the Vancouver Charter. Unlike Seattle, our close neighbour to the south, Vancouver has no separate politicized legislative branch. Essentially, the mayor and councillors act as a board of directors and are paid accordingly. Former mayor Mike Harcourt used to jest that council members were the part-time employees of the City. On the other hand, City administration is handled by a strong, vested civil service that is deeply professionalized, carefully selected and promoted, long sitting, and paid very well. The chief operating officer is the city manager, who has an array of powers, not the least of which is control of the management team. Various department heads are vested with specific powers, not just by council but also through the Vancouver Charter. For example, the charter designates the director of planning as the approval authority for typical development within existing zoning, even though, as will be described later, this has been elaborated with a board of officials responsible for development permissions for big projects. Although council hires and fires senior bureaucrats, and oversees all civic business, the bureaucracy runs the day-to-day work of the organization. All employees report to the city manager rather than to council. This strong civil service system has provided a long-standing discipline to the City and the way in which it makes and implements decisions. A solid policy framework has been built through the years, and most decisions adhere to it, even if the philosophy and political bias of council shift from mandate to mandate. Generally, the strong bureaucracy facilitates long-term thinking and planning, and it secures a very long horizon for applying a consistent civic vision. Political checks and balances keep the bureaucracy on its toes and honest. Though a sea change in council can result in widespread reform by firing the old guard and bringing in new leadership, this tends to happen only once in a generation or so.

Of course, this system is reinforced when the bureaucratic leaders such as the chief planners earn the trust of the politicians by fighting battle after battle through the years with positive and popular outcomes. The system can wobble if that trust does not exist. In our time, on a solid framework of trust built initially by Ray Spaxman and expanded and consolidated very carefully and through a lot of hard work by Ann McAfee and myself, the planning service clicked along relatively coherently and quite predictably. After adopting new directions, the agency was profoundly motivated to make them happen over many years and many councils, and through the contributions of thousands of people, in a plethora of consistent decisions. In a sense, this was a planner's dream for how local government should work. I always felt blessed. Our ideas for a better Vancouver, after intensive discussion by the community and political debate, after adoption by council, and after an orientation for the organization, were actually implemented and also elaborated and diversified to remain relevant as things changed and as we learned more.

There is no doubt that we built a strong consensus around our work, not only at city hall but also out in the community and with the development industry. Frankly, it floundered to some degree and for some time after we left and has only recently been restabilized. But it would not have carried the day without the powerful organization in which we worked. The point is that a stable, consistent, and strong bureaucracy, coupled with the solid trust of politicians in officials, supported innovation and then innovation on top of innovation.

**2.2** Vancouverites are no less fond of their single-family homes than anyone else in North America but, in a significant counter-trend, they have become increasingly open to and interested in living closer together. This photo of ground-oriented apartments in Mount Pleasant shows a delicate version of multiple-family living that appeals to many.

**2.3** Until the 1990s, flight to the suburbs was as prevalent in Vancouver as in any other North American city. Major multi-government initiatives for several decades, to revitalize older decaying inner-city neighbourhoods, effectively stemmed the flow. Places such as Mount Pleasant became popular alternatives, with conversion of larger homes to apartments and infill of rear-yard houses, which set the stage for higher-density offerings. ▶

## ATTITUDES ABOUT LIVING

Now I want to take a completely different perspective on the general attitude of supporting community and tolerance that seems to characterize Canadians and certainly characterizes Vancouverites. I want to talk about living patterns. One of the many ironies of this country is that, though we possess a vast territory, we have become increasingly open to and interested in living closer together than in the past (see Figure 2.2).

Like most of North America, coming out of the Great War, Canadians spread their habitat all over the landscape in a phenomenon of suburbanization that was as pervasive as anywhere in the world. This seemed to suggest that we liked privacy and independence above all else. It also illustrated the dislike, even hatred, that most people felt for density – a widespread attitude that still prevails throughout the country because, traditionally, most density has been so poorly realized.

But alternative attitudes started to surface as early as the 1970s, when we effectively turned down the flow to the suburbs by rejuvenating older neighbour-hoods (see Figure 2.3), which will be discussed in Chapter 4. More and more people – still a minority but an increasingly important one – came to appreciate and enjoy the benefits of a living situation that brought them a little closer together. Instead of just the single-family dwelling being the aspiration of most households, we started to embrace home conversions, townhouses, and apartments as viable if not necessarily equal alternative choices. Of course, the reasons for this trend went beyond a simple change in outlook. The rising cost of housing, the diminishing supply of land for development, and the arrival of immigrants who were familiar with high-density living played a role as well. But the result was that an increasing number of people became interested in multiple living, at least theoretically, some of whom even saw it as chic and superior to separate villa living. This trend was evident to a greater or lesser degree in most Canadian cities, as the child-bearing years of the baby-boom generation wound down, even though, admittedly, most people still preferred the single-family suburbs. Because Vancouver's land availability is so tight and perhaps because its beautiful views become more accessible as one builds up, we were well poised to take advantage of the demographic shift earlier than elsewhere because people saw other benefits of apartment life. This was a fundamental shift of attitudes by enough people that gave Vancouverism a chance, both politically and in the marketplace. Because it is about densification and diversification, the new Vancouver style, brought first to the inner-city, would have died on the vine (or, more truthfully, in our minds) if consumers had not felt at least a nascent inclination to try it out and, having done so, to adopt it. Chapter 7 explains how we exploited this inclination.

## A CLEVER REGIONAL PLAN CONTEXTUALIZES VANCOUVERISM

The birth of Vancouverism was hosted by more than a hospitable attitude among the public and an amenable government structure. It was also enabled by a context of supportable public policy. I have already mentioned CityPlan, the Central Area Plan,[4] and a tradition of local area plans as part of the genealogy of Vancouverism.

Much further back, in the 1970s, a clever and forward-looking regional planning effort really set the stage for all that was to follow. Called the Liveable Region Plan, it was completed for the GVRD by Harry Lash, one of the last century's most gifted, dedicated, progressive, and energetic urban planners.[5] Lash was the first director of regional planning at the GVRD. The regional plan he created brought an urban interest to the regional perspective in Greater Vancouver, which before then had been mostly concerned with rural and agricultural matters. His planning process included the most extensive public participation that our part of the world had yet seen. These were Lash's primary passions, and they remain important legacies. His plan dealt with the full extent of the region, including the Fraser River Delta and the mountainsides that make up the Lower Mainland. The tenets of the plan continue to shape the region to this day, after several major updates through the years,[6] and its component themes have been refined over several iterations into more detailed plans and policies. The process through which it was produced set a high expectation of both public engagement and technical analysis that remains the gold standard for planning in our part of the world. One of Lash's greatest achievements was building a compelling public and political consensus around his ideas that has been passed on in an organic way for more than three generations. Years later, Ken Cameron, a distinguished and powerful regional planner, revamped and revitalized the plan before handing it on. The Liveable Region Plan remains essentially unchallenged, though many other ideas for progressive cities have come and gone. It is so clear and logical that it naturally convinces every observer without the need for interpreters or advocates. It simply makes sense – it did when it was invented, and it does just as much today.

The Liveable Region Plan expresses a profoundly simple concept for converting the Lower Mainland's thin skin of low-density post-war urban sprawl into a hierarchy of more intensive, diverse, and differentiated urban places called "regional town centres" (see Figure 2.4). Ultimately, these centres will be connected by a complete transit network. This pattern of centres and transit stretches from end to end of the region like a pervasive web. The Liveable Region Plan was and is a plan to mature an urban system. It is physically reshaping urban patterns in a deliberate way, and augmenting what already exists within that urban system rather than devaluing it.

For transportation, the plan offered the framework for differentiation of travel options into a mutually reinforcing multi-modal system with a diversity of movement: rail transit, buses, cars, bikes, and walking. Rapid transit became the key new scaffold for all other movement networks rather than the road system (see Figure 2.5). In a car-romanced society, this opened up the potential to shift priority from the car without challenging its legitimacy, a measure that was politically popular. When the plan's approach to transportation was added to Vancouver's anti-freeway strategy, the result for average people was to set in play development of practical transportation choices that few newly built cities can boast of, certainly not in North America.

For historical land-use patterns and lifestyles, the plan provided a way to rejuvenate and support areas without destabilization or displacement. In the immediate hinterland of existing low-density housing and neighbourhoods, the regional town centres are becoming the transactional hubs that serve most day-to-day needs. They are becoming the predominant local places – jobs centres, locations for mixing in new housing types, retail nodes, and recreation bases. And this land-use principle of clustering also facilitated the transportation modes that are most dependent on proximity – cycling and walking. Concentrating on town centres was a particularly clever feature of Lash's plan because it took the bite out of suburbanites' anxieties that each new development would be one more nail in the coffin of what they preferred as a place to live and a way to live. It left most of the lower-density neighbourhoods alone. It showed that new dimensions could be added without sacrificing what many people dearly loved. But it also added things that people found missing in their home locale.

**2.4** The Liveable Region Plan from the 1970s, undertaken by the regional government, then called the Greater Vancouver Regional District, was a smart proposition to cluster density into town centres, which are now coming together, with the inner-city as their apex. In the foreground of this panorama is one of the important regional town centres, Metrotown in Burnaby, with downtown Vancouver in the distance.

**2.5** In the Liveable Region Plan, rapid transit was proposed to connect all the town centres. This pattern is now being completed, as seen here in Vancouver's Joyce area, which lies at the edge of Burnaby's Metrotown.

For urban design, the plan furnished a logic for differentiated placemaking within what was previously a one-dimensional cityscape, building upon and extending from the few highlights that already existed. These included the core downtown area of Vancouver and the traditional downtowns of Lonsdale in North Vancouver and New Westminster, which had once been separate historical centres. Each regional town centre was meant to find its own unique land-use mix, density, scale, and character as competitive anchors for its part of the region. Here again, we see Lash at his best. Dealing as he was with many municipal authorities, all anxious not to be outdone by the others, he offered a huge value-add to each of them in the form of a competitive centre that they could design and grow in their own image, in their own time, and in their own way. He allotted one or more huge projects to each municipality, which are still being implemented almost fifty years later in new growth nodes in such places as Coquitlam and even Port Moody, communities far to the east of Vancouver.

You might say that the plan was sustainable before sustainability came along. It presented an opportunity to save the green lungs of the region for the health and enjoyment of a fast expanding new population. Clustering development within already built areas would diminish the pressure on remaining green expanses. Through the years, this idea was elaborated into a specific protected green zone that, along with the provincial ALR for farmland, has saved over 50 percent of the regional land area from urbanization. The pattern of differentiated scale and density also enabled the more sustainable delivery of utilities and more economic delivery of municipal services.

There is no doubt that the Liveable Region Plan was a smart framework for the Lower Mainland or that every municipality should be grateful for it. But it was especially helpful in the core of the region – in downtown Vancouver – as we put together the various dimensions of Vancouverism. First of all, it provided a coherent pattern within which to nest Vancouverism. Within the hierarchy of places, downtown Vancouver is at the apex of the regional town centres. Looking at the logic of the Liveable Region Plan, with its quest for a balance between jobs and housing, one could see the imperative and opportunity to dramatically increase the population of the core because it already had more than its fair share of jobs.

Second, creating many town centres meant that no single one, including the inner-city, would hinder the growth of the others because all of them had the same freedom to innovate and diversify. I think of the creative growth of the Surrey City Centre or Metrotown in Burnaby, both suburban nodes, as urban energy points that are not oppressed in the least by our adventure of Vancouverism at the heart of the region.

Third, the language and ideas of the plan contained hints for most of the necessary measures to make downtown Vancouver a special place. The Liveable Region Plan offered numerous cues that we could exploit in our detailed area planning. It gave an agenda of intensity and diversity for all regional town centres even as it advocated that each one be unique. We took that agenda to heart. It has been a pleasure to see that the architectural and urban design models of Vancouverism also found expression in many town centres throughout the region – not as copies but as localized versions that reflect district differences.

Fourth, the clever transportation strategy that would eventually start a shift in modes has had the effect of dramatically opening up accessibility of our inner-city through rapid transit. At the same time, now obsolete automobile infrastructure in the inner-city is being dismantled to open up valuable land for more productive uses.

And finally, I have always seen the Liveable Region Plan as the key policy context that gave us the confidence to add a significantly large population to the inner-city. We could do this knowing that essential green areas, so necessary as respite for a massive metropolitan population and for ecological performance, were not being squandered. Instead, they were being protected. The vital ALR was doing the same job to protect open lands that would be needed to grow food nearby.

To me, all of this has meant that the progressive story of Vancouverism might one day not just be a localized downtown phenomenon but would find expression throughout our little patch of the province, giving a coherent structure and form to the entire Lower Mainland. As you take off or land at YVR, you need only look out the airplane window at the complete, though ever-changing, patterns of our magnificent delta to see that it is all of one magnificent logic – a giant human composition that holds its own even within the spectacular arms of the mountains and the sparkle of the sea.

## OTHER TANGENTS

It is always hard to explain why new ideas pop up and are embraced in a specific time and place and with a specific group of people. There is something mysterious about that. I know that the factors I describe here are important because I have seen the particular causes and effects. I am sure other interpreters will find their own reasons. But to round out my views, let me put several other tangents on the table that I think had some influence in fostering Vancouverism.

I have already mentioned the flat-lined economic times around the beginning of the 1980s that necessitated new thinking for how we might all make a living in Vancouver in the future. The best ideas often arise from anxious necessity. Desperation sometimes provokes people to latch on to what looks promising even if unproven. Think of a community that had lived, if not lavishly at least very happily, off the bounty of its natural resources for about a century. Think of the security and complacency that this would have engendered. And then, think of it all gone away through global corporate restructuring. That was so jarring that many Vancouverites were open to new propositions for the future. I remember when everybody embraced the ideas of Grace McCarthy, an influential provincial cabinet minister, who advocated that we make tourism our dynamo economic sector. She said that we must see the magnificence of our province as a destination, train our people to be good hosts, bring our beauty to the attention of the world, and build an infrastructure to accommodate masses of visitors that we might then expect. Grace (by the way, everyone called her Grace rather than Mrs. McCarthy or Madam Minister or any other formal name, and that was just the way she liked it) became the agent and sponsor of all kinds of smart initiatives to achieve these ends. British Columbia and Vancouver owe Grace a great debt because she gave us the lifeline from our past to our future. Then, her idea was fertilized by another idea, which was that we could draw people not only to visit Vancouver but to immigrate and make their lives here simply because it was such a lovely, hospitable place. Everyone latched on to the idea that a big cohort of these new arrivals might be the creative thinkers in the various ideas industries – high tech, animation, filmmaking, and any other dimension of imagination. The tag for these propositions was simple: henceforth, Vancouver would live off its "wits and good looks." We would live off that already mentioned sobriquet, "super, natural British Columbia," which Grace's team invented. Well, Vancouverism, being all about making a city as enthralling as its setting, was just the ticket for this new economy. No civic strategy could have been more in line with the economic realities and prospects of the day.

The final factor that is worth mentioning has to do with a feature of Vancouver's culture that distinguishes it from the other big cities in Canada, especially the pacesetters of Toronto and Montreal. Vancouver is a new city. Founded only in 1886, it has a very short history. It has almost no vested, long-in-control establishment. It has no conservative bedrock of attitudes that would quash new and independent thinking. It started out with very little great wealth that could wash out any proposal that did not suit the established interests. It is a city of new people – immigrants who think in their own way, who bring their own ideas with them, who are blind to social constraints, and who are naturally quite free thinkers. In Vancouver, status is very much based on merit and hard work – we are a striving community that grabs good ideas and runs with them, that goes after the main chance. We are a worldly people – not just because we come from all over the globe but also because we travel everywhere in the world. That makes us inquisitive, critical, and I would even say, aspiring of the very best we can make for our own homes, our own families, and our own fortunes. I have never understood why we were given that epithet of lotus-eaters, because I've never seen much evidence of sloth during my half-century here. Given all this, it would have been surprising if Vancouverism had not been invented here. I won't downplay the fact that most people had a status quo view of city imperatives and forces. I'm sure they were shocked by some of the propositions for Vancouverism as they were initially presented. They rolled their eyes and were skeptical. But there were enough people who did not share their view to build a movement for change. Even most of the skeptics were at least open-minded. And that gave us our launchpad. We had a problem, we had some great cues locally and abroad, we created the idea, we enjoyed both fortuitous support and built deliberate support, and we tenaciously made it happen. In this context, Vancouverism can be seen as actually spontaneous.

In its very spontaneity, it is not surprising that Vancouverism sprang less from the established truths for city building than from a fresh view of how this might be done to suit the unique circumstances of our city. The next chapter explores what were seen as rather strange mindsets at the time.

**3.1** Urbanism is our friend. Vancouverism has been an urban rather than a sub-urban adventure, with a tight focus on the inner-city. This photo captures the essence of our interests, with its density coupled with amenity. It shows the edge of False Creek on the down-town peninsula.

# 3

# COUNTER-INTUITIVE PERSPECTIVES FOR SHAPING A CITY

**THE BEST CITY** building I know is always based upon principles. In Chapter 1, I listed the principles that drove Vancouverism: we adopted the neighbourhood unit as our basic building block, broadened transportation choices, incorporated diversity into new areas, relied on urban design, became increasingly committed to environmental responsibility, and fostered collaboration among all the forces and agents of city building. These six principles came together out of wide public involvement, overt policy formulation, deliberate design processes, strategic political action, and careful development management. But something much more subtle was at play that enabled Vancouverism to be birthed and to thrive. I've already said that ours was a community of new people. As such, we brought a set of counter-intuitive perspectives to our work. These were liberating mindsets underpinning all of our thinking. These mindsets were contrary to the common wisdom of their time and, therefore, opened doors of inquiry that would otherwise have remained firmly closed.

When TEAM took over city hall in 1973, Vancouver was a very average town, with predictable opinions and, frankly, predictable outcomes. But the TEAM reformers set about to change all of that. In part, they did this in the dramatic and, at the time, shocking decisions they made about the future of the city, such as their rejection of freeways. In part, they did this by bringing new blood into the civic organization and into civic affairs, including people who thought very differently from the old guard. You thrived if you looked forward, and you languished if you looked back. Even though the great majority of Vancouverites had not yet embraced the new agenda and the new way of conceptualizing the city, many vital seeds for change had been planted. Now, we fast-forward about two decades. We find those seeds have taken root and all kinds of new ideas are flourishing.

If you could have dug into the minds of the key thinkers who were formulating Vancouverism in our generation, you would have discovered what, at the time, were considered very quirky attitudes. I have often wondered why that was the case. On the face of it, we did not appear to be particularly unusual. Some of us were immigrants, bringing ideas and precedents from other places. I was one of those people. Our leader, Ray Spaxman, was an Englishman who came to us via Toronto. Admittedly, a few people were refugees from an American experience that no longer worked for them. Most were native-born Canadians with what I feel is an anchoring perspective – a touch of the free spirit and a strain of optimism, undistorted by foreign imperatives and foreign history. That was a great advantage. We were mostly young and somewhat naive. But a few of us, who were older and wiser, often guided the way and sounded the alarm that avoided disaster. Ron Youngberg, a senior deputy in the planning department, comes to mind as one of the wisest souls. Most of us had matured as professionals during the precedent generation, within the dynamic if often debilitating culture of city hall at that time. That generation was high on principles, low on compromise, fed up with past ways, and aggressively looking for new directions. We inherited most of that, though we handled it in a different way. We took nothing as given, questioned everything, questioned each other, debated everything, and were fearless, at least within the confines of our supportive organization.

Of course, we had to cope with a few crotchety old-timers who were peppered throughout the civic departments. They were entrenched long before the reform leaders came on the scene, and they were powerful. But in the end, our wave was just too strong, and we had a certain advantage – they would ride into the sunset long before we did. In fact, we drew camaraderie from comparison with the old-timers and from our struggles with them. But the sands were shifting in our favour, creating new beachheads for doing business our way. The bureaucratic culture that prevailed during our early formative years was pretty tricky. I call it the "time of the warlords." The major civic departments, such as engineering and planning, were led by virtual princes who marshalled vast armies of bureaucrats to fight battle after battle for hegemony. By the time we took the reins, everyone was pretty fed up with all the drama, and it was clear that a lot of excellence had been sacrificed for the thrill of victory. Even the princes had mellowed or departed, so we had a unique opportunity to think and do things differently. And that is just what we did.

Five mindsets coalesced and became pervasive. I like to call them our five friends of the heart and of the brain. They were so widely held that we seldom challenged or even talked about them – they were just there within our belief systems, under the surface, quietly guiding each one of us. They were absolutely contrary to most thinking at the time, and had we expressed them overtly, which we virtually never did, most people would have laughed. But they played out in everything that I describe in this book. Let me now, on behalf of a whole generation, testify to those mindsets.

### URBANISM IS OUR FRIEND

If there is one demographic fact that characterized the years leading up to the new thinking about Vancouver, it is the flight to the suburbs. Some people at city hall might have dreamed of a different kind of inner-city, but a lot of people just wanted to get the hell out of the place. They wanted a fundamentally different suburban dream away from the problems and the history of the central city. Their views were reinforced by television shows that painted a bleak picture of old downtowns and by marketers who trumpeted the virtues of life in the spacious forests and farms of the hinterland. They were a strong majority, and their exodus jeopardized the future of the city as much as any other single factor. Such consumer trends can become tidal waves and are very powerful.

By contrast, the inventors of Vancouverism were thinking exactly the opposite. A profound bias that we brought to our paradigm was that the inner-city is where the urban soul resides (see Figure 3.1). This was both our great given and our great blindness, handed on as a challenge to the generation that followed us. But our view is understandable. After all, Vancouver, all of it, is essentially the inner-city. It is comprised of the core, on and near the downtown peninsula, a constellation of first neighbourhoods, and then a constellation of second neighbourhoods, much of it built out and very settled by the 1950s (with infill brownfield exceptions that grabbed a lot of our attention). There were no greenfield sites within its boundaries. This was not the urban fringe or outer post-war suburbs – those were part of the nineteen municipalities that border the city of Vancouver on three sides. We were outsiders to those municipalities.

So, ours was an urban perspective. The ideas and accomplishments of Vancouverism are inner-city constructs. They were somewhat strange for the rest of the growing city, even though they were clearly cradled in the Liveable Region Plan. Very little of what we invented can be transferred to a suburban setting, at least not without major rejigging. Other than the town centres and rapid transit lines, mentioned in the last chapter, the basic fabric, pattern, and scale of the Vancouver suburbs have evolved very little, which can also be said for Canadian suburbs generally. This poses the single greatest challenge for planners of the next generation. How will they make these suburbs, where over 65 percent of Canadians continue to live, fulfilling, sustainable, and resilient?

The blunt truth is that, in our time, we really didn't care much about the suburbs or their problems – they were not on our agenda. The Liveable Region Plan supplied all the answers on that subject. People used to kid me that my eyes would glaze over if I went east of Boundary Road, where I would be stepping into vague suburban territory. We all felt that way. The prevailing message was "urbanism is our friend."

### CONGESTION IS OUR FRIEND

When the work of our generation got fully under way, most people really liked cars, even though, politically, they had rejected freeways. They aspired to car ownership, invested a lot of energy in choosing a car that best expressed their personality, often had several cars in one household, and used their cars spontaneously for almost every kind of trip. And they wanted the car well looked after in our urban schemes. The car was king – period.

And so, the key urban thinkers in the Vancouver of our generation held a somewhat peculiar attitude about cars. Even though many of these people drove cars, lived outside the inner-city and, like most people, fought every day to go back and forth to work (Ann McAfee listened to entire audio books during her long daily trek), the needs of the car were just not a high priority for the city we were designing. I myself lived in the city core, less than a thirty-minute walk from city hall, first in the West End and then in Granville Slopes, one of the new neighbourhoods built during our tenure. But I owned a car, drove to work, and used my car constantly during the work day. I think I was pretty typical. But what we *did* and what we *said* were not necessarily in accord. In fact, the language we used all the time was to "tame" the car. So, during our time, we stopped accommodating the car. The generation before us had denied freeways into the core – the big move that remained phenomenally popular among my generation of planners. Now, we drew a line in the sand for further, more modest, allocations for the car. And every year, more and more of the City's traffic engineers joined our way of thinking. There were no more street widenings. There were no more intersection expansions. There were no more curb cuts along sidewalks. The car would have its primary space and that was that.

This became endemic once we understood what we were facing regarding the journey to work, the one set of trips each day that absolutely determined the shape of the whole city and region (which we will come back to in Chapter 5). After pondering the typical transportation fixes without any hope that they would succeed, the breakthrough in our thinking was the realization that the ultimate answer to this dilemma would be a land-use answer. We would have to bring home and work closer together – proximity would tame the monster on the road.

Well, theory is one thing; practice is quite something else. Active transportation improvements were definitely in the cards, though significantly upgrading the system to be pervasive and, therefore, more organically attractive would take many years. The nascent town centres strategy in the Liveable Region Plan would create more proximity between jobs and home, and the "living first" strategy in the core would be a big offering to that same end. There was very little argument that the centres would make alternative transportation modes more attractive, particularly walking and cycling. But we are talking about long-term change and prying people out of a long-held habit of using their cars for the daily commute and everything else – and loving their cars. What else might motivate them to make such a complete reversal of inclinations?

Intuitively and never articulated in formal policy, we came to realize that traffic congestion could be very helpful (see Figure 3.2). The day-to-day frustration that people experience from increased congestion might prompt them to start thinking differently about where they choose to live and about the most comfortable way of getting back and forth to work. Congestion might be the most motivating aspect of all in order to broadly change public behaviour in the right direction. Frankly, we hoped that, of their own accord, people might decide to live closer to their jobs, thus avoiding the daily hell of a long, congested commute. We also hoped that they would then start spontaneously walking to work and, indeed, start walking more for their other trips. Or, given that the rapid transit system moved separately from the clogged street network, they might at least opt for it for their biggest trip each day. So, without making a big deal of it, Vancouverism became about two carrots and one stick: bringing appealing, diverse, and accessible housing close to core jobs; enhancing transit whenever

**3.2** Congestion is our friend. On most major streets coming into downtown, traffic can be bumper-to-bumper, as on Burrard Street, shown here at rush hour. We felt the experience of traffic would motivate people to live downtown, close to work to cut the commute.

**3.3** Density is our friend. We knew this even from the 1960s, when the West End was planned, as glimpsed here from English Bay. Density brings proximity of origins and destinations, but it also makes for vibrancy and efficiencies.

possible and backing that up with better arrangements for walking and cycling; and then just letting the street system languish in comparison to the upgrading work and expansion that would typically happen in most cities. We begin to whisper, "congestion is our friend."

## DENSITY IS OUR FRIEND

Most people in the modern Western world detest density. They find it oppressive, ugly, confusing, dangerous, and exploitative. That was true when we started our repopulation of Vancouver's inner-city, and it remains true to this very day in most cities, especially in North America. Even the otherwise progressive TEAM political caucus was nonplussed about too much density, and stalled it when they felt it was becoming too oppressive. Most people strongly agreed with this attitude. But, in absolute contradiction to that popular perspective, the planners in Vancouver of our generation were on a different track – and a very contrary track. Even before sustainability was on the table, the benefits of densification were crystal clear to us (see Figure 3.3).

Ironically, most of our predecessors agreed with our citizens, feeling just the opposite about density than we did. The struggle played out in most city halls from the mid-1950s onward was a wrangle between planners and developers about density. Many developers made their money from increasing the allowable development on their property – a tendency that Chapter 9 explains more fully – which, of course, is about increasing density. Many planners might tolerate dense downtown office buildings, but they could see the worrisome impacts of what they felt was over-densification of housing – pervasive building coverage of lots with loss of landscape, heights out of scale with the surroundings, and loss of spaciousness, privacy, and other factors of livability. For proof, the planners and the people need only point to project after project that had been built through the years.

The fact that we did not carry on with that tradition nor stay in league with most citizens has always been a little puzzling. I could say we had no choice, because Vancouver had no extra land to expand into – the core is very small and it is surrounded by older revitalized neighbourhoods that were sacrosanct – so we had to go dense and go up. That perhaps explains why we sponsored more density but not why we embraced it so wholeheartedly. I can think of two causes for our about-face. One opened our eyes to density, and the other motivated us to exploit it fully.

The first cause was an intellectual one. We were inspired by what we saw elsewhere – in places where there was a palpable vibe, such as New York or the old European urban centres. We saw the benefits of density if it was done right. Yes, it offered efficiencies of living closer together with tight proximity of origins and destinations. But it also offered cost savings for government in delivering municipal services. It offered a richness of culture and daily experience that brought in a cool, hip factor. It even offered a closeness for neighbourly support and community self-help that would naturally appeal to residents. After all, in the precedent generation, we had cut our teeth on density in the commercial downtown and the residential West End, and we thought we knew something about how to make it work. Maybe our tolerance for and interest in density was experiential, because many of us lived in West End apartments or what, in those days, were called "Mary Tyler Moore–style" home conversions in inner-city neighbourhoods and had discovered the benefits by living them every day. Maybe it was nostalgic, from our reading of the vibrant and exciting urban descriptions sketched by Jane Jacobs, Lewis Mumford, and the other lyrical writers who tried to envision more intensive alternatives to the suburbs.[1] In Chapter 7, I'll come back to the key urban design thinkers who influenced us. Maybe it was feeling like vanguards of a movement, because many of us were active participants in the just then developing network of the New Urbanism,[2] a small but influential group of urbanists who constantly talked up density, even though they were touchy about tall buildings when combined with density. In principle, we had no objections to towers, so we were outriders to that group, but we were nonetheless involved and fascinated with the rest of their vision. Maybe it was just romantic, because we had been captivated by the images of elegant older cities, where forms other than single-family homes in sprawling suburbs prevailed. I, for one, had not lived in a single-family house since I left my family's home to go to university. I revelled in the lifestyle of the West End. I adored the old cities such as Boston, Philadelphia, Savannah, and London. The Georgian townhouses clustered around their lovely green squares just took my heart away. Whatever the reasons, we intuitively embraced density, for housing as much as for offices, and this was reinforced absolutely when we later learned about the parameters of sustainability.

The second cause was a strategic one. As our regulatory system evolved to include incentives for better development performance and to garner public goods, the tender at play was density. I return to this in Chapter 9, but the logic was compelling. If we wanted all the good things we talked about for Vancouver in the future, we would have to find a way to make peace with densification because density is what delivered those things. Certainly, we could not depend on raising local taxes for the new goodies that tended to serve new areas rather than existing ones. The existing taxpayers would have rebelled. Nor could we rely on grants from senior governments. These were being cut back every year, as governments struggled to balance their budgets. And local user fees would barely cover the operating costs of the amenities we needed. So, we turned our sights on the developers and put our development approval process to strategic use. If developers agreed to provide the glorious amenity package and artful urbanism we had in mind, we would approve the densification of their projects thus providing the extra profits to pay for those public goods. In other words, density became an incentive. It was that simple.

Then, we were faced with a dilemma. We had to agree with our predecessors that most of the density we had seen in Vancouver in the past, particularly for housing, had been quite negative, insensitive to people's needs, and generally dull. It may have achieved some social and cultural benefits, but it definitely did not embellish either the city or the lives of our citizens. It was generally unpopular and did not enhance the image of Vancouver for visitors. So, we could see that a big agenda for us would be to "tame" density, mitigating its negative effects, cramming it full of qualities and amenities that people wanted, and giving it a high design edge. We had to make it stylish and popular. We had to reshape it into an image that would be attractive to the average person. And on this score, we were just a little audacious if not downright naive. We were confident that we could do all of this partly because we had some new ideas for what might work and partly because we would engage with people for their own ideas about successful living, but mostly because we had that special regulatory system as a tool that we knew could deliver results. Well, it ended up being harder than we thought, but we didn't know that at the time. So, through our inclinations and with the strength of our assumptions about reshaping the urban housing model, we began to echo with confidence that "density is our friend."

## PROCESS IS OUR FRIEND

When you think of government and its engagement with citizens, there is usually a litany of complaints about process. Many argue that the process with bureaucracy is too long, it is confusing, it requires too much information, it is expensive, it distorts the simple things you want to do. It's a pain in the butt. For as long as anyone can remember, that is what most people have told us. Some politicians have made a name for themselves by diving into troublesome processes to streamline them – to make them faster, simpler, cheaper, more predictable, and less in our faces. Developers claim that too much time is spent on planning and adjudication when time is money. It is a popular narrative. And yet, since as far back as the first TEAM councils in the early 1970s, this anti-process perspective has not been very influential at Vancouver City Hall. Nor did our generation worry about it as we invented Vancouverism. In fact, we took the opposite view. We felt that processes had great benefits, so we devoted time and energy to elaborating the ones that we needed for planning and development management (see Figure 3.4). It is important to understand why that was the case.

Remember that many of our views and aspirations were up against the status quo. We could not expect that either the public or city council would automatically take the time to understand what we were trying to do. They would certainly not automatically endorse the directions we were advocating. Through early losses, we soon began to realize that the public and council needed to be given time and opportunities to come to grips with our planning agenda – to become conversant with our vision of the city, to test new ideas in their minds and with others, to have input into our new directions, and to integrate these different ideas into their own thinking. To achieve that, we needed a process. Just as importantly, we realized that we had to build all kinds of constituencies for our alternative view of the city. Constituencies do not happen spontaneously or quickly. You must reach out to people and inspire them one at a time to change their thinking. Again, that is a process.

But a philosophical element was involved as well. Our attitudes were not just born out of the political assessment we faced. We were children of the 1960s;

**3.4** Process is our friend and regulation is our friend. Having fun as we conceived our transformation was a big part of the efforts. Public input and collaboration depend upon people and planners working together, as in this public session. In the end, we carefully enshrined all the results in clear and extensive regulations.

the time of radical action, community involvement, and breaking down social and government barriers; the time of liberalizing everything. We fundamentally believed in public engagement, and Ray Spaxman had pressed that into our thinking from his first days at city hall. We also believed profoundly in opening up all our procedures and arrangements for everyone to see and become part of – this principle of transparency put us on the side of the angels.

There was also a very practical imperative for embracing process. Inventing a new way of living required that we deeply understand what people preferred, what they would and would not accept, what made them excited, even happy. It required that we talk to people by the thousands in many different ways and on many different specific topics throughout every project we worked on. Not only

did we have processes for that, but we had many kinds of processes with a lot of experimentation about what would and would not fly. We also realized that we needed to tap into the expert knowledge, skills, and talents that were in Vancouver, outside city hall. We had to acknowledge our own fallibility as we pushed what we saw as the cutting edge. We enjoyed a sophisticated design community that could be called upon for peer review, a smart business community that could advise on economic development, an academic community willing to tell us about social and cultural trends, and a well-travelled and savvy citizenry that could populate a planning commission. So, when we planned new districts, adjudicated a particular development proposal, or thought about broad new policies for the future, we needed all these people in the tent with us. We organized an agenda to make that happen.

We inquired about process efficiencies. For big projects that were going through the approval process, we brought in facilitators to help manage the way with as few roadblocks as possible. Several times, the discretionary development management system was subjected to independent review, with improvements recommended and implemented. We diversified public outreach to make it more fun and fulfilling. The planning department took over public engagement from developers, offering better results than they had previously seen, so they were more tolerant of the rest that they faced. But I have to say that all of this was polishing the apple – the critics never even slightly phased our dedication to process. Contrary to the tenor of the times, we were confident in believing, quietly but surely, that "process is our friend."

## REGULATION IS OUR FRIEND

If people hate process, they hate regulation even more. One of the biggest counter-government themes of our time is the strong belief that society is over-regulated. We often see regulatory frameworks that are outdated, generate results that differ from what was originally intended, or serve one interest seemingly at the expense of other interests. Anyone who calls for an end to regulations and a simplification of laws will be part of a crowded space – I am sure that is why so many politicians enjoy going there. Being against regulations is a widespread view that seems to transcend political parties and political philosophies.

Yet Vancouver, to achieve the dimensions of Vancouverism that are so popular at home and inspiring around the world, is among the most regulated cities of modern times. Those of us who were a part of putting that together never had any meaningful anxiety about the regulations that we set in place. Yes, we too wanted to be rid of outdated regulations. Yes, we wanted regulations that were sensible and understandable and implementable. Yes, we wanted regulations to be applied in a consistent, fair way. But the idea of regulations – their power, their effectiveness, and their need – was never doubted by our generation or the precedent generation before us.

We were never shy about constructing a law to fit exactly what we wanted rather than the other way around. With our emphasis on design, inclusion, and sustainability, and our imperative to engender an evocative personal urban experience, we conceived and implemented layers of regulations that ventured into areas seldom touched by government and development management elsewhere. We now have thousands of pages of laws, guidelines, standards, and other policies. Critics talk about our jungle of by-laws, guidelines, and policies that, in some dark moments, even I find daunting. But the regulations exist for important reasons, which is why they were second nature to us as we invented Vancouverism. I often say that cities are complicated, so the regulations that shape them inevitably need to also be complicated.

The first reason that we were always quite sanguine about regulations is that Vancouverism is all about physical design. Urban design is about both private and public interests. The private side takes care of itself. The public side has to be well codified. A design-based regulatory system has to fully cover and explain all preferred public interests in the design of a place or building or these interests will often get lost. That takes a lot of regulatory detail. In contrast, a policy-based regulatory system, primarily focused on land use, as generally seen in most cities, needs fewer regulations. Design is usually discretionary and the public interests for a design are just left out. In each particular development case, the policy is translated into a design not actually previously thought about or, more often than not, the arrangement is simply laid out from a set of specified standards. There is no pre-conceived physical form that incorporates public interests to carry forward from inception to results, so no need for regulations to do that job. A developer takes the policy, decides how to achieve it, and drafts a scheme that satisfies the developer's private intentions but, too often, the public aspirations of design are left as a crap shoot. This is why policy-makers are often surprised at the physical results of their policies and often quite unhappy.

The second reason that regulations were vital for us was because we were directly answerable to the public. We felt compelled to fully and richly reflect the array of public interests that was articulated through all our inclusive public engagement processes. We felt we had to guarantee to the public that what we had pictured together would actually get built. We knew that the big moves of Vancouver's transformation would be effected over a long period and by many actors, who might not be part of the original community dream. So, it was urgent that they understood the dream, which of course meant a bedrock of requirements, solidly tied down in policies and by-laws, overlaid by a constellation of expectations and best intentions, expressed in interpretive design guidelines. We were open to new ideas as implementation unfolded, and our discretionary system was better than most at embracing the novel and the different, but we felt that the original vision must be well understood and that new directions must at least be judged from the benchmark of the initial conclusions and preferences.

As the years unfolded, we saw how well this careful attention to detail worked to translate plans and images into brick, concrete, and landscape on the ground. We actually built what was initially conceived and put down on paper, and we actually achieved the kinds of places and experiences that we had dreamed about together with thousands of citizens, in collaboration with developers, many years previously. And, because people really liked the results and supported the innovations, a consensus began to gel without any kind of official acknowledgment that "regulation is our friend."

**LIMITS ON INSIGHTS**

These five "friends" never found their way into the public record and were never explicitly debated by the people. They were secret friends, subconscious companions, helping us navigate through endless choices, avoiding the cul-de-sac of thinking that can steal so much time and energy from any inquiry. Would I recommend these same mindsets to another generation of urbanists taking on other challenges? Well, the answer is a little "yes" and a little "no."

We now know that our urban bias limits the application of Vancouverism in the greater struggle to reshape the totality of the city to be more sustainable and liveable – essentially, I refer to suburban change here. Some of the latest additions to the formula, which tackle diversification in the older neighbourhoods, will have a more general appeal and application – things such as laneway houses and multiple units in one house. Our tolerance and innovations for process and regulation will be helpful in the suburbs. But, in the final analysis, we were somewhat narrow-minded, so we left a lot on the table in regard to the issues of the greater regional city that are still there to be grappled with. We were agents of big density and major social integration and diversification, which are still too aggressive in most suburban situations. In hindsight, I am sorry for our blindness because the energy of our inventive process could have stretched wider than it did, at least giving a head start to the new generation. But I am also grateful for our urban bias because it gave us a very fresh row to hoe and a tight focus. At the time, we really needed that. I think the next generation will need its own bias – a suburban bias, with perhaps a more gentle touch. Having a bias helps you slice through the fog to find new solutions.

Though it is undoubtedly true that traffic congestion did motivate many people to make better choices about where they lived and did open their consciousness to different formats for living, the fact is that such congestion is still a bad thing. It may have been helpful for a particular time, but it was a backhanded help that created its own victims. Congestion diminishes the quality of daily life for a vast number of people who do not choose to live near downtown or who cannot afford it. It certainly limits the free flow of goods and even bus transit. It is a distinct black mark on Vancouver's image. I think we were right to limit further incursions of the car's footprint within the urban scene, but we were wrong not to optimize the space already dedicated to the car and to make the street system work at its best level of efficiency. I think my generation of urbanists was fed up with the car and its many distortions of walkable places. We were angry and we overreacted – and then we cooled down. Gradually, we moved from an anti-car attitude to one that aspires to transportation choices, where all the various modes have a role to play. No one can deny that the car is one of the most vital modes, which will become more apparent with autonomous driving and car sharing.

Our bias for density remains as relevant today as it was when we started our quest for Vancouverism, but it is still a very tricky issue and will have to be tackled with delicacy in the suburbs. The general skepticism about density remains strong, and though efforts to tame it have created tolerance among citizens and consumers, the questions of where and how to achieve it are still front and centre. For too many people, the answer all around is still "not in my backyard." All the evidence reinforces the principle that densification is essential to sustainability, resilience, government efficiencies, and even cultural vibrancy – so it remains very much our friend. But the next generation must find a new language to talk about density – it is just too much of a dirty word – and will have to wrap their heads around many more levels and types of density and scale. As a way of pervasively rebuilding a city pattern – not just at focal points, but everywhere – high-rise high density will simply flop in the suburbs. But recent work shows that some forms of density will be applicable. These include hidden density, gentle density, low-scaled mid-rise density, and, yes, clustering of density in transit-oriented nodes or along major streets, separated from adjacent low-scaled neighbourhoods. These may very well find support in the suburbs. And many urbanists are coming to believe that these more modest applications of density will be more than enough to achieve all we need for sustainability, economic efficiency, and vibrancy. At least, that is the hypothesis that the next generation needs to test.

Our comfort with elaborated processes and extensive regulations will also remain helpful as the totality of the city is rethought for the future. If you can't walk the walk because you don't have the necessary tools or methods at hand, you might as well not talk the talk in the first place. You only raise people's hopes and then you cannot deliver. Really understanding and codifying lifestyle needs and preferences inevitably demands extensive processes and regulations. That was true for our inner-city high-density design inventions, and it will be even more essential out in the suburbs, where things are so comfortably settled. In suburbia, we must go the extra mile – or maybe many extra miles – to convince citizens and consumers about a shift in their living arrangements and settings to achieve sustainability goals while protecting what is precious to them. But we must also be sensitive to the impacts of lengthy processes and complex regulations, and do everything in our power to shorten and simplify. The last thing we need is a popular revolt against the contemporary urban agenda because we could not roll it out effectively, did not keep people fascinated, or could not efficiently manage the transition from plans to approvals. People have more limited attention spans than ever before, so our processes and regulations must be adapted to fit the shorter and shorter time people will make available to us.

Even with all these caveats, however, I will always be thankful that we enjoyed a pervasive consensus about our five basic mindsets because it gave us dependable common ground from which to create what we had to create and challenge what we had to challenge. It cut through a lot of confusion and contradictions, enabling us to play our cards together, in a mutually predictable way, even if in hindsight we might question some of the innate wisdom behind this clarity and consensus.

With the background fleshed out – the principles and basic attitudes and the context within which Vancouverism would grow and flourish – let's now explore in more detail the primary themes that were embraced. The first of these themes offers the basic building block of Vancouver's transformation – the neighbourhood.

The heights give us the views. The intensity gives us the vibrancy. The water gives us our unending pleasures. This is the natural touch combined with the human touch that is the essential urban artistry of Vancouverism.

# PART 2

# THE KEY URBAN PRINCIPLES OF VANCOUVERISM

**4.1** The neighbourhood unit was an obvious planning concept for Vancouver's transformation. The whole city is structured in a pattern of settled neighbourhoods, each exciting great loyalty from locals. Like popular Kitsilano shown here, the neighbourhoods have been regularly reinforced and revitalized by city hall. People have a neighbourhood consciousness in addition to a city and a world consciousness.

# NEIGHBOURHOODS

**VANCOUVER IS A** city that has been profoundly shaped by its neighbourhoods, so this became the prime template for the urban arrangements of Vancouverism (see Figure 4.1). The city is composed of a constellation of well-established neighbourhoods that residents feel a close affinity with and work within to build networks of mutual support. The City officially identifies twenty-three neighbourhood areas,[1] but, of course, their boundaries are fluid, so people make their own count. The number is less important than the sheer robustness of this concept. As we entered the digital age, many said that the old-fashioned structure of neighbourhoods would become irrelevant and fall apart, an expectation that was not unrealistic. But it didn't happen in Vancouver. Yes, Vancouverites are just as tuned in to wide networks as any other urban population. In fact, the city thrives and grows because of its place in world networks. But people seem to have kept a second loyalty. They continue to be true to their own local place within a small enough group of people and a small enough geography that they can feel the daily benefits of community life, help define the character of their home ground, and touch the place close around them in a tangible, direct way.

Now, this is partly because of the natural inclination of people, making their own choices in their own ways, but it is also because the local government embraced certain consistent policy priorities over the years – a distinctly place-based policy framework. The City has never had a department of neighbourhoods or neighbourhood-based funding for community groups, as seen in some cities, such as Portland, Oregon. But governance has systematically focused on and reinforced local areas. The planning framework has been neighbourhood-based.

Capital priorities have been determined by neighbourhood-defined demands. Parks and recreation services have been organized within neighbourhood boundaries. The concept of neighbourhoods has been deeply embedded in both service delivery and special initiatives by most civic departments.

Consumer preferences and public policy have closely mirrored one another, so the government and the people have been in sync regarding how to organize their affairs. With the advent of Vancouverism, facing the prospect of massive development and change, particularly in the inner-city, we quite spontaneously and naturally adopted the template of the neighbourhood as the way to plan and build. In this chapter, I outline our basic neighbourhood model, explain in some detail the roots of our policies, and offer commentary about where there are still enhancements that could be made.

## A LONG COMMITMENT TO NEIGHBOURHOODS

Of course, this all started with the initial formation of Vancouver, which expanded out from the core, from the early 1900s, in a pattern of new suburbs. These were later known as streetcar suburbs because they were located and shaped by the construction of a streetcar network. Initially, the streetcar alignments set the priority of development, and the location of stops along the line set the scale of each community. Shops and commerce that served local needs clustered around each important stop. And the housing developed around these clusters, sometimes as apartments over shops but mostly as single-family homes that were laid out in a grid. Local municipal services and facilities followed in the same way. Some residents were employed in their neighbourhoods, but most jobs were in the central city, the terminal point of all the streetcar routes. This pattern was formalized by the Bartholomew Plan of 1928,[2] completed by the American planner and urban designer who laid out the extensions of the original city. The pattern is not at all unique. It was replicated all over North America and beyond as the key shaper of cities until the great wars. In Vancouver, unlike in other towns, sadly, the streetcar system soon became obsolete, overwhelmed by the car. Wouldn't we be excited to have it in service now? But, happily, unlike in many cities, the neighbourhood pattern set by the streetcar system has prevailed as the way local people see and use their city on a day-to-day basis. This is probably because the walking distance to neighbourhood services and amenities is very short, and the walk is usually pleasant. Or, because the local streets were never widened, driving was a bit of a hassle. But I suspect it is also because the community centres and schools were built out with the housing and shops, so people had an established community network and affinity that met their needs. Of course, these "suburbs" now form the core neighbourhoods of the region, within the boundaries of the City of Vancouver, and are no longer considered suburbs at all.

The inclination toward neighbourhoods was reinforced by two initiatives that unfolded long before Vancouverism came to the fore. As they played out over many years, these programs confirmed the loyalties of Vancouverites ever more firmly to the neighbourhood mode. For me, they were very special because this is where I got my start as a planner, first in several specific neighbourhoods and then as the senior area planner, looking after all the local planning programs. In fact, many of the players that I celebrate in this book, in the later story of Vancouverism, got their starts as the foot soldiers of these programs.

One influence was a way of planning that was introduced by Ray Spaxman. He recognized the natural vitality of neighbourhoods but also saw that after almost a century of existence, they needed revitalization. He determined that this could best be planned for and carried out on a neighbourhood-by-neighbourhood basis, working closely with local people, in a process called local area planning, shortened as LAP. No doubt his thinking was also influenced by the negative process of urban renewal that had fallen into disrepute at this same time because of its brutal impact on older communities throughout North America. But Spaxman's was a positive, proactive process that caught the imagination of Vancouverites. In the 1970s and 1980s, LAP teams worked with people in most of the iconic neighbourhoods, constantly reinforcing neighbourhood life. Then, the Expo Line came along in the early 1980s, the first fixed rapid transit line with stations, commonly called SkyTrain because it ran on elevated tracks from New Westminster to downtown Vancouver. This spawned a further round of local planning. Branded as station area planning, it concentrated on the vicinity of the new Expo Line stations within Vancouver. The ultimate elaboration of localized planning, in my mind, was the community development effort in the early 2000s undertaken in the Downtown Eastside over a number of years by Nathan Edelson and others.

The second influence was a pair of programs that were intended to revitalize declining neighbourhoods as an alternative to urban renewal. Offered nationally, they were sponsored by all three levels of government and were partly invented in Vancouver. The main program was the Neighbourhood Improvement Program, or NIP. After a neighbourhood was identified as needing special attention, it was allocated a budget for upgrading community facilities, which was shared equally by the three levels of government. Then it was assigned a planning team that worked closely with locals, usually through an ongoing committee, to decide how to spend the money to optimize revitalization. This is where I got my start in Vancouver, in 1976, as a neighbourhood planner in an area called Riley Park. We exploded this funding program into a full strategy of local area planning for the complete revival of these struggling communities. This laudable program was supported by an even more helpful parallel program, the Residential Rehabilitation Assistance Program, or RRAP. Loans and grants were given to individual resident homeowners who were of modest income, matching their personal investment, to repair and upgrade their often dilapidated homes. This set the home up as fit for another generation of living. Together, these programs represented one of the few times when national and provincial policy directly shaped cities by bringing many neighbourhoods back from steep decline. Because these programs touched people so personally, they were another popular inspiration for a local-oriented attitude.

So, a long tradition of neighbourhood planning and intervention prevailed in Vancouver. It was much stronger than any one overall plan for the city, which might have homogenized things in the interests of consistency or even equity. Put together with the early venture of rezoning the West End for its high-rise future and the planning of False Creek South as a diverse, complete mid-rise community, it was only natural that the neighbourhood concept would be deep in the minds of planners and citizens in the late 1980s, when the megaprojects came along after Expo 86. Since the neighbourhood template was most carefully elaborated at that point, I want to discuss it fully.

But first, let me complete the story of neighbourhood planning, showing how resilient the concept is by remembering even more recent initiatives than those already described. As I mentioned earlier, Vancouver had no strong overall plan until CityPlan was adopted in 1995. This plan had wide and deep community input. Through that discussion, the template of neighbourhoods again bubbled to the surface, acknowledging that upgrading was still needed for some areas. Many of the themes of CityPlan were implemented through a continuation of localized planning in one of the most efficient programs the City ever mounted – the Community Visions Program, starting in the late 1990s and continuing through the turn of the century. Planners Ronda Howard, Trish French, and Susan Anderson developed their own systematic process of offering local planning in a new way. It involved working intensively with local people to help them determine how their communities should evolve on a wide range of CityPlan topics, including introducing new housing types, improving local shopping areas, and addressing their transportation, community facilities, and other needs. Over the years, they worked their way through nine communities outside the central part of the city, none of which had previously had local planning. This was followed by another initiative called the Neighbourhood Centres Program that went into several communities in even more detail, developing specific zoning and street improvements for shopping areas. Using these programs, area planners brought another round of care and attention that residents and local businesses really appreciated.

## MEGAPROJECTS BRING THE NEIGHBOURHOOD ARRANGEMENT TO A NEW STANDARD

With the advent of the megaprojects through the 1990s, we had a strong consciousness that the neighbourhood unit was the right module for growth. We also now had a blank canvas, where we could bring this template to a greater level of specificity in completely new development. This planning was much more deliberate than we could do in the past. We were essentially starting from scratch. So the planning was comprehensive, with few of the barriers or limitations that always constrained the revamp of sitting communities. Also, we could think more holistically and more theoretically. And we could enjoy a creative and wide-ranging conversation with the whole city population about what these places should include and could look like. Because we were working with developers who were ready to put spade in the ground, we were sure we would get things built rather than just sketching ideas on paper. Because the developers did not enjoy already entrenched rights to build out their property, we were also sure that, through the negotiations, the results would look and feel like the places we had designed and promised the stakeholders. These were big projects, unprecedented in our experience, so they were well resourced at city hall and by the various private development companies. We were very lucky with all the development groups – they were cooperative, creative, open to engagement, and patient. Everything I am going to tell you about was conceived through a collaboration between the local government and these progressive developers. Starting with False Creek North at the turn into the 1990s, all the way through to Southeast False Creek in the early 2000s, each project added new elements to what was an evolving definition of the ideal neighbourhood unit. Each, of course, also had its own unique features and quirks, which we exploited.

With each large development area, we started by setting the footprint for each neighbourhood. Sometimes, as in the case of False Creek East, the site could accommodate only one module, which today lines Main Street. Sometimes, as in False Creek North, several neighbourhoods were defined and built in stages – resulting in Granville Slopes, the Beach Neighbourhood (around George Wainborn Park), New Yaletown, and International Village as identifiable places, with Northeast False Creek as another area yet to come. Sometimes, the area of development had to be merged with an adjacent area to get the necessary minimum scale. For example, Southeast False Creek was consolidated with the adjacent blocks around it. Always, we were searching for what would commonly be perceived as a humane, walkable scale, though admittedly, we usually had to more or less fit the template to the available land.

Also of interest was how the development on the megaproject sites would set off development nearby. So, when planning False Creek North, we also had to plan its northerly neighbour, Downtown South, and fortunately we had a recent, robust plan for the adjacent historic Yaletown. For Coal Harbour, we also had to plan its southerly neighbour, Triangle West. These adjacent areas would obviously be prey to speculation and spiralling land values, and we knew that the only way to manage this eventuality was to clearly articulate in specific plans how they would develop. By coordinating all these efforts generally at the same time, we were able to fit everything into a coherent whole that could grow together in an organic way.

## THE NEIGHBOURHOOD TEMPLATE SPECIFIED: TEN PARAMETERS

Vancouver's neighbourhood template was based not only on the broad experience garnered over the years but also on the principles of complete communities that were in wide circulation at the time. However, we did not simply pick the template up off the shelf – it came together as a policy framework quite gradually. This was the result of a long dialogue at city hall, intense debate with the developers, and diverse inputs through engagement with thousands of citizens. It came together from many studies and reports on one aspect or another, stretching over several years. Though it was an incremental invention, it nonetheless gelled into a coherent proposition that we could confidently apply in new areas. First, I will describe the ten parameters of the neighbourhood template and then I will tell you how it was actually operationalized on the ground in various locations.

## Local structure

The first neighbourhood parameter is the basic structure of the place (see Figure 4.2). Each neighbourhood has a central place (sometimes several high streets), where local commerce and community facilities are clustered. Extending out from this, its hinterland consists of housing but sometimes also includes workplaces. Small convenience stores are sometimes mixed in with the housing, often on local street corners.

## Physical integration

The second neighbourhood parameter is full integration into its surroundings (see Figure 4.3). The key way to achieve this is to extend already existing street and walkway patterns into the new areas, offering multiple access points and compatible scale of development plots. Gated or limited-access areas are not supported. New buildings are scaled and massed to echo adjacent existing patterns. These moves create a seamless transition between old and new that settles over time as the new construction ages. Eventually, boundaries are not even perceived.

This all got tested right up front with False Creek North, the first megaproject that moved forward for development. When the developer purchased the land from the provincial government after Expo 86, part of the deal involved the conceptualization of a preferred development scenario by the developer without the involvement of city hall. The developer's design team came up with what was called the "lagoons scheme," which consisted of a series of islands separated from the existing shore by shallow waterways. Unfortunately, there were only a few ways of traversing between the islands or connecting to the existing city. City hall reacted negatively to this proposal from the outset. So did the public and ultimately city council. The main problem with the scheme was that the proposed development would be essentially disconnected and absolutely not integrated within the city setting. The separation would have made it hard to navigate through the area, making it feel very unfriendly. There was also a sense of "eliteness" about the proposed design that offended many people. The rejection of that scheme by almost everyone confirmed our design intention for tight integration of the old and the new, which became a typical design requirement for future megaprojects through the years. Of course, it has to be said that the scheme had a few other problems. The one that caused most people to chuckle was that the lagoons were only about a metre deep and they would have been disconnected from the real waters of False Creek. That would have seemed very

**4.2** Each neighbourhood needs one or more central places for local commerce and services. Here is an important one in Downtown South, with Nesters Market, a local grocery store, as the magnet. Nearby are other local shops and community facilities. These anchor people's fondness for their home base.

**4.3** Each neighbourhood must be tightly connected to adjacent places through the many connections of streets, parks, walkways, and bikeways. Davie Street, downtown, ties together several West End subdistricts, False Creek North, Yaletown, and Downtown South, not to mention that it connects English Bay to False Creek across the peninsula. No gates, many ways in and out, seamless patterns.

false and unnatural – and we just didn't want that kind of fakery in our town! In any event, the lagoons scheme was quickly thrown out and the developer and city hall worked together in a joint design effort, achieving the plan that led to what is built today.

### Open space as a framework

The third neighbourhood parameter is the integrated pattern of built areas and open spaces (see Figure 4.4). An overlay of parks was the initial and single-most powerful form-giver for the ensemble of neighbourhoods that we designed for these large, inner-city infill sites. Each new megaproject neighbourhood was provided with the standard of local-oriented parks, which was similar to that enjoyed by typical neighbourhoods throughout the city. The standard was set at 1.1 hectares (2.75 acres) per thousand people.[3] Generally, these parks were located to serve their neighbourhood but also to separate neighbourhoods for better community legibility. They were sited next to elementary schools so that they could overlap with the school play yards to save scarce land (see Figure 4.5). Negotiating this sharing between the civic parks and school authorities was difficult because of understandable concerns for the security of students at recess, but in all the years this sharing has been in place, there has not been one incident to cause regret.

Then, because the megaprojects were waterfront sites, and most people told us that they would prefer parks on or very near the water, the pattern of parks was distributed along the shorelines. In addition, a non-negotiable requirement was that the water's edge must be dedicated as a public walkway-bikeway (see Figure 4.6). Overall, this was set at a width of 10.6 metres (35 feet). Its walkway portion, which ran adjacent to the water, was set at a width of 7.6 metres (25 feet). Its bikeway portion, which ran parallel upland of the walkway was set at a width of 3.0 metres (10 feet). Then, buildings were required to be set back a further 4.6 metres (15 feet) or more from the upland edge of this dedicated alignment.[4] The parks, together with the walkway-bikeway system, created what has become known as a green string of pearls that now defines the inner-city image of Vancouver as much as any other single feature.

Upland from the megaproject sites, where associated new neighbourhoods were also being designed, we were not able to meet the same park standard – there was not enough available land, and the land that could be used for parks was very expensive. In these cases, we tailored the park provision to what

**4.4** Each neighbourhood needs parks at its heart and edges, resulting in a green recreational framework among neighbourhoods. Here, the intensity of Coal Harbour is offset by its shoreline park, which connects to other parks via a waterfront walkway-bikeway. The Stanley Park forest is at the upper right, just beyond the Bayshore Hotel.

**4.5** Because space is at a premium in Vancouver's downtown, parks and schoolyards are one and the same. David Lam Park, which is also Elsie Roy Elementary's playground, is shown here. The first example of park-schoolyard integration, it has had no problems of either security or management, as had been feared.

**4.6** The continuous waterfront walkway-bikeway ties many parks and neighbourhoods together and has become one of the most iconic features of contemporary Vancouver's image. It started during the 1920s, with the Stanley Park seawall, which took one man virtually his entire working life to complete. This shot shows a newer section in False Creek North.

land we could get, with the expectation that residents of these areas would tend to migrate toward the water and enjoy the lavish parks in the megaprojects. Nonetheless, we did create several new inland parks that became vital to their areas, such as Emery Barnes Park in Downtown South (see Figure 4.7). Chapter 7 will come back to the design, finishing, and furnishing of parks, but it is notable that design ideas diversified through the years, starting with the obvious improvements such as organized sports fields and children's playgrounds but then adding lots of areas for relaxation and people watching (see Figure 4.8). In recently constructed areas, arrangements have become even more specialized, with such things as dog runs and individual garden plots. Of course, on top of all the new park provisions, the downtown peninsula also enjoys the vast, iconic 405-hectare (1,000-plus acre) Stanley Park, the very first park, established in 1886 with incorporation of the City, and a wonderful spread of beaches along English Bay. So, by most inner-city standards around the world, Vancouver is quite well endowed with a hierarchy of parks and open spaces that we added to as we developed the new neighbourhoods.

### Walkable scale

The fourth neighbourhood parameter is an optimal scale for walking and supporting local services (see Figure 4.9). The preferred size of the neighbourhood unit was set such that the average person could walk from centre to edge in about five to seven minutes. This preferred scale was intended to facilitate what are often called the active modes as the best ways to move around locally – walking, cycling, and even skating. These modes are backed up by good transit accessibility. The transportation strategy of Vancouverism will be discussed more fully in Chapter 5. The optimal population size was set based on the number of people needed to support a small full-service grocery store (see Figure 4.10). Thus, the base was set starting at about ten thousand people with better support for a fuller array of local retail services offered if their numbers could be expanded to about twenty thousand, which was preferred. The boundary between neighbourhoods was less important than the relative location and identity of the centre. After all, the centre is where the action is.

### Jobs-housing balance

The fifth neighbourhood parameter is the mix of housing and workplaces (see Figure 4.11). For this consideration, we did not follow the typical principle of complete communities, which is to create a balance of jobs and housing in a

**4.7** As a place to live, Downtown South was incomplete until Emery Barnes Park opened. It is now at the centre of everyday community life.

**4.8** Here in Harbour Green, Coal Harbour's expansive waterfront park, the emphasis is on people watching, gossiping, and enjoying a moment with the little one. Parks play a vital role as the living rooms of the community and are fitted out accordingly.

**4.9** Every neighbourhood must have a walkable scale – just a few minutes to the shops, as shown here at the intersection of the Pacific Boulevard and Davie Street shopping district. With these kinds of distances, people naturally prefer walking, so the sidewalks are packed.

**4.10** This IGA grocer on Burrard Street easily serves the more than twenty thousand people who live in its walkable catchment area. With this population base, grocery stores and other local convenience retailing can thrive.

fine-grained mix within each neighbourhood unit – usually one of the most significant concerns. Instead, because the new neighbourhoods would cluster near a business core of over 170,000 jobs, which in and of itself had created a major imbalance at a regional sector level, we intensified their housing. We pushed only for the jobs that came naturally with the delivery of local services (but we also supported any other job proposal within a specific area, such as we began to see occasionally in Downtown South). Our target was to bring a better balance within the whole central area, on and near the downtown peninsula, to radically shorten the journey to work and cause a shift in the favoured modes for that journey. This was practical because the entire area was of manageable size. It is possible to walk across the downtown peninsula from end to end in either direction in about forty-five minutes or less, so we were sure that clustering housing and workplaces, even with some differentiation of uses, would encourage active modes for the commute to work, rather than perpetuating reliance on the car.

## Local commercial services

The sixth neighbourhood parameter is the provision of commercial services in the local centre (see Figure 4.12). For this, we had a simple concept regarding the basic retail package that was necessary to support localized community life. We ensured that enough space was set aside for these commercial uses in each neighbourhood plan. Occasionally, we facilitated components of this basic retail package with the developer or directly with the retail companies themselves. Most often, we let the market sort everything out, which it usually did quite naturally because the potential demand on offer was so significant. As anchors, we pushed for a grocery store, targeted at a minimum of about 600 square metres (about 25,000 square feet), a pharmacy, and a liquor store. At the time, the provincial government was the primary vendor of alcohol, so its liquor outlets had to be specifically planned for separately from other commodities. In False Creek North, the grocery store got confirmed in a handy way. At the last minute when the plan was being approved, Councillor Libby Davies moved an innocent little motion, passed unanimously, that said the developer had to ensure the opening of a grocery store (the civic lawyers later worried that her motion might not have been strictly within the powers of the City, but that was a sidebar that made no difference to what happened). Her logic was that the grocery store would naturally draw around it the other local retailers. Well, she certainly knew what she was doing and she was right, but the developer had to subsidize the grocery store rent for several years before enough consumers were

**4.11** All neighbourhoods need a mix of housing and workplaces. One way or another, an organic balance of jobs and homes must be found. The high-rise housing of Downtown South towers above an office block, and the nearby business core features even more workplaces within easy walking distance.

**4.12** Each neighbourhood must have its full complement of commercial services, anchored with a food store, pharmacy, and liquor outlet (in British Columbia, government sells spirits, so separate outlets have to be planned). These shops are clustered along Seymour Street near the grocery store shown in Figure 4.2. The other basics are nearby.

on the scene to make it truly profitable. Fortunately, ultimately it became very successful, and the developer recouped any initial losses. And that success – the grocery store is called Urban Fare – became the status quo that took any fight out of the provision of the basic retail grouping for any of the future megaproject plans. I also tried to speed up the interest of the grocery store chains, which were very suburban-oriented, by meeting with almost all of them to convince them that a huge population growth was inevitable on the downtown peninsula. I must say, they became very responsive, so downtown Vancouver now has a full offering of food stores.

Back to our initial local commercial strategy, we also made a point of allocating enough retail space for such outlets as a laundry/drycleaner, hairdresser/barbershop, specialty food shops, and similar typical local commerce, preferably positioned near the grocery store. Then, we added in what are called "third places," a concept invented by Ray Oldenburg.[5] These are the cafes, coffee shops, bars, and other meeting places where neighbours get to know one another and create their own localized culture. In any neighbourhood, these are the third-most important places, after home and work. All our neighbourhood centre plans made room for them (see Figure 4.13). The scale of these provisions was not standardized. Instead, it was worked out on a case-by-case basis according to the consumer base that was estimated for each area.

One thing we did with all the retail and local commerce was to bring everything right to the edge of the sidewalk as much as possible for a tight urban feel. So, we required continuous retail frontage in specified locations and widened key sidewalks for outdoor seating and open-air merchandising.

## Local community services

The seventh neighbourhood parameter is the provision of localized municipal public recreational and community services (see Figure 4.14). Because the megaprojects were being comprehensively developed, we confirmed specific standards for the basic required facilities, as the second set of anchors in the neighbourhood centres, complementing the commercial anchors. The key public facilities in each neighbourhood, or shared between them, were the community centre (scaled at about 0.21 square metres or 2.29 square feet per person) and the elementary school (approximately two hundred children per full-program school). Because the downtown peninsula already had its senior school, with a long and distinguished history, we needed only to secure the junior schools, which was lucky because the delivery of schools became a difficult situation, as

**4.13** Neighbourhoods need what are called the "third places" – cafes and other hangouts that are just as essential to locals as where they live and work. The Village at Southeast False Creek has its share of these spots, as shown here.

**4.14** Each neighbourhood must have its basic public facilities and services, starting with a school and a community centre. Elsie Roy Elementary is the family base for False Creek North. The Roundhouse community centre is right across the street.

I discuss later in this chapter. For each neighbourhood, we required childcare centres (with a complicated formula of #spaces = #family units x 0.3 x 0.6 x 0.72). They were the one type of facility that we did not cluster, choosing instead to spread them throughout the residential setting for easy, direct access (see Figure 4.15). As with the senior school, the downtown already boasted a recently built central library and a branch library in the West End, with state-of-the-art services and facilities. The central library is very walkable from anywhere on the downtown peninsula, including the newly developing sites, so no new facilities were needed, although developers did contribute funds (at the time set at $41 per capita) to increase library services in existing facilities. To round out the list of standards, we also included a specification for public art (see Figure 4.16) of $10.76 to be spent per square metre (originally stated as $1.00 per leasable square foot).[6]

## Social diversity

The eighth neighbourhood parameter is social mix (see Figure 4.17). In each neighbourhood, we worked hard to provide a range of households to achieve a pleasant diversity for all to enjoy. We felt the inner-city should not just be a place for young singles and empty nesters, who naturally tend to migrate there. It should also accommodate families with children. It should not just be a place for well-to-do people; it should also include modest-income people. It should not just be a place for typical apartments; it should include alternative kinds of units to suit many types of households and ways of living. Ironically, some young people accustomed to having a downtown night-time playground free of intrusions and limitations were not happy with our approach. I remember a particularly raucous meeting at one of the universities where the point was very loudly voiced by students. They said we were actually suburbanizing the urban core by making it a place for everyone. I was more than happy to take credit for this particular criticism. But we did also have a solution for the party crowd in our back pocket when we created what has come to be called the "entertainment district" of late-night clubs and restaurants along the downtown portion of Granville Street, slightly separated from most housing. The logic and strategies for achieving social mix are fully covered in Chapter 6. The point here is that we wanted neighbourhoods to be far more than just dormitories. We wanted genuine, rich places for full community life, experience, surprise, opportunity, and learning. If we were to achieve this, a social mix would have to be an essential part of the neighbourhood template. Oh, if we had only realized then just how difficult it would prove to keep the social mix diverse over the long run.

**4.15** Childcare is central to the equation of neighbourhood public facilities and services. False Creek North has Sea Star, shown here, on the west, Dorothy Lam Children's Centre, attached to Elsie Roy Elementary, in the middle, and a third facility at the base of a social-housing building to the east.

**4.16** Public art is an essential neighbourhood amenity. This popular installation in the heart of the Village at Southeast False Creek showcases the orca and raven designs created for the Olympic and Paralympic medals by First Nations artist Corrine Hunt.

**4.17** Each neighbourhood benefits from a diverse social mix. Families enjoy and support one another in Downtown South but also appreciate the young singles, empty nesters, and, increasingly, the social housing. Emery Barnes Park, shown here, is one of the hangouts where everyone meets.

**4.18** Neighbourhoods need both a structure and an agenda for sustainability. Southeast False Creek provides a model, which starts with close proximity of origins and destinations, as well as an emphasis on walking and cycling. This little tyke is just getting into cycling.

## Sustainability

The ninth neighbourhood parameter is sustainability (see Figure 4.18). Although the mixed-use and density objectives in the False Creek North and Coal Harbour megaprojects and their associated upland areas were consistent with later theories of sustainability, only with the planning of Southeast False Creek did sustainability become an explicit policy objective. By the early 2000s, both the theory of sustainability and a strong grassroots advocacy network for it were well established in Vancouver. How we engaged this green constituency and the full dimensions of the resulting sustainability agenda will be covered in Chapter 8, in regard to both the urban structural and infrastructural aspects. The key, at the neighbourhood level, was to emphasize localized district utility systems and to situate a full provision of day-to-day origins and destinations close together to cut travel and, therefore, carbon use.

## Local character

The tenth and final neighbourhood parameter is what we might call "locale" – local character and identity. This is a quality that is very hard to describe but is nonetheless important – the achievement of a certain place-based uniqueness that differentiates one area from another, imbues it with its own personality, and gives its residents something they can feel is very special (see Figure 4.19). It may be derived from an existing feature or character that needs to be carefully protected and enhanced. The extraordinary, one-of-a-kind views of the mountains and Stanley Park from Coal Harbour offer a vivid example of strong identity that was brought out and confirmed by careful planning and design. I chaired a series of intense meetings involving the developer, upland property owners and residents, and a cadre of their architects and lawyers. We spent weeks moving buildings around, shaping them and slimming them until we had attained balanced and protected views for everyone. Otherwise, the lovely vistas – this area's most character-defining aspect – would have been lost for all but a very few lucky residents, which would have been a shame. Alternatively, local character and identity may be added when nothing on the ground offers a starting point. For instance, in Downtown South, the creation of Emery Barnes Park and then, facing onto it, the Vancouver International Film Centre, a special cinema for the film festival, and the Scotiabank Dance Centre around the corner, injected a lively cultural character into surroundings that were otherwise somewhat flat and predictable (see Figure 4.20). This transformed a bedroom community into

**4.19** Each neighbourhood has to channel its own special character and uniqueness. In Coal Harbour, the view of the water and mountains is the essential personality of the place, so everything was deliberately designed around it.

**4.20** Here is the Vancouver International Film Centre, seen from Emery Barnes Park. The film centre and the Scotiabank Dance Centre just around the corner brought out a cultural dimension in Downtown South that has become a unique defining quality of the neighbourhood.

a real people place. What we discovered early in our learning about neighbourhood development was that this is not just about planning, to get all the uses and supports right. It is also about design, to make a place loveable and memorable and fulfilling. We will return to this in Chapter 7, which examines the urban design dimension of Vancouverism.

## APPLYING THE NEIGHBOURHOOD TEMPLATE: CUSTOMIZATION ON THE GROUND

Having specified the neighbourhood template, I have to say that it actually never came together in the kind of complete and obvious way that might be expected with such a clear definition of what we needed to achieve. The fact is that planning is more an art than a science. Results tend to be better and more compelling when templates or standards are customized to particular situations. Partly, this is because of the imperative to stay true to the specialness of a particular place, as I have just described. Partly, this is because each neighbourhood area offers unique assets and limitations in size or configuration or adjacencies – some things can be done and some cannot. But, as much as anything, customization is vital because it is the only way to offer rich urban choices for people in how they wish to particularly live. Tailored design is the real art that needs to be understood in the repertoire of Vancouverism. The specific juggling that we had to do is central to the results that we achieved.

### Organic balances among uses

For one thing, when you mix uses, you must have the right combination, which must come on stream at the right time. For example, as the area around the extension of Davie Street in False Creek North was built out, I recall feeling real anxiety because the initial results were surprising. This was one of the most important traditional local shopping streets of the West End, so our team had very carefully designed the extension several years before. Lots of apartments were built and many residents were in place, but the sidewalks, although beautifully finished, were just empty of people. I felt we must have made some mistake because our public realm was simply not enticing people to come out and use it. Then, Urban Fare opened its doors, the streets were instantly full of pedestrians, and all was well (see Figure 4.21). I discovered that, until the grocery store arrived, most new residents had been descending by elevator from their apartments to their underground parking and driving to their old neighbourhoods to pick up groceries and everything else they needed. They had no reason to come out and engage with their new community. Once the mix was complete and there were offerings nearby, people started using them. That was one anxiety I was very glad to leave behind as a neighbourhood designer – but people came to the sidewalks only when the right combination of uses was actually in place.

Tailoring mixed-use also entails getting the proportions right between the various uses. Each use must reinforce its companion uses – there must be an organic balance of supply and demand between them. For example, if a grocery store is to flourish, there must be enough people in its catchment area to support it. But the store must also be of a size and diversification to meet the needs of these consumers or they simply won't patronize it. If this combination is out of sync, the place does not work. The same kind of compatible balances must be set for every use combination. So, planners cannot simply tick off the items on a list of preferred uses. They must ensure that the uses are there in the right numbers to complement each other in very specific terms. To some degree, this has to be negotiated between planners and developers. There is a commercial ecology that must be balanced, along with a cultural ecology and a social ecology. None of this can be left to chance.

### Cross-sharing of community services

Sometimes, practical reasons obliged us to tweak the specified standards for municipal services, which also had a diversifying effect on community character. This was the case for Downtown South and False Creek North because of the differing specifications for their respective community centres. In Downtown South, we developed the Gathering Place, a special kind of community centre that caters to the unique needs of modest-income people, including support for the homeless (see Figure 4.22). Social housing now clusters around the Gathering Place, mixing comfortably with market buildings of smaller apartments for single people and couples. Due to the resulting streetlife, homeless people feel safe in coming for their daily services – they do not feel intimidated. Everything fits together in a positive way. In contrast, in False Creek North, we developed a different kind of community centre, called the Roundhouse, which focuses on services and facilities for families with children. It also offers arts-related programming (see Figure 4.23). The Roundhouse sits cheek by jowl with a school, a childcare centre, a shared park and schoolyard, a pre-teen play yard, and a public plaza designed for arts and cultural gatherings and general community use. Family housing bunches nearby, so the place is filled with children of all ages. These families mix happily with the often older couples that also live in the area.

Again, it all fits together. There is no doubt that families with children come from Downtown South to the Roundhouse for recreation or that adults and singles from False Creek North, particularly if they have special needs, walk over to the Gathering Place for the services and supports they require. That's just fine. It all works because the distances are short – so we get convenience without giving up a very localized personality for each area.

### Using anchor facilities to engender area personality

Some cities have used investment in arts and cultural facilities and programming, along with sports venues, as anchors for revitalization and to draw people back to languishing districts. This is often called the "strategy of the spectacle." It can work but it can also backfire if the requirements of the facilities themselves, such as parking, or the impact of mass gathering, such as noise, traffic, and security, neutralize everything around them. Vancouver has not adopted this strategy, because a rich mix of land uses and activities has been more important to us, along with that strong interest in inner-city housing. But we have designed and used the cultural and sports facilities we have invested in as a way to add personality to our different neighbourhood mixes. Again, it's all about land-use choreography and tailoring. The area around the new central

**4.21** When the essential services are available and close by in a neighbourhood, the place comes alive and thrives. One could say that, as a community, False Creek North was born when the grocery store, Urban Fare, opened its doors on Davie Street.

**4.22** In a healthy and tightly knit community, public amenities and facilities can be shared across neighbourhoods to fulfill differing needs. In Downtown South, the Gathering Place Community Centre caters to modest-income singles and people with special needs. Residents of nearby False Creek North also use its services.

**4.23** Community sharing happens in many directions. The family-oriented services and arts programming of the Roundhouse in False Creek North are regularly enjoyed by people who live next door in Downtown South.

**4.24** Treatments in the public realm can go a long way in expressing an area's character. These book-shaped inserts with literary quotes, around all the trees in the neighbourhood, are a clever identifier for the district of the main library.

**4.25** Squeezed between Chinatown and the escarpment of downtown, International Village, as its name suggests, has a distinctive identity as a crossroad of cultures, signalled by this evocative globe at the heart of the area. ▸

library, along Robson Street, in the northern part of Downtown South, has taken on an ambience that appeals to a certain group of people. The same is true for the southern part of Downtown South, around the intersection of Davie and Richards Streets, where the Scotiabank Dance Centre and Vancouver International Film Centre (already mentioned) attract yet another demographic. A third example is the area hosting the Queen Elizabeth Theatre, Playhouse, Rogers Arena, and BC Place Stadium, densely mixed with workplaces, housing, and hotels, forming a strong entertainment district with a real buzz. Anyone who likes sports and entertainment would want to live or work there. All these areas represent a mix, but each puts it together in a different way for different interests and appeal. Of course, there is also an element of spontaneity, as large facilities and sites have been designated based upon land availability and costs. But a lot of deliberate localized planning brings in the rest of the neighbourhood mix, to finish the public realm as an area identifier (see Figure 4.24), to add public art and landscape, to insert support facilities and services, and to limit parking in the big-event spaces for traffic control.

Occasionally, adjacencies have made a big contribution to a distinctive identity, offering a unique neighbourhood choice to consumers. Take the case of International Village, which is squeezed between the escarpment of the downtown core and Chinatown (see Figure 4.25). Its location is perfect for easy access to downtown jobs and the constellation of language schools that teach English to over forty thousand students at a time. International Village fills out what was once the blank edge of historic Chinatown. As its name implies, it has taken on an international flavour, particularly that of Asian cultures. It has one of the best

Asian-cuisine supermarkets in the city, and its shops cater to various cultural interests and tastes. But it also offers quality new housing for people who might enjoy the historic character in the vicinity but who also want all the mod cons. It integrates old and new in a picturesque area with abundant street colour and energy that draws its own aficionados.

As it turns out, applying the neighbourhood template in Vancouver has been a lot like cooking. We start with a recipe, rejig it to take advantage of the ingredients at hand, shape it to please the special tastes of our hoped-for guests, add a pinch of our own favourite spice, and then bring it all together with a kind of faith that it will be delicious. Are Vancouver's new neighbourhoods delicious? You only have to take a walk, have a taste of the experience, see what you see, and then you can decide for yourself. Maybe you'll agree with Lonely Planet,[7] who put neighbourhoods first on its list of the best attractions in our city.

## STAYING TRUE TO THE NEIGHBOURHOOD FRAMEWORK

Even with all its variations, the neighbourhood template remains important in Vancouver, so it is relevant to continue to enhance and update it when necessary and to support its application in a thoughtful way. There is no question that neighbourhoods have staying power. The strong identity of the new neighbourhoods has inspired a deep-seated loyalty that more than matches what people continue to feel for traditional neighbourhoods. The formula for the new, though quite straightforward, has been complete enough to replicate the key prevailing conditions that allow the older places to work. But some problems have arisen, and it is useful to put these on the table.

One difficulty that might have caused much else to unravel is that the delivery of elementary schools has lagged behind the construction and occupancy of their catchment neighbourhoods. Schools are the heart of any complete neighbourhood that includes families with children, and without them there is no way that neighbourhood life can truly thrive. This has been a significant problem for inner-city revitalization in America that we had hoped to avoid in Vancouver. The public-school system in our province provides consistent excellent education, so we thought at least we started with a leg up from the American experience. But it was not the quality of the system that proved difficult. Instead, it was the attitude of its leaders that caused a real problem. The Vancouver School Board is elected separately from the municipal council and is responsible to the provincial ministry of education. From the beginning of our downtown planning efforts in the late 1980s, there was an expressed skepticism among school authorities that our plans would successfully draw children into the new areas. With no solid proof of student demand, school officials were not prepared to support the construction of new schools that they would be forced to staff and operate. Even though the sites and new school buildings would have been provided and paid for totally by the developers, like all other public amenities, the school authorities remained intransigent. Instead, they insisted they would pay for the schools and build them only when and if they felt they were truly needed – although they did agree to accept school sites for gratis from the megaproject developers. They were certainly not prepared to gamble on the outcome or to use a school investment as an enticement for new families. They argued that they faced too many competing demands elsewhere. And so, though each neighbourhood plan included a designated site for an elementary school, those sites remained vacant for years on end. One of my biggest frustrations of those years was not being able to change the consciousness of the school board.

More than anything, a caprice of fortune saved the day. In the New Yaletown area of False Creek North, families moved in much faster than even we, the planners, had expected. These new families exerted their own political pressure on the school board. The board saw that the demand was real, so funding and construction of the first elementary school, Elsie Roy, was finally completed. It was slightly later than we had hoped but earlier than we had feared. And Elsie Roy proved a great success. Its attendance is regularly over-subscribed, and the quality of its education has met everyone's expectations. The school plays a contributing role in the community and is so popular that an extension has already been added. So, with this school, along with the rehab of a long-existing school in the West End, we managed to bridge the gap, even though demand for schools continues to grow. Finally, after many years, a second new school has come on stream, Crosstown Elementary School in the International Village neighbourhood, and only two more sites remain in reserve.

I always felt disappointed that we could not use the availability of a good public school to sell our message of sustainable inner-city living to more young families. It would undoubtedly have been a big drawing card for our whole development strategy, and today we might be enjoying even more families with children than we currently see. Anyone who applies the neighbourhood template in the future would be well advised to make the right arrangements for the delivery of schools right up front. Sadly, the Vancouver School Board continues to drag its feet. The proposed schools in Coal Harbour and Southeast False Creek remain elusive, even though much of the private development has been completed. Shame on them.

Some people have looked at our neighbourhood template and noticed what, for them, is one major glaring deficiency – an error that in their minds would guarantee that our new areas could never be complete. They noticed that nowhere did we include provisions or standards for places of religious worship – churches, synagogues, mosques, or temples. And this is absolutely true. Though we never debated the topic very fully, I can offer our logic, which is two-fold. First, the inner-city already had a relatively full tally of Christian facilities within walking distance, most of which were losing membership, so we felt that new development would help to regenerate their congregations. Of course, this logic falls short for non-Christian places of worship, for which there was growing demand but a general lack of options. Second, our planning philosophy was admittedly secular and did not see religious facilities and venues as a public responsibility. If new ones were needed, we reasoned, the market would supply them. In hindsight, I feel that both of these "excuses" are quite lame. I can see now that we should have dealt more sensitively with this public need. Regardless of one's religion or beliefs, many people see spiritual support as a basic part of community life. Creating sites for such uses and generating a process for allocating the sites could have been a positive thing. This should be added to the neighbourhood template.

A final unfulfilling aspect of the neighbourhood strategy has to do with inclusiveness. I mention it here briefly only because it will be more fully discussed in Chapter 6, but it is just too important to ignore in this list of deficiencies. As applied so far, the neighbourhood template has not been able to fend off the spectre of expensive housing and how it completely edits out some groups of people. In situations of private development, no economically viable formula has yet been found to adequately secure the full range of diversity that is such a strong preference for neighbourhood life.[8] When we invented Vancouverism, we did not perceive how overwhelmingly this problem would come to consume the attention of our whole city. But that is not a good excuse. Though our planning did allot sites to low-income social housing, we should have worked harder to create affordable housing for middle-income and special-needs residents. We should have made more provision for the homeless. We should have built every single low-income housing unit sooner rather than later. We weren't able to do all of this, and it is a continuing regret.

Beyond regret, several further lessons from our neighbourhoods strategy can enhance future efforts and any similar initiative elsewhere. An important insight that became more evident as one after another of our new areas came on stream is that neighbourhoods are not just physical or even social realities. They are dynamic, living cultures. They can and should be deliberately planned, for which our template was, undoubtedly, a useful guide. But we may have been able to help them come to life faster and better, with more inclusiveness, if we had offered a more systematic kick-start for that cultural side. This definitely could have included some kind of programming and perhaps initial funding to help new residents settle in. Some of this was happening in the new areas, where our park-board-managed community centres have a long history of thoughtful programming and funding – and that is all to the good. But the support might have gone much further. The City's social planning department could have offered a standard package of social support to new residents. Meet-and-greet events could have been arranged. Assistance could have been provided with setting up foundational community self-help institutions. New people with similar interests could have been brought together through introductory programming. And nearby long-standing communities could have been engaged to mentor their new neighbours. Given that the people who were moving in came from all over the world, or from a drastically different suburban lifestyle, these kinds of outreaches and linkages would have helped them settle in faster, create the networks they needed, and start the natural community development that ultimately allows neighbours to invent just the kind of social arrangements for a place they can call home for a long time.

Another aspect of the natural dynamics of neighbourhoods is that they are constantly changing, constantly evolving, constantly getting better or worse, depending upon circumstances. A proactive planning service must be cognizant of that reality and must move to assist positive change and to forestall decline. Some of the neighbourhoods that came together during the heyday of Vancouverism are now approaching their twentieth anniversary. They are beginning to show their age. There are new ideas that need to be accommodated – opportunities to enhance the experience of long-time residents. And, to some degree, it can be helpful for people just to have a good conversation about the local situation to build new friendships and networks. The current civic administration might take its cue from the Community Visions Program of the 1990s, establishing a carefully calibrated, systematic, limited-time planning agenda to assess and fix difficulties before they become a crisis. These neighbourhoods are valuable long-term assets to the City and to their residents. With just a little effort and a little money, their resilience could be enhanced and soundly guaranteed.

## THE VIEW FROM HOME: POST-OCCUPANCY EVALUATION

In 2007, with a dedicated group of analysts, I conducted a post-occupancy evaluation of False Creek North. Returning to a neighbourhood after it is built to see how people use, judge, and value it can be an insightful experience. Unfortunately, though, planners almost never get to do this simply because time and money are scarce, and because they usually move on quickly to new assignments. In contrast, soon after my retirement from civic government, a unique opportunity presented itself to counter this tendency, and I just could not let it pass. Through my role as a part-time professor at the University of British Columbia, I was able to put together a series of courses on post-occupancy evaluation, and False Creek North became the students' case study. Even if our study was limited to just one area, I knew we would acquire useful information about all the areas we had conceived because all were drawn from similar roots. I was able to team up with a visiting professor from Australia, Wendy Sarkissian, an acknowledged expert on community design. Together with twenty-four students, we spent more than four semesters getting the job done. We professors acted as the guides, but the students were the real creative and questioning force in the research. They kept us objective, relevant, and on point. We looked at the performance of the neighbourhood from a variety of perspectives, engaging all kinds of residents in many ways, reaching out to small children and their parents as well as couples and singles and seniors. Among our techniques, we used a community-wide questionnaire, an engaging "have your say" discussion workshop at the community centre, a students' workshop at Elsie Roy School, and a series of in-depth interviews. In all, we engaged over a thousand residents of False Creek North. There was enough overlap in these methods that the findings from one angle could be checked against the results from another angle. So, we became very confident about our results.

By that time, False Creek North was well established, with a full population base, retail high streets, parks, and local facilities. Things were settled. It was a genuine community in every sense. People had had time to consider what worked and did not work for them. And they were not shy about telling us what they thought.

The results, generally, were gratifying.[9] Here's an interesting sampling of what we discovered. We were glad to find a major level of diversity – we found the youth, with a significant portion of the population under the age of 19; we found the renters, with over a third of households renting; we found the international set, with almost half of households for whom English was not their first language at home. We were unable to tie down tightly the specifics of the types of households, which would come later from civic research, but the information we gathered strongly suggested that a very comfortable mix of people lived in this community. One thing was absolutely clear, even without knowing the specific numbers – many more children lived within the community than one would expect at this kind of density in an inner-city location. We learned that people actually knew their neighbours and that neighbour-to-neighbour linkages and supports were important in their daily lives. Residents talked about adjacencies but also about the neighbourliness within a building and, for townhouses, along a sidewalk. It seemed evident that a neighbourhood culture was thriving.

Though people had many good things to say, they were not quiet about deficiencies. They were bluntly critical when they felt they needed to be. They talked extensively about two aspects of False Creek North where they were distinctly not satisfied. They told us there was unfinished business in building their community and vital gaps in its ongoing management. Given the demographic profile that had come together over the years, with a big presence of young families with children, their points were not surprising even though they were somewhat disconcerting.

First, respondents called for a much fuller provision of children's facilities at a standard that reflected the reality of local needs. They reminded us that Elsie Roy School, the single elementary school that had been opened in False Creek North, though highly rated, was overcrowded and that it had a waiting list for students. They expressed anger that the other schools remained unbuilt. They said that childcare facilities were too few and that waiting lists for childcare could be demoralizing to parents who were trying to invent a new way of living at close quarters with their children. They listed other missing amenities to enhance family living, such as children's clubs and a babysitting registry. Pointing out that the parks had been designed solely for team sports and small children, they suggested that interesting things needed to be added to appeal to older children and teens. They felt that, in fact, teens had been left out of the equation for facilities, and meeting spots or hangouts were needed for them. Many people complained that we seemed to have forgotten about dogs, which they reminded us are very popular for all kinds of households. They felt that dog owners had not received enough support and that dog runs could have been installed. Fortunately, this has been remedied in more recent developments (see Figure 4.26).

At a completely different level, residents noted that affordable housing for families was becoming increasingly scarce – some of them said they were sure they would soon be forced to leave the area. They questioned why we had not secured more middle-income and rental housing during our planning. They saw the neighbourhood's undeveloped social-housing sites as a black eye and could not understand why these remained unbuilt.

Second, on a topic we had not expected, residents demanded more consistent management and maintenance in their neighbourhood and in their buildings. Many called for a wider range of retail shops to offer better local choice and affordability of goods, especially things needed every day. They felt there needed to be more retail competition, particularly among grocery stores, to keep prices reasonable. Others complained that litter was not picked up enough and could not understand why such a well-designed public-space system received such sloppy upkeep and repair. Not surprisingly, people who were new to multi-family life expressed concern about noise, late-night street activity, and dim lighting in parks. A common complaint focused on visitor parking in individual buildings, which was not well managed, creating security concerns.

**4.26** In a post-occupancy evaluation of False Creek North, locals told us that we needed to make provisions for dogs. High-density residents are passionately fond of their dogs, but not everyone is a fan. Designated dog parks were the solution, like this one at the east end of the neighbourhood.

**4.27** It was fulfilling to learn that more than 90 percent of respondents in our neighbourhood survey recommended False Creek North as a place to live. They clearly like the area and intend to stay. This view of a favourite gathering spot on Davie Street certainly confirms the sentiment – it is all very comfortable and settled.

These are the small domestic truths that reveal what it is like to live in a place and call it home. They are the truths of personal and intimate experience. And such messages should not be denied or ignored, especially not by a local government that made a profound promise to its citizens while offering them a new form of intensive inner-city living. As, together, we invented that lifestyle, the civic government said loudly to potential residents that it would be there for them, a promise that needs to be honoured. On the one hand, the neighbourhood template needs further detailed calibrations for better results in the future. On the other hand, there is ongoing civic responsibility for deficiencies in the recent inner-city neighbourhoods that need serious attention.

One final question was at the heart of our inquiry: Overall, what did residents feel about False Creek North? We were surprised by the answer – in fact, we were unable to find such a result in any similar studies that we could put our hands on. Over 90 percent of respondents said they would recommend the area as a place to live. Even in the face of many specific concerns, this is undoubtedly a place that people want to live. It is not merely a stopping point on their way to a suburban dream or a spot to hole up after cashing in a suburban home (see Figure 4.27). It offers a preferred way of life, and in North American terms, that is the vital breakthrough of Vancouverism.

With this sense that Vancouverism is a place-making venture based on neighbourhoods, let's now turn to how these areas are best connected – our second theme, transportation.

**5.1** From an early period, Vancouverites have enjoyed a comfortable and convenient bus system. This was a good foundation from which to build a diversified transportation system rather than simply depending on the private car.

# 5

# TRANSPORTATION CHOICES

**IF YOU GET** right down to it, it may have been a tiny group of frightened and pissed off people, back in the early 1970s, who changed Vancouver forever – some might speculate it was even one specific family among this small group, the Chans of Chinatown and Strathcona. After all, they were lead activists in this little band, fighting the fight of all fights with the monster of all monsters – the Vancouver freeway monster that was about to land on the historic city with a phenomenal thud and gobble it all up in the interest of civic progress. That would be cutting the complexity of history a bit fine, but it is a romantic way to remember that momentous time. It was the point when Vancouver went contrary to a vast worldwide consensus of what cities must do to be competitive, and contrary to a solid local establishment consensus that Vancouver had to get on this worldwide bandwagon. Instead, Vancouver citizens just decided to kill that one freeway planned to come from the east into the downtown and, with that, to kill the whole freeway culture in our town. Of course, history isn't that simple. There were key anti-freeway fights going on in many cities at about the same time, such as the famous examples led by Jane Jacobs in New York and Toronto. The Vancouver activists were certainly inspired by those campaigns. Sadly, most of those challenges failed, and those cities remain well tied up in their freeways to this day.

Back in Vancouver, there were hundreds of local people who joined in common cause against the freeway, and there were many individual leaders and activists among them. Then there were the sympathetic people throughout the city who joined the fight, ultimately resulting in the formation of the reform party, TEAM, which Frances Bula and I have already described. Personalities such as Mike Harcourt, Art Phillips, Walter Hardwick, Darlene Marzari, and Setty Pendakur became household names, ultimately city councillors and progressive leaders for a new kind of Vancouver. Shirley Chan, a daughter of the Chan family, became a national political figure after a long stint at city hall, working for Harcourt. Some will argue that all their efforts would have been for naught if the federal money needed for the freeway had come through on time. Some have said that the key decision to kill the freeway happened before TEAM officially came to power to strike the final death blow. But the truth is that these courageous people killed the damn thing one way or the other, through sustained effort, over a number of years, outside and inside government. In doing so, they took control over the whole city and sent it in a new direction. Theirs was a fight about saving the fragile historic areas of the city – particularly Chinatown but equally anxious about Strathcona and Gastown. It was also about saving a vast corridor of neighbourhoods of modest homes and shops extending across the East End of the city.

But the whole freeway story was even more frightening. In the original engineering drawings, an elevated section of the route ran along the waterfront until it entered a tunnel to North Vancouver. If that had been constructed, you could have forgotten about ever linking our downtown to the water. You could have forgotten about the convention centre complex, the hotels, and most of the housing, parks, and amenities that are now thriving as the Coal Harbour community. It was a terrible story that gave us the scars of the Georgia and Dunsmuir Viaducts, the only parts of the freeway that were ever built. When they were completed in 1971, it was felt the viaducts were needed, with or without the rest of the freeway, because they carried people over what was an unpleasant industrial district. Ironically, had these viaducts not been in our way, this part of False Creek North could have been one of our first choices for redevelopment – rather than the last. Only now are we finally getting on with the completion of a lovely new neighbourhood by scrapping these unsightly viaducts.

But even that was not the end of the nightmare. Another major road would have crashed through the north shore of False Creek – goodbye to that community of fifteen-thousand-plus people who now live there happily. And, of course, you can be sure that all of this would have been chapter one of a much more draconian story for our delicate inner-city. Put bluntly, it would have been a disaster for Vancouver, as it was for many other cities. But thankfully, we avoided it all. Instead, we started to constrain the car because of its impacts, which ultimately evolved into an explicit strategy to put in place a balanced diversity of transportation choices.

In the first instance, this is a land-use story – people rescuing places that they loved from complete obliteration. They may not have opposed freeways in principle, but they certainly opposed this particular example, which was so unbelievably insensitive and destructive. But, as the fight was fought, I think people began to seriously learn about transportation alternatives as they searched for a different way to handle movement that would not depend upon that one nasty freeway. They gained insights about a contrary kind of future. So, as events unfolded, the anti-freeway victory became a transportation story. It became an eye-opener for a different way to think about how people might move around in a modern North American city, and all of this happened before the die had been cast for a freeway culture in this city. So, it set us on an alternative trajectory that I have already referenced and now want to explore in some detail as one of the most profound dimensions of Vancouverism. To be clear, though, almost nothing else we will explore in this chapter would have been possible without that one fundamental progressive decision way back at the very beginning of the roots of Vancouverism.

## SMART LAND USE BEGETS SMART TRANSPORTATION

I would dare say that Vancouver has often backed its way into transportation innovation. Alternative transportation directions have generally followed alternative land-use moves – not for us the strategy of making transportation investments to shape the city. The regional plans of the mid-1990s – the Regional Transportation Plan of 1993 and the Liveable Region Strategic Plan update of 1996 – were developed as a package and had land use and transportation policy tightly tied together.[1] But there is no question that both of these plans were based upon the regional land-use plan of 1975 that first posited the theme of town centres.[2] In other words, we decided first the kind of place – the structure of our city – that we wanted. Then we considered how best to service that with transportation – rapid transit expansion between town centres, transportation demand management to change travel behaviour in favour of transit, and walkable community design. We see this over and over again. CityPlan, embracing neighbourhood centres, came in 1995 and was not followed by the Vancouver Transportation Plan until 1997.[3] The Central Area Plan was adopted in 1991, but the Downtown Transportation Plan did not arrive until 2002.[4] Even with that initial anxiety back in the 1970s and 1980s about how to finance an expanded auto infrastructure in our complicated region, which I discussed in Chapter 1, the problem was primarily tackled as a land-use matter. A common theme often cited by officials in Vancouver is that the best transportation plan is a good land-use plan. Instead of searching for transportation fixes that might replace the car, we first thought about just achieving better proximity of homes and jobs.

From the beginning, we were skeptical about the car. We also enjoyed a convenient and comfortable bus system that was well used and positively received by all kinds of people (see Figure 5.1). And we started building our first rapid transit line in the early 1980s, which was a tangible example to people of a viable alternative movement choice to the car. But, first and foremost, Vancouverism has been about placemaking and engendering positive urban experience, and then we thought about how to create the flows that would tie all these places and experiences together. Our generation offered the land-use side of a sustainable city-building template that is now being elegantly elaborated on the transportation side by the current generation, as I shall explain later. But it all started quite hesitantly.

## INITIAL TENDENCIES

In hindsight, the first incremental moves can be seen as somewhat reticent. Without challenging the car or building a practical network of transit alternatives, we concentrated mostly on the proximity of key origins and destinations, as I noted above. We followed a simple logic: getting everything closer together would cut the number and length of trips, and would also shift how they were made, from mechanical movement (cars and transit) to active movement (walking and cycling). Since the biggest component of trips in any city is always the journey to work, the link between homes and jobs was our biggest focus. This first logic led to the second obvious logic: the way to achieve proximity was through densification and diversity or mixed-use. So, before we seriously pondered a policy for alternative transportation, we set off to rearrange how things were laid out in the city. We set off to populate downtown Vancouver with more and more residents, close to the largest employment concentration in the region. We also started to densify along our local shopping streets outside of the inner-city. Out in the suburbs, plans started to come together for the various regional town centres, often reinforced by other subsidiary centres. Only later did these morph into true transit-oriented developments. After all, how could there be transit-oriented development when we did not yet have transit? Policies were also put in place in some instances to damper the development of office parks located away from the identified regional town centres and probable future transit routes. These are always car magnets because the workers have no alternative.

Within the downtown and the regional town centres, we started thinking about the organic balance between jobs, housing, and retail. And, in all these efforts, we were talking about many factors of experience in placemaking that went beyond just the implications for movement. Yes, we hoped that the necessary rapid transit network would ultimately be built and that the bus network would be made more fine-grained. Also, we were sure that our arrangements would motivate a quite natural shift to walking and cycling because the distances would be so short. But we did not wait for any of that to gel before reshaping the city. We just had faith that it would gel.

### FURTHER INCREMENTAL MOVES

A parallel set of further incremental measures proved to be a little more proactive – they had to do with starting to tame the hegemony of the car within the pattern of the city. In a nascent form, this began simply enough. One of Ray Spaxman's skilful moves in the 1970s was to change the quality and incidence of surface parking lots in the inner-city. He imposed tighter zoning allowances, stiff design guidelines, and temporary permits for surface parking. For all significant new development, underground parking simply became a non-negotiable requirement. Visitors today often comment on the absence of surface parking lots in the core city. This was not an explicit alternative transportation move, but it was surely symbolic. For the first time, the City indicated that cars could not just go anywhere and be everywhere, regardless of how they might impact the vital urban activities all around all those cars. For the first time, we indicated that there were more attractive things to look at in the urban scene than a sea of cars.

Another helpful zoning change in the 1970s within office districts was to establish secure bicycle parking requirements and specifications for changing rooms so that cyclists could get out of riding gear into their business attire. Soon we began to see not only cars parked underground but also bicycles.

More progressive was what is now seen as a set of audacious steps taken in the same period of the 1970s. One was an aggressive traffic-calming program in the West End, and the other was a peculiar mixing of pedestrians and auto traffic in the redevelopment of Granville Island. Using diametrically opposite strategies, these two efforts proved that in different kinds of situations the car could, indeed, be tamed.

As the West End had converted to an apartment community, a downside that no one had addressed was the huge volume of commuter traffic on its residential streets. People who worked in the inner-city or who drove through it on their way to the North Shore often used the West End as a shortcut. This created noise, danger, and general unpleasantness, particularly west of Denman Street. Planners and local residents got together and worked out a clever pattern of mini-parks set within street rights-of-way, coupled with traffic diverters, which transformed the area into an obstacle course for motorists (see Figure 5.2). Outsiders started to avoid the place, the area reclaimed its calm, and the problem was solved. At a political level, where for years it had been thought that the car was king, this program proved that this just did not need to be so and that commuter patterns could be managed in the interest of other local needs.

In the redesign of Granville Island, turning it from an industrial past into an arts, entertainment, and shopping precinct, the designers of its public realm, architects Norm Hotson and Joost Bakker, did something fundamentally unique in regard to transportation. They simply thumbed their noses at the car by making the pedestrian area pervasive from building wall to building wall throughout the island (see Figure 5.3). Cars and pedestrians were all mixed up, and people on foot essentially took over the place, leaving drivers to make headway as best they could. This was one of the earliest experiments in the world of removing barriers between cars and people. It proved that this kind of mix resulted in greater safety for everyone. There have been no serious accidents, right up to this day. Needless to say, as the new reality on the island settled in comfortably, it was inspirational for those in Vancouver who were searching for a new balance between cars and all the alternatives.

Building on these early moves, we began to see an increasing tendency at city hall into the 1990s to limit the dedications of public space to the car and big vehicles. No longer would streets be expanded and sidewalks narrowed, just to facilitate auto flow. Some dedicated right-turn lanes at corners were removed, reclaiming sidewalk space and leaving drivers to wait in the travel lane for their right turn. We started to see pedestrian bulges installed at intersections and even, occasionally, curbside parking spaces pre-empted for sidewalk activities (see Figure 5.4). Lines of parking and occasionally entire traffic lanes were taken back for buses only. For the first time in living memory, planners and engineers at city hall started challenging the very generous standards that had long been in place for fire truck access, causing our local streets to be unnecessarily wide. In

**5.2** Along with other street diverters, this mini-park on a closed street in the West End is one of many installed during the 1970s, in an early effort to control traffic intruding into the neighbourhood.

**5.3** The revitalization of Granville Island in the 1970s included one of the world's early experiments of mixing cars and pedestrians. It has been a complete success, with little friction and no serious accidents.

**5.4** From the 1970s on, Vancouver began to limit the commitment of public space to the car. As shown in this more recent example on Robson Street, we also started reclaiming areas, such as parking spaces, for people on foot. This seating takes away several parking spaces.

**5.5** Sometimes, taking back the streetscape for pedestrian activities is only temporary, such as this use of several blocks of Howe Street downtown for a public market.

newly developing areas, we started designing narrower streets, with boulevard landscape and finishes that could be trampled by a fire truck in the rare circumstance when that was necessary. Parking access was restricted to back lanes where possible, limiting the number of curb cuts and driveways that allowed cars to intrude across sidewalks. Automobile loading areas were constrained on-site and limited along streets if they required cut-ins to sidewalks. Truck routes were rationalized. In the past, the automobile footprint had been almost casually expanded every time there was a spot of congestion. Now, the opposite became true. We almost casually began to take back the streetscape, sometimes on a temporary basis and sometimes permanently, for diverse use by people on foot (see Figure 5.5).

In the 1990s, we also drew for the first time a very important line in the sand. We established the principle that auto capacity would be limited to the existing auto network, without incremental expansion. Several unnecessary one-way streets were converted back to two-way streets. One important policy was not to allow further expansion of traffic lanes into the inner-city. This was tested in 2000, when the Lions Gate Bridge was renovated. Built during the 1930s, this key bridge shuttles traffic from the North Shore into downtown. It has just three lanes, but the direction of traffic in the middle lane is reversed throughout the day to accommodate the primary traffic flow. Many people said the rehab project was the time to expand the bridge to at least four lanes. It is still three lanes today.

As we implemented higher-density housing areas, we also started experimenting with parking standards. Starting historically with quite high parking requirements and an aggressive attitude to get as much parking as possible, we began very slowly to move in the opposite direction. Economic factors were partially responsible for this – underground parking is very expensive to build, so there was pressure to forego some of that cost. Also, we started to see a lot of unused underground parking spaces in new buildings and realized that car ownership must be declining more quickly than predicted. Throughout the 1990s and into the new century, parking requirements have been decreasing. More recently, we have started talking about parking maximums instead of parking minimums.

## A NEW BREED OF ENGINEERS

Knowing the typical culture of traffic engineers and the civic engineering establishment throughout North America, some might wonder how any of this was possible, especially on an incremental basis. In many places, the engineers represent the status quo, supporting automobile pre-eminence within the civic bureaucracy, and they protect this vigilantly. Well, in the early years we had some tough battles, which I particularly remember as a neighbourhood planner. Even our tiny victories were big victories because there were so few of them. Historically, Vancouver started with its own very conservative engineering department right through to the 1980s, but after that time, and the retirement of several particularly conservative engineers, the interests and attitudes of the City's engineers started to change. I credit a lot of this to a very forward-looking chief engineer by the name of Dave Rudberg, a professional who started at city hall as a strong deputy before taking on the top leadership role. One might describe Rudberg as an engineer's engineer, with complete command of the traditional framework of civic engineering practice. He could out-argue even his most conservative colleagues, using their own language and professional ethos. But he was also a real city-builder who could see that cities had to change – that they must discard their outdated mid-century standards. He was politically savvy and could see the growing demand for a more sustainable and livable form of city. I also came to see that he was a genuine visionary, who wanted Vancouver to mark a new trail for transportation and, in fact, many other dimensions of sustainable infrastructure and prudent environmental management of urban assets. Rudberg quietly but deliberately sponsored many of the early moves to tame the car and shift emphasis to other modes. It could not have been done without his consent.

At the operational level, Rudberg was backed up by Lon LaClaire, another engineer who proved to be pivotal to the new transportation paradigm that was coming together. LaClaire possessed transportation expertise and a command of the most sophisticated transportation modelling that was then under way, but he was also a person with great sensitivity to the urban design outcomes that we could achieve in our city. At the time, most engineers neither understood nor embraced urban design intensions. In my view, he became one of our best urban designers, without ever being identified as one – interestingly, he was an accomplished mural artist on the side. Instead of letting his computer modelling determine the fate of a progressive urban design initiative, LaClaire used those same models to show alternative traffic solutions that accommodated the urban design move. Or he proved with the models that traffic would not be significantly affected by a more diverse use of street rights-of-way. LaClaire was always, and still remains, a key ally for a quality public realm.

But, like much of the story of Vancouverism, the transportation innovation in Vancouver was not led or carried forward by just a few smart, informed people. Early on, and under the leadership of Rudberg, the whole department of engineers became a hotbed of alternative thinking, first about transportation and more recently about all the technical aspects of urban sustainability. Throughout the department, engineers attuned themselves to the best practices of urban design, complete community building, and sustainable city infrastruc-ture. In subjects where planners were at best novices, these engineers pushed the boundaries on the utility side and transportation side that have become such an integral part of the sustainable Vancouver model. My direct experience was that, every year, the gap between the attitudes, theories, and experience of planners and engineers was narrowing. Early on, we bickered a lot. Later on, we became partners in very innovative initiatives. More recently, those partnerships have been enhanced by initiatives taken separately but totally in alignment with one another. Today, these progressive attitudes and understandings absolutely lead the department, in the hands of the more recent chief engineers Peter Judd and now Jerry Dobrovolny, both of whom grew up in this changing system, led many of the moves from within the ranks, and helped to craft a forward-looking engineering ethos. I say now that Vancouver's engineers are as good as its planners in public engagement, urban design, and sustainable invention. That may be one of the most important reasons why Vancouverism has been so fully realized and integrated into the practices of city hall.

## VANCOUVERISM PLAYS OUT ITS TRANSPORTATION AGENDA

Most of the early tentative, experimental moves, undertaken with the help of the engineering leaders mentioned above, finally became enshrined as official public policy with the adoption of the 1997 Vancouver Transportation Plan.[5] Tellingly, it resulted from a tight collaborative effort between the planning and engineering departments – Ann McAfee led the way on our side, and I supported her one hundred percent. The seven guiding principles of the 1997 plan offered a very clear expression of intentions for transportation in Vancouver, as well as local hopes for the larger region, as the new millennium approached. It informs our story well to summarize these principles. I'll interpret these in my own words rather than those officially in the document. Here is what those principles set out as goals for the city and to some degree the region, even though responsibility for the larger area is outside the local control of Vancouver:

- Vancouver would henceforth accommodate growth in auto demand by using the existing road network, without increasing road capacity.
- Vancouver and the region would accommodate overall growth in transportation demand by improving facilities and arrangements for the alternative modes to the car, these being transit, walking, and cycling (this was especially targeted to the inner-city on the downtown peninsula).
- Vancouver would motivate residents of the city and the region to leave their cars at home and use alternatives where practical, recognizing that the major

part of success would rest on spontaneous individual choices on a day-to-day basis.

- Acknowledging that the car will continue to be the major form of transport, particularly for areas not well served by transit, Vancouver would emphasize and advocate management of traffic demand, including implementing carpooling, parking limits, and tolling of bridges and other electronic road charges (this last idea was a bit of a stretch back in 1997 and remains controversial to this day).
- In the face of continued prevalence of the car and the lack of freeways, Vancouver would undertake traffic-calming measures to slow the speed of traffic and prevent shortcutting to reduce the impacts of vehicles moving through neighbourhoods.
- Remembering that good truck access is vital to the local economy, particularly related to the port and the airport, Vancouver would maintain a clear and complete truck network and, where impacts could be managed, pursue better truck access to key logistics sites.
- Vancouver would implement planning and development policies that support local retailing, personal services, business outlets, and community facilities so that residents can find more of what they need, including jobs, closer to home.

This was a progressive plan, but it was also a practical one. One of its main themes was that the City should foster wide transportation choices, inclusive of all modes, but that there should also be priorities set among those modes. Thus, for the first time, we officially said that we would spend money, provide space, and shape policy to reflect the following priorities: first walking, then cycling, transit, goods movement, and finally private vehicle use (see Figure 5.6). In essence, this was a rebalancing act to bring the evidence and availability of the other modes up in stature while continuing to reduce reliance on the automobile. The aspiration was that people would choose the mode that best suited the particular type of trip they were making and best suited their particular personal needs. I would say this was the point at which the progressives made peace with the ongoing presence and utility of the private car, and at the same time, the traditionalists realized that other modes were needed in the city and could even benefit car enthusiasts by taking others off the road for many kinds of trips. It was a virtuous accord.

To push things ahead, targets were also set for the various modes in 1997. It is interesting to track those over the years, both in terms of changing aspirations of

**5.6** For the first time in 1997, public policy confirmed transportation priorities: walking, cycling, transit, goods movement, and then private cars, in that order. This scene, with me taking the picture as the pedestrian, illustrates the top three priorities.

the targets themselves but also in performance.[6] Let me set the stage by remembering where we started. In the mid-1990s, the city as a whole had a status quo mode-split as follows: walking and cycling 15 percent, transit use 15 percent, and private automobile use 70 percent. The situation in the inner-city was a little more balanced: walking and cycling 15 percent, transit use 23 percent, and private automobile use 62 percent. In the 1997 plan, the following mode-split targets were officially declared: walking and cycling 18 percent, transit use 23 percent, and private automobile use 59 percent.

The 1997 plan was not just idle talk. In the document, over seventy major initiatives were adopted, and a specific work program was approved with the plan. This work program was aggressively implemented, with a progress report in 2001 quantifying the momentum.

By the turn of the century, Vancouverism's unique land-use model had real traction, especially in the downtown. The place looked and felt dramatically different from just twenty years before. The early incremental transportation moves, coupled with the deliberate application of the strategies in the 1997 plan, could now be augmented and consolidated. Mode-split performance was beginning to shift. By 2004, the overall city split was, roughly, walking 17 percent, cycling 3 percent, transit use 17 percent, and private automobile use 62 percent. (By way of comparison, the overall regional numbers were more what would be expected: walking 11 percent, cycling 2 percent, transit use 10 percent, and car use 77 percent.) The new Downtown Transportation Plan,[7] unveiled in 2002, included over eighty further initiatives to really secure a balanced transportation system, at least serving the inner-city. Then, the 1997 plan was reviewed in 2006,[8] which indicated that many of the targets had already been achieved. In these efforts, the principle of genuine transportation choice was confirmed and the modal priorities of the overall city transportation plan were again echoed and even more aggressive targets were carried forward for the inner-city. These were walking and cycling 18 percent, transit use 34 percent, and private automobile use 48 percent. In my view, this round is when the drive of land-use innovation was finally surpassed by the drive of transportation innovation. This was possible because citizens now had a lot of tolerance for new transportation ideas in the inner-city because they were enjoying the benefits of close-in living.

This brings us up to the end of the initiatives of the generation that formulated Vancouverism. The picture by this time did not look too bad from a transportation angle. Growth had been phenomenal since Expo 86: by 2015, over 100,000 more people were living in the city of Vancouver, most of them anchored downtown. There were over twenty thousand new jobs in the inner-city. All had been accommodated without allowing anything more for the private automobile culture. Many people had said it could not be done, but now it was done.

The integration of land-use and transportation planning and implementation became standard practice. Everyone in our generation, at least in Vancouver proper, pushed hard for the realization of fully complete neighbourhoods, striving for explicit balances of housing, services, and commercial supports. In the inner-city, even with all the growth, there is less car use than in the past, down by 34 percent from 2007. A private car is just no longer a day-to-day necessity. Many people and a lot of households have discovered that foregoing a car, or multiple cars, puts a great deal of money back into their pockets – money that, for example, can be used to invest in a more expensive home, which is a solid asset tending to increase in value in our economy rather than a consumer good ever decreasing in value. People walk or bike more than in many modern cities, and they do so in shorter trips (see Figure 5.7). This all reflects a somewhat contrasting household model for budgeting money and time than you normally see in North America. People spend less money on transportation and less time moving around. They have more valuable time with their families, including a growing tradition in the inner-city of a parent walking the children to school. They testify to feeling less stress from the everyday drama of commuting. They have more money for investments that build their wealth. Looking back at the overall picture, the in-migration of massive population took a lot of commuter trips from outside the downtown peninsula out of the equation. As significantly more people moved downtown, over 75 percent of those people who also work downtown began to walk to their jobs. They are totally out of the commuter rat race. You can imagine their emotional state when they arrive comfortably at work.

The dual initiatives of restricting road capacity while increasing transit have worked better than most people expected for those longer trips that still need to be made every day by people who have not desired to leave the suburbs. Fortunately, regional transit development has effectively mirrored City policy directions, with positive results all round. In the core city, though the population has increased by 75 percent and jobs are up by 26 percent, the volume of incoming cars in the daily commute has dropped by 20 percent. Even at the overall city boundary, the number of incoming cars has declined – it is down about 5 percent. The growth in demand for commuter trips has essentially been accommodated by transit – people have actually switched how they travel to work in the positive direction (see Figure 5.8).

The all-government commitment to expanded rapid transit since the late 1990s has been extraordinary by any standard. It must be remembered that transit is not controlled by the City, so all of our plans might have been for naught if senior governments had not been understanding and interested. Like its predecessors, the regional transportation agency TransLink manages transit. Expansions are paid for by a partnership of the provincial and federal governments, along with local governments. Rapid transit started with SkyTrain, then a peculiar technology of driverless trains on a grade-separated track, selected only because senior government politicians wanted to be seen as at the cutting edge of transit technology. SkyTrain began with a single route in 1986, called the Expo Line (built for Expo 86, from downtown, serving the southwest out to New Westminster and then later on to Surrey). The next fifteen years saw implementation of the Millennium Line (serving the eastern suburbs), the Canada Line (built for the Olympic Games, extending south from downtown to Richmond and the airport), and the introduction of the West Coast Express commuter rail service (coming in from the farther-out easterly suburbs). The capacity of the Expo

**5.7** On foot is the way to go in Vancouver's inner-city. We walk and bike more than the residents of most modern North American cities, and our trips are shorter or combined with transit.

**5.8** The automobile infra-structure of Vancouver has been constrained, and transit has filled the gap for more and more commuters, particularly in the inner-city. As you see here, it is not a bad way to travel.

Line has increased by 30 percent since its inception. Bus routes and service hours were also dramatically expanded. And now, beyond the time frame of our story, we have recently seen the addition of the Evergreen Line in 2016 (extending service in the eastern suburbs). Further expansion of the bus system is in the works. Also, SeaBus, the passenger-only ferry service to the North Shore, started in 1977 and now a vital part of the transit network, is expanding. Figure 5.9 shows the overall picture. Extension of rapid transit from central Vancouver to the west along Broadway and more transit in Surrey are the current top priorities. Despite all this growth, though, the biggest problem now is keeping transit capacity in pace with growing demand. Think of the contrast with most North American cities, where transit demand is at best stable or in decline. In this region, we simply cannot build enough transit and have a long way to go before we achieve what could be called a pervasive system.

Traffic-calming measures (see Figure 5.10) have been implemented in many Vancouver communities to stop what was originally called "rat running" – that practice of motorists shortcutting through a community on local streets when arterials are jammed. Vancouver has a complete and well-scaled grid of streets that offers a great array of opportunities to accommodate auto routes – another gift of the 1928 Bartholomew Plan that I mentioned in Chapter 4.[9] Given that we forewent the freeway approach, we are lucky to have such a tight network of streets as an alternative. But that same grid can also be a major problem in trying to protect the safety, livability, and integrity of neighbourhoods if there is unrestricted auto flow on all streets, especially within otherwise quiet neighbourhoods. So, traffic-calming features have been installed in all kinds of neighbourhoods throughout the city to deflect drivers back to the arterials (see Figure 5.11). In laying out the new downtown neighbourhoods, we built the calming in from the beginning, making strategic disconnections of some streets, dramatically limiting continuity of auto access along the water, and placing car deflective measures where they were needed. In this work, we invented a colourful jargon by calling the resulting protected precincts "areas of tranquility." This is one of the things inner-city residents often tell us they appreciate most about the neighbourhoods they live in.

Even though many other challenges remained to be addressed, the combination of core transformation, consolidation of neighbourhood centres, intensification along commuter streets, upgrading of the transit network, and constraining the auto infrastructure was showing important results by the turn of the century. At the city level, already by 2008, the proportion of trips undertaken by

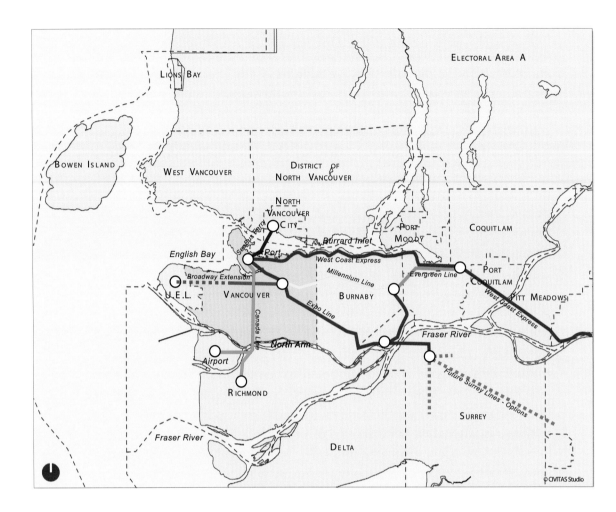

**5.9** A primary network of rapid transit fans out from downtown Vancouver. A much denser bus network overlays these spines. Existing rapid transit lines are the Expo Line, Millennium Line, Canada Line, and Evergreen Line. Also shown are the West Coast Express commuter rail line and the SeaBus ferry. Soon to be added are Broadway and Surrey extensions.

**5.10** Traffic-calming measures, such as this roundabout in Kitsilano, have been added to many neighbourhood streets. A second one is visible in the distance. These small efforts have big results for safety and quietness.

**5.11** This West End traffic deflector on Comox Street helps to fend off commuter "rat runners," creating what we call "neighbourhood areas of tranquility."

foot, bikes, or transit in Vancouver overall had topped 40 percent, and recent study indicates that the 50 percent mark has now been surpassed – not bad for a city that, like all the rest in North America, sprawls all over the landscape and is inhabited by people deeply in love with the romance and image of the automobile culture. There is no doubt that the Vancouver region is still car-centric, but the city itself has made the shift, and I am confident it will spread.

The cycling story during the time of the emergence of Vancouverism is a little more tentative. The 1997 plan certainly called for more bike routes. The plan drew out a grid of bike routes throughout the city to improve the convenience and safety for cyclists. No doubt, this would increase the appeal of bicycle travel. Vancouver has a very temperate climate, so it was reasonable to expect that cycling could become more significant as a dependable mode of travel. A share-bike program has enhanced this potential. This whole initiative was stalled for several years while a solution was found to a tough conundrum. Provincial law says that all cyclists must wear helmets, but helmets are tricky to offer in a share arrangement because of all kinds of little problems. Fortunately, everything was solved, the share-bike program has now settled in and become popular, and you see helmets hanging beside parked share-bikes (see Figure 5.12). Our system, in which cycling lanes are separated from car lanes, has spread quickly (see Figure 5.13) but putting this in place has not been easy. This is a touchy situation, where people who prefer different modes or feel impacts stare one another down, face to face. As separated, dedicated bikeways are insinuated into existing streetscapes, driving lanes are edited out, and auto capacity is diminished. Drivers often begrudge the whittling away of their turf. They get mad. As curbside parking is given over to bikeways, and options for front-door loading and valet parking are cut back, retailers and restaurateurs feel the pinch. They also get mad. Sometimes, even residents become upset when the flexibility of their street is constrained or a stand of share-bikes suddenly pops up in front of their home. And, of course, many car fans just viscerally resent the intrusion of bike culture in what they see as the natural domain of the automobile. So, to some degree, implementing the grid of bikeways was a thankless task, until we started to see the numbers (see Figure 5.14). After a multi-year program of new bikeways, cycling is up in a significant way – in recent years, it has topped 7 percent of all trips, and biking to work has broken the 10 percent mark in Vancouver as a whole. My generation made little progress in ratcheting up cycling, but the current generation has surely made up for lost time. But I am getting ahead of the story.

**5.12** The share-bike program, replicating what is now common in many progressive cities, is a popular addition to Vancouver's cycling culture.

**5.13** Upping the ante for cycling, a network of separate bikeways, such as here on Hornby Street downtown, is spreading quickly throughout the city.

**5.14** The use of separated bikeways is increasing significantly, which justifies the initial difficulties of implementation. The Hornby bikeway is crowded during peak hours. Now, we hope that cyclists will learn to better respect pedestrians, who are, after all, the top priority.

## THE NEXT GENERATION SHIFTS THE AGENDA

As Chapter 8 describes, the focus on the initial themes of Vancouverism became less relevant as the city moved into the 2010s. Innovative people began to concentrate on the fresh challenge of how to make Vancouver a truly green city. The new generation would build upon the land-use model of Vancouverism and the transportation advances. But it would also expand the agenda into infrastructure reform, social advancement, and the potentials of new economic approaches.

So, in 2012, when an updated transportation plan was presented, we saw a completely novel kind of document. It has a quite conventional title, "Transportation 2040: Moving Forward,"[10] but, after reading that, an old-timer would initially have trouble finding the hard transportation focus. That, in fact, is a good thing. It shows that Vancouverites have become more sophisticated since the early foundational measures already described. The 2012 plan is no longer just about transportation or even allocations for use of land. It situates transportation within a much more comprehensive paradigm that reflects a full sustainability agenda, integrating environmental, social, economic, and cultural considerations. Transportation has become a means to an end rather than an end in itself. To make the point, I'll summarize the list of intentions with which the plan opens. It still emphasizes the challenges posed by overall growth, limited road space, and demand for transit, but it now gives pride of place to the health costs of sedentary lifestyles, the economic consequences of high housing and fuel prices, the social requirements of an aging population, and the environmental implications of climate change. To confront these challenges, the objectives of the plan do not stand alone. Instead, they are drawn from the comprehensive greenest city agenda that was being invented at the same time – one of ten green plans. The transportation vision and intentions are expressed as "green transportation goals" and organized on the basis of economy, people, and the environment. This is not a traditional engineer's plan. It has a refreshingly wider scope and intent.

But when the 2012 plan gets to the point of transportation, it really gets to the point in no uncertain terms. The 2008 mode-share performance for the overall city had been 40 percent by foot, bikes, and transit, with still 60 percent by cars, a ratio that was seen as amazing at the time. The target for 2040 is now set to topple that performance on its head: 67 percent by foot, bikes, and transit, with only 33 percent left to the car. The distance for every car trip is set to decrease by 20 percent from the 2007 status quo. And, in a new measure, taking inspiration from the Nordic countries, it is targeted that by 2040, there will be zero traffic-related fatalities.

It is not my intent to fully describe or comment on the 2012 transportation plan, because it is not an integral part of the story I am unfolding about Vancouverism – it comes after our story and represents a completely new story in and of itself. But I cannot help but highlight a few of the detailed features because they are just so much in the tradition of what we were dreaming about in my generation. The specific policies attack automobile dependence from very interesting directions. At a land-use level, it is not surprising to see continued emphasis on proximity of origins and destinations to facilitate walking and cycling, through density and mixed-use within the private realm. But now we also see proposals for better, more diverse, and creative use of the public realm of street rights-of-way.

We finally see specific proposals to enhance the environment for walking, with the target to increase the proportion of pedestrian trips to over 20 percent from the much lower 2007 status quo. This has been a sorely missed aspect of the transportation story from the very beginning. We had talked a lot about the top priority of pedestrian supports, but not much actually made it to ground. We still use standard sidewalk materials and landscaping in most instances, so you would be hard put to read priority for walking in the average streetscape. Yes, we have emphasized sidewalk indentions for wheelchair access, which has been good for the principle of universal accessibility. Yes, we have changed the crosswalk signals in many locations to enhance the chances for safe walking across busy streets. Yes, we have many years of adding rain protection on building walls adjacent to sidewalks. But, no, we have closed very few street or lane rights-of-way to traffic, as has been seen more and more in cities around the world. No, we have not sorted out key gaps in the continuity of a comfortable pedestrian network. No, we have not resolved many unsafe situations for walkers along busy streets. No, we have not redesigned streets to be friendlier to pedestrians than they are to cars. No, we have not found a dependable way to keep our pedestrian places both garbage-free and well maintained, even where we have put in the few decorative treatments that are such important cues to pedestrians. No, we have not declared the pedestrian to have one hundred percent right-of-way in traffic management. To step into any of the new bike lanes is taking your life in your own hands. Many cyclists now seem to enjoy the new designated lanes as a bicycle freeway, where pedestrians are the enemy if not actually a target. We have lots to learn as designers and as cyclists on this front. The bottom line is that we have simply not done enough, and until the laudable intentions of the 2012 plan are fully realized, Vancouver will remain a less than ideal place to walk around. To my mind, this area of the current plan portends to have as big an impact as any other aspect because the pedestrian realm has been so overlooked for so long.

The 2012 plan also has high aspirations for cycling and transit. I have already referred to the advances that were made in the dedicated, separated bicycle network – these were initiated through the plan, along with more to come. The plan intends to build upon the advances made in the downtown over the last decade by aiming for the proportion of trips by bike in the whole city to increase to 12 percent from the 2007 status quo. The transit evolution in the region has also been outlined above. Although much of the 2012 plan's intentions will be achieved only if TransLink, the regional transportation agency, does its job well and if senior governments are forthcoming with the huge amount of necessary funding, the target to grow the proportion of transit trips from the 2017 status quo to about 33 percent is a positive yet practical one. This will also be essential to achieve the target that about a third of travellers forego their cars by 2040.

The implementation side of the 2012 plan is interesting because it is so specific and so focused on transformative projects that are of a scale to genuinely enhance our green brand. It's all about big ideas that, one by one, are already changing the face of Vancouver as each one is put on the ground. As expected, removing the Georgia and Dunsmuir Viaducts is included (something we original Vancouverism agents always talked about but found totally elusive), this being the final bludgeon to that original freeway monstrosity. Preserving continuous rail corridors for other uses is a big theme. The Broadway subway extension, along with new transit on the old rail corridors, heralds a long-term strategy to provide a grid of transit rather than the current radial system that fans out from downtown. For the bridges that connect downtown to the south, across False Creek – the Burrard, Granville, and Cambie Bridges – cool revamps are posited for lavish pedestrian and bicycle routes. The heritage of the Burrard Bridge has just been enhanced as a treasure, along with installing dedicated bike lanes. Furnishing the Granville Bridge with a lush greenway spine for walking and cycling down the middle, and fitting it with an elevator down to the popular tourist attraction of Granville Island are stylish moves that many people eagerly anticipate. This is just a taste of the projects that are now officially on the docket, along with more improvements in all aspects of active movement. One has to admire the chutzpah of this big thinking.

So, the generation that followed in the footsteps of those of us at the centre of the original invention of Vancouverism has become very bold in its transportation aspirations for the future city. In fact, these kinds of audacious gestures would seem out of character in any other North American city and are even at the edge of what Vancouver culture might suggest is probable, but their nervy forward vision is part of their serious appeal. There can be no doubt that if the measures that are specified in the 2012 plan are fully realized, Vancouver will truly be a different city than ever imagined, and it will be a truly green city by any standard. It will have transcended the intentions of Vancouverism, even though I would dare suggest that those of us who came before will be egging on this next generation to make it so and to push it even further.

### WILL WE CONTINUE TO WALK THE TALK?

Even with all our progress, Vancouver's transportation situation remains a tenuous one, fraught with difficulties. This new urban land-use model that we conjured up, successful as it has proven to be, does not yet have a fully formed transportation concept to go with it. A parallel movement paradigm still needs to be invented or, at least, further elaborated. Though Vancouver is generally scored highly by the rating agencies of the world for livability, traffic tie-ups and limitations on goods movement always pull us down. The better we perform in transit, the more demand we create, keeping a balanced capacity just out of our reach. Cycling advances create cycling critics, as I have already described. Pedestrians are told that they are priority one, but when they venture on and along the street, as everyone urges them to do, they often have difficulty believing it.

Recent initiatives are on the right track, but they will have to go all the way – and probably further – in every aspect that is contemplated if they are to have a chance to engender a land-use and transportation balance. I think the secret of the Vancouverism paradigm, writ large for transportation, is that the transit system has to be pervasive, the cycling pattern has to be pervasive, and a hospitable setting for walking has to be pervasive – all in addition to a consistent pattern of intensification, mixed-use, and jobs-housing balance everywhere.

Without freeways – which, in my mind, remains a defining positive feature of Vancouver – the management of traffic within the existing street network will never be successful unless we get more of those cars off the streets. This is where "mobility pricing" comes in – this is the pay-as-you-go tolling system for use of the auto infrastructure, also called "road pricing." In the future, mobility pricing is inevitable. Otherwise, every driver will increasingly pay dearly in both time and frustration every single day. We will have to price our bridges, our commuter streets into the city, and probably even the specific links into the downtown, the epicentre of the region. This is certainly the experience of other congested cities, such as Singapore and London. Vancouverites have not yet come to this realization. Mobility pricing remains unpopular, primarily because the alternatives to the car are still not good enough. But, in the end, I am convinced there will be no way to avoid it.

Transit will also need significant further elaboration if it is to become an alternative that works for most people. Over the last several generations, the region has done a good job in expanding the rapid transit system but not nearly enough for the kind of fine grid that will be essential in the future. The intentions of the Transportation 2040 plan are laudable, but the proposed initiatives in that plan will not be enough. And in any event, transit will not be determined just by the City, because it is a regional and even a provincial responsibility. Almost every major commuter street will ultimately need a rapid transit capacity of one kind or another. My colleague Patrick Condon has been a strong advocate for an overlay of trams – a light rail alternative like that in Portland, Oregon – within the wider grid of rapid transit. I agree that, in many districts, a tram network would be sensible for many arterials. But, to my mind, the further enhancement of our already good bus system is the more logical next step forward throughout the region. Currently, suburban riders can wait a very long time before the bus arrives, which will simply not be tolerable once the car constraints are in full force. As we fight our way toward a better rapid transit network, more applications of express buses, what TransLink calls the "B-Lines," will be a handy first step (see Figure 5.15). Tram alignments or light rapid transit can then be put in place as ridership increases.

We must also get much better at securing transit funding. For as long as anyone can remember, this funding has been neither planned nor systematic. Instead, it has been granted on an opportunistic basis, depending upon the political interests of the moment. Acquiring funding for expansions is always a big battle. Given the extraordinary difficulties that we have historically had with transit funding, the plans for the future that I have just described seem like

**5.15** On key growth corridors, express buses that make few stops will build transit use and shape transit-oriented development. Called "B-Lines" in Vancouver, these routes are being expanded by TransLink, the regional transit agency.

an impossible dream. They will be an impossible dream until the senior governments realize that creating a genuine alternative to the automobile infrastructure is in the national, provincial, and regional interests – not merely to make movement more comfortable for all our citizens but also to lubricate the economy. New, more dependable funding mechanisms must be put in place, and funding must no longer be treated as a political football or, worse yet, a political pork barrel.

But I would go even further when it comes to transit. Right now, the most comfortable way to move around is in the sanctity of the car. It is private, it is climate-controlled, it has music, it can be luxurious. It goes specifically from the exact origin to destination you require. It is at your fingertips exactly when you need it – no queuing in the rain. Even with the clogged traffic people often find annoying, how can we balance the advantages of the car with collective movement? We need to pay a lot more attention to the experience of transit in terms of both comfort and convenience – both rapid transit and the bus (see Figure 5.16). These will not be engineering solutions. They will be design, programming, and marketing solutions. Could we create more personal space in the trains? Could we up the quality of the interiors of buses and trains and that of their stations? Are there services that we could add? Could we offer live entertainment or education? Could we make every trip a lottery, with the chance to win free transit or maybe occasionally a free trip to Europe? We certainly need a fun and creative

**5.16** As well as providing attractive routes and timing, transit needs to offer comfort and appeal if it is to compete with the amenity of the private car. Improving the transit experience, by limiting crowding, such as you see here, and improving other aspects of the trip must be a continuing priority.

loyalty program to reward transit use, such as now seen in Bologna. I am not trying to promote specific embellishments here, but I do suggest that such embellishments be given serious and creative consideration.

Perhaps the biggest embellishment for transit could be a more tailored customized trip. Surely, there could be more alternatives for that first and last link that every transit rider must organize – home to transit and transit to home. Or, taking it one step further, we need to join the worldwide trend of what is called "integrated mobility," where people use a phone app to select and connect all the modes for an overall trip that will deliver the best convenience, cost, and experience. They make a single payment to cover the entire journey, all of which cuts their reliance on a private car. Think of public transit, taxis, share-cars, share-bikes, rental cars, and ride-hailing all considered together in one-trip planning and linked with associated services. Hannover launched an early version back in 2004, and cities as different as Helsinki, Seoul, Birmingham, and Los Angeles, among many others, are implementing systems of one kind or another. As an integrated transportation agency, TransLink might be perfectly positioned to run the whole show in Greater Vancouver. I wonder if share-cars, share-bikes, or a TransLink-organized version of ride-hailing might at least take the place of bus links to rapid transit stations or for many different kinds of short trips. Also, for tangential origins and destinations that are off the beaten path, TransLink has started to experiment with custom transit in small privately driven buses. This idea, in my view, has a big future as a way to make public movement more compelling and personalized.

I have already worried about the lack of advances in support of walking in Vancouver. A fascinating idea that could offer great pedestrian benefits for our city is what the planners of Rotterdam call the "City Lounge" program, echoed by similar programs in New York, Copenhagen, Dublin, and a few other smart cities, though lacking the clever name. In these initiatives, each city is searching its public domain for spots and even networks to reclaim for active civic life. Furnishings and finishes are improved dramatically from traditional standards. Trees and landscaping are added. Public art is added. And then programming is arranged – starting with buskers. The clear message in these places is that pedestrians have priority and that walking is encouraged. It is not a policy communication but an experiential one – which is far more powerful for the average person (see Figure 5.17).

Goods movement, a simmering difficulty for both Vancouver and the region, has not yet received the kind of innovative thinking that I have otherwise been describing in this chapter (see Figure 5.18). When a city does not have freeways, it also does not have express corridors for goods movement. Goods have to be transported through the regular street system, with predictable limits on efficiency and impacts on those adjacent to major streets. Only recently, in 2017, was an overall goods-movement strategy adopted at the regional level. Called "Moving the Economy,"[11] it was completed by TransLink, in collaboration with the local governments and the business community. Current efforts emphasize protecting rail corridors, maintaining and confirming truck routes, improving access to the port and airport, and standardizing freight vehicle licensing. Perhaps the most forward-looking aspect of all this current work is the initiative to found a regional freight council of business, government, and community leaders to really tackle the tough issues in an innovative way. There is no doubt that, without a freeway system, a new paradigm for goods movement will be needed as the region continues to expand and densify. One can imagine dedicated freight corridors or even public transit for freight, limitations on truck size with installation of smaller-scaled dispersed logistics centres, and other measures that have simply been unthinkable to date and were never even broached in all the inventions of Vancouverism.

My most serious concern for the future rests not with direct transportation policy but, rather, with the ongoing attitude about land-use policy that will either support or not support active mobility. There are moments, as I survey the current planning moves now under way, that I have begun to question if the principle of complete communities is still embraced at city hall in Vancouver.

One example shows why I have begun to worry – the recently approved plan for the False Creek Flats. This vast area, a low-scaled district just to the southeast of the downtown peninsula, will undoubtedly be the biggest growth area of the inner-city for the foreseeable future (see Figure 5.19). It includes key rail lines, some important infrastructure installations, a future major hospital campus, and some vital industry but also much obsolescence and huge swathes of open developable property. In mid-2017, after many months of intense study and strongly articulated passion about saving industry and encouraging high tech, the planners unveiled a plan. Adopted by city council, it enshrines a very narrow range of uses, does not foster intensity or mixed-use, makes almost no attempt to bring jobs and homes closer together, offers few if any of the ancillary services and amenities that working people need and want on a day-to-day basis, and takes only glancing advantage of two new transit stations that will soon serve the area. If the envisioned workplaces are developed as intended, there is no doubt that the employees will be car people. Even those who are lucky enough

**5.17** Robson Square downtown has been permanently closed to car traffic and is now dedicated to pedestrian use and all kinds of community activities, from informal gatherings to events. Here the jazz festival takes centre stage. These "city lounges" need to proliferate.

**5.18** Innovation in goods movement has lagged in Vancouver. Recent policy directions from TransLink may help. Large trucks on small streets, with all the resulting noise and disruption, is not an optimal situation.

**5.19** Land-use solutions, focused on principles such as complete communities and transit-oriented development, have as much potential as technical fixes in resolving transportation glitches, possibly more. Sadly, Vancouver's largest inner-city growth area, the False Creek Flats, shown from atop the local transit station, has recently been zoned without either principle in mind. Let's hope this is only a holding action and that the zoning will soon be changed.

to work near those transit stops will probably use their cars because very few restaurants, cafes, gyms, shops, or almost anything else they need during the day will be within walking distance of their workplaces. The basic idea of complete communities, upon which the whole strategy of modal shift to active transportation is based, is simply left out of the picture in this plan. If the understanding and consciousness are missing to make complete communities an absolute requirement in *this* area, where a wholesale redevelopment will inevitably occur, I cannot imagine what will be planned for more incrementally changing areas. I urge a refreshed dedication by city hall to the basic principle of balanced, mixed, complete communities. The profound benefits of simple proximity have to be freshly emphasized. I can only be optimistic that these kinds of recent prevailing attitudes at city hall will change quickly.

### THE BIGGER UNKNOWNS

The heirs of Vancouverism will have to cope with some very tricky new inventions as they move ahead – inventions that were not even in world consciousness when my generation was in charge. These inventions will take fresh thinking and may put to the test many of the progressive ideas for transportation that have guided thinking up to this point.

Exciting the world right now are the diverse opportunities that have been opened up by the new themes of the sharing economy. Vancouver has seen a dramatic increase in car sharing – membership in share-car associations in Vancouver is the highest by far than in any other North American city (see Figure 5.20). We are at the forefront in at least this one aspect of the new trend of sharing. In the inner-city in particular, people who have given up private car ownership have signed up to share-car collectives, which gives them access to cars when they need them, without the ongoing expense of ownership, maintenance, and storage. Buying is out, sharing is in (car ownership in the inner-city has stabilized at about 0.4 cars per capita, no longer with an upward trend). Almost 30 percent of Vancouver drivers are members of at least one car-share co-op. The dense, mixed-use urban structure makes this practical for residents. In contrast, the City and Province are only now starting to embrace ride-hailing systems such as Uber and Lyft. The potential for ride-hailing arrangements linked to transit, as a more dependable alternative to taxis, has not been exploited. It remains to be seen how the city and region will insinuate the many possible transportation aspects of a sharing economy into the status quo.

**5.20** Vancouver has been swept up in car sharing. We use share-cars more than any other North American city. Our tight urban pattern and diversity certainly encourage this. These share-cars downtown are ready for the next member to grab the keys.

It is equally unclear how the driverless vehicle will enter into the Vancouver lexicon of transportation. As cities all over the world struggle to understand the implications of autonomous driving, one thing is becoming evident. The self-driving car will draw people away from transit more than from any other mode. So, transit agencies, including TransLink in Metro Vancouver, will have to think hard about how to make transit more competitive than in the past. To keep transit riders, we may be on the verge of having to offer free transit trips and find some other way to pay for our transit system as a fundamental utility. The earlier we make this shift, the better. Habits are hard to break, and once people settle into autonomous driving, luring them back to transit will be difficult.

But, autonomous mobility may have much more profound implications than even the challenge to transit. It may dramatically affect the whole public realm. Pundits predict two contrasting futures, depending on how self-driving is allowed. The first suggests that, if autonomous driving is introduced into the urban movement system through privately owned vehicles, the number of cars on the road could increase exponentially. Households could own multiple autonomous vehicles, maybe one for each member of the family. After dropping off commuters, the cars could circulate around town all day rather than parking, or they could head back home, returning at quitting time to pick up their owners, which would at least double commuter trips each day. The second future suggests that, if autonomous cars are linked exclusively through car sharing and not allowed otherwise, significantly fewer cars than we now see could be on the streets at

**5.21** Like everywhere else, Vancouver is anticipating the future culture of autonomous driving. But, because we have constrained the realm of the car, including narrowing newer streets, as here in Southeast False Creek, self-driving vehicles may be possible only through a share-car system.

any one time. Cars would be on the road only as people need them. I would not dare to speculate on the exact numbers and proportions – I have not reviewed the detailed analysis – but the contrasting futures are vividly suggestive. In suburban situations, with a long history of building wide streets, well beyond real needs, these alternatives may represent real choices for a local government and its citizens to contemplate.

In the case of Vancouver, where the car infrastructure has been increasingly constrained for a very long time (see Figure 5.21), at least since the late 1980s, I suspect there may not be a choice. The future may have already been pre-ordained. It may be inevitable that the share-car approach will be the only viable approach for autonomous driving because the alternative would simply swamp the street system, creating chaos and bringing all private movement, and most goods movement, to a standstill. On the other hand, the scenario where there are vastly fewer cars within the road system may create never-before-seen opportunities for expansion of the active mobility culture. Of course, this whole question remains a fascinating speculation but also a very serious one because the outcome of this profound choice for transportation may ultimately determine if the future of Vancouverism will be as a long-term new way of building cities or simply a cul-de-sac affectation of the late twentieth century.

As I have said, transportation, as exemplified by the current generation of thinking about Vancouver mobility, has become a sub-set of the bigger question of the ways and means that Vancouver will become a more sustainable city – and so it should be. We will explore this in Chapter 8. But, having made the point in this chapter that proximity is pivotal to the active transportation strategy of Vancouverism, and that a fine mixing of uses and activities is central to proximity, I'll now turn to the social side of the Vancouverism paradigm, where this is dealt with – the quest for diversity. This is the subject of the next chapter.

**6.1** "Living first" was our prime mantra for transforming Vancouver's inner-city into a people place. These people in Emery Barnes Park are living our dream every day – over 110,000 of them downtown.

# 6

# DIVERSITY

**"LIVING FIRST" IS** the phrase that we came to use to evoke the essence of the land-use mix that transformed Vancouver's inner-city (see Figure 6.1). Many would say it is the prime motive of Vancouverism. Provided with a very traditional mid-century, nine-to-five downtown of office buildings and retail, as a new generation took the reins of planning in Vancouver, the idea took root to mix up all this commerce with housing – as much housing as could be drawn to the area and as many types of homes as could be accommodated. Of course, we concentrated on that jobs-housing link that I discussed in Chapter 5. We said we would support housing over any other use in the inner-city – it would come first in our priorities because there were already so many jobs in the downtown core. At the same time, there was a growing anxiety that the local economy was cooling, with the globalization of the resource sector, and a hope that new housing and the spinoff services and activities that came with it might just be enough to anchor revitalization, creating new kinds of jobs. I remember exactly how "living first" came into our lexicon. Initially, I had coined my own phrase that I thought was apt – I had said that what we were doing was a "residential first" strategy. Early on, we had the opportunity to present our approach at the Harvard School of Design in Boston because the professors there had heard about what we were trying to do and were very interested to hear about it. After our presentation, the chair of the school, Alex Krieger, offered a commentary in which he said that what we were actually up to was *living* first" because we not only wanted housing but also everything that goes with it to offer complete community life. Of course, we grabbed those words and they became our mantra. Many years later, after I had retired from government, Krieger became a close colleague in my work in Dallas. When I reminded him of this story, he said he thought *we* had invented the moniker and that he had just picked up on it – so go the vagaries of memory. The point is that Vancouver created a plan for a profound mix of work-places and housing, with an emphasis on housing – the 1991 Central Area Plan that I spoke about in Chapter 1.[1] It led us into the ever more interesting and neces-sary land-use and social mixes that I will fully describe in this chapter. Also in this chapter, I will talk about some of the blindness in our approach and the difficulties that still plague the city as a place that aspires to welcome everyone with open arms.

## CONSOLIDATING THE PRINCIPLE OF URBAN DIVERSITY

The 1991 Central Area Plan helped to crystalize our ideas. But the roots of Van-couver's experience were much deeper and much older than that. It started back in the mid-1950s and on into the early 1970s, initiated with a rezoning of the West End, which came together in a short but intensive redevelopment drama long before the era of Vancouverism. This very quickly rebuilt the western side of the downtown peninsula, on an admittedly somewhat random basis, into Vancouver's first high-density residential community (see Figure 6.2). Through this massive change, our community learned for the first time how to live in a high-density setting, even though the emphasis was mostly on small suites, rental units, and a distinctly younger and older population. Outsiders were often disdainful – there were many stories about the area's transient and casual living, overcrowding, and almost flippant take on what is important in life. People said that West Enders were crammed together like seabirds on a cliff. For West Enders, there was exactly the opposite attitude. They enjoyed an exciting new living experience, a flourishing community spirit, diverse kinds of neigh-bours, and both a hip urban vibe and the convenience of walking to work, all unavailable in an otherwise suburbanizing world. Their attitude finally pre-vailed in the collective consciousness of Vancouverites, both as consumers and voters, which set the stage for more and more associations of housing and work-places in increasingly closer proximity.

And then, again, well before the advent of Vancouverism, during the 1970s, another initiative changed the way that everyone looked at planning, adding the idea that the City could not only encourage densification through blanket rezon-ing, but could also achieve it in a logical and organized way, by creating identifi-able neighbourhoods with explicit urban design and social and quality-of-life

**6.2** The West End, shown here, introduced
Vancouver to high-density living and
social mix. It built out through the 1960s.

objectives. That initiative was the deliberate and planned development of False
Creek South (see Figure 6.3), now often called Southwest False Creek to differentiate it from Southeast False Creek, which was developed much later for the 2010
Olympic Games. In this area of City-owned obsolete industrial lands, the planners of the 1970s used a planning method that was characterized by both urban
design and social design prowess, coupled with public engagement. And it was
all managed through the strong hand of the local government. It is hard now to
understand how revolutionary that thinking was for this city at the time. We
were moving from a past when development had been determined solely by market forces, as interpreted by the developers themselves. Now, the community
would lead the visioning and detailing of what it wanted itself to be in the future.
False Creek South brought all kinds of innovations, but one that played a central

**6.3** False Creek South, pictured here, now often called Southwest False Creek, was the first deliberately designed higher-density inner-city community. It proved that we could integrate design, social, and other public objectives to engender a high quality of life. It built out through the 1970s. Now, diversity became explicit policy.

**6.4** Another breakthrough for Vancouver, Granville Island was completed by the federal government in the 1970s, confirming that smart design and deterministic policy could achieve outstanding results. This included the fascinating idea of employing profitable uses to subsidize desired low-profit uses – mixing up the mix.

role in the later social story of Vancouverism was the notion that housing should be available for a wide spectrum of people, not just those who could secure it in the open marketplace. The community plan for False Creek South targeted an expansive mix of housing. About a third of it consisted of subsidized low-income units, with the remaining two-thirds divided equally between middle-income units with secure rents and free-market higher-income units. Housing for seniors and people with special needs was added to the mix. Of course, the fact that the lands were City-owned and would be long-term leased rather than sold made a big difference. Public ownership meant that the mix could be realized through writing down the value of the land for some of the units, which brought development costs down and lease costs down, along with other entrepreneurial business arrangements rather than just through municipal regulation. This made the mix practical to achieve. Readily available federal funding also helped. But the idea of mandating a housing mix and the proof that it could be achieved have influenced all that has been done since that time. Let's just hope that this optimal mix holds steady as the long-term leases, now coming to maturity, are considered for renewal.

The West End and False Creek South experiences were reinforced by a third initiative – the conversion of Granville Island, launched during the 1970s by its owner, the federal government (see Figure 6.4). Sponsored by cabinet minister Ron Basford, the consummate government insider, the scheme simply confirmed that proactive and deterministic planning was the right way to go for Vancouver and that it could yield an even richer mix by including primary uses and activities that were not just market-based. This project was a game-changer. The island sits at a highly visible location in False Creek under the Granville Bridge, right adjacent to the downtown peninsula. It was converted from a messy and obsolete industrial district to a cool precinct for retail, recreation, and education, with a strong arts, crafts, and culture identity, lots of innovation, and a preference for independent ventures rather than corporate and chain dominance. The big anchor of the conversion was a large public farmers' market, with all the bells and whistles that created what was called a "festival market" at the time. It was equal to or better than any such market on the West Coast – Pike Place Market in Seattle was the reference for comparison. The thing that caught everyone's attention was that it was so deliberate – from the progressive, all-encompassing public realm plan by architects Norm Hotson and Joost Bakker that I talked about in Chapter 5 to the establishment of the Granville Island Trust. The trust was created to oversee the island but mostly to manage the cross-subsidy of profitable ventures that underwrote the unprofitable cultural, arts, and crafts activities. Just as in False Creek South, the conversion of Granville Island showed that government could plan and guide wonderful new urban experiments to take Vancouver to a new level. It could leverage social and economic objectives that just could not be contemplated in the past by the random interplay of market forces.

Then, along came Expo 86, the world's fair that put Vancouver on the global map but also opened the eyes of our citizens to a whole new aspiration for urban accomplishment. With recent experience, we were ready to undertake a bit of social engineering in Vancouver, and our new megaprojects right after the fair gave us the stage to act out these intentions. At this moment, the social aspirations of Vancouverism really took off.

In the late 1980s and early 1990s, I well remember the contrasts at city hall between the frenetic, unpredictable negotiations with developers and the quiet, deliberate policy formulation by staff, though all were focused on the same topics.

In one location, the huge False Creek North megaproject sometimes prompted abrupt, loud, ad-hoc bartering and brokering, all played out against a backdrop of three-dimensional models. The smart and accomplished private development team was led by the genius of Stanley Kwok and the artistry of designers Rick Hulbert, Barry Downs, James Cheng, and Don Vaughan. The equally articulate civic multi-departmental team was guided by planner Pat Wotherspoon, with Elaine Duvall from social planning and Jim Lowden from the park board. I myself led the negotiations, which could be stormy because the interests were vital and often contradictory, the players were sharp, and the emotions often ran high. One memory is so indicative. We were in an intensive discussion around a model one day. I felt that too much density had been crammed into one location so I quietly took one of the building models and slipped it into my pocket when I thought no one was paying attention. Less building mass felt better to me. A little later, I noticed Stanley Kwok quietly putting one of the extra building models back on the board when he thought no one was looking. I suspect more building mass felt more profitable to him. The fact is that there was always a tacit smile between us that extended in both directions, and so the chess match continued.

Contrast these sessions with the in-house systematic and rigorous planning analysis, in a separate location very nearby, that we juggled as we invented the social agenda that shapes Vancouver to this day. These were the careful discussions, centred on data collection, geographic allocations, testing of land-use combinations, and public consultations by my Central Area Plan team – policy guru Ronda Howard working with Trish French and Nathan Edelson. Again, I was at the centre, leading the discussions with this intelligent and highly principled team, which could out-debate anyone. Howard was a wizard who could look you in the eye, without blinking, and coolly list off ten arguments full of facts without a single pause. She would break eye contact only when she realized you had given it your best shot and could not possibly win the argument on the merit of your counter-arguments. So, with this group, there was no intellectual cutting of corners just to soothe the political edges.

Discoveries and ideas would pop up in one place and need to be introduced in the other. Contradictory ideas had to be reconciled. Potentials in one place had to be operationalized in the other. All the results had to be reviewed and accepted by what was called the "Major Projects Steering Committee," which included all the key department heads. Tough issues needing guidance had to be discussed with the city council in specially convened work sessions. At times, I felt like a juggler. It was a heady time – and an admittedly stressful time – and it resulted in a community framework, including a social agenda, that we have to some degree accomplished and to some degree used from then on as the gold standard that we have yet to fully accomplish. That it may have missed key factors that have become evident decades later, such as the inclination in a successful city for gentrification, does not diminish that in its day it was way out there on the edge of invention – a somewhat dangerous place to be in the cauldron of civic politics.

Floating above all the specific ideas was a commonly held, deep belief in the simple principle of urban diversity that I have emphasized from the beginning of our story. The consensus about diversity – and I recall it as a seldom-challenged consensus – went beyond the historic examples just described, which created opportunity, and even the transportation reasons outlined in Chapter 5, which created necessity. For most of the contributors to the social formula that was to emerge, this principle of diversity had a profound ethical basis, grounded much more solidly than in practical considerations. From study and experience, we could see that no city could be truly genuine unless it accommodated a great variety of people and activities. It must be inclusive – which, at that time, was one hundred percent focused on the low-income left out and on embracing more and more types of people (a narrower lens than planners would have today, hopefully). Theory and practice reinforced the idea that culture, energy, creativity, uniqueness, mutual assistance, and the many other features that we wanted for a competitive and fulfilling Vancouver in the world in the future could be guaranteed only if we could dramatically expand our diversity. For many others, diversity was also an imperative for market success. They argued that we could not build the kind of demand that would be able to shape the trajectory of Vancouver, especially in the core city, unless we widened the appeal of what we were building to include as many people as possible. Their differing wants and needs could fuel wave after wave of growth. You have to remember that those were the days when the private market took care of high-income and middle-income people quite handily, and almost no one doubted that this situation would always be the case. The market also easily hosted typical types of households in the form of housing that had been their conventional preference – singles in apartments, families in houses. But it just left out so many other people. So, diversity, of all kinds, was seen as a vehicle for social responsibility, economic resilience, and optimal efficiencies – and this was long before the thinkers of the world added environmental sustainability to the urban equation. We now know that urban sustainability is fostered by natural diversity and even more urban diversity than the policymakers of Vancouver had in mind when the social agenda was first set off.

In hindsight, perhaps the most fascinating if not surprising aspect of diversity to shape Vancouver was the consolidation of that shared sense of social responsibility into commanding public policy – we see that acted out to this day, as planners actively tackle the crisis of affordable housing for middle-income residents. It is hard to understand how it happened in this place, when it was so much later in coming to other cities, at least in our country. It is still a quite weak dimension in the planning service and governance of many Canadian cities and with our senior governments. To understand the Vancouver situation, we have to look back, again before the rise of Vancouverism, to several experiences that strongly shaped civic thinking. Let me describe two of the most important of these root influences.

Over the last century in Canada, it is worth remembering that the nation and provinces had a long history of housing programs that served people in need. Coming out of the Second World War, veterans could choose between grants and loans for either education or housing. From the 1950s on, there were government partnerships for investment in public housing (called social housing in Canada), as was occurring throughout North America. I have already referenced the Residential Rehabilitation Assistance Program of the 1970s, the tri-government assistance program that funded utility upgrades in private homes. Up until the 1980s, there was a strong tradition of non-profit mixed-income cooperative housing across the country and a program of tax advantages for the creation of market-rental housing. I trust the memory of Cameron Gray, a social development specialist and, in later years, the director of the City's housing centre. We will come back to Gray a little later. He reminisces about what he calls a golden age of social-housing achievements, the late 1970s and early 1980s (admittedly, an all too brief golden age), when many projects were completed. Most provided housing for what is now being called the "missing middle" – households that were not poor but could not afford to buy a single-family home. The government-underwritten non-profit co-op program of the day was particularly focused on these groups. In contrast to the profit based, expensive, and exclusive co-ops that exist in places such as New York City, the co-ops in this program were a form of non-profit home ownership, whereby the householder shared ownership of the overall building as a member of the co-op, with occupancy rights to a particular unit but limits on transfer of the membership. Both the government-sponsored rental projects and non-profit co-ops were required to set aside only 15 percent of their units for households that could not afford market rents, though in fact the percentage was generally higher, typically over a third. Gray remembers Doug Sutcliffe, the City's development manager for False Creek South, being very explicit that, in using these programs, he was not creating a neighbourhood for low-income households. Rather, the term he used for the households he accommodated in social housing was "modest income" households. This held true for Champlain Heights, an early comprehensive development on the far easterly edge of Vancouver, and for most of the scattered social housing built at that time. My purpose here is not to fully describe the history and content of these programs but, rather, to use those mentioned as testimony that government assistance for housing was not a new idea, even with the general standoffishness of senior governments to local concerns. Across the country, we had models and expertise and public support.

Then, in the 1980s, in that wave of Reaganomics that hit not just the United States but also our country, we began to see a pulling back from housing spending by governments. Less and less money was made available for housing, and increasingly the money that could be cobbled together by housing officials and advocates was focused on those in greatest need, the lowest-income population and those with very special requirements – in other words, those who had absolutely no way to compete in the housing marketplace. As Cameron Gray remembers, the Province took over social-housing development during this decade and required all the households in its projects to be for those who were unable to afford market rents. There was never enough money, there were long waiting lists for social housing, and we regularly began to see people on the streets without housing of any kind. And for anyone just above the lowest income, there was simply nothing. This travesty was amplified by other similar Reaganomic-like moves, such as disinvestment in facilities for those with mental illnesses, including closing down institutions and shutting down programs for people with substance-abuse problems. The result was that homelessness became a regular and, sadly, accepted reality on our streets and in our language, which we have yet to eradicate.

During this downturn, Vancouver was unusual in keeping the faith with social housing, probably because it was one of the first cities in Canada to have an official social planning department and because its directors, Maurice Egan, followed by Max Beck and Joyce Preston, were articulate spokespeople for all the needs of the poor. They had some hard fighters in their corner in Doug Purdy and John Jessup, who worked against all odds to deliver projects. Ann McAfee, then one of the most distinguished housing planners in the country, also played a pivotal role, writing policy after policy to establish the social-housing framework.

This brings us back to Cameron Gray – one of the real heroes of Vancouverism. With Purdy, Jessup, and McAfee, he kept the social-housing agenda alive through the dark times. When the City's housing centre was founded in 1991 and he took it over, he bridged all the housing efforts from the past to the future – he was tenacious and innovative in social-housing projects, both when funds were scarce and later, when we developed strong partnerships that I will talk about in this chapter. Founded as a spinoff from the social planning and properties departments, the housing centre was assigned to advocate and operationalize the social-housing agenda. It was a complicated business. Gray reminded me of the limited civic mandate that they all had to live with. He remembers that the City, until quite recent years, was largely reactive to the social-housing programs and the funding that was made available by the senior governments. The City government saw itself as a junior partner, facilitating the implementation of senior government programs. It was an active junior partner, in the buying of sites and the development of policy to facilitate the investment of federal and provincial social-housing funds, but it didn't do a lot on its own. This somewhat opportunistic approach meant that the City had to cope as the senior government funding taps turned on and off. It also meant the City had to live with whatever requirements were set for the use of the money, which shifted as political parties in power came and went. And so it has gone with changes every decade. The result has been a kind of swiss cheese, with social-housing programs that are full of holes. The overall portfolio has some of everything – but never enough of anything. Even with all this chaos, Gray pulled projects together every year, using whatever resources were at hand. He used land and equity from the City's land bank, called the Property Endowment Fund. He applied for whatever senior government money might potentially be on offer. He used other City funding that he could grab. He led the way as the City advanced the practice of community amenity contributions from developers in larger new projects and then, as one of many applications, made this source of funding available to respond to housing needs. In particular, Gray helped to develop a very intelligent approach to zoning bonusing and community amenity contributions, using not just set values but detailed proforma analysis of each private project in order to tightly calibrate what was offered to developers and received in return by the City. I will fully describe proformas and community amenity contributions in Chapter 9. Due to these efforts, regardless of the scarcity of funding, the City managed to deliver at least a modicum of low-income housing every year – never enough but also never nothing. So, this vital thread of social-housing practice and capacity was there to be expanded as the idea of diversity regained ground in the 1990s, as a part of the flourishing of Vancouverism. This influence on the social agenda cannot be emphasized enough.

The other influence that engendered the growing sense of social responsibility in Vancouver came from a group of tireless and aggressive advocates especially characterized by one of the key personalities of the city – activist and later city councillor Jim Green. This influence was grounded in the harsh streets of the toughest area of the city and the organization founded by a very important threesome in Vancouver's social history, the indomitable and courageous Bruce Eriksen, Libby Davies, and Jean Swanson. The group they founded in 1973 was called the Downtown Eastside Residents Association, or DERA, and ultimately it was led by Jim Green in the 1980s. These four, along with the powerful labour lawyer and poverty advocate Harry Rankin, need a whole book of their own for accomplishments that soared in defence of and assistance to the poor and disenfranchised people of Vancouver. One such accomplishment was their leadership in the other local political party that helped set the pace in these formative years, the Coalition of Progressive Electors, called COPE. Davies, Eriksen, and Rankin were COPE city councillors for many years. Davies went on to national service as a member of parliament.

The Downtown Eastside, as its name suggests, is an older inner-city cluster of areas east of the downtown, extending over to Clark Drive. It had become a low-income district, home to poor families, older resource workers, Indigenous people, very modest-income service employees, and new immigrants. It was also home to residents whom social workers would describe as "at risk" due to mental illness, substance abuse, or other disabilities, and to people who were just "worked out" in the punishing labour jobs in the resource hinterland of the province. The community had its infrastructure of services and facilities for those in need and significant public housing. It also contained most of the older small hotels in which low-income people lived; their monthly rents matched the housing allocation in a welfare cheque. Later, these hotel units were officially designated as SROs, or "single room occupancy" units. Fortunately, the district had that strong, dedicated cadre of people, led by Eriksen, Davies, Swanson, Rankin, and Green, who cared enough to devote their lives to helping those less fortunate than themselves. Somehow, for many years, it all hung together.

Expo 86 changed all of that. With all the benefits it brought to the larger community and economy of the city, the big dis-benefit it brought to the Downtown Eastside was a dramatic destabilization of that community. Rents started to go up because the area was so close to the Expo site. The SROs started to be converted back to modest tourist accommodation, pushing out long-term low-income residents. Too many people were left with no option but the streets. It was not a good scene by any standard. Frankly, a lot of Vancouverites were so dazzled by the glitter of Expo that they were in denial about its destructive impact on the Downtown Eastside. Jim Green and DERA, supported by Councillors Davies, Eriksen, and Rankin, along with the strong community voice of Swanson, refused to let the crisis be ignored. They made a lot of noise. They spoke out; they organized people to express their plight; they protested; and they joined into the political fray, acting inside and outside of the political process as need be. They worked tirelessly, not only to deal with the direct consequences that were there for all to see in the Downtown Eastside – advocacy for specific individuals who were especially hard hit by the displacement that was starting to occur – but also to establish the principle that low-income people could not just be left behind to fend for themselves as the greater city moved forward with all of its new opportunities.

The struggle of the dispossessed in the Downtown Eastside, the sheer tenacity of DERA, and the unavoidable truth they exposed became huge influences on the thinking at city hall as the era of Vancouverism began. City hall started shifting gears. Advocates, rightfully so, said that not enough was being done by the City, but at least something began to be done. Many people resented the noise, but at least that noise led to some remediation. But, more than most at the time could have understood, what was happening was that a principle was being consolidated at city hall to the effect that a consistent portion of citizens would not be able to participate in the traditional housing market, and they would need help and support. It clarified a long-term imperative to try to do a better job than in the past to house those citizens. That principle has been further elaborated to this day, and it has been handed on as people have retired. We have not solved the problems of housing that, sadly, are becoming worse with all our other success (which I will come back to later in this chapter). But nor have we been complacent. That is the legacy of Jim Green and the others, the foundation for everything else I am going to describe in the housing strategies, policies, and practices of Vancouver. Theirs was a prime contribution.

Diversity, in what was then felt to be its key dimensions, as much as we could achieve it or leverage it, became the overarching drive that represents one of the key planks of Vancouverism.

## DIVERSITY THROUGH LAND-USE MIX

One side of diversity was the profound land-use mix that I have already started to describe. Beginning with nearby associations of offices and housing, Vancouver started experimenting with how to bring these uses into even closer proximity and how to add other uses to the mix. Of course, some mixes came naturally, such as retail at the base of housing or office buildings along successful shopping streets. Ray Spaxman had the bright idea to try to leverage one use with another. He felt a high-value use could carry the cost of a lower-value use if a developer was rewarded to do this with more density for the high-value use. That reward was called a bonus. He tested this first in the 1970s in the downtown zoning, with modest but indicative success, by adding housing as the lower-value use to be added along with a density bonus to office projects. At that time, most consumers just did not see housing as a favoured use in the commercial core, but there was a frenzy under way to build more and more offices. He felt that some people would enjoy the mix as residents, and it would certainly support walkability. Once this bonus approach was established, other uses were added to the equation. We offered non-market housing projects a higher base density in the zoning than that offered to market uses on the same sites. If developers added cultural and community amenities to their projects, we rewarded them with greater office density. If they provided a park within or adjacent to their scheme, we offered a bonus. The experience of Granville Island showed that low-profit but appealing activities, such as arts, crafts, and cultural ventures, could actually be supported by the profitable high-value uses if they could be linked into a business and zoning formula.

Ronda Howard reminded me of one of the biggest breakthroughs of the Central Area Plan, which was how to bridge the gap between the extremes of no mix and any mix. Endless thinking, research, and learning during the formation of the Central Area Plan went into what clusters of uses were synergistic and compatible – not all uses mix well. Instead of getting caught up in the tightest circumstances of mixed-use within buildings, the analysis found more potential in mixed-use within differing types of districts where circumstances allowed a great variety of compatible combinations. Groups of activities thrive in distinctive clusters, and the clusters can become quite complex and exciting if you think through each component carefully. Howard and her team pondered what went best with head offices in the central business district, what could best co-exist within housing areas, and how to diversify uses in industrial locations. This mélange within the district became a notable aspect of our use-mix formula.

Then, into this increasing stew of offices, housing, retail, arts, and culture, the planning of the megaprojects quickly added the ingredient of systematically required community and recreation amenities, based upon standards that I reviewed in Chapter 4. All these experiments challenged one of the fundamental premises of land-use zoning that had prevailed since its invention almost a century before – that for health and safety reasons, uses must be separated, not just between buildings but also between districts. People were reacting everywhere against the homogeneity that resulted from this approach, and every new mix that was tested in Vancouver reinforced the idea that this city did not have to continue in the sterile image that the old approach of zoning had created. The planners were certainly convinced of this, and growing numbers of citizens and consumers obviously agreed, because mixed-use projects and areas were increasingly popular.

The development community also had to find a way of thriving in this new kind of urban stew. Not surprisingly, the pervasive single-use zoning system had encouraged most development companies to specialize – some companies did housing, others offices, others retail. But now, they diversified. The opening up of regulations may not have been entirely responsible for this, although it certainly helped. Perhaps more because of the limited land in the inner-city of Vancouver, developers saw opportunity in mixing uses as they intensified their projects. They saw more efficiencies and more curb appeal and more profits. The development sector swiftly repositioned itself to handle any use that was deemed both necessary and compatible with a complete community or a preferred market image. Most companies dropped their traditional specializations, and mixed-use buildings became the norm. Some mixed different uses, such as housing and retail (see Figure 6.5), others mixed public and private uses, such as housing with childcare or cultural outlets, and others mixed different expressions of the same use, such as apartments with townhouses.

That diversification continues and it is spreading. Through the work of Michael Gordon in the planning department during the late 1990s, some inner-city industrial sites were opened up for artists' studios and artists' live-work spaces (see Figure 6.6). Now, people are starting to think more and more about what other kinds of uses can be mixed within industrial zones, particularly as industrial types themselves are being redefined through globalization. With the growth of high technology as a vital new sector of Vancouver's economy, ever new combinations are coming together as high-tech production increasingly looks and feels very clean compared to traditional industry, with few impacts. Whether these technology firms are focused on invention with production elsewhere, or invention tied directly to on-site production, or invention with production and marketing digitally, they often prefer spaces that differ markedly from the typical office formats – they need larger floorplates and cheaper rents, especially at the start-up level, so they search for compatibilities among types of uses that traditional offices just could not tolerate. That includes compatibilities with industry and warehousing, and even reuse of those mini-malls in secondary locations that have become obsolete. Of course, one cannot lump all high-tech activity together – the typical office works for some companies, or at least they can shoehorn themselves into a conventional space to take advantage of a great location. To complicate things even further, early on in the redefinition of "work," especially for technology jobs, a cross-over was seen back to housing. Increasingly, all apartments were seen as potential work-at-home sites, so zoning allowances were put in place to define and manage that.

All these new options were broadening the market and adding rich land-use diversity to the city.

**6.5** Vancouver developers and their architects have become accomplished at building mixed-use buildings, such as this excellent model on Cambie Street, which includes housing, offices, retail, and restaurants. This mix gives the city a vital land-use diversity.

**6.6** Allowing artists' live-work studios on low-value industrial lands has helped modest-income artists survive in an increasingly expensive city – this set of studios is on Great Northern Way at the edge of Mount Pleasant. However, as land values continue to rise, even this advantage may become a thing of the past.

## DIVERSITY THROUGH SOCIAL MIX: THE PRECEDENTS

The other side of diversity was the even more profound social mix that I now want to look at in some detail.

Let me start with an irony. From the 1960s on, an unusual phenomenon arose in the otherwise law-abiding society that has always characterized Vancouver. Social diversity in Vancouver was actually started by outlaws. Now, I am not talking about the mafia or the criminal element that the word "outlaw" normally conjures up. I am talking about upstanding middle-class people who took the law into their own hands. From the outset of the formation of the ring of older inner-city neighbourhoods, houses were often constructed to contain separate secondary accommodation to house multi-generational families or just to meet the extra demand from a growing population. These suites even became protected during the Second World War. After the war, with more plentiful housing, Vancouver and many other cities made these secondary suites illegal. Both from this tradition and with rising home prices, many homeowners chose to disregard the law. They kept their secondary suites or cobbled new suites into officially single-family homes. They were generally in the basement and were often called "basement suites." They were mortgage-helpers for young families, spaces for extended family members in immigrant households, separate digs for a family's maturing children, and rental flats for students or single-parent families or starting-up couples or lone modest-income adults. Their proportions varied from district to district, but sometimes over half the houses had these secondary units. Since the rents tended to be lower than for legal units, these secondary suites really helped those who, otherwise, might not have had any place they could afford to live. This was a very good thing. But there were problems – building-code deficiencies that caused safety concerns and were expensive to fix (particularly lower-than-allowed ceiling heights in basements), tax evasion by landlords, tight parking on residential streets, and just the discomfort of otherwise good citizens breaking the law.

In 1988, the City finally took the matter in hand with an initiative spearheaded by planner Nathan Edelson. He crafted a by-law to permit family suites but with a very broad definition of what constituted a family. Each neighbourhood was then asked to vote on whether or not it wanted a community discussion on how secondary suites for non-family members might be legalized in its area. Edelson started with an older neighbourhood called Riley Park, which had widespread illegal suites. He faced more contention there than some might have expected but ultimately legalized over 60 percent of the suites while also

**6.7** Diversifying housing options downtown has been key to drawing many types of new residents for more vibrancy. Newly constructed on Seymour Street, these lofts, with their double-height ceilings, are popular.

**6.8** Further land-use diversity has been engendered by adding live-work and live-retail units, such as these on Hornby Street. ▶

learning how to make the program more effective. Over the next decade, streamlined variations of this process were carried out by another planner, Dave Thomsett, to determine if and how illegal units might be made legal. Many neighbourhoods took up the option, and you might say that the outlaws were finally able to go straight. Ultimately, in 2004, as a result of COPE's election victory and a promise it had made in its campaign, secondary suites were legalized in all previously single-family zones. This shows just how long some necessary situations need to gestate before they become the status quo. But it has to be emphasized that secondary suites did their part in adding to the social diversity of Vancouver in a way that was very close to home for many citizens – from their own personal experience, many people saw that they could comfortably embrace a social mix.

Once the dense multiple-family housing market took off after Expo 86, the private sector, with the support of city hall, really starting experimenting with its own ideas for viable housing mixes. Responding to wave after wave of new demand, particularly in the core city, the market started delivering a range of household sizes and bedroom counts in new apartment complexes, building diversity as it went along. We started seeing what became known as "mingles suites," where the unit included two master suites, each with bedroom and bath, so that two unattached people could share a mortgage and each build equity or where two people could share rent without more intimate ties. Then, "loft" units were added to the mix – these being units with two-storey living spaces (see Figure 6.7). Later, thanks to the urging of realtor Bob Rennie,

live-work and live-retail units were added, particularly for ground-oriented spaces close to downtown businesses (see Figure 6.8). In these units, for the first time, we allowed flex space – that is to say, either use, interchangeably, could claim the space from time to time. Rennie even chose one of these flex spaces for his corporate head office. Townhouses became common features at the base of apartment buildings, though this was a trend that was driven as much or more by urban design concerns as by an interest in social mix (I'll return to this in Chapter 7). In downtown marinas, floating homes were allowed. Granville Island had a complete floating-home village (see Figure 6.9). Units designed and fitted out specifically for in-home offices helped some consumers find ownership in an increasingly expensive housing market because "office rent" could subsidize a mortgage. For the inner-city, all this diversification was pivotal because it increasingly made a downtown housing choice more practical for consumers. The high growth in demand that resulted has not abated to this day.

Sometimes, to ensure a modicum of social mix, we had to take protective action. The small SRO hotels that I mentioned above are a case in point. Starting with Expo 86, the frantic development in the inner-city put unusual pressure on these and similar buildings. It appeared that these buildings were doomed to be

lost, with lots of vulnerable people displaced. Seemingly, there was little that city hall could do to forestall the losses. Finally, Jill Davidson, a key planner in the City's housing centre, led an initiative to change all that. Working with Nathan Edelson, by then our Downtown Eastside planner, and Celine Mauboules, Davidson developed a regulatory strategy to protect SROs from closure and demolition. Ultimately, in 2003, they were able to request provincial support, through an amendment to the Vancouver Charter, to put that strategy in action. This resulted in the Single Room Accommodation (SRA) By-law, which protects SROs, rooming houses, and other tiny low-cost flats. There is no doubt that this has saved many of the lowest-priced market units from being removed, even though, by 2007, the value of protected properties had become so high that additional protections had to be added to the by-law. Retaining SROs continues to be more and more of a struggle every year. Although no one would argue that they are a

**6.9** Houseboats have been fostered in inner-city marinas. These offer another way to live while adding "eyes on the street" for safety, even when there is no street. This is an entire floating-home village, moored at Granville Island.

**6.10** Losing the small old hotels lived in at welfare-rate rents has been traumatic for Vancouver. These buildings, called SROs, are now preserved, but sometimes a rundown old structure is replaced by a comfortable new one. This was achieved with the new L'Hermitage Hotel, built by the Malek brothers on Richards Street. The low-income units sit adjacent to the luxury hotel, securing a fine-grained social mix. Walk up from the elegant doorway and you will find an attractive arched entrance to the social housing.

sustainable solution for low-income housing, they have surely provided a stop-gap until better solutions can be found. The initiative to protect SROs led to a number of arrangements where new construction involved the unavoidable demolition of this older housing. SRO-type units, but delivered to a better minimum standard, have been integrated into new buildings as part of the developers' community amenity requirement (see Figure 6.10). Too bad we were not able to get this started way back in 1985, when Jim Green first made public the loss of SROs leading up to the tourism of the fair.

There are two directions where municipal public policy has been consistently focused and evolved into a fine science for diversity – the mix of housing by income level and by type of household. I now want to describe each of these directions in detail.

The time when housing specifications came to a clear policy urgency was the turn into the 1990s, just after Expo 86, when we started detailed planning of our downtown megaprojects. Rightfully so, the developers of False Creek North and Coal Harbour said to the City that clarity of housing policy was essential for them because targeted housing would surely be at the heart of civic requirements in response to the significant additional development that they wanted. This would undoubtedly be a big part of their project costs. Given the history that I have already described, interested citizens and organizations were clamouring for the same kind of clarity. Politicians knew that clarity was necessary for political peace and stability. In particular, Mayor Gordon Campbell provided strong political sponsorship for the prime housing policies that set the pace in Vancouver. And for the planners – community, social, and housing planners – crafting a clear housing policy for the megaprojects was of vital importance because no one wanted the massive new developments to exacerbate even further the tendency toward ghettoization of low-income people or the creation of dull, one-dimensional new neighbourhoods.

And so, a policy process was initiated to set the framework for household diversity. In one form or another, with varying proportions, it has been applied to all larger projects in the city since its inception. It can be characterized in very few words: 20 percent of all units in a development area must be designated for non-market housing, and 25 percent of all market units in each new building must be suitable for families with children. Of course, the explanation of the detailing of all of this is a lot more complicated.

## DIVERSITY THROUGH SOCIAL MIX: THE INCOMES FACTOR

During the period of our story, the key factor that has generally been at the top of the government agenda for housing assistance has been simply to provide for people at different modest-income levels, primarily because the market just does not serve them well – they tend to be left out or are offered the lowest-quality options. With the fresh thinking related to the megaprojects, city hall aspirations went well beyond just that fundamental concern. We were thinking as much or more about the kind of community that we wanted to create and the kind of communities that might spring up around the new developments. There were two other compelling purposes – planning purposes – behind the megaprojects' social-housing agenda than just housing the disadvantaged. First, we wanted to facilitate benefits that would come from a community with mixed incomes – things such as mutual assistance, the day-to-day enjoyment of difference, offering quality community living regardless of wealth, and reflecting a larger social profile. Second, we wanted to avoid the disadvantages that would result if all the wealthy people lived in the new areas and all the poor were increasingly pushed into substandard older areas. We knew what we *didn't* want – the nightmare of North America's modern urban ghettos, where vulnerable people are clustered together, isolated from jobs and provided with virtually no resources. Constantly declining, the ghettos are redlined by banks as places too risky for rehab

**6.11** In recently constructed areas of Vancouver, 20 percent of units are required to house low- and modest-income people, thus achieving an economic mix. This building, the Roundhouse Co-op, in False Creek North, near the Roundhouse community centre, is home to households who cannot afford to pay market rents.

loans and are disinvested by local governments, with fewer and fewer traditional services, but over-invested by governments in social services that became dependent upon sustaining poverty. We had one place like that, the Downtown Eastside, that we all wanted to fix, so we definitely did not want to be the people responsible for the spread of such awful trends. It did not take a lot of analysis to come to the conclusion that we had to do better than what might just naturally happen (see Figure 6.11).

At the same time, looking in hindsight, I now realize that we took a somewhat narrow, if practical or expedient, view of the social mix. Because of the prevailing attitudes of the day, we put our energy into the low end of the income spectrum, rather than pushing a broader program of social mix. Partly, this was because we worked within senior government parameters and because funding from senior governments initially supported only the low-income portion of the megaproject social-housing formula. Later, during the 1990s, as funding flexibility was loosened up, at least we were able to add the low-end-of-market modest-income group back in. We were able to push a modestly mixed-income housing scenario. But the limits remained pretty tight. In those days, it was widely believed that middle-income people could find a place within the market offerings and would rise over time from a tenuous start as they built equity. So, they did not need special help. During the 1990s in Vancouver, that was still generally true, and almost nobody predicted that this would change. Reinforcing this, many people said that public taxes should not subsidize those who could compete on their own in the market – that it was unfair for some taxpayers to subsidize other taxpayers just to up the quality of their housing, even if there might be community-wide benefits. And besides, they said, subtracting buyers from the market for modest housing might depress that market. Recently, I have heard people say that we could at least have focused on rental housing that might have spread some diversity from the high end down the income spectrum. Some have also pointed to rent controls, which existed in New York at the time, asking why we did not go that route. I am sorry to say that those people miss the most important two-edged point. On the one hand, we faced a crisis of low-income exclusion that took all the resources we could command – we never had all the money we needed as the problem got worse and worse. On the other hand, the middle-income plight of today was simply not in our consciousness because it did not then exist, so we were not about to spend scarce resources or political capital on a problem that we could not discern. We surely could not defend that. So, public policy gave priority to the low end of household financial capacity – a blindness that now upsets me, as we all see housing prices soaring in Vancouver. If only we could have seen this coming. I will come back to the housing affordability challenge at the end of the chapter as the biggest problem the city has going forward.

Of course, we had to define the specific poor to be served. For this, we took a somewhat theoretical view of several key considerations.

### The social-housing community share

The first consideration was the level of income to be supported. The City decided to reflect the regional profile of household incomes. About 20 percent of Vancouver's regional population were the lowest-income households, so the target for this lowest-income segment in new areas was set at 20 percent of each new area's overall population. Since household wealth varies across any region, the City also decided that those to be served would be the lowest 20 percent of household incomes *within* the districts where the new megaprojects were located. We called these "core-need households."

### The social-housing community mix

The second consideration was how to spread social housing within a whole neighbourhood. Around North America at this time, there were various experiments about the best way to achieve social integration of various income groups. Of course, the customary way was for the poor to be housed in large segregated projects that often set the character of their entire neighbourhoods. The downside of this was becoming well known, as I have already described. In reaction, another approach was to pepper low-income units within every market building in an area so that there was no perceivable clustering – a small number of units would be insinuated into every building, perhaps a few per floor, preferably with no discernible pattern or sub-grouping. This resulted in a concept called "inclusionary zoning," which has been quite effectively used in some places, although the overall yield is often limited by the high cost of this approach. However, even with its appeal for very intimate social integration, this is not the way we decided to go in Vancouver. Social service delivery agencies worried about the difficulty of efficiently serving their clients if they were widely dispersed. Condo marketers told us that people would be reluctant to pay the market price for a unit if an identical one right next door was highly subsidized. Social-housing developers told us that the necessary partnerships to construct and manage the buildings would simply be too complicated and vulnerable. Some low-income people said they might not feel quite at home in that kind of intimate mix. So, in Vancouver, the policy we adopted was that social-housing buildings would be separated from market-housing buildings (see Figure 6.12) but with several caveats. First, they would be evenly spread within the community, including on preferred sites (see Figure 6.13). Second, they would be kept to a manageable size overall. Originally, that was set at a maximum of fifty units per building for those with primarily families and a hundred units per building for others. But, quite early and through the 1990s, this standard became less fixed when we started the mixed-income projects, because the spectre of the old mass public-housing social problems was no longer a concern. Third, social-housing buildings would be built to be virtually indistinguishable from market-housing ones (see Figure 6.14). Actually, in some cases, the megaproject developer contributed to construction budgets for social housing to up the quality of building finishes to match nearby buildings. This was perfectly acceptable to these large developers because it enhanced the ambiance of areas where they were often selling many buildings at the same time.

### The social-housing household mix

The third consideration was the nature of the low-income households to be supported. Statistics indicated that about half of the low-income households in the

**6.12** Non-market and market units are not mixed within a building in Vancouver, but they are fully integrated in separate buildings within the neighbourhood. Which of these two buildings consists of social housing?

**6.13** This lovely social-housing building, primarily for low- and modest-income families, is on Marinaside Crescent, right on the park and waterfront in False Creek North – not relegated to a second-rate site. It has a childcare centre on the ground floor.

**6.14** If social housing is to avoid stigmatization, it must be built to the same standards as the market housing around it. This non-market family housing building on Pacific Boulevard at the edge of historic Yaletown is considered by many to be the best-designed building in the vicinity.

**6.15** Social housing for those with special needs has been the government priority since the early 2000s. It is often co-located with support services, like this Coast Mental Health Resource Centre in Downtown South. This housing is essential, but we must remember that accommodation for low-income singles and families without such special needs is also in great demand.

region were families with children, including single-parent families. So, a target was set that, in each neighbourhood area, 50 percent of social housing would be made available for families with children. This allowed some buildings to be specifically designated for seniors or special needs and most buildings to have a mix of households with and without children, while also more or less reflecting the general demographics. Senior government funding also supported this at that time, so most of the megaproject social housing had a strong family factor. That would change as the trauma of homelessness emerged. Again, we are back to the difficulty of shifting senior government attitudes. In the 1990s, government concentrated on supporting family housing, but from about 2000 on, shelters and housing for the homeless and those with special needs took priority (see Figure 6.15). At any one time, one or more segments of need have been sidelined. Over the last two decades, that has been families with children, which is simply regrettable.

However, as I look back now, I cannot help but see that our thinking about the nature of subsidized households may have been somewhat narrow-minded. We felt that housing for seniors and those with special needs could just be handled separately, without targets and on separate sites. There were different funding streams for these types of households. They each had their own special profile of building-service needs and programming. In some cases, people expressed anxiety that certain populations could be difficult for neighbours to live with, which suggested some separation – such as, for example, transition-house residents or those with significant mental challenges (although the truth of this has never really been consistently confirmed). In any event, the main social-housing agenda was targeted for the more typical household rather than those with special needs, differentiated only by whether or not children were included. We're back to the swiss cheese, though, because in the 1990s, government funding was not allocated for seniors' housing, so we see less of it in the megaprojects than I would have hoped. In recent years, this has been remedied to some degree, as provincial funding has shifted to housing for low-income singles with needs beyond affordability. This focus resulted in assisted-living projects for seniors, which were developed during the early 2000s. Supportive housing for the homeless and those suffering from addiction and/or mental illness has followed since then. Most of these clients are on welfare and aren't just low-income but very low-income. But needless to say, money was way short of what was needed for this sector.

### The social-housing income mix

The fourth consideration was the proportion of low-income households in any one building. It did not take a deep analysis to understand that the huge public-housing projects throughout North America were dysfunctional – creating a worry about what would result with 100 percent low-income people in residence, as had originally been mandated by the government funding. The result was that a policy objective was set to have at least a modest mix of incomes within each building. Fortunately, senior government policy had also shifted, so this was soon allowable.

This all sounds good until you realize that the 20 percent formula for core-need households was set at the point when all the units were intended for core-need residents. Once we added a modest-income segment, we started to put the needs of the poor at odds with the desire for mixed-income housing. We couldn't increase the proportion of social housing, which was more-or-less fixed through a toughly negotiated accord with the developers. So, as the mix settled in, it became unavoidable that we actually housed fewer of those with profound need than was originally intended. By the mid-1990s, when most of the megaproject social-housing projects were put together, the principle of mix had really taken hold. Government funding supported up to 40 percent of households at modest market rent, 30 percent of what was called shallow core-need (the top 25 percent of core need), and 30 percent of deep core-need (with rents set at what welfare would allow). It was great for community building and acceptable to developers, but, from the perspective of pure need, it left some people out. This all stopped in the early 2000s, when provincial funding directed almost all the cash to people with special needs, most of whom were low-income. There is no doubt that the 20 percent social-housing policy for the megaprojects has suffered from being developed for a specific federal-provincial social-housing program that was then cancelled just two years after the first legal agreements with the developers were signed, setting the stage for all that would come later. It should have been designed to accommodate changing programs.

### The social-housing partnership

Having what became known as the "20 percent social-housing policy" in place was a good thing, but the big question remained of how to implement it. Social housing is expensive to build, manage, and replace. It definitely could not simply be totally financed by the private developers, and there was no way they were prepared to take on ongoing responsibilities. Governments increasingly could not afford expensive land, and they too were unwilling to cover all the costs or build the infrastructure to manage a huge inventory of units. So, Vancouver developed a viable and practical partnership model.

In the megaprojects, the social-housing partnership had five partners – the developers, both the senior governments, federal and provincial, non-profit housing societies, and the City. The various roles were straightforward. The developers were required to designate the land in their area plans and then to provide that property at a discounted value to the City. Then, once funding was secure, the developers acted as the contractors to construct the buildings. The senior governments shared the cost of building the housing through various programs that changed over the years. The non-profit societies took on the operation of the housing as leasees of the City. The City held ownership of the land and ultimately the buildings, but the big job, as landowner, was to put together the agreements for development and to find solutions to particular glitches, which in later years involved coping with the changing funding programs of senior governments. How this all came together was more complicated.

It was easy to locate and designate the sites within the megaproject plans because the areas being laid out were so spacious, and design of the detailed plans was being done by the developer and civic designers working together. We had a lot of freedom with densities that would be set for all the development sites, particularly the market ones. If we made the market condo sites slightly more dense, with a smaller footprint, space was opened up to insinuate the non-market housing sites. Since we preferred the non-market social-housing sites to be smaller and well distributed within the market neighbourhoods, we found many opportunities within the geometry of the various area plans to fit in all the sites we needed to meet the targeted housing mix.

Tying down the sites was more tricky. In buying the land from the developers, the City could pay only a value that was agreed upon by the senior governments, who provided the funding for that land purchase as well as for the construction costs. The senior governments' funding programs always specified the value they were prepared to support for land at a set rate across all the projects they funded – a per-unit land allocation averaged over both urban and less-urban land values. The idea was to maximize the housing yielded from their funding. They were more concerned about maximizing units on cheaper land than about achieving a community mix, which might mean that some individual non-market buildings would be on more expensive land. Of course, inner-city Vancouver was always the most valuable land to build upon, so this arrangement actually represented a significant subsidy by the megaproject developers for social housing. Let me explain. Policy required securing a social mix as a requirement of rezoning. The rezoning provided the increased development allowance the developers wanted. No other public money was available to plug the gap in land values for the social mix, so the developers had to put it up or forego the rezoning. This social-housing land subsidy became part of the overall community amenity contribution required of developers in any rezoning to cover the costs of increased public services and facilities demanded by the new residents they were building for. Needless to say, the land subsidy was ultimately quite costly for the developers, but the picture was not all bad for them in the partnership. From selling the sites up front to the City, through options to purchase in favour of the City registered on the land title, the developers received an early cash flow as the first social housing projects were built (or, where projects were not constructed, at least an early security on future land sales). This was a welcomed infusion to help them pay the significant initial costs of the entitlement process. Also, as the construction contractors for the non-market buildings, the developers enjoyed the construction profits. Construction was done at market rates, with the normal market profitability. In the end, for the developers it was not an unacceptable deal.

But, of course, the deal worked as a good partnership only if the projects were actually built. Thankfully, most were built and the partnership yielded the planned results. But the straitjacket of the agreements, with parameters absolutely set with the assumption of imminent development, has proven to be a problem, making it particularly difficult to implement over time as government funding programs and developer circumstances changed. We have sites to this day, covered by agreements from the early 1990s, which are only now gearing up for development because the specifics of the agreements are hard to reconcile with current circumstances. Many think, in hindsight, that it would have been better for the City simply to have taken ownership of the sites from day one, with no strings attached, and brought them to development when and how it could manage it. This would probably have had about the same impacts for the developers.

As I have already said, for their part in the partnership, the senior governments, through whatever funding programs were operational at the time, provided the money to actually erect the buildings – either in cash or through underwriting construction and mortgage loans. They provided the lion's share of the funding. The Province also managed the allocation of units to eligible occupants through a provincial agency called BC Housing, which maintained selection criteria and a careful list of housing applicants.

The City part of the partnership, in addition to securing and holding the land, was to make everything happen and to resolve any problems that might block implementation. The senior government program requirements and standards were strict, and the funding formulas were tight. This often led to financial shortfalls in actual projects. Most of these were resolved by the partners. But the land-value premium was one typical shortfall for which the City had to find the extra money. For the megaprojects, initially this was not a problem because the developers covered the gap. Years later, Cameron Gray had to get creative by cashing in some sites to raise money to cover the cost of social housing on other sites. Elsewhere, City-owned land might be made available for free or at a discount to suit the allowable land component in the senior funding. Of course, the City also spent significant resources on social housing, just to coordinate all the players, negotiate all the typical agreements, deal with public inputs, and put the housing propositions together, as well as direct everything with meaningful social-housing policy and targets.

Essential to this partnership was the non-profit housing sector. These are non-profit housing organizations that develop and manage social housing. For ongoing operations, they use government funding for construction, welfare rent rates and other subsidies for most units to house low-income residents, market rent rates for some units to house modest-income residents, and support program funding from government or through philanthropy. Typically, these groups became the operators of the housing on an ongoing basis. With various mandates and financial supporters, they each had their own style and preferred client base, but overall, there was enough variety to cover everyone. In many respects, the housing societies were the unacknowledged agents that made the whole system work. They still are. Other partners have been active or passive, but the non-profit housing societies have stayed through thick and thin to make sure the housing was offered, maintained, and sustained.

Although the megaprojects set the pace, both the 20 percent social-housing policy and the partnership for its realization have become generalized as a component of complete communities in Vancouver. It is harder to secure sites when they are not made available from the property base of a megaproject and have to be purchased on the open market. In this case, the requirement of development cost levies (essentially a development tax) was put in place, as will be discussed in Chapter 9, and one application of this alternative source of funding for public goods has been what is called "replacement affordable housing." This became an important source of funds to purchase property for social housing in more incrementally developing areas – many contributions from small developments that add up to make social housing possible. The role and contributions of the other partners in the social-housing partnership remain similar to that already described.

### Results

Some would say that this is an overly complex system. When it was cobbled together, it reflected the potentials of its day, but as we would now judge, it has not delivered all that had been hoped for. In most major developing areas of the city, the full expression of 20 percent low-income housing remains an aspiration, primarily because the contributions of the senior governments have not been consistent and the partnership mechanisms were too inflexible. The City and the non-profits have stayed true to the partnership, but the provincial and federal political agendas sometimes support housing and sometimes do not. When senior government funding flows, social housing comes on stream; when this funding trickles, the delivery of social housing stalls – or, certainly, slows down. This ebb and flow has varied widely over the years. During the ebb, sometimes the City had to get very creative with funding to allow for some social housing to take place. Still, I estimate that in most areas, we may have secured about 15 percent social housing, a pretty commendable performance, compared to that of many cities. But there are still those sites that have lagged behind.

Instead of cashing in sites for cash, it is interesting to see what Cameron Gray tried to do in the early 2000s. As usual for Gray, he brought a very clever alternative formula to the table for at least one project. He proposed a higher-density building on a social-housing site than had originally been designated. Then, he allocated the additional development to market-rental housing and channelled these market rents to underwrite the borrowing to build the building. Through this formula, the market rents carried the low-income housing during the life of the construction loan, and thereafter, more and more of the market units could be reassigned to low-income users as the long-term building mortgage was paid off – with the final mix depending upon ongoing operating costs (see Figure 6.16). This is an appealing self-sustaining model, not dependent upon senior government funding assistance. The downside is that it takes a long time before a lot of the social housing comes on stream. Gray's model has not caught on as the primary way to bring on social housing in the absence of the kinds of partnerships that I have described, but it still has great potential to do so in the future. Like so many others, Gray has now retired, and his kind of push just does not seem to be there anymore. I am grateful that Michael Flanigan, the former real estate guru at city hall and now a leader at BC Housing, has taken up the challenge. He may be the only person who can untangle the bureaucratic knots with a smart entrepreneurial funding approach for the future.

Even as a flawed model, hobbled by changes in senior government policy, the social-housing strategy has been vital in Vancouver. It secured much more diversity than would otherwise have been the case. It delivered a significant stock of social housing within very complete, well-endowed new communities that provide better living for many low-income households. A touching moment for me before I left government was a public meeting where a single mom living in a social-housing unit with her son in the Coal Harbour area came up to me to say how much better and safer and more optimistic their lives had become since moving into the community. What more testimony could anyone need to know this is a good thing? Has it been enough? Probably not. Has it been better than nothing? Definitely so.

## DIVERSITY THROUGH SOCIAL MIX: THE FAMILIES FACTOR

The factor of families with children living comfortably in high-density multiple housing is one of the most innovative and unique aspects of the social agenda of Vancouverism, setting it apart from most contemporary North American cities. This is particularly true in the inner-city, where an aggressive policy to attract

**6.16** As conceived by Cameron Gray, this innovative building in Coal Harbour mixes non-market and market rental housing. As the construction mortgage is paid down through the years, the proportion of social housing will be increased. Many units are suitable for families. This is desperately needed at this expensive location.

**6.17** In recently constructed areas of Vancouver, 25 percent of units in every residential building must be suitable for families with children, thus achieving a mix of types of households. We do not require that families with children occupy these units, but we carefully design for them. This strategy has worked well. As you see here, children are everywhere in our new neighbourhoods.

**6.18** In downtown Vancouver, people are surprised to see families with children rather than the singles and empty nesters who naturally gravitate to high-density living.

and serve families has applied to every neighbourhood since the early 1990s, when the "living first" strategy came into being. Children are everywhere on the urban scene in Vancouver, creating a different personality for the city than is seen in other places – not just in the traditional older neighbourhoods but right at the heart of the city in the highest-density areas that cluster on the downtown peninsula (see Figure 6.17). Children range freely throughout the inner-city, leaving their mark on the housing, crowding the services that have been built for them, and setting an image of family living in areas where many people are very surprised to see anyone other than young singles or older people (see Figure 6.18). It can be quite a spectacle at times (see Figure 6.19). Of course, it's a genuine joy to see kids of any age all around, but the presence of the ten-year-old is particularly telling. That's the sign that the family is there to stay and not just waiting for the kid to walk, when they feel they have to move on for the supports of the suburbs (see Figure 6.20). But, beyond the simple pleasure of kids in the mix, the implications for social diversity, market reach and community stability, as well as resilience are quite profound. The presence of the child is the key fea-

**6.19** The presence of children in our dense down-town is an iconic part of the city's image. As they engage with the world around them, and we engage with them, the culture of children and families creates a splendid kids zone.

**6.20** Are families living downtown temporarily, or do they choose to stay? One indicator is the evidence of the ten-year-olds. Once kids reach school age, a family has to make a definitive decision – to stay and make it work or move to the suburbs, which are well kitted out for children. The presence of these young fellows in Vancouver's downtown – and there are hundreds like them – indicate which option their parents chose.

**6.21** Sometimes a city can seem a harsh reality but the mere presence of children domesticates all around them as seen here with this band of kids on their daily trek to school. The place feels better for everyone when children are on the scene. We also found that designing for children creates a place that works better for others, such as seniors and those with special needs. ▶

ture that domesticated our ever-intensifying city and made it relevant to the broadest possible spectrum of people (see Figure 6.21). It is a success story in no uncertain terms. The big question: How did we make it happen?

## What families need and want

In modern North American cities, when we think of children, we generally assume they will be living in detached homes, ground-level townhouses at best, located within a modest-scale setting, usually in the suburbs. If we think about families in apartments, we usually assume they have no other choice – we assume they are of very modest income, perhaps single-parent households. But, as Vancouver started to play with multiple-housing development during the 1970s, a lot of people starting asking why that needed to be the case. Looking at European cities and a few surviving examples in historic eastern North American cities, people questioned why families would not want to live in apartments. Thinking of young couples who had enjoyed an urban lifestyle before they had their kids, for example in the West End, people wondered if they would like to continue with that lifestyle even with their kids in tow. One person in the City government, in particular, started asking questions early on. Ann McAfee, then still in her role as senior housing planner for the City, put together a systematic empirical research program to inquire with the families themselves about the pros and cons of having children in multiple housing, publishing her first findings when we were still in the early years of intensification. McAfee discovered two important realities. First, she found that there were many families who would be happy to consider a multiple-family lifestyle – this was something that was inherently attractive to many potential urban family households. Second, however, she learned that most multiple-family housing was just not workable for families with children. The unit and building designs did not accommodate the needs of parents and their kids. The neighbourhoods generally were deficient in children's services, from childcare to recreation, and were not designed in a child-friendly or even child-referenced way. Basically, interested families told McAfee that, like it or not, they had little choice but to move to the suburbs when their children were no longer toddlers. So McAfee, with a colleague, Andrew Malczewski, took all her data and developed an articulate set of guidelines for family-oriented multiple-housing,[2] as a general advisory reference for interested developers. This was approved and went into use in 1978. Although not mandatory, these guidelines, just because they were so sensible, had a big influence on South False Creek, then in the process of development.

Then, with the advent of the megaprojects, the interest in dense family housing became one of the biggest topics of conversation. Simply put, we felt we had to include family housing not only to diversify the communities that we were creating and offer a new kind of lifestyle choice for families that we now knew were very interested, but also to reflect the fact that most workers in the inner-city came from households with children. Nearby housing would not be attractive to them if it was not designed for them. Pragmatically, we were also certain we had to broaden out the multiple-housing market to create enough of a consumer base to feed the "living first" machine. In 1992, McAfee's earlier research was updated, applying it to even higher densities than she had initially contemplated, and we sent it forward for city council adoption as a clear set of guidelines for housing families with children at high density.[3] These guidelines ultimately changed the way that dense multiple housing was built in Vancouver and dramatically changed the profile of the communities that resulted.

The guidelines were very specific and detailed. I do not want to cover all aspects of the guidelines here, but it is informative to give a flavour of what is

**6.22** Families have returned downtown because we tailored it for them. Detailed guidelines shape the family habitat, specifying requirements for the unit, building, and community. Protected children's play areas close to and visible from family units, even on high-level terraces, is one such specification. In the case shown here in Downtown South, the street is about ten floors down.

**6.23** Fun features are endlessly appealing to families, as this public piano demonstrates. Such things must be deliberately planned and programmed into all public areas.

specified (see Figure 6.22). The guidelines outline requirements for the unit, the building, and the nearby community. For the unit, among other concerns, there are guidelines on bedroom count and size, floor finishes, storage, noise abatement, and private outdoor play space on a terrace or balcony. For the building, guidelines include those for public play areas within a specified distance of a family unit, overview of play areas by adult-oriented facilities such as laundry rooms for supervision, safety measures for building facilities, and clustering of family units for mutual aid and support. For the nearby community, there are requirements for all the normal children's facilities that one would expect, along with safe pathways to schools and parks, not interrupted by major streets, as well as community play space and areas of natural landscape. Because the guidelines had been derived from extensive conversations with families with children, we were convinced that the provisions were comprehensive. We hoped they would spontaneously draw families in large numbers to a living situation that had previously not been seen as relevant or good for children (see Figure 6.23).

### Securing family housing

For the megaprojects, the question was how to make these guidelines mandatory rather than just advisory. This took several important steps.

First, within the megaproject policy framework, we set a requirement that 25 percent of all the units in a building would have to meet the new guidelines. This figure was not very scientifically derived, but we did feel that this was more-or-less the proportion of a community's households that generally included children in our region. This was on top of the requirement outlined earlier that 50 percent of social-housing units in an area had to be allocated to families with children. Taken together, these were more than just marginal family housing requirements.

Second, we had to end a practice that was quite widespread in our city – landlords often banning children from apartment buildings, at their discretion. We passed an ordinance to make that illegal, except for specially designated housing, such as for seniors or those with special needs.

Third, we had to decide how to determine if a project met the 25 percent family housing requirement. For this, solid training was provided for the staff who reviewed development applications for approval. No bonus or incentive was given to developers to support the requirements for family units. They were expected to achieve these requirements within their normal project costing. Also, there was no rule that every family-designated unit must actually be occupied by a family with children. We set no limitations or barriers on who lived in these units. That was left to the marketplace. Our attitude was to believe in probabilities – if a unit was truly suitable for children, we felt that a family would be most likely to choose it and that over time the unit would settle in as a child-occupied space. Happily, that faith has been largely borne out over the years. And with the ever-increasing high cost of separate family homes and the shift of young families to apartments, fortunately we have built up a good stock of suitable units that are more affordable simply because they are older. However, as I will worry about later, this may be a temporary state of grace, as middle-income households are pushed right out of the market.

And lastly, we had to ensure that the community side of the equation – the battery of services and facilities needed by families – would actually find its way into the new communities and that these communities would be safe for children and generally child-friendly. For that, of course, we set required standards for schools, community facilities, and other services that I discussed in Chapter 4. But, in addition, the social planning department appointed what was called a children's advocate. The first children's advocate, Rita Chudnovsky, made a big impact through her tenacious efforts. She operationalized a whole program of change to make the city more child-oriented. For example, she started to address, at the civic level, childcare funding and operations, which up until then had been handled generally by senior governments quite randomly – still an issue in both our city and our country. She became an agent to secure more regularized government support. Childcare became a requirement in new developments where the City had leverage to make this so. For the megaprojects, Chudnovsky became the key adjudicator of performance for children's concerns. She reviewed all the neighbourhood plans to make sure that safety and security for children were well handled – even to the point of specifying that the landscaping near playgrounds must contain no toxic plants. She pushed to get schools built. She advocated for family-oriented programs in new community centres. All in all, the children's advocate was the voice to guarantee for new family residents coming to live at high density that they would find a community that actually did meet their needs.

### Results

As a result of this aggressive strategy, housing for families with children has now been deeply integrated into all the new communities of Vancouver (see Figure 6.24). Standards that once applied only to megaprojects are now targeted

**6.24** The policy for household mix, attracting families with children, has been phenomenally successful. Research indicates that 29 percent of new housing includes children. More than seven thousand children now live downtown. Our strategy actively enticed them with all the supports necessary for family life.

**6.25** This tai chi circle of Chinese Canadian women in Queen Elizabeth Park shows the spontaneous result of open immigration policies in Canada over many years. The City had no need to officially diversify at a cultural or ethnic level. Our planning did have to deal with sensitive issues for comfortable integration.

for all community developments and in some cases have even been increased. On the downtown peninsula, according to the last census, there are about seven thousand children, more than in any one of the nearby traditional residential communities that surround the inner-city. Schools are at capacity and demand is strong for more to be built. In a City study completed in 2008, Michael Gordon found that fully 29 percent of new units in the core city now accommodate children – more than the initial 25 percent target set for the megaprojects and far more than the 6 percent reality that had long been a natural outcome in the West End, without any public policy.

The cost factor that is now rearing its ugly head in Vancouver may draw back these results to some degree. It has undoubtedly hindered families from living at high densities in other expensive cities, but the die is definitely cast for family living in Vancouver's inner-city. I do not see this changing any time soon. Regardless of income levels, most units designed for children still have children living in them, and the amenity of downtown Vancouver for these children will always be a draw. As the City takes on the middle-income housing challenge, particularly by facilitating more rental housing, it will be essential to apply the family-housing parameters to this new rental stock. More and more, families are not seeing home ownership as the pension plan that it was for our generation, so rental housing will be attractive to them – that is, if it is built to suit their needs.

## A DIVERSITY THAT WAS NOT PURSUED: ETHNICITY

For some observers of Vancouver's expansion of diversity, one direction of social policy that was not pursued is quite interesting. The City has never tried to officially diversify at a cultural or ethnic level (see Figure 6.25). Partly, this is because everyone always agreed that this was a tricky row to hoe under any circumstances – differentiation too easily can become discrimination. Mostly, though, it was because we did not need local government involvement to achieve levels of ethnic and cultural diversity that have now become a featured characteristic of Vancouver. The open immigration policies of the federal government in modern times have done that job very well for our city and for many other cities in our country. Canada is now one of the most multicultural nations in the world, and ethnic diversity is the norm in all of our urban regions. Vancouver and Toronto are the most identified multicultural cities in the country, and they enjoy their cultural diversity in relative harmony. That is not to say that there have not been difficulties through the years and that racism and chauvinism have not shown their ugly faces. Like many places, early Vancouver was often hostile to people of Chinese or South Asian or Japanese descent, and we continue to struggle with the place of Indigenous communities within the city, including redressing the undeniable wrongs of the past. But, generally speaking, except for the knotty issues for First Nations that remain a fundamental challenge, when you compare our day-to-day experience of cultural and ethnic diversity with that of many cities, Vancouver has found its footing, at least from the point of view of city planning and the urban issues I discuss in this book.

One reason for this is an attitude that was cultivated at city hall and out from there. The City fostered a strong sense that cultural differences were to be carefully respected and even celebrated. I attribute the consolidation of this ethic to one person in particular – that is, Judy Rogers and a wide-ranging program she framed as "managing diversity." This started long before she became city manager. First at city hall's equal employment opportunity office and then through the Hastings Institute, which she helped to found, and a program called "Kingswood," she pushed a sustained, multi-year training effort to bring gender and multicultural understanding and sensitivity to the city. Her mission was to teach all aspects of social diversity to every single civic employee, as well as those of other governments, Crown corporations, non-profit organizations, and private companies. There is no doubt that she had a broad impact on attitudes that one could feel as a municipal public official. I was certainly motivated positively by the Kingswood message in our planning activities. For example, most public outreach came to be done in the key languages of the city. For subtle issues that had a potentially racist or anti-immigrant dimension, a tweaking of policies and by-laws was pushed as soon as the issue became noticeable. We constrained the size of what were pejoratively called "monster houses." These very big new homes built to maximum zoning capacity, which often popped up in areas of generally smaller homes, were associated with immigrant investment. In fact, the immigrant homeowners usually had nothing to do with their initial redevelopment, but long-time residents commonly blamed them for it. Similarly, we tightly limited the cutting down of large old trees. Justifiably or not, felling trees was often associated with new immigrants, who were unaware that Vancouverites revered these trees. Ethnic enclaves and districts were facilitated, even though sometimes these were more a marketing image than a reality and sometimes more historical than contemporary. For example, we have civic street and area signage in districts that identify cultural associations. Nonetheless, even with massive new growth, these enclaves remain identifiable, and most people seem to appreciate them because in modern times they have never become negative ghettos. But, otherwise, no one felt it was necessary or appropriate to use civic planning policy to shape or diversify any kind of cultural or ethnic social mix – even though some people say that we could have done more to integrate Indigenous communities.

## THE CHALLENGE OF DIVERSITY: A CONTINUING QUEST

On the social-engineering front, there is only so much any government can do and should do. The beauty of a robust urban system is that it finds its own complexities, and a civic personality builds around the unique socio-economic mix that results. There is no question that this has happened in Vancouver such that the city now has a memorable and compelling character and identity. Thousands of people have made their own special contribution – big and small – to the personality of Vancouverism. Nonetheless, like all North American cities, Vancouver works within an imperfect market, which, if left to its own devices, leaves out some people and serves others poorly. Certain potential market sectors will languish simply by being overlooked or misunderstood. Also, the local market operates within a larger national and international market that can sometimes undermine local interests. There is a role for local government to offer leadership and take action when the market consistently cannot do the job or distorts local conditions. There is also a role for local government to shape the nature of the place, based upon the vision of the whole community, as expressed through the democratic process. That is the essential foundation for the social agenda that I have described for contemporary Vancouverism.

And yet, one always seems to be left with a level of disquiet on this topic. Has the City done enough? Was the City insightful enough about the implications of its own actions and the implications of the changing place of Vancouver in the world? In hindsight, I must acknowledge that we could have done more. Let me close this chapter by describing where Vancouverism has not met the intentions that were so important to us at the beginning. Mostly, this has to do with the inability to predict the future.

To some degree, Vancouver is becoming a victim of its own success (see Figure 6.26). As the city has been opened to the world through the years, it has drawn more and more people, talent, and wealth, all clamouring for their piece of the rock in what has become known as a "sanctuary city" in a troubled world. This has led to a kind of urban malignancy that is starting to eat away at the very formula of diversity that we have so carefully put together since the early 1990s.

**6.26** This headline from the *Vancouver Sun* in 2014 says it all – the biggest issue facing our city in its quest for diversity is the shrinking affordability of both housing and work-places, now hitting not just low-income people but many others.

That malignancy is the dominance of the richest, resulting in spiralling land values, echoed in rising prices for housing and workplaces, which edits out activities and people just about as fast as actions can be taken to edit in those same people and activities.

An early casualty has been what could be called the lower-order uses within that mixed-use of which we are so proud. Vulnerable since at least the late 1980s has been traditional industry, along with warehousing and a range of city-serving supports. Industry was never a strong suit in Vancouver, even though we originally lived off our lumber sector and, more recently, have had our stars, such as garment production. For as long as anyone can remember, industry has had difficulty competing for its properties. I do not buy into the argument that says *we* actually made this happen as we converted the inner-city mega-projects and then upland development areas from low-intensity infrastructure – essentially railyards and warehousing – to high-density urban uses. Uses on these sites were clearly already obsolete, and the railroads in particular had taken their own initiative to relocate. Adjacent uses were dependent upon the rail operations and became redundant once the rails moved. All the megaproject sites and districts were more than ready for reconstruction, and the benefits of their transformation far outweigh the resulting losses. However, because the process was so sweeping and so profitable, this transition also carried away a plethora of interstitial uses that were little valued but are undeniably essential as support for any urban core. I am talking about such things as low-end commercial support services, wholesaling, warehousing, repair shops, and auto services. Also, as housing became more valuable, even office sites started to be grabbed for residential use in the inner-city, leading to significant worry about office capacity for the business needs of the future. For many years, with very restrictive zoning, we protected some areas close to downtown for lower-order uses, such as Burrard Slopes and the False Creek Flats, along with the areas northeast of city hall and east of Gastown. But we forgot that this was at best an interim solution that would ultimately be overwhelmed by rising land values – and that has now occurred. For the housing-office competition downtown, Ronda Howard undertook what became known as the "Metro Core Study,"[4] which led to protection of office sites. Again, probably at best, this gave us breathing room. Soaring land values, set by world demand and almost immune to local control, need a new response to secure preferred local uses. Instead, we continue to rely on protective zoning, even though many people now understand this will simply no longer be effective. The same argument applies to another use that every city needs – that is, low-rent space for start-ups and marginal businesses and most of the creative sector. The same can be said for high-technology production, a whole new sector that is revitalizing what had become moribund industrial districts. All of these uses are under stress in today's marketplace, with nothing seemingly in sight that will change that. We now need a strategy that embraces the inevitability of high land values rather than trying to fend off or collapse those values. This will take us back to an old idea that Ray Spaxman originally gave to the city and that I have already talked about – leveraging through bonusing. To bring long-term security to the lower-order uses that we want – whether it is industry or high-tech production or start-ups or creative space – we must use zoning to tie them to the higher-order uses that can cope with the rents from high land values. The lower-order uses must become *required* and must be included in any building that houses the higher-order uses. This will be a future of tight mixed-use buildings and sites and districts that are choreographed in a partnership between government and the private sector to bring everything necessary into the urban equation and keep the mixes secure over time. Time will tell if we have the inventiveness to bring this about.

As land values soar, the social mix has proven to be just as vulnerable as the land-use mix. In the social sphere, there is a long-used term for what is happening with rising costs. It is "gentrification," which essentially means that wealthy people outbid less wealthy people for housing and worksites, thereby displacing those who cannot compete. We should have seen this coming in this increasingly popular and successful city. We should have seen this coming as we made "living first" not just a planners' theme but a very chic, stylish and hip trend for more and more consumers, more and more kinds of households in the marketplace. But then again, this may be the inevitable wisdom of hindsight. It is a quandary. We put most of our public-sector eggs in one basket – housing for the low end of the income spectrum – because at that time we had to and we did very little to secure anyone else's housing. Yes, we secured some income mix, but it touched only the bottom edge of the range of middle-income households, leaving most of the middle class out of the equation. Even with all the work for family housing, we got the right housing built but did not secure it for families whose average household incomes we should have expected (and could have estimated). Then, in about 2000, senior governments stopped funding most family social housing and mixed-income social housing. And for seniors' housing and special-needs housing, we more or less went with the flow, securing whatever housing we found ready money to support rather than setting any kind of specific target for this housing. Surely, we could have foreseen that, with an aging population, we would need so much more secure housing targeted to seniors and the disabled. Again, we see that clarity of hindsight. Instead, we thought the status quo of those days would just go on and on. I've said it before, in the early 1990s, it was still true that most families, even with middle incomes, could find a comfortable place to live. They could buy that housing and then ride a wave of capital gains overtaking the mortgage, trading up, and even underwriting various family obligations from time to time. More recently, as prices went up, the common story has been that parents dip into their own housing equity or savings to subsidize their children for their first homes. One way or the other, until relatively recently, middle-income people found their places in the market, and all was well. Also, in those days, seniors who owned a suburban home could expect that its sale would support them as their needs changed or they became disabled. But times have changed and all of these assumptions are just no longer dependable. We should have realized that long ago, during the formation of Vancouver's social agenda, not just now, after the fact, because now it all seems so absolutely predictable.

So, today, Vancouver finds itself in a crisis of affordability – of housing and workplaces and even retail spaces, not to mention special-purpose places. The crisis is so overwhelming that it could take apart the extraordinary progress in diversity and inclusiveness that has been one of the prime hallmarks of

Vancouverism. In fact, this issue is so profound that it could bring this proud city to its knees.

The affordability crisis needs an aggressive and sustained response. This will take a renewed commitment to the principle of inclusiveness because the solutions to the problems of affordability will challenge our prevailing theories and principles. Here are just a few ideas that have to be developed.

To civic housing targets, we will definitely have to add a specific middle-income target – maybe returning to the original formula that applied in False Creek South, where a third of housing consisted of subsidized low-income units, a third was secure middle-income units, and a third was free-market higher-income units. How to achieve this in completely private developments will be the problem to solve. We will also have to return to that golden age of mixed-income social housing that Cameron Gray talks about – maybe reflecting the regional proportionality of middle-income households or maybe tying middle-income targets to types of households, such as those for families or seniors. One way or the other, if we want an inclusive city, those in the income middle can no longer just be left to fend for themselves. The City has already experimented with some forms of this focused attention. In 2007, during negotiations with the developer of Southeast False Creek, the City confirmed that a middle-income component of secure rental housing would apply in the area for at least the next twenty years, representing about 30 percent of the first phase of housing. In 2013, through the new West End Community Plan, replacement rental housing was made a requirement when such housing was displaced by new development.[5] But, for the most part, the missing middle is still the missing middle. In addition to housing, we may also have to do something similar with other essential uses, such as independent retailing and special-purpose workspaces. Crafting a secure socio-economic mix, though it grates on our sense of the freedom of the marketplace, will become essential the more successful Vancouver becomes as one of the world's destination cities.

But merely setting targets will not be enough. Delivering the targets will take all the ingenuity and money that we can muster. As our history with low-income housing has vividly illustrated, intervening in the housing market is very expensive. The more we spread that intervention, the more expensive it will become. In some places, such as the Nordic countries, we are seeing experiments that may need to be tried in Vancouver. At Sege Park, in Malmo, Sweden, with the emergence of the sharing economy, various forms of co-housing are being explored – they are talking about how people might share spaces or equipment or services to bring their housing prices down. Rather than simply moving to a more remote location to find affordability, these creative people are in the process of actually redefining the housing commodity itself by looking at its component parts and how much privacy and exclusiveness are needed with each component. Back to Vancouver, we have had a few tentative examples of multiple housing that can be rearranged from time to time at the discretion of the owner/occupier to carve out a separate, lockable secondary rental suite, which can assist affordability just as the traditional secondary suite did for the single-family home in times past. Clever experiments to this end have been completed in the government-supported communities developed at both the University of British Columbia and Simon Fraser University. This whole range of inquiry has rich potential, but it will challenge everything we know about zoning and home building and marketing.

On another front, it is time to look to the financing and development sectors to assist us with the problem of the missing middle. For consumers right now, we offer the option of full home ownership if they can afford it, underwritten by a privately financed mortgage. Or they can rent. Tenants have no housing debt or equity, but a rent cheque is lost to them forever once the landlord cashes it. Surely, there has to be a middle ground between these two alternatives. We need to offer options that provide various levels of benefit with various levels of cost. Perhaps rents could be modestly subsidized by increasing development on non-profit property, freeing up tenants' cash flow for other purposes. Perhaps long-time tenants could receive some form of rent rebate. Perhaps a portion of rent could go to an automatic savings program for tenants. Perhaps people could become homeowners, building equity, but without the option of accessing capital gains, so prices will be significantly lower for any given location. There may be other forms of home ownership involving short-of-freehold tenure. There should be shared ownership supported by the finance industry. We need to experiment with home tenure. We need to experiment with the nature of the housing builder – non-profit rather than for-profit builders. We need to experiment with home financing. A group called Options for Homes in central Canada and the not-for-profit housing societies in Rotterdam are illustrative of the direction that Vancouver must now start to consider. But this thinking will be out of the box, big time.

It will take a new kind of courage, even audacity, by the current cadre of planners and builders and property managers and financiers to bring to heel the

**6.27** Meeting tomorrow's challenges for diversity will require the same kind of courage as was seen when we targeted families with children to live downtown. During the 1980s, people claimed that most families would never want to live in high-density settings, especially not in what was often seen as a dangerous part of town. Yet our "living first" strategy depended on these new-comers. This shot shows how wrong the critics were.

**6.28** The mission of this downtown social-housing building is expressed in its name, which also applies to the fundamental mission of Vancouver-ism. We need the roofs, but, indeed, it is about "more than a roof."

monster of unaffordability. It feels like the same kind of courage that was at play at the outset of Vancouverism. We had it then, as the record now confirms (see Figure 6.27). Even with the critique others and I have offered, the social accomplishments of Vancouverism have been extraordinary and exemplary (see Figure 6.28). I hope this new generation will have their own kind of courage and tenacity to tackle what may be the hardest of all their challenges.

## THE BIGGEST BLACK EYE IN THIS WHOLE STORY

If a community embraces diversity, what responsibilities come with that? In Vancouver, we found that the answer to this question is much more complicated than it at first appeared. As I have described in this chapter, we focused on diversity of land uses and housing, with some, if not complete, success. But true diversity is about taking the fullness of human experience, the difficult as well as the laudable, within the culture of your city. And, on this front, one area of Vancouver always brought us up short. In this area, we faced a daunting challenge when we started our work, the City struggled with it throughout the years of our tenure, and it remains a vicious problem to this very day. I am talking about the Downtown Eastside, with its deplorable social circumstances of poverty, mental illness, and addiction. I have already introduced this neighbourhood and described how it came to be a community under sustained stress. But there is more to this situation, and it must be told because it is the biggest single tragedy of Vancouverism.

In addition to the pressures on existing modest-income housing in the Downtown Eastside, turfing long-time residents, the area has become the centre of homelessness for the whole region. The reasons are complex and overlapping, and it would take a whole book to truly dissect all the negative forces at play. That is not my purpose here – in fact, I am not competent to do that – but I do have to summarize the key vectors. To start with, of course, our whole economy has not been able to make a dent in the basic endemic poverty that is especially evident in the Downtown Eastside. Instead, as the city became more and more economically successful, the gap between poor and rich has become greater over the years. That poverty often brings its own victims and cast-off souls. Then, in the 1990s, because of well-meaning insistence from patient advocacy groups and new theories of treatment, among other things, the Province, as elsewhere in North America, started a process of deinstitutionalizing mentally ill patients from the traditional hospitals, with the intention of reintegrating them into community-based care facilities. But in a parallel trend, this was the very time when all the senior governments became politically driven to cut deficits and even balance budgets, so it was not difficult to just scratch off the funding list the extensive investments that were necessary for all the new facilities. That funding could just be deferred. I remember years later, in the early 2000s, provincial government reps came to city hall to start talking about at least a modicum of investment in facilities, but it really did not amount to much. In any event, no one had seemingly even thought about the probability of neighbourhood opposition to such a re-mix, which was very real, like it or not. So we began to see more and more mentally ill people on our streets, with no place to go, very little support, often becoming homeless or perhaps just not able to find the housing that might have been available for them. The Downtown Eastside became an epicentre because at least it had some long-existing support services. But the services that were in place became more-or-less overwhelmed. Then to this commentary must be folded in the expansion of the drug culture in those same years. Adding to the population at risk in the Downtown Eastside were teens and young adults pulverized by drug addiction, along with the mentally tortured people that many analysts saw as self-medicating with those same drugs. This simply compounded the impacts of alcohol addiction that had long been a reality of the Downtown Eastside, particularly hitting older resource workers simply spent from hard labour and Indigenous people. In very little time, a difficult status quo was pushed out of control into a wholesale crisis, by a contradiction of public policy, neglect, increasing social blindness, and denial. And that is where things sit to this moment in time.

Looking around the Downtown Eastside today, you might conclude that no one has done anything through the years, which, of course, would be the ultimate indictment for Vancouverism. In fact, such was not the case. Over the years, particularly under the guidance of city managers Ken Dobell and Judy Rogers, many initiatives were attempted. Services were added. The funding of service agencies was reviewed, with the intent of rationalizing what was seen as a random puzzle of services in order to channel more money directly to those in need. A needle-exchange was established. This all culminated in an initiative that had much greater positive impacts than one might imagine. It was called the "Vancouver Agreement," unfolded under the direct leadership and tutelage of city manager Judy Rogers and operationalized by an aggressive and smart bureaucratic activist, Donald MacPherson, as North America's first civic "drug policy coordinator." This was a five-year tri-government agreement, signed in 2000 and renewed for one additional five-year stint, to holistically address all aspects of the Downtown Eastside dilemma. This was an initiative that I, personally, supported but was not directly involved in, but I will always be thankful that it became a top civic priority because, otherwise, the situation would have spun out of control long ago. The Vancouver Agreement had many achievements, a story that is best told by those at the centre of the action, but one particular cluster of efforts stands out for me. Vancouver employed what became known as the four pillar drug strategy. This was invented in Europe during the 1990s and had been implemented in such places as Geneva, Frankfurt, and Sydney before it was adopted for our city. The pillars are prevention, treatment, enforcement, and harm reduction. That last pillar, harm reduction, is by far the most progressive and has restructured how Vancouver deals with addicted people. The principle is that no harm should come to those suffering from addiction, because that addiction is seen as an illness rather than an illegal choice. The measures coming out of this strategy are extensive, but the most important by far has been the supervised safe injection site in the Downtown Eastside, called "Insite," which opened in late 2003, the first such facility in North America. This was coupled with expansion and diversification of needle-exchange programs. And, without a doubt, the net effects have been positive, according to City documentation: a reduction in drug users consuming drugs on the street; a significant drop in overdose deaths; and a reduction in infection rates for HIV and hepatitis.[6] God forbid what might be the situation today if the Vancouver Agreement and all of its spinoffs had not happened.

And yet, the situation today seems to be worse than ever. The fentanyl crisis has been a particularly bad setback. That's why I see it as a dark shadow in the tale of Vancouverism because the tenacity that we brought to bear in our other inventions has simply not been as consistent in this case, even with the extraordinary efforts of the Vancouver Agreement. The numbers of those at risk on the streets, with little aid and support, are increasing. Homelessness, even with the City's best efforts, is not decreasing. The life tragedy of the mentally ill and addicted has not abated and is there every day for all to see. The poor are poorer, and their plight is in such harsh contrast to that of Vancouver's rich, who are richer. The whole social fabric and physical fabric of the Downtown Eastside seems more frayed than ever. And that is really not good enough in a city that prides itself in all its other city-building achievements. We should have done better.

I cannot help but feel that the City needs to try once again to see what can be done to improve the situation. We need a new priority civic initiative – a vigorous drive – like that sponsored by Judy Rogers almost two decades ago. We need all the governments to put their minds and their resources to the task. We need the best forensic thinkers to put their minds to the task. We need everyone to pitch in. The potential solutions are not as clear as are those for the other current challenges of Vancouverism, but two things are obvious. First, there will have to be significant legal and organizational reforms in how people at risk are viewed, served, and assisted, reforms that will challenge current attitudes and laws. Second, the City will have to take a leadership role because the problems are more or less ours, and they are certainly right on our doorstep.

The Downtown Eastside, regardless of city hall efforts and local advocacy efforts, remains the negative contrast to the progressive story of Vancouverism. Our social agenda achieved much more than most other cities during the same period, but so much more needs to be done, as this one key community so cogently illustrates. This is the unfinished business for the next generation.

Having gained a sense of the social side of Vancouverism, let's now see how it was put together in the physical form of the city. Vancouver is famous for its contemporary style and elegance, and excellence in urban design has been at the centre of its principles for over forty years. The next chapter will sketch what that has been all about.

**7.1** When most people think of Vancouverism, they think of one building type – a point tower, with its low-rise podium extending along the street. Here is a fine example in Downtown South. Our urban design agenda has a much richer set of intentions and results, but there is no doubt that this form for high-density living has become an important contribution to urban typologies.

# URBAN DESIGN

**TOWER + PODIUM:** this is the image that is conjured up in most people's minds when they hear the word "Vancouverism." They think of a street-level low-rise building crowned by a slim tower (see Figure 7.1). Though this may be a common application of the word, this one aspect of urban form is only the tip of the iceberg of what we conceived for the urban design of Vancouver over the years. Vancouverism now comprises a host of design expectations that have brought coherence, character, and livability to the contemporary dense city. Compared to that of other cities, development management in Vancouver has a very strong imperative for private development to reflect a public agenda of urban design in every single building and open space that is built. This did not come quickly or easily, but the public agenda came to be pervasively codified and applied by the local government, backed up by credentialed urban design experts, skilled design negotiators, design peer review, heavy public input, and a discretionary regulatory framework that brings truth to the idea (and underlying legal fact) that development is a privilege conferred by the community and not a fundamental right.

In this chapter, I will outline the unique Vancouver factors that shaped our urban design synthesis over the years, the history of some of the most vital ideas, and the holistic agenda for, first, the public realm and then the private realm that has come together as a major dimension of Vancouverism that is bigger than the sum of its parts. Then, I will offer my critique of some of the missing elements and weaknesses still evident in the existing agenda and challenges that remain for Vancouver's urban design evolution in the future. In Chapter 9, we will come back to the regulatory tools and processes that were invented to apply what I describe in this chapter.

## INFLUENCES SHAPING VANCOUVERISM

It has been said that the basic scenario of the tall thin tower sitting on a podium was imported from Asia, when Asian development companies and Asian consumers came to the city, particularly with the turnover of Hong Kong to the People's Republic of China in the 1990s. This is simply wrong. It is invented history, by people who were not a part of the organic, locally based genesis of the podium-and-tower form and its related urban design concepts. In fact, in addition to what Frances Bula has already described, there were five factors that had significant influence in the thinking at city hall, the development community, and the design community over the years when intensive development was also under way, and these ideas became the status quo very quickly. The so-called "Hong Kong factor" was never a strong determinant. Let me summarize the truly important influences.

The first influence was the setting itself – the geography and climate. As I summarized in Chapter 1, Vancouver has the dual nature of being hemmed in and drawn out. It has a fixed land area, with no way to expand its living space. But the lovely water bodies and striking majesty of its mountains to the north are unendingly beguiling. The fundamental urban condition that prevails is that of limited space with a spectacular edge. This created the necessity to use land efficiently, which means building up, reinforced by an imperative to lift people up from grade for the dramatic views that open up all around them with height.

This setting also offers a very moody climate – the city sits within a cool, often overcast rain forest. As Vancouver's greatest homegrown architect, Arthur Erickson, always emphasized, this is a "white-sky town," with many grey days and lack of regular sunlight. So, light is important. This has led to the tradition of glassy buildings open to as much light as possible. It has also necessitated careful management of sun access for sidewalks and public spaces, which has tended to pull tight the profiles of tall buildings so they create less shadows and to separate tall buildings from one another to keep corridors of light that can penetrate down to ground level.

The second influence was the historical tight grid of streets and small-lot subdivision of land in the inner-city. The size and layout of Vancouver blocks, lanes, and streets are very similar to that seen in the older sections of many North American cities. As Patrick Condon explains in his book *Seven Rules for*

*Sustainable Communities,*[1] this pattern is very amenable to many scales of development, from single homes to high-rises. Yet, paradoxically, the small-lot subdivision and ownership patterns created a countervailing influence to keep many individual building sites of manageable scale. Assembling properties for a larger site was very tough and expensive because the city has such a uniquely limited land base. Naturally, there were some exceptions. In areas that offered panoramic views where higher rents could be expected, the developer would sometimes acquire a cluster of properties that permitted the erection of a particularly big skyscraper. In such a case, we usually got a well-separated but somewhat isolated tall concrete structure surrounded by landscape. But just as often, or more often, smaller sites were exploited, so many tall buildings came to sit side by side along the streets. Both conditions had their benefits and problems, as we shall see. A further uniqueness had to do with a feature of our building code that does not exist in most North American cities. For fire exits, the building code permits an efficient configuration called a "scissor stair" that wraps around the elevator, taking much less room than a conventional staircase. The result is that towers have been very practical as intensification has taken off, but their floorplates have remained unusually small by North American standards. To see how this happened quite naturally, one need only survey the West End, where such tall thin towers, either tightly side by side or sitting spaciously within a green site, were the order of the day starting back in the mid-1950s. Reacting to several unpopular view-blocking "slab" buildings that had also sprouted on a few larger sites, the West End planners who designed this first tower community of the city locked down the thin tower preference, with zoning rules to require it and facilitate it. All these factors set the public and design consciousness clearly with a bias for what became known as the "point tower" – tall, thin, and very elegantly proportioned. But there were reservations, which further evolved the parti – as I will now explain.

The third influence was the experience of planners and consumers of that mid-century high-rise pattern of the West End that I have just referenced. Though many people came to enjoy the dense, tall development of the West End – it was and is a very popular neighbourhood – they also told Vancouver urban designers two key things based upon the conditions that they experienced. First, where many small sites had developed along a street, people said that tall buildings were getting too close together, creating privacy issues. This led to a study of privacy distances in the early 1990s that ultimately set a 24.4-metre (80-foot) separation between tall residential buildings throughout the city. Second, where large sites hosted a single tower, people told us, almost contrarily, that the sidewalks were becoming too anonymous and even unsafe, bereft of people and activity, because everyone was up in the towers, leaving vast, empty ground-level spaces between the buildings. Trish French, one of the era's most important urban design policy-makers, borrowed a term from the Muppets when she called such hefty isolated buildings such as these West End types "pigs in space." People told us that landscaping alone was not a viable alternative to people-generating functions – Le Corbusier's idea of the "towers in the park" is not all it's cracked up to be.[2] As we moved forward, we decided to avoid that outcome of densification in Vancouver, so we started pressing new development design to locate some building mass right on the line of the sidewalk, at least for a few storeys, thus beginning the tradition of the podium. Oh, by the way, beyond building shapes, people also told us that the luxury of magnificent Stanley Park, at the edge of the West End, was not enough for the open space needs of the community. They said they needed nearby smaller park spaces; they needed close-by escape from the concrete intensity of the immediate setting. This set off a whole range of park design policies to integrate buildings and green space everywhere. Overall, the influence of the West End was to confirm for Vancouverites that density is good but only if it is carefully shaped to minimize impacts and maximize day-to-day livability.

Then, as time moved on, the fourth influence became the existence of those vast megaproject properties cheek by jowl with the old city core, in contrast to the relatively small blocks and lots within the core. These sites gave us a playground to test the building shapes and urban design formulas that grew out of the other influences, already described, and to apply them over a wide area in a short time. These megaprojects took our theoretical thinking to practical implementation at a scale so that we could truly understand the veracity of our ideas and fix them within our design equation for the whole city. As we tested the alternatives, it became increasingly clear to us that the thin, carefully proportioned, carefully spaced point tower, with a gracious apron along the street, just performed so well in regard to our setting and consumer preferences.

The fifth influence was probably as important as all the other factors put together. The transformation process was set off at a very good time in the evolution of the community's design capacity and philosophy. The urbanist intelligentsia of Vancouver – those who provided the creative directions for rethinking the form and character of the city – were well versed in the best ideas afloat in the re-emerging art of urban design. This may have been more pronounced in Vancouver than in many other cities because a lot of these people were immigrants, coming from mature, sophisticated home cities all over the world. They were well travelled and had real experience of the urban forms that could be morphed to meet the needs of their adopted city. Of course, it is also possible that having a particularly clever group of designers thrown together in the same place at the same time might just have been a happy coincidence. Whatever the case, among other influences, they were empowered and educated by what is now called "New Urbanism," a movement that was sweeping North America at the time,[3] although they never seemed to buy into the low-rise bias that dominated that movement. But the attention to deliberate urban design rather than random growth was compelling. So, a strong physical design consciousness and sophisticated theoretical foundation influenced their perspective of what a city needed to be and what it needed to achieve for its citizens. Often, they were products of the mid-twentieth-century counterculture movements that challenged the status quo, reformed government, and embraced a wide and active public democracy. I remember many intense discussions about both the relative elegance of various tall, thin building forms and the scale that building walls along streets needed to be for pedestrians to feel comfortable. I remember similar debates within the community that influenced all our thinking. The people who initially shaped the process and those who followed in fully realizing those initial directions were all very well endowed with a prowess for civic design while being liberated from past practices that might have limited the application of their creative thinking.

So, instead of just importing fully formed urban design solutions from other places, Vancouverism was about creating a fitting urban design formula that grew out of our unique local situation, our unique local experience, and our unique local thinking. Yes, the fact that we had consumers who came from dense origins, particularly in Asia, and accepted high-rises, gave us market credibility. The fact that some Asian-based developers brought a technical capacity to build tall and complex buildings made things easier. And the fact that we had architects, developers, politicians, and especially buyers who had visited workable dense places, especially in Europe and old parts of North American cities, made our own solutions more defensible because we could say we had seen something like them somewhere else. But our homegrown urban design agenda was quite new and was put together in quite a special way – which is the big lesson of this chapter. It is vital that every place carefully assess its advantages and disadvantages, and conceive its city shape from what urban designer Scot

Hein ironically calls its DNA (its "distinguishing neighbourhood attributes," Hein's own play on words). That is how we will secure and protect at least some diversity and individuality of our cities in a time of pervasive globalization.

## THE ORGANIC EVOLUTION OF VANCOUVERISM
## URBAN DESIGN TRADITIONS

Almost never in the evolution of urban design traditions in Vancouver did an idea come out initially as a fully formed proposition. In almost every case, a design theme found a first expression and then was tested and refined over many years and many applications. To give a sense of this, let me describe the changing nature of just a few of the practices that now have become synonymous with Vancouverism.

*Tower-podium*

First, let's stay with the tower-podium parti that I referred to at the beginning of this chapter. I have already described how this concept was a response to the empty interstitial spaces that we were creating in the West End in its first iteration of redevelopment. But the idea also had another separate root. When Ray Spaxman arrived on the scene in the early 1970s, he brought the first systematic thinking about urban design into the city since the place had been initially laid out during the first third of the century. Spaxman had a very sophisticated view of the physical design of cities, engendered in part by his roots in England but also by his fascination with cities all over the world and his voracious reading on the topic. He brought Vancouver's attention to the ideas of people such as Gordon Cullen, Christopher Alexander, Kevin Lynch, and Ian McHarg.[4] At that time, Vancouver was in a development boom for commercial high-rises in the core city, and the office-building formats that were popular in many places were quite naturally brought forward for this city. Essentially, these were tall towers, often of some girth, which sat within pointless, empty plazas. Everywhere, people were beginning to notice that these plazas were not working the way the designers initially hoped, as urban embellishments and respite. Instead, they were becoming an urban blight, dead spaces, not particularly friendly to everyday users, and often unsafe, especially during off hours. After conducting research in the United States, William (Holly) Whyte brought this out in the open in his seminal book, *The Social Life of Small Urban Spaces*.[5] This book had a big impact among the planners and urban designers in Vancouver right through the 1980s. Spaxman agreed with its findings, but he also saw that due to the addition of the open plazas, the streets themselves were losing their visual coherence and iden-tity. They were no longer defined and contained by any building mass. Spaxman took decisive action in his new downtown plan and zoning by putting in place and then carefully implementing a policy of street-oriented buildings that became the other early expression of the podium, along with the West End response already discussed. The word he brought into the Vancouver vocabulary was "streetwall," and it became a basic for proposals coming into city hall for new downtown buildings. I remember with embarrassment that local politicians used to make fun of Spaxman and the rest of us about the use of that word and challenged us on what it meant and why we thought it was so important.

But that is not the end of the story, because Spaxman's solution had a few problems of its own. These streetwall building elements needed to be not just structured mass. They needed to be useable spaces. In the early years, as can still be seen in some locations today, the volume was just that – architectural caprice and massing, with nothing really going on within the architectural framework. The podiums did provide a wall for the street but not much by way of energy or activity. The obvious answer was to fit them with retail shops along the side-walks, as is seen in most other cities. But, alas, Vancouver is not like other cities. It is somewhat isolated, sitting apart from other modern megalopolises, such as one sees on the east coast of America, the totality of which generates strong retail demand that can seemingly fill endless retail frontage. In Vancouver, all was fine with local neighbourhood shopping areas that served day-to-day con-sumer needs. But demand for general, high-order retail that would target a downtown was limited. We discovered that we could not fill all the spaces cre-ated by the new downtown commercial streetwall frontages that were being built. We tried a few mitigation measures, one being to create spaces that could be used as lobbies in the short-run and converted to retail in the future as demand grew. But mostly, the streetwall policy limped along, solving well the issues it was meant to solve, with some retail, some architectural caprice, some "future" retail allocations, and frankly, a lot of retail vacancies that were not a happy result on the street. What may have saved us from more pervasive future problems was that the market for commercial office buildings, with their inte-grated retail spaces, cooled significantly, starting in the late 1980s. This was happening almost everywhere in the Western world because there had been so much overbuilding of this building type, creating unprecedented vacancy rates. Almost no important large-scale office building was constructed in Vancouver for over a decade, so that also stopped the proliferation of the excess retail at the base that had tagged along with these buildings. With the slow growth of retail demand over time, the vacant retail space created in the early Spaxman years was finally absorbed – problem solved.

But even that is not the end of the tower-podium story. Once residential demand took off in the inner-city in the 1990s, we had another set of opportunities to exploit and extend the podium idea in a new context. Faced with the same problems already described – dead ground space and towers too close together – we were able to explore other uses for the podiums that were specifically needed to support residential use. The first new opportunity came with the realization that residents needed a lot more ancillary spaces and facilities than office workers did – things like spas and pools and meeting rooms. So, these uses became important content for podiums in residential complexes (see Figure 7.2). That was all to the good, but these were inward-oriented uses, so they still did not generate the kind of activity and overview at the sidewalk that makes for desirable and safe public space. And then, we made a discovery. I do not really know if any one person made the link – I was one strong early advocate, urban designers Trish French and Ralph Segal were others. We discovered that in our residential policy framework we were leaving behind ground-oriented housing, even though many people told us that they wanted to avoid apartments in a tower even with higher density living. They might have a dog that needed daily walking or children to let out to play but keep an eye on. Maybe they were afraid of heights or had a phobia about people living over them. Some people said they just wanted the identity of their own front door, as they had when they lived in a typical house. Also, admittedly, there was a bit of romantic thinking at play as well. Many of us admired the lovely streetscapes of rowhouses that we had experienced in historic cities, from London to Boston and Savannah (frankly, I had Bath, in England, in mind when I pushed for the crescent of rowhouses that now gives the name to Marinaside Crescent in False Creek North). We thought something like those historic frontages – evolved, of course, for a contemporary application and for the local setting – could add to the ambience and character of Vancouver streets. At any rate, we settled on the idea that we needed townhouses or rowhouses of some kind – and this offered almost endless utility for the use of residential podiums at a very hospitable scale of from two to four storeys along sidewalks (see Figure 7.3). This, yet again, transformed the concept of the podium because now it could be very active, offer good observation of the streetscape, and provide permeability (doors and windows) for easy access and safety. You can hear the spirit of Jane Jacobs in these aspirations, and it has to be

**7.2** Early podiums were often equipped with amenities for residents. In this case on Pacific Boulevard, the podium houses a pool and spa, above a line of ground-floor shops.

**7.3** Rowhouses extend from a Coal Harbour tower – the ultimate expression of the podium and its most typical use. Such townhouses along the streets and open spaces of Vancouver have become central to the city's contemporary image.

said that her book *Death and Life of Great American Cities* was a big influence in Vancouver.[6] At first, developers resisted the idea of rowhouses because they doubted that any consumers would prefer a ground connection instead of those lovely views. Early on, I had some mean arguments with developers and their architects just to get these rowhouses included. These were quite the battles – one architect facetiously said that only a streetwalker would opt for a rowhouse because the commute to work would be short.

They soon discovered they were wrong, as the first rowhouses were quickly snapped up. Most importantly, the rowhouse meant that the sunken costs of the required podium could be transformed into a money-maker for developers. That certainly sweetened their inclination to include them in a building's design. We now have thousands of these rowhouses in the podiums that line most of our streets in Vancouver's core city and even out in the suburban town centres.

And then the last bit of the story was a finding that the rowhouse format could also work in commercial and transition areas for live-work units, where we found a growing demand, as working at home became more common.

So, what started out as a simple urban design affectation has been evolved into a way of building a streetscape that is not only emblematic of Vancouver but offers a wide variety of applications and is very marketable. It has converted consumer attitudes from anti-density to density-happy and is perhaps one of the most essential contributions to the day-to-day livability of Vancouver.

## Courtyard

Now, let's turn to the urban courtyard as another example of the evolution of an idea. Once the streetwall podium had been established in the vernacular of Vancouverism and was being regularly applied in the intensification of areas in the inner-city, we began to worry about the loss of open space in these areas. Where we had the advantage of unusually large sites, as in every one of the megaproject locations, we started massing whole blocks at one time, and as the streetwall claimed the street edge, we usually had leftover space in the centre of the blocks. These spaces quite naturally provided the opportunity for court-yards, from which we could see great benefits as an expansion of the open-space offerings in a community. So, the courtyard idea was born for Vancouver, re-inforced by the appeal of these kinds of spaces that we saw in cities all over the world, from Paris to Cordoba to Beijing.

In the first round of courtyard development, as you can see today in the waterfront sites of Granville Slopes on the north side of False Creek, adjacent to

**7.4** On large housing sites, the podiums created interior courtyards. Early examples, such as this one in Granville Slopes, were open to streets or walkways, which expanded the public realm. Although this was beneficial, especially in park-deficient precincts, residents of the building worried about security and privacy. Visitors wondered if they were welcome.

the Burrard Bridge (see Figure 7.4), the urban designers pressed hard to have these courtyards open on at least one side to the public area of the sidewalk or seawall walkway so they could augment the green spaciousness of the public realm in the absence of dedicated parks. In some cases, even if the courtyard was fully surrounded by podiums, city hall still required developers to make the space public, through a public-use agreement, so anyone could ask to be admitted and could not be turned away. It all sounded good, and so, in these areas in this first generation of courtyards, they were developed that way. However, it turned out that almost no one was enthusiastic about this arrangement. During our post-occupancy conversations with them, residents told us that the courtyards were too public, not nearly private enough to be used in a secure, intimate way, like a backyard. For non-resident visitors, the courtyards were too private, not nearly public enough to make them feel welcome and less like intruders. Also, no one knew which courtyards were subject to public-use agreements, so these became irrelevant. The bottom line was that few people were using these courtyards, so the space, desperately needed at higher densities, was essentially wasted.

In the second iteration of the courtyard, we fixed this by giving up on the public-use aspiration and accepting that a courtyard could and should be primarily a private space. Well, actually, it was semi-public because it was accessible for all the residents in a building complex – but it was private to that small cluster of residents, who are more likely to know one another as neighbours (see Figure 7.5). This was a controversial move that caused a lot of squabbling among city hall staff because some people saw these spaces as part of the public equity of the place. But we stood our ground on this. Once the courtyards became private, they could be well furnished and lushly landscaped without the worry of vandalism or theft. Play equipment became typical because these spaces were safe for children at play, with only modest supervision. And in some cases, they could even be programmed for things like children's birthday parties and weddings and building picnics. The result is that use patterns increased dramatically over that seen in the earliest courtyards, and the value of the courtyard became integral to the value of the units having access to it – a real marketing feature for those units.

In the final version of courtyards, we started seeing proposals to raise the courtyard along with its surrounding townhouses one or several levels above the street. This came about because the courtyard with townhouses typology was becoming very popular, so developers wanted to have these features even when they had other uses for the building's at-grade frontage along the sidewalk, such as shops or restaurants along with their back-of-house supports such as tucked-away parking (see Figure 7.6). Also, consumers preferred these courtyards to be as private and secure as possible because they were truly becoming the communal backyards of their building complexes – popular places for such pastimes as children's play, sunbathing, allotment gardening, and other quite private family activities.

So, again, an urban design conceit that was initially grasped as an attractive green feature has evolved into not just a green amenity but also a very vital part of the spectrum of public-to-private open space that we came to understand was essential for high-density living. Now, almost every newer building includes some kind of courtyard, at various levels, almost always semi-private, hosting all kinds of resident activities and engendering a happy neighbourliness. There

**7.5** As courtyards evolved, it became standard to fully enclose them. They became very popular for residents at high densities. Landscape architects saw them as the perfect canvas for artful design. I live on this lovely example in a later building in Granville Slopes.

**7.6** Courtyards have become so popular that residents want them even if retail is located along the sidewalk. Because retail has a much deeper footprint, including its utility support, it would displace a courtyard at the same level. In such cases, courtyards were raised to a higher level. This example on Cambie Street sits above big box stores. Surrounded by housing, it includes green play space and allotment gardens for residents. The full building is shown in Figure 7.13.

are now scores of these courtyards, and most are elegant canvases for the fine art of landscape architecture.

## View corridors

A third and final example of the evolution of urban design thinking in the city has to do with view corridors. I remember Ray Spaxman describing his first reaction when he arrived in Vancouver and saw its extraordinary setting of mountains and water. He immediately worried that the enjoyment of these unique and special features, especially from key public places on and near the downtown peninsula, would be lost as the city further built out. So, in an early move, he hastened to protect views from at least the ends of streets, even those extending across private property, in the case of the central waterfront (see Figure 7.7). First, buildings would not be allowed to close off the view by being built across the alignment of view streets. Second, as buildings located closer to the edge of the peninsula, they were set back, respecting an angle that opened up the view as one approached it, travelling along one of these public thoroughfares.

But Spaxman knew this first policy would not be enough to protect the experience of the city's evocative setting. He knew that people cherished other more spacious views from key public spaces and that they highly valued private views, with apartment prices being significantly enhanced if they had access to good views. So, he set in place a policy that every new building proposal would be evaluated from the perspective of public and private view gains and losses. The architects quickly created a methodology for defining and analyzing the views that would be gained and lost from both the new building and the surrounding ones. From that point on, the City starting managing the public-views resources, which were increasingly understood as part of the essential commonwealth of Vancouver, as well as brokering the plethora of private views that were gained and lost with each new building.

However, there was a downside to the City taking on such views management. Many people began to blame the City if they found themselves on the losing end of a views decision. Also, every single development with views issues became a political hot potato. I remember harsh moments in front of council and the Development Permit Board, arguing to save views with developers and architects whom I admired, on projects that, other than destroying important views, were delightful proposals. These were difficult dramas. There seemed to be too many variables at play in views analysis and too much judgment call necessary with each variable. Essentially, understanding, valuing, and brokering views is a messy business. One of the biggest vulnerabilities was the determination on a case-by-case basis of what public views were important and then staying consistent about that as the City adjudicated many separate development proposals over time. In the late 1980s, the mayor of the day, Gordon Campbell, made it clear that something more had to be done. He urged Spaxman to convene a full views analysis of the important public views of the city, to have it completed by independent consultants in liaison with City staff, and to include very wide public input. And that is what happened. As one of Spaxman's deputies at that time, in charge of the downtown, I managed a consultancy with planner Mike Kemble, undertaken with great effectiveness by consultant Peter Busby, one of Vancouver's most up-and-coming architects. Back then, the work was pretty unprecedented. Some cities had protected the odd view of a historic building, as in London, or limited all heights to ensure that a public building retained its prominence, as in Washington. Ottawa had limited downtown heights so that the profile of Parliament Hill would not be lost. But we could not find any place that had taken on the entire views resource as a public equity to be carefully nurtured and brokered. Working with staff and the general public, Busby and his colleague Bob Thompson, with economic evaluation and advice from economist Jay Wollenberg, identified the most important public views, the objects and scope of those views, and the implications of protecting those views on the development rights and values of individual properties throughout the inner-city. Their work was primarily concentrated on the core city because very little high-rise development was happening elsewhere in Vancouver at that time. For those few high-rise proposals scattered around town outside the core, we felt that our original customized evaluation process could apply to them. In the inner-city, the members of Busby's team found the views, they documented them, they determined the specific affected development sites, and they told us specifically what the impacts on development would be, such as cutting the development allowance, limiting heights, or forcing a building to have to shift location on its site. Then they completed a public process that took input from thousands of citizens. They were very thorough and city council enthusiastically adopted their findings (see Figure 7.8).

The result of this massive effort was to bring enough clarity to the question of protected public views that it stripped the heat out of the issue for almost all future development proposals. The same happened with private views preservation as computer applications made the identification and brokering of these views more efficient and effective. For vital public views, the City has been able

**7.7** In Vancouver, we initially secured the views along downtown streets out to the evocative setting. In this protected view corridor along Burrard Street, you can see it all – the water, mountains, and Lonsdale community across the harbour. Such views subtly bring the natural beauty into the heart of the city.

**7.8** High above the ground, officially designated view corridors extend across the entire downtown. No building is permitted to intrude within these 3-D cones. This map, the result of extensive analysis and public discussion in the late 1980s, is from the official plan. The cones save views of spectacular mountain features from public places south of False Creek and do double duty as corridors for delightful views out from the heart of the city. All of these views are now a vital part of the commonwealth of Vancouver.

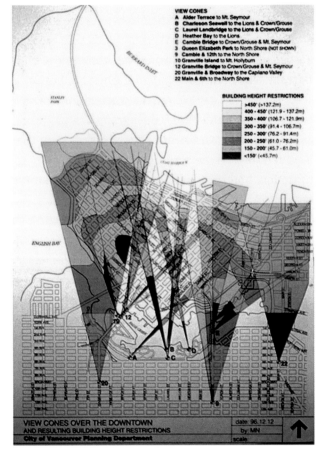

to conserve a wide array of perspectives across the downtown skyline to the mountains and out from within the downtown to both the mountains and the water – even in a time of unprecedented new development. Some architects and developers still resent this intrusion into their design freedom and push the edges from time to time. But the protected views are now part of the essence of Vancouver, a treasured public benefit and resource, hopefully in perpetuity. This was confirmed some twenty years later, in the late 2000s, when Brent Toderian, during his time as chief planner upon my departure, undertook a review of the view corridor policy. He concluded that it had done and continues to do what was initially intended, that it continues to be strongly supported by citizens, and that it has had almost no negative impact on the trends or profitability of development.

A final iteration of the story of view corridors is nothing less than true icing on the cake – being able to shape the skyline of downtown as a work of art rather than just a result of commerce and the market. Having managed protected views for a decade or so, we started to hear commentary from people that perhaps the resulting skyline was becoming too flat and undifferentiated. We realized that we needed to consider its overall profile, not just the view corridors that ran between the buildings. In the late 1990s, I asked Ray Spaxman, now in retirement from the City, to systematically complete the assessment. He and Michael Gordon at city hall compared our skyline to the evocative skylines of other cities, "growing" it in various ways through computer simulations derived from a digital model of the actual city with real sites that were available for new construction. Then they sought the response of thousands of people on the options. It was an urban beauty contest. Ultimately, we augmented the view corridors policy by selecting a few carefully pinpointed locations outside the corridors, where a tall building of unprecedented height could be added to punctuate the skyline and provide a much more articulated and expressive profile. It is a very sophisticated state of the urban design of Vancouverism to cover not just the function and economy of the city but also its overall grace and beauty (see Figure 7.9). I do not know any other place in the world that is deliberately sculpting its skyline in this way.

THE THREE EXAMPLES discussed above show the agility and evolution of Vancouver's urban design agenda. I could have drawn similar portrayals for almost all the urban design moves that matter for Vancouverism. Equally important is to understand how the various key urban design policies have come together,

**7.9** The downtown skyline has been specific-ally designed as a work of art, having referenced the differing skyline expres-sions of cities around the world. Heights are set to establish a certain overall pro-file of buildings with artful punctuations, all against the mountain backdrop. This is urban design as public art.

reinforcing one another to create a compelling whole. That is now where I want to turn, focusing first on the ordering of the public structure of the city as a framework and then shaping the private components within that structure.

## CREATING THE PUBLIC URBAN DESIGN FRAMEWORK FOR VANCOUVERISM

Unlike some cities, Vancouver has never depended upon a one-off, dramatic architectural gesture to either achieve the quality and character it needs or to set the direction for what it might become. Instead, we have taken a holistic perspective, attending to the overall structure and coherence of our various important places, attending to the continuity of detailing of these places across many different projects, attending to the relative fit of one initiative with another as each new piece was added, and in recent years, attending more and more all the time to the imperatives of sustainability (I will cover this fully in Chapter 8). It has been like putting a puzzle together when you know the final image will only be discovered at the end. No one building or space dominates – this is an urban design approach of patterns and networks and themes. And this all starts with the public realm of Vancouver, or what we might view as the public container within which the private culture of the city is hosted and thrives. The design agenda of this public framework can be summarized through five essential propositions.

### Urban structure

The first proposition has to do with basic community structure. As transformation geared up, we paid a great deal of attention to the component community units that would make up the resulting city. Whether we were pursuing change through the revitalization or reuse of existing areas or by starting from scratch in the layout of the large megaproject sites, we consistently set up the overarching local structure first and then let individual initiatives go from there. The most fundamental planning and urban design format to manage change has been the localized area plan. City-wide urban design schemes have been almost non-existent. The last overall design plan for the city was way back in 1928, the Bartholomew Plan,[7] which I have already referenced. When CityPlan came along in 1995,[8] it was more an articulation of policy than a design-oriented plan. In Vancouver, the planning focus has always been on local areas. In Chapter 4, I talked about the neighbourhood as an organizing principle for new inner-city change. In addition to neighbourhood plans, we have commercial precinct plans, historic district plans, and plans for special places. There is a rich tapestry of localized area plans that overlay each other to offer the total picture for Vancouverism.

Localized area plans set the scale and pattern of streets and development sites (generally accepting historic patterns already on the ground and defining the overall new subdivisions for sites of wholesale change). They define the open space network of parks, pedestrian pathways, walkable streets, and bikeways. They direct traffic, diverting volumes to create quieter traffic areas for safety and noise management. They identify the local centres for commercial services and the infrastructure of public social and recreational facilities. And they identify for special attention any unique features of character or local attachment that need to be preserved or even enhanced. These plan areas are of many different sizes, depending in part upon natural boundaries or patterns of property ownership but also with a consciousness to make them complete walkable districts with a general intention for the five- to seven-minute walking radius from an area centre to its edges that I posited in Chapter 4.

### Urban patterns integration

The second proposition is to emphasize integration. As described in Chapter 4's discussion of the neighbourhood template, the basic intention is that new areas and existing areas should flow seamlessly into one another with maximum permeability between them. So, unlike many other cities, Vancouver has avoided that closed, inward-oriented development scenario for new urban interventions that focuses on internal coherence and limits access at the edges, sometimes to the extent of even being gated. I have already described how streets for new areas extend the prevailing alignment, pattern, and scale of the existing connecting street system. We want many links between areas, not just a few. The seawall walkway-bikeway runs continuously along the water's edge regardless of adjacent ownership, now stretching some twenty-four kilometres (fifteen miles) within the inner-city. An overlay bikeway network within the street grid is being implemented to link areas. As described earlier, an overlay of protected public views has been secured. And the morphology of buildings has been choreographed so that scale, mass, and space blend comfortably.

### Streetscapes

The third proposition is the tailored detailing of streetscapes. Urban design in Vancouver has started to move away from the simple application of street standards and zoning that is the practice in most modern jurisdictions as the way to expand or revamp the city. At least for a few important streets, instead, the functions and preferred scale are determined and then both the building massing along the street and the actual configuration of the street and sidewalk setting are custom designed for an integrated effect (see Figure 7.10). You might say it is like having clothes tailored for you rather than buying off the rack. I wish we could make this the common approach rather than one only for the special exceptions. But a start is a start.

Sometimes, the key job is to maintain and perpetuate what is already there. The elements and scale of many streetscapes have been in place for a long time, and care is taken to maintain the coherence of these places and to differentiate them from one another. As discussed in Chapter 4, the initial development form around the streetcar lines at the beginning of the last century set a pattern that remains effective today. Locally scaled retail high streets were established that today form the backbone of modern neighbourhoods. These streets and other relevant arterial streets have been magnets for densification, taking pressure off adjacent areas. Revitalization of these inner suburbs, starting in the 1970s, stayed true to these historic patterns, reinforcing and enhancing them as part of the neighbourhood retrofit.

The identity and treatment of streetscapes that extended through the inner suburbs of the original city have been inspirational for new areas in the core city where we were starting from scratch and where densification has been targeted. Guidelines for most new retail high streets include a modest setback of the retail frontage along the sidewalk to facilitate outdoor merchandising and cafe seating without overcrowding the sidewalk (see Figure 7.11). There are also guidelines on the width of individual store frontages so as to avoid blank walls and to maximize access points. There is careful formulation of the list of allowable retail uses to ensure the continuity that helps retail thrive. There are requirements for awnings and other protective overhangs, which have been aggressively implemented in our rainy climate.

In several recent initiatives, the City has also taken on the challenge of how to integrate big box retail into the streetscape without wiping out the intimate scale and character that are so desirable. Essentially, the big boxers have to break down their offerings into component parts that can be expressed and even accessed along the street. Large floorplate retail outlets often occupy upper floors, leaving smaller shops at the sidewalk (see Figure 7.12). In one case, the big box stores are overlaid by housing at the next level up, creating a true

**7.10** Like many cities, Vancouver has struggled against utilitarian street standards to bring character and uniqueness to districts, as expressed by their streets. This custom-designed example, Pacific Boulevard, is by famous street design gurus Allan Jacobs and Elizabeth MacDonald. It includes a special pattern of street trees, boulevard landscape, artful sidewalks, and custom furnishings. We can never do enough of this in Vancouver.

**7.11** This bicycle shop at the south end of Davie Street has taken full advantage of the small building setback from the property line. Other retailers along the street have outdoor cafe seating and merchandising, all without crowding pedestrians. This results in a fascinating streetscape.

mixed-use arrangement (see Figure 7.13). Parking in all cases has to be grade-separated, generally underground but in several cases up on the roof, where it can be integrated with compatible retailing such as a garden centre or auto-accessories outlet.

The story of the residential streetscape is quite different from that of retail. What exemplifies almost any typical suburban residential streetscape in most people's minds, of course, is the frontyard setback and associated landscaping. That can certainly be reinforced in revitalization of those suburbs, but it cannot be imported to higher-density streetscapes. Yet, in Vancouver as elsewhere, the initial history of residential frontages in high-density areas consisted of either blank space or blank walls and so did not satisfy contemporary needs and expectations. We had to create a new residential streetscape arrangement that would deliver the kind of livability and identity that many people wanted in their housing. We often said that we had to "domesticate" the high-density residential streetscape (see Figure 7.14).

I have already described how we came to the idea of rowhouses in the podiums of tall buildings. Now let me describe how we domesticated those townhouse frontages. We could not import the form or spaciousness of suburban residential streets, but we did take inspiration from them. We noticed that people seemed to value a component of private space at the entrance to their homes, both to use and to express their personal identity. We noticed that people liked landscaping out front. We noticed that people valued an entry or "front door" experience. So, these features became guidelines for the frontages of rowhouses. The guidelines for Downtown South, in the heart of the downtown peninsula, developed by planner Jill Davidson and urban designer Trish French, offer the typical example (see Figure 7.15). We set the front wall of the rowhouse back slightly to leave room for a small front garden. Generally, this area is landscaped to soften the hard edges of the building along the sidewalk, and residents often add their own gardening efforts to artfully personalize these spaces. To reinforce this, the boulevard area along residential streets (that space between the curb and the sidewalk) is required to be soft-landscaped rather than paved. We have had mixed results with this because the foot traffic along high-density streets can punish the grass much more than in suburban areas, but the green theme is certainly extended when at least some of this area avoids a hard, generally concrete, finishing. For each unit, we require a primary entrance directly off the sidewalk rather than off a hallway inside the building. The guidelines favour a somewhat formal expression of the front entrance so that it visually declares

**7.12** To engender retail energy along a sidewalk, it is essential to have small shop frontages and many doors, but this can be interrupted by large outlets such as food stores. One solution, as here on Robson Street, is to move the grocer upstairs to the second level, maintaining a line of small stores and other services along the sidewalk.

**7.13** This building on Cambie Street accommodates big box stores by requiring multiple entrances and discrete activities along the sidewalk, and placement of expansive floor space upstairs. The addition of housing above the retail makes it a mixed-use model. Big boxers can be intrusive, even if consumers do like them, but they can be inserted into a vibrant urban streetscape without deadening the sidewalk.

**7.14** Residential streets in apartment areas can become anonymous, with only one door along an entire block. Replicating the appeal of front doors in individual homes, this typical line of rowhouses along Richards Street features many doors and stoops. This domesticates the street for safety, interest, and personal identity.

itself and the main door (see Figure 7.16). We then require the floor of the unit to be set a few feet above the sidewalk. In part, this secures the visual privacy that people need, but it also creates a porch or stoop that evokes a house-like image, clearly communicating that the frontage is residential and not for some other use. Of course, the many front doors and stoops along the sidewalk also offer a quality of safety, and perhaps even real safety, because walkers have a sense that any door might be a sanctuary at an unsafe moment.

In addition to the special features of retail and residential streetscapes, a big theme in the Vancouver agenda is that most streets be pedestrian-friendly and walkable. This primarily requires these streets to be pedestrian-scaled, which is why the podium height is so important, but the most effective way we secure this is through the planting of trees. The general requirement is that all streets have to be lined with trees, and at higher densities in the downtown, streets without retail are planted with a double row of trees on each side of the street, one row on the grass boulevard at one edge of the sidewalk and the other row just within the property line at the other edge of the sidewalk (see Figure 7.17). This planting clearly defines a pedestrian corridor, creates a delightful green canopy that screens tall buildings, cools the sidewalk, and makes the setting much more gracious for people on foot. Arthur Erickson, the architect of Robson Square, a major government building in the heart of the city, started this approach when he planted a double row of trees all around that building complex, which was instantly popular.

In many areas, the tree-planting program is reinforced by two other important features. One is pedestrian-level lighting. Instead of lighting focused solely on the street, useful mostly to people in cars, the sidewalk has its own lighting pattern that is scaled to pedestrians. Many smart cities have installed this form of lighting, and it makes a big difference in the ambience and safety of the sidewalk after dark. The second feature consists of special decorative detailing to offer interest and delight as people walk along the sidewalk. In one neighbourhood, Triangle West, this includes manhole covers that are decorated with an Indigenous motif. In another neighbourhood, Downtown South, the concrete sidewalks are stamped with a random pattern of leaves to remind walkers of nature (see Figure 7.18). For one important retail sidewalk, along Pacific Boulevard, a colourful plaid pattern of concrete and pavers has been used (see Figure 7.19). Farther along this same sidewalk, a public art installation plays with words to echo the prehistory of the area. If only we had consistently followed through with more diversity of paving and sidewalk detailing. The quite forgettable basic

**7.15** In Downtown South, as shown by these rowhouses on Richards Street, a small setback provides a touch of landscaping that softens the hard edges of the building. A short flight of stairs adds privacy and separation. This approach has become typical for Vancouver rowhouses.

**7.16** Enlivened by summer flowers, this formal front door arrangement offers a special entrance experience. Residents express themselves by personalizing their doors and porches.

**7.17** An appealing feature in downtown residential districts, as shown here on Homer Street, is the double row of trees on each side of the street that provides a green canopy, screens tall buildings, and gives a sense of protection from adjacent traffic.

standards are still too prevalent. To counteract this in some cases, the City does sponsor a neighbourhood gardening program on public rights-of-way that was introduced as part of a city-wide effort to calm local traffic. It applies to such features as traffic circles and sidewalk bulges and the centre of cul-de-sacs in dense areas, where local people can plant whatever kind of garden features that they like and wish to pay for. It's called the "Green Streets" program, and where it has been taken up, it offers a delightful local touch. These kinds of features transform a utility application into a caprice that engages people and enhances the experience of walking.

Looking back, I wish we would have done more of all kinds of pedestrian detailing in more locations. Our experience was nothing but positive in these efforts because they so delicately humanize a part of the city, the street rights-of-way, that have been dominated by the car for far too long. These areas need to be aggressively claimed back for people on foot, and the only way to do that is to refinish them and refurnish them for walking and all the activities that come with walking. People walk more when they feel safe, comfortable, and visually engaged with interesting things along their route. We could have made this a higher priority, and the next generation should take up the baton on this.

### Amenities

The fourth proposition in the public design agenda of Vancouverism is the aggressive provision of amenities. I have already outlined the community-amenity strategy of facilities and services at the neighbourhood level (Chapter 4), but this bias toward public amenities also shapes the design of places. Vancouverism is about living fully and joyfully in public space and having the public provisions of the city enhance day-to-day livability. We have already surveyed how the City tied down the important public amenity of views, which is now seen as one of the basic attractions of the city. The amenity agenda comes to ground in the open spaces of the city with several particular imperatives.

It has been important for Vancouver that the park system is not just seen as a space of respite for the buildings nearby but that parks become the effective living rooms of the community. This means special governance, special funding, special programming, special furnishings, and designations for special uses. For decades, the residents' associations at community centres co-managed their facilities with the park board. They were assigned a budget to spend as they chose on programming at their centres and the parks in their communities. They also raised more money for projects that could not otherwise be funded. This

**7.18** In some areas, Vancouver has experimented with custom paving designs, such as the leaf shapes stamped into the concrete of this Downtown South sidewalk. It is an artful metaphor of nature. There is still much to be done to expand this tailored design attitude into other areas.

**7.19** Along the retail streets of False Creek North, where the developer, Concord Pacific, provided ample funding, an expressive plaid paving pattern provides memorable character. This view of Pacific Boulevard also shows the building setback.

fundraising has now been standardized across the city to offer more equity between neighbourhoods of differing income levels, but program funding is available, and community groups can fit programming to the needs of their particular population. A good example of distinctive programming is offered by the Roundhouse community centre in False Creek North. This centre has designated itself as an "arts" community centre, so it specializes in hosting all kinds of arts initiatives, activities, and events. It also brings neighbourhood activities and celebrations into nearby parks (see Figure 7.20).

As densities increased, we realized that the long-applied civic policy of having parks and schoolyards in separate spaces just did not work – it took up too much land. So, as described in Chapter 4, in the core city in newly developing areas, these are combined. The effect is that parks are energized by children at play on a day-to-day basis, not just when parents decide it will happen but, also, regularly and constantly by the school recess. It makes for a lively scene, where everyone more-or-less mixes up in the parks. Interestingly, initial concerns about the safety of children outside the security of the schoolyard have proven unfounded. There have been no problems, and the sharing works very well.

In the inner-city, the continuity of the seawall walkway-bikeway along the foreshore has had another benefit that shows the opportunity of networks versus separated public spaces. As the large megaprojects developed, we located their neighbourhood parks along the water, where most people preferred to be. With the seawall, they became a chain of interconnected spaces that offer a much more pervasive experience of green spaciousness and respite from the intense city than would have been available if they had been separated and isolated from one another. Stanley Park connects to the downtown beaches, which connect to all the parks that line False Creek, which connect to the English Bay beaches in Kitsilano and out to distant Jericho in Point Grey – a majestic assembly that could be replicated in any city that sees public space not just as a local resource but also as a web of connected amenity. Of course, when a consciousness of environmental systems is added to the equation, local ecological patterns can also be woven into the urban scene. This has not been systematically accomplished in Vancouver, but the potential is definitely there.

The amenity of parks is also achieved by a fine distribution of spaces. We provide a development bonus if a project delivers a space in a location where there is deficiency. We also allow transfers of bonus density to open up vest-pocket parks and other infill spaces. In Chapter 5, I described an early successful traffic-calming experiment in the West End, where portions of streets were closed, with

the spinoff benefit of creating dispersed mini-parks. We now often include closed or semi-closed spaces only useable by cars to access underground parking that would otherwise have been street area (what we call "mews" spaces) to provide small, intimate mini-parks (see Figure 7.21).

Public amenity comes from special designations of use and appropriate furnishings of parks. Of course, for use designations there are the templates for active play and sports that one sees in every city – the softball diamonds, basketball courts, soccer pitches, and tennis courts. Parks standards ensure that facilities for these high-demand activities exist in every community. Park board booking arrangements ensure maximum use and sharing. But the Vancouver parks agenda goes well beyond that. Three examples of other arrangements will give a sense of how parks are further diversified. First, there is an emphasis on articulated and designated children's playgrounds. Once we enticed young families with children to live at high density, as I described in Chapter 6, we had to provide playgrounds for those children. A diversity of play designs makes that real – play yards with the typical equipment you would expect (see Figure 7.22), water playgrounds (see Figure 7.23), water's edge exploration areas, and ecological adventure sites where kids can see nature in action. We took care that no

**7.20** Programming from the nearby Round-house community centre spills out onto David Lam Park. Such activities bring the whole area to life for local people.

**7.21** In a traditional layout, this area in False Creek North would have been an access street for underground parking. In a move to claim more space for people, it has been closed to through traffic, planted, and furnished. The parking ramp is just behind me as I took this picture. In an amusing metaphor, we came to call this a "mews" because local cars still access the ramp down to the parking – cars being the horses of today.

**7.22** Downtown parks are specially fitted out for children in the interest of drawing families to live in the inner-city. This portion of David Lam Park is typical.

**7.23** Several water parks expand the inner-city appeal for families. This one on Granville Island is especially popular on sunny days.

**7.24** In post-occupancy evaluations, downtown residents told us that dogs were important to apartment dwellers, regardless of whether they are single or have children. As a result, dog runs, like this one in Southeast False Creek became more evident in recent park designs.

poisonous vegetation was planted in these locations. We looked at design for safety and overviewing. And we saw the play equipment itself as an opportunity for serendipity. Second, we are increasingly designating and specially furnishing areas for dog runs (see Figure 7.24). We found that dogs are very important to apartment dwellers, especially for people who live alone. But sometimes there can be conflicts between dog owners and others. Creating dog parks and dog-friendly areas within parks help to diminish the friction between dog owners and dog critics. Third, a strong demand for gardening led to the allocation of garden plots in many parks and also on many leftover public lands in the city (see Figure 7.25). We learned that even when people willingly move away from single-family living, they miss the pleasures and benefits of gardening, so we are adding more locations every year for these endlessly popular personal garden allotments.

This idea of securing high amenity also stretches within the public realm beyond the officially dedicated parks – let me offer several examples.

The street tree-planting program that I discussed earlier also anchors a broader theme advocated by our arborists as the "urban forest." Trees are integral to the image of Vancouverism, but, as in most places, the spread of urbanism generally leads to their loss. To stave off these losses, our arborists are working to reinstate trees, concentrating on both their sheer numbers and their diversity. On streets and in parks, tree species are mixed to improve resilience against diseases. A strong regulatory program prohibits the random cutting down of trees on private property, with a permit required for removing them. And the old, glorious specimen trees that flourish all around the city are given special respect. We break the normal design rules in our efforts to retain them (see Figure 7.26).

Public art is now an integral part of Vancouver public spaces through a City program started in the early 1990s and expanded over the years. It includes a civic art commitment, where all new capital projects include a component of public art, a community art program of local initiatives supported by the City, and a developer requirement for public art in new projects. The result is an expanding collection of art in public places that enhances day-to-day experience in those places. Even though a recent review revealed that the program has had its ups and downs, there is no question that this art is a significant amenity that Vancouverites highly value. The developer requirement, particularly, gets top marks for consistently insinuating fine art into many locations, in comparison with similar policies in peer cities. On top of the government program, a private, non-profit initiative has had a big bang in the city. It is called the "Vancouver

**7.25** People who moved from single-family homes told us they missed their gardens. The solution was to sponsor allotment gardens in parks, such as this West End example in Nelson Park.

**7.26** Vancouverites love their majestic old trees, so we fit new street and sidewalk designs around their old favourites.

**7.27** Public art features prominently in the new Vancouver. This bronze sculpture, called *A-maze-ing Laughter,* by famous Chinese artist Yue Minjun, was installed in 2009 by the Vancouver International Sculpture Biennale. Highly popular with children and tourists, it now permanently embellishes Morton Park, at the edge of English Bay Beach in the West End, thanks to the generosity of the Wilson family.

**7.28** Another sculpture from the biennale, *King and Queen,* by Sorel Etrog, is endlessly popular in Coal Harbour Park. It certainly is a magnet for these teens.

International Sculpture Biennale," or the "Vancouver Biennale" for short. Founded in the late 1990s by art entrepreneur Barrie Mowatt, it brings world-renowned public sculpture to the city in eighteen-month-long exhibitions in parks and other public sites. When the show ends, some pieces become part of the City's permanent collection (see Figure 7.27). The Vancouver Biennale is non-government-funded and is managed in partnership with the local government. Support for the permanent installations comes from private philanthropists. The program and its regular outcomes are wildly popular with the public (see Figure 7.28).

Support for character areas is important in the repertoire of Vancouverism. Later in this chapter, I will discuss how the City manages its limited but valued heritage buildings and districts. In addition to those, however, there are many other areas that have evolved a special character or personality over the years, and these qualities are also valued, with ongoing efforts made to maintain and enhance them. This includes districts as diverse as Fairview Slopes and Burrard Slopes, south of False Creek, and the neighbourhoods of Kitsilano and Point Grey on the west side of the city. The character of these kinds of areas has to do with scale of buildings, detailing of architecture, consistency of materials, and patterns of landscape. How new development infills into these settings is a major concern. To manage this, a set of guidelines has been adopted for each area, and all new development must reflect these guidelines. In new schemes, the design community is challenged to stay compatible with the character of the setting as articulated by the guidelines while also satisfying their clients' normal expectations for the development program and contemporary needs of consumers. Since compatibility with local character is such a delicate art, these guidelines are not hard-and-fast rules. Rather, they offer a sense of direction and expectation that have to be creatively interpreted by the architects and landscape architects as they do their jobs. The result, over time and through many interventions, is that these areas have been maintained and enhanced so that they genuinely contribute to the diversity of experience that people enjoy and appreciate across the whole city.

At the top of the amenity list in any city will be its social and cultural offerings. Of course, Vancouver has its typical cultural facilities, the civic theatres, art gallery, and concert venues that connect any city to the world of culture and are generally paid from the public purse and philanthropy. But support for local culture is also important, even though there never seems to be enough money to underwrite all the programs and facilities that are called for. Vancouver leverages many of these facilities through its development management system, bonused through discretionary zoning or negotiated in rezonings. This initiative delivers diverse cultural and community offerings, from childcare centres to seniors' centres to a contemporary art gallery, a dance centre, and a film centre, and many other kinds of outlets that house non-profit cultural, social, and community activities. The mechanics for this will be covered in Chapter 9.

## Universal accessibility

The fifth and last proposition on the public side of Vancouver's urban design is universal accessibility. Mayor Art Phillips first sponsored this back in the 1970s, with a program of curb ramps on sidewalks. In the late 1980s and early 1990s, as the thinking that would result in Vancouverism was gearing up, the civic engineers realized that the responsibility for accessibility went beyond ramps. They realized that the city was not easily useable by people with mobility and visual challenges – not just the profoundly disabled but also older people and even children. This set off a continuing effort of investigation, study, and experimentation to improve performance in the public realm that is now well integrated in policy and consistently budgeted. The idea is to deliver the highest possible level of barrier-free accessibility. In the search for mobility inclusion, the City adopted seven principles of universal design, as articulated by Ronald Mace, the founder of this idea. These principles are equitable use, flexible use, simple and intuitive use, perceptible information, tolerance for error, low physical effort, and providing size and space for both approach and use.[9] The engineering documents give a clear sense of inclusiveness: "Things to consider when designing a pedestrian environment are the natural surroundings, including the weather and the users, including people that are large, people that are small, people that use wheelchairs, scooters, guide dogs, white canes, people who have hearing impairments and people who have learning disabilities."[10] Attention has been given to sidewalks and paths – size, flow patterns, surfaces, furnishings, root systems of trees, and lighting – curb ramps, road crossings, bus stop design, signage design, and parking for the disabled. This comprehensive program is retrofitting older areas to perform better and is setting high standards for newly developing areas. The megaprojects have been a good testing ground. I have heard one wheelchair-bound politician, former mayor Sam Sullivan, say that he lives in Downtown South because all the new areas are genuinely and easily accessible, so he can navigate comfortably. The same considerations extend into the design of new buildings, so the pattern of accessibility is truly becoming pervasive. This is not to say that contradictions never arise or that trade-offs are never made. Occasionally, they have to be. For example, as I described earlier, the front doors of rowhouses are reached by a short flight of stairs, and the small scale of the entrances makes the addition of ramps unrealistic. There are cogent urban design reasons for keeping the steps, so we are increasingly providing a wheelchair accessible "back door" to the units via the main building entrance. In this case, we felt the trade-off was worth the array of benefits provided to most users – an uncomfortable view but one nonetheless taken.

THROUGH ALL OF these diverse urban design efforts and considerations, the public realm is organized to bring an overall coherence to the city and to accommodate a wide use of public spaces that will augment and support what is happening on private property. But Vancouverism has also shaped the private side of the city in a pervasive way to bring the public agenda strongly into every new private project. The idea is that there should be a seamless integrity across the whole cityscape that optimizes what both government and the private sector are offering.

## MANAGING PRIVATE URBAN DESIGN PERFORMANCE FOR VANCOUVERISM

It is fair to say that there is more influence, some would even say intrusion, by the public agenda into the design and development of private property in

Vancouver than one might see in most cities. City hall tries to keep its fingers out of the style and architectural expression of a building, but it does have expectations through development approvals of aspects of massing, orientation, interfaces, adjacencies, and performance that fall within what the community has defined as the public interest. This brings a coherence and continuity to the street experience that is often admired about Vancouver, even though the tenacity to get there had to be acted out between City staff and development proponents in struggle after struggle on the detailed design of building after building. No building is exempt from this process. We worked this out and accomplished what we accomplished through a well-articulated framework of design guidelines that are administered through discretionary decisions.

*Neighbourliness*

Back in the 1970s, Ray Spaxman argued that, all too often, insensitive relationships among buildings caused unnecessary conflicts between neighbours and created a sense of crowding and claustrophobia that thoughtful design could have avoided. He suggested that, if nothing else, new buildings should be compatible with adjacent buildings and spaces, and should minimize their impact on nearby uses and people. He popularized a term that has now become one of the central words in the vocabulary of Vancouverism – he called this "neighbourliness."

The insistence on compatibility, or fit, requires that new development carefully respect, reflect, and extend its context, including the prevailing features of general local character, and that it offer comfortable direct adjacencies. This involves streetscape patterns and relative building scale, along with transitions in scale, setbacks, and components of area character. We first pursued this compatibility through the neighbourhood revitalization planning, discussed in Chapter 4, which started in the 1970s, with broad community input. Early guidelines dealt extensively with low- and mid-rise buildings, and the features of neighbourhood character to be replicated could get very specific, including building style, detailing, and materials. In other words, the guidelines were very much intruding into the details of architectural expression. There was a significant backlash from the design community and homeowners, as well as a growing understanding that fit could be achieved without always looking back to the past and while protecting the integrity of the designer to control the artful expression of the building in a contemporary way. So, a somewhat tenuous compromise was reached. In lower-density areas, where domestic issues of fit and character are controversial, style-related guidelines remain in place and have been expanded. For example, in traditional residential settings where peaked roofs are the norm, there are continuing debates about flat roofs. The key battle-grounds for this tug-of-war have often been in what are called the "conversion zones," where single-family patterns are slowly being diversified into modest-scaled multiple-family occupancy, as in Kitsilano and Grandview-Woodland. In guidelines for these areas, you will see phrases such as "blend in" and "not a place for new ground to be broken on architectural style," with urging to "use traditional architectural forms."[11] This has not led to what might be considered cutting-edge architecture in these settings, but it does offer a visual calmness that seems to appeal to many local people. Then, in the early 2000s, even the lowest-density multiple-housing zones – areas with two and three units per property – became subject to style directions if people wanted to build just a lit-tle bit more than the basic allowance. Style directions remain a focus of inquiry in these low-density character areas. Of course, historic areas get a lot of style attention because this issue is so controversial. Contrasting style can quickly blemish heritage character. A good example is the designated historic district of Shaughnessy, a locale of lovely Edwardian homes. In this area, securing details of character in new construction is felt to be vital to the preservation of the herit-age buildings themselves, along with the graciousness of the district. However, outside these areas, and as densities have increased, a more permissive, flexible attitude prevails, where compatibility and fit find quite diverse expression, as judged by the architects with a little direction from city hall. One of the senior development adjudicators for many years, Ralph Segal, offers a good example of this more tailored approach. In the early 2000s, when he and I were dealing with the expansion of the Vancouver Trade and Convention Centre, our main concern was that the building should not be a kind of black box, inwardly focused and cut off from its surroundings. We wanted to turn it inside out so that it would posi-tively engage with its waterfront setting. We also worked to carefully integrate the many-levelled public realm around the whole building. We focused on those issues in a dialogue with the architects and otherwise paid little attention to the actual architectural style of the building, although we did facilitate the dra-matic green roof that now characterizes the whole complex (see Figure 7.29).

Neighbourliness is about the interface between buildings, especially in resi-dential settings. It is about how people who live close together co-exist comfort-ably, with as much freedom as possible but also with constraints on that freedom if it negatively affects someone else. Typical considerations when new buildings infill near existing buildings include access to daylight, protection of privacy,

noise attenuation, and ensuring that one development does not compromise the development potential of adjacent sites. As in most places, attention is paid to the horizontal angles of daylight, with a requirement that all rooms receive natural light and that neighbouring buildings not block out that light. Over-shadowing of private yards is evaluated when new construction intrudes beyond the prevailing line of existing building facades – tailored setbacks may be required or the stepping down of building heights. We work with designers to juggle window openings and the distance between windows to avoid visual overviewing or at least to bring enough distance so that overviewing is not intru-sive. Screening is required when there is overviewing of private open space. Unit orientation might be shifted to take primary habitable rooms away from public walkways. We have acoustic standards for buildings and open spaces, with a lot of shifting of open areas to quieter zones where possible. To maintain adjacent developability, terracing of a building may be required. Fine-tuning proposals for neighbourliness is a sustained concern of regulation and the approval process.

One typical form of development in Vancouver, what we commonly call the "shophouse" (see Figure 7.30), exemplifies these general concerns for neigh-

**7.29** On the Coal Harbour waterfront, the Vancouver Trade and Convention Centre engages with its setting, generating activity all around the complex. Through the input of civic urban designers, the "black box" potential of such a facility was turned inside out. The vast green roof makes the building a compatible neighbour to adjacent towers.

**7.30** Mid-rise "shophouse" buildings line most local shopping streets throughout Vancouver, bringing diversity to established communities of single homes. Shophouses have retail at the sidewalk and apartments and/or offices above. Here is a typical example on Broadway, near MacKenzie Street in Kitsilano.

bourliness and fit. Over the years, the shophouse has been evolved and applied with such attention that it is now used as a model in other cities. Generally four or five storeys high, shophouses line many of Vancouver's older retail streets, threading through lower-density residential districts, with shops on the ground floor, several floors of apartments above, and maybe a floor of offices added in between.

Often, only a lane separates the shophouses from the adjacent single-family homes. This proximity can cause difficulties among neighbours, so Trish French carefully redrew the shophouse guidelines in the early 2000s. To respect the scale and privacy of nearby buildings and to create a comfortable fit between buildings, the revised guidelines include setbacks and terracing at the back of the shophouses, interfacing with the homes (see Figure 7.31). The guidelines also include neighbourliness specifications, such as I have already described, allowances for enclosed balconies, and respectful arrangements for garbage handling and loading. The resulting buildings offer clear identity as local centres, a positive framing of their streets, supportive setting for their retail, comfortable adjacency with their neighbours, and highly livable conditions for their residents.

*Livability*

Once high density and high-rise development arrived on the Vancouver scene in a big way, it became evident, as I have emphasized before, that most people do not see density as inherently good. Early dense buildings in our city, whether in the West End or Kerrisdale, tended to be austere and insensitive to people's needs and wants. They were seen as dormitories or warehouses for people who had no better alternatives. They were certainly not stylish and were seldom considered hip in the marketplace (see Figure 7.32). Unsurprisingly, many people did not find density attractive. In fact, they often avidly disliked dense buildings and districts, and they certainly had no desire to live in them. Yet with our space limitations, our growing understanding of the link between density and sustainability, and the expressed desire of people to access our majestic views, we were sure that densification and height would be good for our city – especially in our core and our distributed town centres. The challenge was to make the density of the city as appealing as, or even more appealing than, the lower-scaled alternatives (see Figure 7.33). Our strategy, as explained in Chapter 3, was to "tame" density, so it might better reflect the preferred image and needs of average consumers. The crucible for this was the complicated question of livability.

In hundreds of public discussions, we came to understand better and better what the concerns were, and we started to work toward solutions. This is why we evolved the iconic building typologies that I have already described. We opted for the slim tower, with an unusually small floorplate and specifications for separation. We added the rowhouse podium, with its very domestic frontage. We set up the hierarchy of public-to-private open space and the fully realized, useable, and attractive courtyard. We established the livable and neighbourly shophouse. Of course, the issues of neighbourliness that were initially on our agenda were pushed up a notch. For all dense buildings, we added the potential to enclose balconies, which is particularly helpful where ambient sound levels, say, from noisy streets, are high and cannot be practically mitigated. We became more systematic in private views management. For tall and dense building proposals, we started reviewing private-view impacts to take whatever measures were reasonable to preserve these views, certainly to avoid capricious blocking of neighbours' views, and even to open up new view opportunities. This has become a very sophisticated analysis in Vancouver because views translate into hard cash in real estate transactions. We became much more caring about the impacts of garbage handling. We started to worry about the interface between housing, shops, and restaurants, including loading noise, smells, and the racket of rowdy

**7.31** The neighbourliness of the shophouse has been a special concern of Vancouver's urban designers. Explicit design guidelines reconcile the relationships between these buildings and nearby single-family homes. Here is the rear facade of the shophouse shown in Figure 7.30, with its setback, terraces, and landscaping.

**7.32** Early dense buildings, like these in the West End, were generally nothing to write home about. They resembled dormitories for people who could not afford single-family houses.

**7.33** This Downtown South building is a vivid contrast to the one shown in Figure 7.32. "Taming" density through compelling building design has been a top priority, not only for developers and their architects but also at city hall. Great design attracts consumers, many consumers have created a trend, and this trend has dramatically repopulated the inner-city.

late-night customers. We started to take more care with signage, particularly to avoid the impacts of sign lighting and kinetic patterns on neighbours. In Chapter 6, I summarized a whole suite of guidelines and requirements to more comfortably house families at high density and to make this housing naturally attractive to households with children. Arriving full circle back where we began, our urgent livability concerns were key drivers in fully realizing the urban design and amenity agenda for public space and complete neighbourhoods that I have already described.

Let me talk more about open space on private property. I have already told the story of courtyards, but significant opportunity to expand the availability and utility of open spaces has also been afforded by the occupation of roofs (see Figure 7.34). Green roofs have had a long history in Vancouver, long before they became popular and a part of the sustainable urbanism tool kit. In our case, the move to green roofs was a very gradual process. In early developments, such as Southwest False Creek and Fairview Slopes, the mid-rise, stepped design vocabulary resulted in private roof gardens as a regular feature, especially on sloped sites. People became accustomed to them, architects enjoyed including them, and developers saw their added value. As we moved into higher density and scale, we naturally saw accessible roofs as the way to dramatically increase unit amenity and appeal. This also extended to commercial buildings and even became a dramatic feature in our new central library. Large terraces became the norm wherever a roof was contiguous with useable indoor space – either for private use or for all the residents of a building (see Figure 7.35). Roofs are landscaped but also fitted out with inviting furnishings. Some roofs have even become market gardens, delivering produce to nearby restaurants and homes. Once the trend was fixed in the public consciousness, we have never looked back, and civic policies have been amended to facilitate green roofs and make them more typical. With front stoops, green courtyards, balconies, enclosed balconies, and green roofs, we achieved the kind of hierarchy of open space in the private realm that is both attractive and useful and that extends similar efforts in the public realm.

Another important area of management at high density is overall building heights. In an urban setting, the ambient scale of buildings can instill a quite intuitive sense of comfort or discomfort – the drive is to decrease heights to maintain a human scale. The exploitation of urban land always puts pressure to increase heights. In principle, we have not seen this as a bad thing in Vancouver, in part because the built mass of the city always seems minor set next to the mountains. But our concern about livability always caused us to want local

**7.34** Green roofs like this one on Homer Street were part of the Vancouver design agenda long before the movement swept North America. When space is tight, any flat surface can become a garden.

**7.35** The roof of this tower on Hornby Street is a garden and event place that is shared by residents. It is part of the hierarchy of public and private open spaces that provides the green setting for most inner-city neighbourhoods.

government to have control of building heights. Outside the inner-city, this was done through quite fixed maximum building heights in residential areas and the commercial precincts that served them. Within the inner-city, the story was a little more complicated. For most of the time after Spaxman put in place the downtown zoning in the early 1970s, as introduced in Chapter 1, there was a pattern of sub-areas of various heights that more or less echoed the topography of the peninsula. These were areas of specified but negotiable maximum heights, but, in addition, no building could exceed an overlaid non-negotiable height of just over 137 metres (450 feet). In practice, most development stayed consistent with the sub-area height that was specified. But the zoning did allow greater height, up to the overall fixed maximum, to be considered by planners on a case-by-case basis, where the developer made a compelling argument of delivering significant public benefits. As time went on and this discretionary system became more regularized, with benefits better codified, more and more height negotiations were successful. So a diversity of heights resulted, but all within the maximum ceiling. This maintained a scale to the city that most people felt was a comfortable balance between impacts on people and compatibility with the mountain setting. The final iteration to diversify heights beyond this ceiling in the inner-city has already been described – the skyline study where, for emphasis, several locations were designated for extra height above the general ceiling. And, then, from this study, further refinements have been made through recent years. Vancouver's tallest building now stands at just over 180 metres (600 feet), and the City continues to be open-minded about additional focal points of height (see Figure 7.36). To be considered for that special opportunity, developers are required to meet the highest standard of design excellence, as judged by a special panel of design peers with explicit expertise in tall buildings, and must offer extraordinary amenities.

In articulating all of these design guidelines and practices, we were essentially looking at high-density living from the consumer perspective, with the intention to deliver a "wow" experience. We hoped people would feel the potential of that positive experience when they first considered high-density living and would enjoy its real benefits when they actually began their adventure in what was a very different lifestyle for most of them.

### Safety and security

The next area of general public concern for private development that garnered significant attention from city hall has been safety and security. Vancouver is

**7.36** Vancouver's inner-city is a place of tall towers, but building heights have always been carefully managed. At predetermined locations, extra height is possible to create emphasis. One of downtown's tallest buildings is seen here, as punctuation in the otherwise undulating skyline.

quite a safe city, with lower crime rates than are often seen in North American cities. Even so, from early on in the development of guidelines, we paid attention to safety and security because high-density living had a bad rap on this front from many consumers. We tried to enhance casual surveillance of public areas (what Jane Jacobs described as "eyes on the street").[12] We fostered what is called "defensible space" by designing in safety features and designing out unsafe aspects. We worked for a sharp definition and identification of the public and private domains – a clarity of boundaries. We urged careful public-access controls for private spaces such as yards or lobbies. We paid attention to security in grade-separated parking facilities – management of access, ease of exiting, and open visibility within the lots. Then, in the 1990s, a movement swept North America – "CPTED," or "crime prevention through environmental design." This movement found rave supporters in Vancouver's local government circle, bringing a deeper attention to safety and security by articulating design considerations that can protect any building and space against common crimes. Urban designer Mary Beth Rondeau worked with police department staff to apply the general CPTED principles to the Vancouver situation and enshrine them in guidelines that were imported into most of the City's regulatory documents.

### Architectural expression

I have already said that, in the design management of private development in Vancouver, planners have tried to stay arm's length from the style of architectural expression chosen by developers and their design teams. This has always been a tricky business in the art of Vancouverism. What represents a component of area character in the articulation or finishing of a building, and what represents the art of architecture for the building designer? The honest truth is that judgments have shifted from time to time and as various people held responsibility for making those judgments. Sometimes, though, wills have simply collided and the results have been acted out on the public stage, leaving confusion in many minds. Take the case of the dark glass that sheathed a downtown building developed by Peter Wall in the early 2000s. The City had a long-standing guideline against dark glass, which was felt to exacerbate the dull greyness of our long winters, so Wall's building was approved with the stipulation that it must use clear glass. However, after construction began, it was noticed that dark glass had been substituted for the approved shade of glass. A stop to construction was issued and after long negotiation, architect James Cheng, at my request, brokered a deal: the City accepted that the dark glass already installed could stay in place, but the remainder of the building must be finished with clear glass. Years later, with a new generation on the scene at city hall, Wall went back to the City, applying to replace the clear glass with dark glass, and that too was approved. So goes the ebb and flow of civic artistic judgment. In another case, at the Athletes Village, built for the 2010 Olympic Games in Southeast False Creek, the developers initially indicated that a form of neo-classical style was in their minds. The City's urban designer, Scot Hein, did not pounce, but he was concerned that the style might not be in line with the image of Vancouver. There were no civic guidelines directing his response or any policy on style, but Hein did tap the views of peers in the design profession to test his reaction. They shared his concern. Through a delicate process of thoughtful discussion, the planners and the developers identified a typology that was acceptable to both, and the issue was sidestepped.

What have been more influential in the architecture that emerged during the time of Vancouverism are three factors. First, our generation concentrated on residential buildings because very few office or cultural buildings were being constructed during this time. For a typical residential building, it is difficult to include those dramatic architectural flourishes that the budgets of commercial and cultural buildings accommodate and that clients insist upon. It is more likely than not that buildings will resemble one another – budgets are tight, consumers worry about ongoing operating costs, developers prefer building designs they know will easily sell, and buildings are often built by one developer in clusters. Residential buildings are usually the background buildings, built very well in Vancouver and with elegant simplicity, but not often as architectural statements (see Figure 7.37). Second, the period of Vancouver's most profound transformation, particularly in the inner-city, was very brief. By contrast, architectural styles and design preferences, like other cultural expressions, go through slow cycles. During the formation of Vancouverism, there were few of these cycles. Certain themes of architectural expression have been popular – such as pale-green glass during the early 2000s – and these have been replicated over and over again, without the insistence or involvement of city hall (see Figure 7.38). Contrary to popular belief, there has never been a design guideline for pale-green glass in Vancouver. Third, and probably most importantly, the overwhelming preference of most of the design community throughout the postwar period in Vancouver has been for a clear and consistent modernism. In a town where design matters and where distinguished designers are put in influential positions on private development teams and in public advisory reviews,

peer pressures have had more impact than any civic guideline. Unlike many cities, Vancouver has had little interest in trends of post-modernism or in replicating historical styles, so conflicts regarding style have actually been few and far between.

### THE SPECIAL ANXIETY FOR HERITAGE

In relative terms, Vancouver is not very old. It has not been embellished with the dense collection of great heritage buildings that can be a powerful component of character and storytelling about a city. In this respect, the city is unlike neighbouring places such as Seattle and Portland to the south that enjoy wide-ranging heritage character. Although long a site of Indigenous villages, little remains except what might be discovered by archaeologists. Europeans did not settle here until the 1860s, and the place was a small town for decades after that. Around the turn into the twentieth century, there was a spurt of major buildings – and quality buildings – as the city took a more prominent place in Canada and the British Empire. After the Second World War, a strong culture of West Coast modernist architectural expression flourished for private homes, but Vancouver's larger downtown buildings were quite typical of many smaller North American cities. The bottom line is that the city has comparatively few

**7.37** In Vancouver, contemporary residential buildings are very well built but tend not to be architectural statements. Instead, they offer a coherent setting for the spectacle of public life, as seen here at the Roundhouse plaza. Recently, developers and their architects have started to explore more expressive designs, which is all to the good.

**7.38** The pale-green glass that is often seen on buildings from the period of Vancouverism – sometimes pervasive, as illustrated by this building ensemble – was not a city hall specification. Architects and their clients freely selected it.

heritage buildings and historic districts, so each heritage resource is all the more valuable.

Having said that, until the 1970s, we were not careful custodians of our heritage. Because the small scale and value of most historic buildings formed such a stark contrast to modern development potential, the real estate and development community found it hard to save old buildings and make a profit at the same time, so those buildings were constantly demolished. Compounding this problem was the fact that the City had almost no civic authority to deal with the situation. Only the Province could designate heritage, but, of course, it was pretty removed from the local scene – although that freeway drama that I have alluded to often in this story did lead to the heritage designation of Gastown and Chinatown in 1971, an early nail in the coffin of what would have been a grotesque demolition. At least in these areas, we could forestall heritage losses and look for alternative solutions to secure what was in place. We now see it as fortunate that these areas were also becoming economic backwaters, so there was little demand for new construction. As in many cities, this may have been the biggest factor in saving Gastown and Chinatown. In 1973, we finally got the civic right to designate properties and create heritage advisory committees. The City moved promptly to confirm unilateral designations of about fifty of the most obvious heritage buildings. But there was a backlash. In 1977, the Province brought in a new heritage conservation act that introduced what some would now see as deliberate ambiguity. The resulting legal interpretation was that a property owner had to freely accept heritage designation – and owners expected compensation for any financial value lost. Few were willing to do this voluntarily, and there was no money or political will for compensation. So, we lost a lot of great buildings.

As the city approached its hundredth birthday in 1986, there was a strong anxiety about this unsatisfactory state of affairs for heritage. Every lost building set off a political struggle, with an ever-growing sense of doom among heritage advocates. But, finally, help was on the way. Mayor Mike Harcourt initiated a program, to be completed for the big civic birthday, to put in place a heritage inventory, a heritage management plan, and a program of public information. Experienced community planners, first Dan Cornejo and then Jeannette Hlavach, led a team of staff, consultants, and a lot of volunteers to do the work, with help from citizens all over the city. In the new inventory, now called the "heritage registry," almost three thousand buildings, areas, landscapes, and archaeological sites were identified. To this day, the registry remains the foundation for securing our heritage – it does not provide protection, but it cues everybody when heritage is in play and starts the process to save it. The registry is updated on an ongoing basis, even though many would say that, after many years, it needs an overhaul to bring it up to date with new thinking that now embraces intangible factors and what are called "cultural landscapes." The management plan that came out of these efforts put in place for the first time incentives to motivate owners to save heritage and accept designation. This included zoning relaxations and fast tracking for civic permits. It also started the City thinking about a heritage foundation that could up the ante even further. This all set the stage for heritage as one of the themes of Vancouverism.

Changing times, attitudes, and governments brought more tools to align interests to proactively save our heritage. In 1994, the Province extensively upgraded the City's heritage powers. A key new tool was the "heritage revitalization agreement" (shorthanded as HRA), which facilitates conservation of a heritage building because it can vary uses and densities. Vancouver was given a then quite unusual power to establish a heritage density transfer system. Under the terms of an "HRA," the owner of the building accepts the heritage designation and agrees to restore and maintain the structure in an agreed upon manner. In exchange, the City grants extra density for development to the heritage site. This density can be built on the site or on another site – in other words, the density can be moved around. Here is how it works. A calculation is done of the cost of a tightly assessed restoration plan along with lost opportunity costs, based upon what is called a "statement of significance" (our "SOS"), defining the heritage features of the building to be saved. This cost is then converted into an equal value of developable density, which is vested on the property through the HRA. Since accommodating this extra density typically involves demolishing or damaging heritage buildings, the owner is allowed to sell the density. In a transaction that is carefully monitored by the City, it is transferred from the heritage site (called the "donor site") to another site (called the "receiver site"). The City ensures that the added density will comfortably fit in with neighbouring buildings on the receiver site. Transactions involving transferred density occur through the open market, without civic regulation or control, as a sub-sector of the wider free real estate market of the city. The HRA framework was the big breakthrough that offered tangible resources for heritage owners to cover their premium costs for rehab of buildings, thus compensating them for accepting the heritage designation. Before the advent of the HRA framework and associated transfer strategy, many owners felt that having a building identified as heritage was a liability. The new tools converted heritage into an opportunity, because the City program covered the extra costs of holding and managing what was seen as a community asset. An untold number of buildings have been saved and restored through this program. When I took over directorship of heritage as one of my co-director portfolios, I used the program avidly. Sadly, a supposedly temporary brake was put on the program in recent years because city hall felt that too much density had accumulated in what was called the "density bank." This is not actually a bank. Rather, it refers to the prevailing total of saleable density held on various sites. In any event, city hall was concerned that the build-up of unused density could cause the value of all that density to collapse. Many in the real estate industry did not see a need to suspend the program, because there was little evidence of market distortion. I worry about the effect of having put the program on hold. The stall may ultimately limit the program in a big way because it might be made available in future to so few buildings, or people might lose confidence in holding density for sale and transfer. That would be a big shame. There is no doubt that positive tools are needed, as without them, heritage seems to just melt away over time.

For the prime heritage districts of Gastown and Chinatown, a more proactive approach has been necessary. Both of these areas are very special. Both are densely packed with heritage buildings and complete heritage streetscapes, which are rare anywhere. Gastown, the original townsite of the city, has a lovely stand of Victorian and Edwardian buildings. Its streetscape had received a make-over in the 1970s, during which the now famous steam clock was added (see Figure 7.39). But the area was languishing and falling into disrepair. Chinatown, the designated district for Chinese immigrants during the time in our early history when there was legal segregation, also has great turn-of-the-century buildings with very evocative Asian motifs (see Figure 7.40). It received a lovely traditional garden, designed by architect Joe Wai, in the 1970s and its own cultural centre shortly thereafter. Fortunately, people of Chinese descent now live everywhere, but there was a downside for Chinatown. Its traditional consumers have dispersed, which led to a slow decline of the area. The economic slump in both areas may have helped to save old buildings from demolition, but it certainly did not motivate their conservation and restoration. I, for one, became very anxious about these districts – they needed a kick-start for revitalization. So, in the early 2000s, I tasked planners Marco d'Agostini and Nathan Edelson to put together a special time-limited program for these areas. It offered the bonus/transfer opportunity as well as grants and other support for facelifts of heritage facades. Tax relief was made available to reinforce the value of bonus density, given the much higher costs of restoring the often poorly constructed buildings. In Gastown, this special program has had a boom effect, particularly because of the efforts of several developers. One key one was Robert Fung who restored and repurposed a cluster of buildings near Gassy Jack Square. He tenanted these buildings with young vibrant tech and design companies as well as housing (see Figure 7.41). Another was the Bendtsen family, which had long anchored its worldwide retail and furniture business, Inform Interiors, in the area. They did a beautiful restoration of several buildings and ignited a lot of other merchant interest. The incentive scheme and the efforts of these pioneers prompted a strong revival of the district. It has now caught on with millennials as a hotbed of high-tech start-ups and with retailers as a hip shopping district. It is also popular because housing, being located in older buildings, is a little more affordable than in other downtown locations. Gastown is no longer the worry that it used to be for heritage aficionados and city planners. Unfortunately, the same cannot be said for Chinatown. The incentive scheme has certainly been taken up in some instances in this district (see Figure 7.42), but several conditions have mitigated its positive impacts. For one thing, many sites are owned by family "tongs," these being clan associations or societies that hold their properties as a legacy of

**7.39** Gastown is the original townsite of Vancouver and a heritage treasure. The popular steam clock, a 1970s addition, entertains tourists on Water Street.

**7.40** Chinatown, one of the largest and most authentic in North America, is also a cherished heritage district in Vancouver. The depth of public affection for Chinatown is indicated by the recently added Millennium Gate, which includes an insightful declaration "Remember the past and look forward to the future."

**7.41** Gastown has been restored and revived for a new hip demographic, kick-started by an attractive civic incentive program taken up by developers such as Robert Fung.

**7.42** The heritage incentive program has had mixed results in Chinatown, but one highlight was realtor Bob Rennie's careful restoration of its oldest buildings, the Wing Sang complex, for both his offices and his private art museum. Density from the old building site was transferred to the new building next door, seen on the right in this photograph, thus removing any future redevelopment option and saving the site's heritage for the foreseeable future.

their long roots in Vancouver but have little inclination to exploit them through normal market opportunities. In 2014, a further grant and support program was approved to conserve the twelve tong heritage buildings, most of which are over a hundred years old. But that may not be enough. There is continuing interest in new development, which has been spurred on by the searing inner-city market. Many people still feel that historic Chinatown and its character are in danger and that more needs to be done.

The heritage march goes on in Vancouver, which is a good thing. In 2009, Gastown was designated a national historic site, followed by Chinatown in 2011. Many people now feel that the battlefront needs to shift away from the obvious buildings to the smaller, less recognized resources that are scattered throughout the city.

## AN INCOMPLETE REALIZATION OF URBAN DESIGN FOR VANCOUVERISM

Although Vancouver has paid very aggressive attention to urban design for the last few generations, there is so much more that needs to be done. Urban designer Trish French and I have reminisced that one of the pleasures of Vancouver's urban design approach has been the flexibility to tackle problems as they become important, to evolve, and to leave some concerns behind – an alertness to challenges, critiques, new situations, and dilemmas. I have already identified some design moves that did not work out the way we had hoped. It remains a quest to improve on these ideas. But even more importantly, there are new realities that need to be further addressed. No story about Vancouverism would be complete without being up front about what could be better.

The most pervasive commentary that has been made about Vancouver's approach to urban design is that it has not led to dramatic architectural expression or extraordinary architectural icons for our city. Many people are critical that the overbearing attention of the City on every project has limited the range of great architecture. They have also argued that this has led to a uniformity of architecture across many buildings and areas. These criticisms are both false and true.

After some early meddling with the specific architecture of buildings, particularly in our lower-density residential character areas, the urban designers at city hall began to discipline themselves on larger proposals to attend to factors of public concern and leave the actual architecture to the architects and their clients. Few of our guidelines for dense areas or comprehensively planned projects target architectural expression or mandate specific detailing or uniformity, and they certainly do not insist on an architectural style. I described earlier the cultural and economic factors that have set the private design agenda. These factors have been much more influential than civic intervention. A lot of the uniformity we see in recent Vancouver architecture has been the result of the free workings of the market and the trends of design culture rather than the oppression of city hall.

Nonetheless, I think we did constrain wide architectural expression in some ways, even if we did not mean to do so. So, as recent chief planner Brent Toderian has advocated, we need to find ways to open up the freedom of design in our city. The clear articulation of City guidelines and the influence that is wielded by the planners who administer them can result, by accident, in architectural reticence, especially when a client pushes the architect to get on with the project. Critical reactions through public engagement can foster, again by accident, conservatism in design. From time to time, it is useful for those who administer the guidelines at city hall to go through a systematic self-assessment to confirm that they are not allowing personal taste and preferences to cloud their judgment on interpretations of guidelines. One easy measure to open up more creativity would be to suspend normal guidelines for especially iconic sites and go, instead, for a one-off dialogue with the proponents. This could also be done consistently for important civic buildings, and city council could add budget and imperative for design excellence, as has been done, for example, with federal court buildings in the United States. Another effort, following a practice set by Toderian, would be to deliberately urge developers to hire innovative architects for important, strategically located sites – with the intent to push the bar higher in all architectural performance. We require this for buildings where developers are going after the highest heights, over the specified limits, but we could throw the net wider, at least through persuasion if not through regulation. It is interesting to see that, in recent times, a few developers have picked up on the benefits of exemplary architecture and, without pressure from city hall, have started sponsoring much more cutting-edge design. Ian Gillespie of Westbank Developments comes to mind, and his recent "Vancouver House" building by Danish architect Bjarke Ingels is an exemplar. These developers have decided that good design sells at a premium, which may be the most influential factor that will enhance the architectural performance in Vancouver for the future. After all, the regulatory process should do the job of denying approval to bad design and insensitive, unneighbourly schemes, but it can never ensure great design. That is the challenge of creative architects and informed builders. But the City has to get out of the way in some respects to let that happen. There is no question that consumer trends will be much more influential than all regulations put together, so we have to focus consumer interest on better design products, as has occurred in other design sectors. If developers produce great architecture, consumers will come to expect more and even better architecture, creating a virtuous circle of demand and supply that is quite independent from any attention at city hall.

Another criticism of Vancouver's high-density urban design is that we have overused towers (see Figure 7.43). In Downtown South, though we set a mid-rise height for all buildings, we rewarded developers if they assembled a site big enough for a tower. Even if such suitable sites could not be put together, developers came to expect that a smaller site could nonetheless achieve its tower if the developer imported bonus density from other locations. Towers came to dominate the whole area. The tower is undoubtedly a great building form, but it can become overwhelming if it is used indiscriminately. Fortunately, we started diversifying our thinking, with the urban design of places where the tower just did not fit in, such as the new Arbutus Neighbourhood, along central Broadway, and in the Burrard Slopes area. This came to a head in the late 1990s in the initial designs for Southeast False Creek, an area I will discuss more fully in Chapter 8. In that case, the City's real estate team led the project because it was on City-owned land. Their designers, along with my team, spent several years sketching tower-based master plans. The Southeast False Creek megaproject is adjacent to Mount Pleasant, a more modest-scaled neighbourhood, with historic patterns and a delicate mix of buildings and uses. As the planning director, I felt increasing anxiety that a forest of tall towers would be out of place in such a district. It was not the way to go. But it was hard to argue against the tower scenario because it generally performs well, is very popular, and offers very little economic risk to developers. Civic real estate staff said, "It works, so why shift away from it?" City hall and politicians were heavily vested in the existing scenario that people had worked hard to put together. I feared this was one of the few times that I might have to put my job on the line by going public and ultimately recommending against the towers scheme. As it happened, members of the design community in Vancouver were having the same second thoughts as I was. I made my views known to them and egged them on to declare their concerns. They started communicating to city hall that a prevalence of towers in that situation was not appropriate. In fact, I dare admit now, all these years later, that I assisted them behind the scenes in their communications with the politicians.

**7.43** Towers are undoubtedly the preferred Vancouver paradigm. Some say we have overused towers and that more building diversity is needed.

**7.44** In the early design of Southeast False Creek, public reaction to yet another tower-podium proposal inspired a dramatic reset in favour of a mid-rise scheme, which produced the lovely buildings shown here. Arthur Erickson's low-rise community centre is prominent in the foreground closest to the water. ▶

They argued that the city needed to have a diversity of neighbourhood types, even at high density, so that people had better choices on where and how they lived. They argued that there is a suitability of scale that makes sense in varying settings. Their arguments were my arguments. With some of the recent alternatives in mind, we joined forces, convincing the city manager and city council to let us sketch an alternative – with the same density and population targets but in a mid-rise form. I commissioned Norm Hotson, a distinguished architect, urban design consultant, and good friend, to conceptualize the new scheme and it became the form-setting direction for the project (see Figure 7.44). The new concept was embraced – problem solved. Then, several years later, the prime developer, the Millennium Development Group, under the artful leadership of the Malek brothers, had many architects deliver the individual buildings. After I had departed from the City, the senior urban designer, Scot Hein, choreographed it all from city hall, addressing the hundreds of issues that really made it work well. Since then, mid-rise building formats have become a more regular part of the repertoire of Vancouverism – the newer buildings along South Cambie Street, sponsored by the planners who took over from my generation, illustrate a whole strategy built on mid-rises. Also, small sites downtown are no longer automatically approved for receipt of transferred density. But I fear we will continue with the tower bias unless we are very sensitive to the uniqueness of differing places

in our city. Some recent projects, situated more-or-less randomly outside the inner-city, are particularly worrisome – especially if citizens start to push back, as they recently did regarding the planning around Commercial and Broadway in Grandview-Woodland and for several tower proposals in Mount Pleasant.

A third issue has to do with affordability. As I have already fully discussed in Chapter 6, affordable housing has become the single biggest issue facing Vancouver as it continues to evolve. In looking for mitigation of high costs, we have not tapped our urban design tradition or prowess. The demand for urban design performance seems to care little for cost factors. I have never believed that a city should trade off its essential quality or character just to make things cheaper, but I do believe that design can be just as much a tool for affordability as it is for luxury. For example, I can see great potential for "sharing" solutions brought into the design of our neighbourhoods. Careful design could show us how to deliver co-housing, not just for a few seniors but also for young families and extended families and alternative households. Careful design could show us how to offer amenities that are shared among buildings rather than being provided separately within each building. Design innovation could show us how to accommodate what are now private home functions in public settings. We are starting to see interesting design solutions for sharing in the Nordic countries, as I mentioned in Chapter 6, which might well find application in Vancouver. And new design solutions could open up ways to overlay multiple functions in any one space and offer options for organizing and allocating space differently over time as household needs and economic circumstances change, bringing much more flexibility in the use of space than is now possible. Vancouver has to empower its sophisticated architects, landscape architects, and interior designers to experiment on the affordability front, and we have to sponsor the results.

A particularly frustrating issue concerns the spotty nature of public-realm improvements and the inconsistent custodianship of the public improvements and design flourishes that have been achieved. In most new developments, especially in the megaprojects, the finishing of public places is characterized by high design (see Figure 7.45). However, quite similar public places in the older parts of the city have languished and fallen into disrepair. A basic and unattractive standard prevails for their sidewalks, with little variation other than raw concrete (see Figure 7.46). No character whatsoever is embedded in these treatments. Furniture forms are basic and utilitarian. Sidewalks are cluttered with random additions collected over time. In a city that prides itself on its good looks, this is a real disappointment, especially because public places remain central to the compelling image of our city.

Maintenance and upkeep are just as problematic. Over the years, cleanup of the public realm has been cut back, in a direction exactly the opposite of most competitive cities. Of course, the culprits have been the politicians and senior officials who set the operating budgets. In recent years, a lot of typical maintenance funding has been diverted to the shiny new toys that are always seen as more popular. This is starting to backfire, big time. Our streets, sidewalks, and parks are littered with garbage and damaged features. Our hodgepodge approach to sidewalk repairs is especially frustrating. A grinding machine randomly slices away concrete if a sidewalk bucks up and is no longer exactly flat. Instead of replacing the sidewalk, the City just grinds away the blip, creating a permanent blight. Regardless of their original finishes, streets and sidewalks

**7.45** This tailored wood paving in Southeast False Creek is reminiscent of a pier, perfectly suited to the waterfront setting.

**7.46** Given what is going on along this downtown street, its standard sidewalk of raw concrete is a sad under-statement – no colour, no texture, no pattern, no character. Yes, it does the job, but in an unnecessarily boring way.

are patched with asphalt, so their aesthetic patterns are obscured under a random assemblage of black blemish after blemish. The City does most of this to cut insurance liabilities because it is a self-insured corporation. It takes the cheapest and fastest approach to fix the glitches to avoid being sued if there are accidents in the public realm. A tough consequence of this expediency is blight of the public realm wherever an insurance liability has been identified. This saves a lot of money for the City, but it costs a lot of money for people who depend upon tourism and other activities that need an attractive setting, not to mention the impacts on citizens in their experience of the city on a day-to-day basis. They see their communities gashed and wounded. It is a high frustration to see the expensive furnishings and finishes of a public area, for which I negotiated so long and hard, demolished in an afternoon, seemingly never to be replaced. This whole practice has to be reformed, and deep-sixing the concrete grinder would be a great, symbolic first step. I have to admit, also, that some of the special treatments we put in place have not been robust enough. Every year, the detailing of the sidewalks in Downtown South falls apart a little more. We should have been mindful of more hardy solutions – and, it has to be said, the current custodians could also be a little more protective.

We urgently need a new dedication to a quality public realm, with high design, ample funding, and top-priority implementation. We also need a new maintenance program that restores finishes and furnishings rather than defaces them. Until this happens, the existing messy status quo will stand as a blunt contradiction to the best of Vancouverism.

As we look to the future, there are two major challenges that Vancouver's urban design culture has to take on in the next generation.

The first challenge is to put our minds to the urban design solutions that will be necessary looking out from the core to more dispersed areas, even within the older districts in Vancouver but also in the suburbs. Outdated settings have to be brought in line with contemporary principles for environmental compatibility and repair as well as contemporary expectations for livability and civic services. The focus during the consolidation of Vancouverism was, first and foremost, on the inner-city and then on a very few outlying districts – making these places better, primarily through clever densification. This included community-upgrade areas, such as in Marpole and the Arbutus Neighbourhood, and large sites, such as the East Fraser Lands along Marine Drive, that have become available from time to time. But the city of the future must be livable and sustainable everywhere – and this has to do with a lot more than just density. Early positive moves in this direction were the legalization of secondary suites and the neighbour-friendly modifications to the shophouses along major suburban streets, both already described. But after that, things went quiet. More recently, beyond the heyday of Vancouverism, the discussion in the close-in older neighbourhoods has been kick-started by the introduction of what is called "eco-density," pushed forward by Brent Toderian from an initial idea by Mayor Sam Sullivan. In the late 2000s, Toderian shepherded an eco-density charter that brought the themes for densification into the neighbourhood policy framework beyond the expectations of past area planning. With planner Ronda Howard, he also led the introduction of laneway houses in the backyards of suburban homes, fostering what he calls "gentle density" (see Figure 7.47). Intensification of the Cambie Corridor was another special focus of attention in these years. But these are only initial moves. Solutions outside the inner-city must go well beyond just the trajectory of densification and developer interest in residential towers on special sites. No one is paying enough attention to other vital aspects, such as the range and cost of housing, the range of types of households accommodated, the quotient of parks and open space, street standards, community facilities, and special features. Just as, in our generation, every aspect of downtown living and working was reviewed and changed, so too will the next generation have to do this for the balance of Vancouver neighbourhoods, echoing the work that was completed back in the 1970s and 1980s, when realities differed radically from those of today. So must the ever-moving wheel of planning continue. Until this happens, all Vancouver's other successes will remain a minority endeavour not touching the larger footprint of the whole city.

The second challenge was brought to my attention by Andrés Duany, the distinguished American New Urbanist. During the early 2000s, we worked together on the East Fraser Lands, one of those suburban development nodes in the southeast sector of Vancouver. At one point, we took the opportunity to survey and discuss the state of Vancouverism up close. Duany expressed admiration for the achievements of our urban design agenda, but he made one unique criticism that I now see as particularly insightful. He noticed that the practice of custom shaping and detailing of our buildings for their designated uses is significantly restricting any flexibility for reuse and shifting use over the long run. He felt that this is becoming more and more evident as densities go up in our building formats. He wondered if this lack of flexibility would limit the resilience of the city to change over time and to meet new demands. As inspiration, if not as actual models, he offered the example of nineteenth-century warehouse buildings and

**7.47** Density is gentle when units and people are delicately added within an existing neighbourhood. A second house has been slotted into the backyard of this Mount Pleasant property – very discreet but eminently livable.

**7.48** From a design perspective, Vancouver is no longer an "accidental" city – it is very deliberately designed in a collaboration of diverse interests that reconciles complex public and private needs. The result is both logical and graceful. ▶

eighteenth-century terrace-house buildings, which seem able to take on almost any use as need be over time. He worried that we would probably have to rebuild our city over the years as new patterns emerge, which will be very expensive as well as environmentally indefensible. I think Andrés Duany is right about this. A big job for the next generation will be to evolve all our building types with a thought for diversity of use and maybe even diversity of tenure so that they will be more and more responsive to whatever is demanded of them as time goes by, without demolition. I cannot see that anyone in Vancouver is thinking about this. My generation certainly did not do so either.

Perhaps this is the very beauty of a dynamic city – the art of it is never complete; it is always in a process of change and reform. When it comes to urban design, the advantage of Vancouverism is that we understood the value of applied design and developed the capacity and skills to achieve design intentions. We felt that design mattered, that it was worth fighting for, that it was valuable, and that it could make our lives better. Hand in hand with the design community, we convinced the public, the consumer, and the development industry that this was true. Through Vancouverism, we have left behind the notion that the accidental city is the only city that we can ever hope to achieve (see Figure 7.48).

Now there is an explosion of consciousness all over the world about environmental responsibility and urban compatibility with nature. This will bring yet a further evolution of the social and physical design of the city. Sustainability is the rising priority of Vancouverism, as the current leadership attempts to position our city in the vanguard of the green movement. The next chapter will explore the roots of this and reflect on what will happen to the city as it makes its green mark.

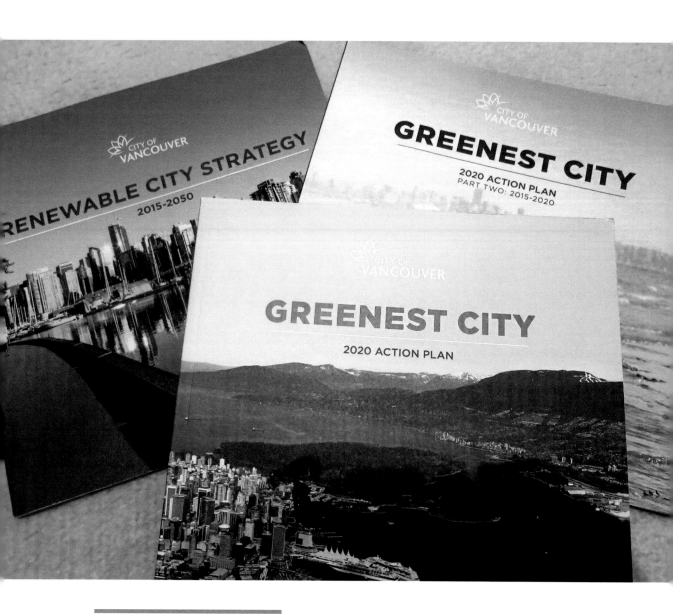

**8.1** These "greenest city" manifestos of a new generation will transcend Vancouverism.

# 8

# ENVIRONMENTAL RESPONSIBILITY

**MY GENERATION PROVIDED** the solid foundations for sustainability, but we cannot take credit for a comprehensive agenda. That came much later. Called the greenest city initiative, it has been elaborated in great detail by the current leadership at city hall into a commendable wide-ranging policy, a set of clear targets, and an aggressive action plan. The intent is to produce significant results in advanced urban sustainability for the whole city as soon as 2020 and profound results by 2050 (see Figure 8.1). But the greenest city advocates did not start with a tabula rasa. I have already mentioned Greenpeace and David Suzuki as Vancouver originals who fostered an early mindset in our city. During the genesis of Vancouverism, we were also setting the stage for sustainability, though without necessarily realizing it. This chapter surveys our initial green moves, perhaps as a prelude to a fuller outline of current and pending sustainability initiatives, which someone else will put on the table. I am sure that they will tell their own story, all in good time.

Yes, from the beginning, we were certain that a more intensive, diverse use of land, taking development pressures off the urban edge, must be good for the environment. But, because land is scarce in Greater Vancouver and always has been, we would naturally have tended to use it more rationally. Yes, we were also sure that shortening the commute to work would cut pollution and set up even more environmental benefits as active modes of movement and transit came into play. Chapter 5 covered this in detail. But for simple economic efficiency in our complex region, we would have pursued land-use solutions to transportation challenges even if saving money had been our only and final motive. Yes, we knew that we needed housing for low-income people. But, providing it would undoubtedly have been on our minds regardless of other intensions because we were heirs to a long tradition of such social concerns. It took some time for these disparate threads to coalesce and then to be woven into a planning imperative with a grander mandate and worldwide endorsement that would extend to everything we did. After all, we planners were not accustomed to dealing with infrastructure and the details of utilities. We were not agile at folding ecological patterns into open space and other designs. We did not devote much thought to the fabric of buildings and the nature of construction. But ultimately, as we learned and as we worked with other knowledgeable thinkers, sustainability did come together as a strong driver of our work.

Fortunately, a civic task force on atmospheric change, composed mostly of private citizens, produced an insightful report in 1990. Shepherded through the strong advocacy of City Councillor Gordon Price, it was aptly titled "Clouds of Change."[1] To my mind, this was the first serious attempt at tackling an environmental approach to city building in our town. I have to admit that the environmental perspective was initially nothing more than a kind of spiritual fascination to most of us planners at city hall. It became even more interesting when the United Nations Brundtland Report introduced the holistic strategy of sustainability in 1987,[2] consolidating environmental urgencies with social and economic concerns. The overall strategy became increasingly relevant to us in the early 1990s, as its message spread around the world. That was surely true for me. I remember convening a series of breakfast meetings in the mid-1990s with smart activists on most of the sustainability topics that I knew very little about. I was the least knowledgeable person in the room, so I just listened as they laid it all out so logically. My colleagues were boning up on one aspect or another of a more responsible city and bringing their findings into our discussions. Ours was a steep learning curve. Early on, I plucked a passionate young planner out of the University of British Columbia planning school, Mark Holland, tasking him with completing a survey of urban environmental factors around the world – defining the relevant components, identifying best practices for each one, and estimating how Vancouver rated on each factor. His survey became the first benchmark for our advance into this brave new world. Other departments in the City were doing the same thing in their own way. Through these experiences, we were teaching ourselves, step by step, about the components that we needed to deal with. So, by the mid-1990s, we began to morph the Vancouverism paradigm to include more and more features of the emerging framework of sustainability – starting with the downtown megaprojects and culminating in Southeast False Creek, which was my generation's most evident outcome, as will be described later. That's when the next generation took over, and they have advanced our work to ever greater heights from our beginnings.

## THE SMART-GROWTH FORMULA AS AN ARMATURE FOR SUSTAINABILITY

As the Brundtland Report's key themes of sustainability were elaborated over time, it became clear that the sustainability strategy had four legs: an environmental agenda, an economic agenda, a social agenda, and more recently, a cultural agenda. The various features that increasingly came into play were all aspects of a smart-growth formula, accepted worldwide, that became fixed in the collective consciousness of city hall and with the development and design community, reinforced by citizen activists. This articulated directions for both the structure and the infrastructure of Vancouver.

From a structural point of view (see Figure 8.2), we already knew that smart-growth was about the form of the city – clustered density and mixed-use and all kinds of diversity and protected open space. It was also about the character of the city – placemaking and quality and local uniqueness. These ideas were easy to embrace in Vancouver because of our long-time focus, for all the reasons I have discussed in earlier chapters. Urban livability and attractiveness had been our mantra from the beginning of the Spaxman years. Adding to this, we quickly learned that the smart-growth formula was also about the fabric of the city – environmentally neutral construction and operation of buildings and spaces. Green construction standards entered the hallowed pages of the building code step by step over the ensuing years, as I will touch on more later.

From an infrastructure point of view (see Figure 8.3), the smart-growth formula was about the servicing arrangements of the city – diverse circulation, more and more transportation choices, such as walking, transit, and cycling, with less and less dependence on the car. Our geography certainly gave us the cue for that, but getting the alternatives off the ground took a long time, and the jurisdiction for transportation went well beyond the City of Vancouver, as I explained in Chapter 5. The formula was also about the community services and social safety net of the city, recreation facilities, childcare, good schools, and all kinds of accommodations for those with special needs. And it was about culture – venues

**8.2** Vancouverism put the "smart-growth" formula into action with the structural aspects of intensity and diversity. This Seymour Street scene in Downtown South, with its multiple uses and maximum use of the land, is indicative.

**8.3** By diversifying transportation options, Vancouverism started the transformation of the essential infrastructural aspects of smart-growth, which is now a major thrust of innovation. In False Creek East, the SkyTrain is emblematic of contemporary transportation priorities. ▷

for local access to the triumphs of world culture and many outlets for the flourishing of a unique local culture. These are the social sides of sustainability. As I portrayed in Chapter 4, these factors grew in our consciousness year after year, as we clarified standards and set new ones that were practical and that could be easily understood by both the public and the development sector.

The big eye-opener was that the smart-growth formula, at an infrastructure level, was also about the utilities of the city. It was about managing water, waste, and energy in a conserving way and, where possible, about accessing local inputs, particularly local food. We realized that smart-growth simply would not happen unless the whole infrastructure system was sustainable. Well, this was completely new ground for most of the planning service at city hall. Just figuring out how to influence the status quo was a tough mountain to climb. Except for electrical energy, which in British Columbia is hydro-produced, Vancouver's utility infrastructure was anything but sustainable. Needless to say, this has been the hardest nut to try to crack, and it remains a profound challenge for the current generation. They will certainly need the "greenest city" imperative that has become the brand of current innovation. Recent policy development for sustainability in Vancouver has started to tackle infrastructure, and that is a very good thing.

Even with the thousands of policy, implementation, and funding difficulties that had to be confronted, there can be no doubt that this holistic formula, as it entered our consciousness, reinforced and gave urgency to the typical program of good, responsible planning, but it also became a big help in moving our thinking forward and in addressing a range of challenges in reconceiving Vancouver. What a useful formula. Of course, it works for the environment. After all, many of our initial "green" ideas were borrowed from the environmental movement. But it also works in addressing our growing health problems, particularly those related to obesity and a sedentary lifestyle, because it gets us out of our cars more. It works for economic development, especially that aspect of diversity. It works to mediate social isolation, a nagging issue of intensive development. It works in facilitating creative cultural expression. For both concerns, the result of getting more people closer together is natural social engagement. It works as a framework to simply enhance the quality of everyday experience, which I have already declared as a prime concern in Vancouver from the beginning. Thus, the formula for smart-growth became a pervasive philosophy. I have summarized its components right up front in this chapter because it offers a logical armature for most of the relevant policies, plans, and programs that came out of Vancouverism and grew into the more recent effort to become a truly green city.

## A SUSTAINABILITY FOUNDATION GROWS THROUGH THE MEGAPROJECTS

As discussed in Chapter 7, the 1990s megaprojects in downtown Vancouver were all about urban design. We were on a quest for the most delightful, hospitable, and amenable place that we could invent for living at high density. We were dealing with high density because, with land being so scarce and values being so high, we had no choice. If we had not accepted high density, then we would not have seen any development at all, simply because it would not have been economic to build. But this very act of embracing and taming density through delicate urban design was a fundamental move in the direction of sustainability at a structural level. This one shift in our paradigm opened up so many other themes of sustainability – diversification, active transportation, protected open space, and economic efficiencies. It also provided a funding source for public goods that are essential to sustainability and to implementing the social agenda, as Chapter 9 covers more fully.

The False Creek North and Coal Harbour megaprojects were the early crucibles for our forward thinking. As we started to plan these areas, in a collaboration with the developers and the public, we always led off by generating what we call a policy statement. As I describe more fully in Chapter 9, a policy statement is a general outline of development intentions for an area that describes what the detailed plan will and will not include. These very conceptual documents offer a quick insight into the primary interests of the day. Judged against current standards, these early statements did not include much about environmental concerns and certainly expressed no cautions about the impacts the area plans might have on either the local ecology or the worldwide crisis of excess greenhouse gases. But, looking more closely, one can discern the beginning of concerns for environmental features as well as the economic and social sides of the sustainability equation as we understand it today.

The policy statements paid virtually no attention to the bigger issues of compatibility between nature and the city – these were not documents for environmental activists. But there were some first moves. For example, there were policy aspirations for regenerating marine and intertidal habitats as we redeveloped the water's edge with the seawall and related features. There was a policy response to the concern for sea-level rise as a result of global warming – a higher standard elevation was declared for the seawall and adjacent development (see Figure 8.4). There was a declared expectation that residents would recycle their household waste and garbage. There were words about diversity of species for street

**8.4** An early policy response to rising levels was to build all the seawalls at a higher elevation, in order to prevent future flooding. This is the Coal Harbour seawall. Thus commenced our efforts toward environmental sustainability. Sadly, we may have underestimated the problem, and further mitigation may yet have to be done.

trees to ensure resilience, even though native species were not emphasized. And the theme was expressed that, if people moving into the area shifted many of their trips to walking, then there would be less pollution.

The policy statements provided very little content on the now commonly understood economic and social components of sustainability. But there was some content. The low-income and family housing requirements were major features that remain at the cutting edge of urban social policy in North American cities to this day (see Figure 8.5). The neighbourhood template, already discussed, made a beginning in regard to social and economic development.

Even though these early expressions of sustainability expectations were somewhat haphazard and even vague, they did lay the groundwork for much more fully articulated policies, as the green agenda gained more traction over the years in each new development or revitalization area. We did offer at least a nascent holistic view from the beginning. It could be said that the table of contents in the policy statements provided for a complete story to be fleshed out as further elaborations of sustainability entered the collective consciousness of the city. And because each policy statement was a baseline to be bettered next time, the framework for sustainability became increasingly filled with real requirements and expectations that could lead to more sustainable performance for the city as a whole.

However, I do not want to downplay the urban design factors that dominated these megaproject plans (see Figure 8.6). They were absolutely primary preconditions for a more fulsome agenda of urban sustainability. As the smart-growth formula makes clear, without some significant level of density and diversity, no big city can ever be sustainable. And yet, as I have often emphasized in this story, most urban consumers are not happy with density and diversity, at least not in North America. Our megaproject urban design advances changed that, at least for our part of the world, thus vesting a model of living and of development that is now being extended to more areas of the city, where there are opportunities for intensification, and more areas of the region, where greenfield and brownfield sites are being constructed as the regional town centres of the future. More intensive living is now readily accepted and even popular. It is embraced by types of households that would not have considered it in the past. It now represents the majority of new housing that is on the market in the region. So, slowly but surely, the urban metropolis of Vancouver is becoming more dense and more diverse, which is a profound structural precondition for the green advances that are increasingly becoming a vivid part of Vancouver's image and that fill out the picture of sustainability.

So, by the late 1990s, when the megaproject planning phase ended, we had a framework for the structural side of sustainability and at least the transportation and community aspects of the infrastructural side. We also had the language and wider-articulated concepts, so the bigger picture was, indeed, starting to become clearer. Suddenly, the word "sustainability" became the most popular word in the English language, and we joked that every planning notion now had to include the word or it just would not be relevant. For a while, I even worried that the word would be devalued from overuse to the point that the concept itself would come into disrepute. Fortunately, I was wrong about that.

**8.5** Headway in social and economic sustainability for Vancouverism was initially represented by inclusive policies that welcomed all kinds of people within the new communities, engendering the kind of social interactions you see here in Emery Barnes Park.

**8.6** Many urban design factors come into play, not only to implement sustainability but also to make it preferred by consumers and therefore marketable. Vancouver's megaprojects, such as here at False Creek North, set a popular stage for later innovations. This photo was taken along Marinaside Crescent.

Also toward the end of the megaproject planning phase, we began to under-stand that the construction of buildings played a significant part in the compat-ibility of the city with the natural environment. As is true everywhere in the world, constructing and operating buildings consumes a lot of energy, so to up the ante on sustainability, we needed to improve their performance. Green build-ings had become a major talking point in North America, with the formation of the United States Green Building Council – followed in our country by the Canadian Green Building Council, thanks in good measure to the leadership of Peter Busby, a forward-thinking Vancouver architect and colleague. These organ-izations were strong advocates for a discretionary approach to improving the green profile of buildings. They initiated a performance-rating system called "LEED" – "leadership in energy and environmental design." Developers could have their buildings rated according to high green standards. The expectation was that consumers preferred green performance and would naturally choose a building with a high LEED rating. This approach had significant benefits. For one thing, it introduced green building performance, but in a gentle way, with prog-ress left to the good graces of the developers and their architects, along with the natural pull of the market. Since, in the beginning, there was a significant pre-mium to pay for building products and systems that improved the green quotient, and prices varied in differing locations, taking the discretionary route was the best way to consolidate the green movement with little opposition. For another, LEED established clear parameters that helped everyone understand the aspects of a building that contributed to better or worse impacts on the environment – along with specifications for various levels of performance. In a clever way, it both demystified green construction and depoliticized its implementation.

In many cities, instead of dealing with the underlying construction require-ments to absolutely secure green construction performance, a simple policy mandates that buildings must meet a certain level of the LEED standard – or an incentive is offered for specified LEED performance. In Vancouver, we started doing this early on and still do, at an increasingly higher level, with large projects seeking rezoning for greater development rights and for publicly funded con-struction. But we began to feel that this was too narrowly targeted. Knowing that the city faced such a high level of construction, we wanted to ensure that all new buildings immediately contributed to sustainability. So, in several iterations through the mid-2000s, the City building department completed a wholesale evaluation of the Vancouver building code. (The Vancouver Charter enables us to have our own tailored building code, securing local requirements as a takeoff of the national building code.) As a result of this review, all the relevant requirements were increased, especially those related to energy performance, to be absolutely confident that anything constructed under a Vancouver building permit would perform at a high green standard. We started tentatively. Over the years, as competitively priced building materials and components became increasingly available and the cost of erecting a green structure therefore came down, we amplified the requirements. It is not my purpose here to chronicle the details of the many adjustments or judge their merits. Instead, I use the matter of green building performance to illustrate that from the turn of the century, Vancouver was coming of age in the philosophy of sustainability. We were no longer novices. Our green building strategy was certainly more aggressive than the discretionary approach of LEED, and in one grand gesture, we moved light-years ahead of most other cities on this key aspect of an environmentally responsible city.

## SOUTHEAST FALSE CREEK CONSOLIDATES THE COMMITMENT TO SUSTAINABILITY

The culmination of our comprehensive planning projects in the inner-city in our generation was the area called Southeast False Creek. It was later fast tracked for development as the Athletes Village for the 2010 Winter Olympic Games (see Figure 8.7). The policy statement for this area, completed in 1999, was a very different beast from those of the past. It was all about sustainability – the urban design components seemed just to tag along for the ride. This aspiration had deep roots, going back to the "Clouds of Change" report of 1990, which I have already referenced. In 1991, when we began to think about the future of Southeast False Creek, city council stated that it must include principles for energy-efficient community design. Council even used the "sustainability" word, probably for the first time in one of its resolutions, by also directing that we should explore the possibilities of the area becoming a model for "sustainable development" (in the resolution, the term was probably put in quotation marks because no one in Vancouver really knew what it meant or might entail in terms of practical implementation). Bringing forward for development the City-owned lands that make up Southeast False Creek involved many bureaucratic steps, and frankly, we had bigger fish to fry with the other active megaprojects through the

early 1990s. So, serious work on the policy statement for Southeast False Creek did not get under way until 1997. By that time, the City had become pretty savvy about sustainable development, along with the rest of the world, and we were no longer merely contemplating the possibility that the area might be a model. Instead, we were bound and determined that it would be.

In case we might have been reticent about that, it has to be said that a big cadre of citizens were going to make sure that we did not lose track of what the planning focus needed to be. Early on, just as the discussion was beginning, a host of environmental groups started to criticize our process because it did not seem to be zeroing in on sustainability fast enough. They came out of the wood-work from every sector of the environmental movement, and they were steady and articulate advocates. Fortunately, instead of shielding ourselves from them, we embraced them as our guide and conscience for the whole effort. They took on a stewardship role for all the green features. Known as the "Southeast False Creek Working Group," they met with us on a regular basis, they became essential to the planning process, and none of us ever looked back.

**8.7** On the sustainability front, the ultimate accomplishment of the initiators of Vancouverism was the planning and design of the Athletes Village for the 2010 Winter Olympic Games, which is now commonly known as the Village at Southeast False Creek. The upcoming generation of urbanists will start from here, as they take sustainability and "one-planet living" to new heights.

**8.8** Southeast False Creek includes a district-based clean energy system, which captures heat from untreated waste water.

Also, when we began to plan Southeast False Creek, we finally had a concept to guide us that you could really wrap your mind around – it was called the "ecological footprint," and it was a genuine Vancouver invention. First presented in writing and given its popular name by William Rees of the University of British Columbia in 1992, the idea was further developed, including a concept for calculating the metrics, by Rees and his student Mathis Wackernagel, in the latter's 1994 dissertation.[3] Two years later, it was bound into a cogent volume, *Our Ecological Footprint: Reducing Human Impact on the Earth,*[4] which was written by both men. So, by 1997, we could talk with some confidence about planning expectations for an environmentally defensible urbanism.

Because of all this, the "Southeast False Creek Policy Statement" was a contrast to its predecessors.[5] For one thing, it declared in no uncertain terms that the area would meet the highest standards for sustainability and would be a model sustainable urban neighbourhood. It defined "sustainable development" and described what a sustainable neighbourhood was all about. It espoused development principles that were drawn directly from the prime Brundtland formula, with which we had become quite conversant. By the time you finish reading the introductory sections, long before even one policy proposal is put forward, you are almost overwhelmed by the aspiration that this community

**8.9** Water management in Southeast False Creek naturally cleans runoff groundwater through creeks in the park before it is let out into False Creek.

will not degrade its natural setting – a thought not even mentioned for the earlier megaprojects.

Unlike earlier statements, the one for Southeast False Creek included a long and detailed section on the environment, with a sharp eye on the utility measures necessary to protect and enhance the local ecology. This entailed innovative proposals for energy generation and use (see Figure 8.8). For the first time, the statement referred to a district-based green energy facility, now a defining feature of the area. Called the "Neighbourhood Energy Utility," it provides heat and hot water to homes by recovering waste heat from untreated waste water headed for the sewers, reinforced by rooftop solar thermal collectors. The area also hosts the first net-zero energy building in Canada – an affordable housing building for seniors that produces as much energy as it consumes.

The statement contained advanced proposals for water management (see Figure 8.9). For example, runoff would be channelled into a creek system in the local park that cleans the water before it is released into False Creek. This is now a lovely and fascinating feature of the park. Also, rainwater would be systematically collected for gardening.

Waste management would be pushed to a new level. The statement targeted greater waste reduction and diversion, prioritized composting, and asserted that the blue box recycling program,[6] then used only in lower-density areas, should also be applied in this multi-family district. At the upstream end of things, the document called for use of local materials and inputs in both the construction and ongoing operation of the area.

The statement included policy directions on remediation of contaminated soils, which earlier statements had mentioned only for the most polluted of circumstances. It also addressed the potential and form of urban agriculture, with the intention of increasing the amount of locally produced food. Community gardens and rooftop gardening were suggested. You may not often see actual urban farmers on the scene, but you will now see a lot of gardeners and a lot of garden plots, which give the area a strongly domestic feel.

In an absolutely new measure, the statement called for the development of a neighbourhood air-quality strategy. It tackled reductions in greenhouse gases and ozone-depleting chemicals, advocated low-impact transportation, and urged the use of oxygen-enhancing landscape design and maintenance. Of course, it specified a high standard of green building technology, including use of material inputs in a conserving, low-impact, environmentally sensitive way. And finally, it proposed organizational action for ongoing environmental stewardship and learning.

For the first time, specific targets were set for all these dimensions of environmental sustainability. And they were more than idle words – there was a drive and guideposts to make sure it all happened. Indeed, most of the innovations were implemented, and so successfully that the United States Green Building Council designated the area a "LEED-Platinum" sustainable neighbourhood. Only one other North American district shares this honour, and it also happens to be in British Columbia (the first one ever designated was a smaller area, Dockside Green, in nearby Victoria).

Of course, the policy statement for Southeast False Creek included all the aspects for structuring a community that typified the earlier megaprojects (see Figure 8.10). But the expectation was that it would ratchet up the earlier base of performance. It had density and mixed-use but in a fresh mid-rise format (see Figure 8.11). It integrated social diversity, both in income and household types, but it set targets for even greater diversity, with specifications for middle-income as well as low-income housing. It offered a complete suite of cultural, community, and local retail facilities to serve day-to-day needs (see Figure 8.12). It had the typical open space requirements, but with more spaciousness in the waterfront walkway-bikeway and a lovely square around which everything is focused

**8.10** Like the other mega-projects, Southeast False Creek was designed as a complete community, with all the local bells and whistles that are now expected in new Vancouver neighbourhoods. This sign summarizes the commercial offerings.

**8.11** Southeast False Creek has density and diversity but in a fresh mid-rise form with a design flair.

**8.12** Southeast False Creek is a genuine community, with all the buzz of people enjoying their lifestyle. Terra Breads, offering healthy and delicious cuisine, is one of the key meeting places.

**8.13** Southeast False Creek meets all the civic parks requirements but in a very urban way, with a main square embellished by memorable public art. *The Birds,* by Myfanwy MacLeod, depicts a pair of house sparrows, a ubiquitous species in Vancouver. Kids are fascinated by these giants.

**8.14** The waterfront walkway-bikeway in Southeast False Creek takes the standard format to new design heights. It is extraordinarily popular.

(see Figure 8.13). It required public art. And it designated active transportation – high transit use, cycling, and especially walking (see Figure 8.14). With all these features, it manifested the area's now popular name, "The Village."

I have called Southeast False Creek the culmination of my generation's work on sustainability because, even as its detailed design commenced, many of us were leaving the scene – we were retiring from city hall. We passed the baton to a new group of civic officials, with only a few old-timers left to carry the flag of Vancouverism into the detailing of the area. Scot Hein, the senior urban designer of the City and the head of the civic design studio, was the key person for continuity. But we need not have worried, because the new generation of planners ultimately outdid our thinking by many measures. They certainly echoed all the themes of Vancouverism that had become the expected norm. But they attacked the challenge of sustainability like tigers. What we dreamed about, they made real. What we had not thought to dream about, they brought into the heart of the development scenario. They made tangible the directions for environmental responsibility, producing the model sustainable community that we had aspired to from the beginning. We did not do that – they did. But for them, Southeast False Creek was only an experimental area. They had a much bigger vision in mind – nothing less than making the whole city a mecca of green urbanism.

## A GREEN AGENDA FOR THE WHOLE CITY: ASPIRATIONS BEYOND VANCOUVERISM

As I have emphasized throughout this book, my task is not to tell the story that unfolded after the salad days of the formulation of Vancouverism. But I do want to be clear that, from the seedlings we initially planted, a very lush forest of sustainable urbanism has been nurtured by those who came after us (not to mix my metaphors). Vancouver is now widely acknowledged as the greenest city in North America – it certainly has the smallest per-capita carbon footprint. We still lag behind the world leaders in the Nordic countries, but we are pulling ahead by a wide margin from all the cities in our part of the world. Look out, Europe, here we come!

I think Vancouver's moment of transition from inquiry and tentative experimentation to full commitment and aggressive, methodical action to become one of the greenest cities on the planet can actually be pinpointed. The year was 2009. A bright, young, and popular politician, Mayor Gregor Robertson, assembled a group of local experts, mostly from outside government, in what was called the "Greenest City Action Team." This informed and inquisitive team surveyed the best practices of the most forward green cities and set the goals and targets that could eventually transform Vancouver into the world's greenest city.

Then, an energetic bureaucracy, steered by then deputy city manager Sadhu Johnston and most of the civic leadership, produced a roadmap to make this all happen, involving thousands of Vancouverites along the way. The result was the "Greenest City: 2020 Action Plan" that I have already referenced.[7] Actually, the document notes that there are ten separate plans, each with a long-term goal for 2050 and medium-term targets for 2020. With this kind of agenda, it is not surprising that Johnston has now become the city manager.

The plan is refreshing because it is comprehensive but also succinct. It offers both the big picture and practical steps forward. Its vision is sweeping, and its specific aspirations are crystal clear. It includes the measures that will be undertaken as soon as possible, as well as later efforts that can build upon initial successes. There is no question that it transcends Vancouverism, even though it extends and elaborates our original intentions. Let me give you a glimpse of what the current generation has on its bucket list, taken directly from the action plan, but using my own words. Of course, in meeting virtually all these aspirations, the City will need the help of the other Lower Mainland municipalities and the regional and provincial authorities. Many of the matters at play come under the jurisdiction of other governments or agencies, so a partnership will be required at every step. Achieving this may be the biggest challenge of this plan, with so many governments and authorities involved, but at least the City is showing that it wants to set an aggressive pace and be a leader.

Of course, the first marker date of 2020 is upon us with some targets in sight and others remaining elusive. There is no doubt that much has been achieved in the first ten years, even though great transformations in sustainability are still to come. But in terms of spurring action and opening doors to new directions, the spirit of the early targets has actually been more important than the specific performance. By 2050, though, it is vital that the targets be actually achieved or even bettered.

For a green economy, the intent is to secure Vancouver's international reputation as a hub of green enterprise. To do this, over the ten-year period up to 2020, it was targeted for the city to double the number of green jobs and double the number of companies that are actively greening their operations.

For climate leadership, the declaration is nothing less than to eliminate dependence on fossil fuels by the outside date of 2050. The immediate target, for 2020, has been to reduce community-based greenhouse gas emissions by 33 percent from 2007 levels. This is all about green construction, active transportation, zero-waste plans, and neighbourhood-scaled renewable energy systems. Southeast False Creek is obviously the inspiration here.

Also, the hope is that Vancouver will lead the world in green building design and construction, which is not unlikely because some of the most cutting-edge green architects are based here. From 2020 onward, all new buildings are to be carbon neutral in operations. Also, energy use and greenhouse gas emissions in existing buildings will drop by at least 20 percent from 2007 levels.

The green transportation agenda – opting for walking, cycling, and public transit – has already been fully described in Chapter 5. By 2020 more than 50 percent of all trips should use these modes, and the average distance of trips by car should come down 20 percent from 2007 levels.

For waste, the intention is ultimately to have none – zero waste. By 2020, solid waste going to the landfill or the incinerator should be reduced by 50 percent from 2008 levels. Household and construction generation of waste must decline drastically and materials must be reused and recycled. The three Rs – reduce, reuse, and recycle – must become a household and corporate mantra. Composting has to become commonplace. Producers have to become more responsible for the ultimate disposition of their products. Building demolition is starting to reform, shifting from brutal destruction to careful disassembly and materials salvage.

Ready access to nature is emphasized. The idea is that Vancouverites should enjoy incomparable access to green spaces, including the world's most spectacular urban forest. A maximum five-minute walk from every home to a green space was set for 2020, along with planting at least 150,000 trees. The latter is a practical goal, given that reforestation of the city's public realm is a long-standing policy and that trees on public and private land are already legally protected. Native species and compatibility with the local eco-system are also emphasized.

For the ecological footprint of the city, the aspiration is to achieve a fair-share, "one-planet" draw on the natural systems of the setting. This means shifting away from the "three-planet" draw that is now estimated as our status quo. The idea is to get our consumption in balance with what we produce or protect for the environment, so that everyone can live happy, healthy lives, leaving space for wildlife and wilderness, all within the limits of our planet. How to attain this, beyond careful metrics, remains quite vague. So, this is a continuing quest.

On the matter of clean water, the goal is that Vancouver will have the best drinking water of any city in the world. First and foremost, this requires meeting

**8.15** A spontaneous initiative for food sustainability is Sole Food Street Farms, which grows fruit and vegetables on temporary sites in the heart of the city, for sale to local people and restaurants. This non-profit also has a strong social mission to employ what other people would have called the unemployable and to donate food for those in need. The farm, along with several market gardens on downtown roofs, is on the cutting edge of Vancouver's green agenda.

or exceeding the highest drinking water quality standards anywhere and, by 2020, having per-capita water consumption down by at least 33 percent. It will be interesting to see if personal habits have shifted as quickly as the policy-makers had hoped.

The same kind of goal is expressed for the air we breathe – that it be the cleanest of any major city in the world. Again, this requires exceeding local and international standards, particularly as expressed by the World Health Organization. Mostly, attaining this objective is about cleaner modes of transportation but also about reducing woodsmoke from homes, along with industrial pollution.

And lastly, the aspiration is that Vancouver will become a global leader in urban food systems. This requires more local food production. The short-term target was to increase city-wide and neighbourhood food production by a minimum of 50 percent over the decade to 2020. Thank goodness we have been so carefully protecting our agricultural lands in the region and province over the past forty-five years. One spontaneous initiative that makes this civic policy aspiration seem almost practical, even in the core city, is a pop-up farming enterprise called Sole Food Street Farms (see Figure 8.15). Launched in 2008, this non-profit venture already uses over 2.5 hectares (6 acres) of surplus parking lots in the inner-city for farming. It grows produce in moveable bins, selling it to local restaurants and households. Even more importantly, it provides jobs and food to disadvantaged people, helping them to restabilize their lives. The City did not start this endeavour – credit for that goes to two socially responsible people, Seann Dory and Michael Ableman, and a vital community organization called "United We Can" – but it does support the effort in various ways. These urban farms are a sight to behold, and this unique and commendable project to my mind has extraordinary potential for both environmental and social progress.

On every one of these fronts, the old-timers who invented Vancouverism will be cheering on each initiative. Many of us wish we were still around to be a part of this wholesale urban reform.

## REMAINING CHALLENGES

I am convinced that the science of sustainability and even our understanding of what constitutes a green city are in their infancy. What looks like progress today will be inadequate tomorrow. The cutting edge changes constantly. So, the remaining challenges are almost undefinable. The fact is that no city in the world is truly sustainable. No city in the world has removed the pressures from its natural setting. No city in the world is actually contributing to the optimal functioning of its host eco-system.

For our part, the sins of omission are, perhaps, forgivable. There is much that we could have done earlier and more fully. We could have made more progress before handing on the responsibilities to a younger generation. The world is littered with stories about what people could have or might have done. I think we did our part to the extent that we understood what was at stake. We were not shy about tackling new concerns as they emerged. And, because the next generation has come so surely to the helm of the great mission of sustainability, our shortsightedness did not result in dramatic harm. On the whole, I feel few regrets.

But there is one area of sustainability where we could have done more. I mentioned this in Chapter 6 and will return to it in Chapter 10. This has to do with the social resilience of our community, and it *was* on our agenda. In our day, we worked hard for low-income people, but there we stopped. We did not look carefully at the bigger picture for a household's budget. Despite all our fine words about a social mix, we did not ask how households of differing capacities, particularly with middle incomes, could survive, much less thrive, in the new communities we were creating, especially if these communities became as successful and popular as we hoped. I will say it many times in these pages – our oversight is especially problematic because its end result may jeopardize most of what I celebrate in this story.

This completes our exploration of the key substantive themes of the paradigm of Vancouverism. How we made it happen, and how we continue our journey, is another level of this chronicle. Implementation is the subject of the next chapter.

**9.1** Vancouverism was nurtured within a free market but also within a government tradition of coordination and management. Wide freedoms are joined with the clear rule of law. I was grateful for our Canadian balance of the public and private sectors because it fostered community interests and made our ideas practical to pursue and realize.

# 9

# PUBLIC AND PRIVATE COLLABORATION

**THE ESSENTIAL PROPELLANT** of all I am going to tell you about the organization, arrangements, and processes of Vancouverism is one very powerful motivator – self-interest. The basic approach of all our work was to find common cause among the various sectors that envision, create, manage, and use the city – I have said from the beginning of this story that collaboration is a prime principle of Vancouverism. No doubt, many people saw the good in what we were trying to do, and we ourselves recognized well-intentioned people when we encountered them. So for sound altruistic reasons there was often a natural inclination to collaborate. But our cooperative approach did not absolutely depend upon that. We did not assume that there was some mystical desire by people in Vancouver to work together, putting aside their differing perspectives and aspirations. Instead, we built a system that taps, brokers, and ultimately reconciles or aligns self-interests among the many public and private forces that make up the body politic and market of the city. People work together because they benefit more by doing so, not just because they wish to bring about some kind of overarching good.

In this chapter, I will describe that system. After looking a little closer at our modus operandi, I will show you how and why we did what we did, in governance and management, to set up a high-yield development management framework, to engage and convene people, to undertake planning and policy making, and to arrange sustainable funding for the necessary public infrastructure. As I go along, I will highlight some of the more unique organizational arrangements that brought all of this together. Then, I will close by outlining some continuing anxieties. Admittedly more technical than the rest of our story, which cannot be avoided, this is the "how to" chapter, which is all about implementing Vancouverism.

## A SYSTEM BASED UPON INTERESTS AND COLLABORATION

Vancouverism came together in a conventional free-market economy, in the Canadian tradition, with lots of freedoms but a clear rule of law (see Figure 9.1). One aspect of Canadian law that distinguishes us from our American cousins has to do with property rights. In Canada, owners do not have inherent property rights – Crown rights supersede. This creates a power balance that shapes our whole approach to change management. This is germane to the two underlying propositions that I have already touched upon – self-interest and collaboration.

This free-market framework is a balancing act, with the equilibrium between public and private interests changing from time to time – how a city sets its own balances determines what results it will get. Unfortunately, all too often, what occurs is a free-for-all between competing self-interests, and the city becomes a chaos, resulting in the lowest common denominator – the collective interest suffers but so do many individual interests. The reform political movements of the generation that preceded Vancouverism, with their strong academic leanings, were fed up with that reality. These reformers wanted a more coherent city. So, in the 1970s, they found their man in the new chief planner, Ray Spaxman, who reorganized everything to lead to a better result. His perspective was that of a visionary, as I celebrated at the beginning of this book, and he had strong views, but he was also an organizer. He felt strongly that a collective image had to prevail for the future city and that people had to work together to achieve it. By "people," he meant those in government, the private sector, particularly developers, non-profit community organizations, and individual citizens. This meant that a power balance had to be created among these sectors – for which, some sectors had to be empowered, and others had to be reined in. This also meant that if you did not involve everyone in a collaborative effort, you could not move forward. Not for him the themes that government should "get out of the way" or that "the experts know better than the average Joe on the street." So, he reset the system of development management and decision making. He reset the system of developer engagement. He reset the system of public involvement. His intention was that the systems have to host collaboration and to motivate people to want to collaborate. His perspective became the perspective of our whole generation. The question we faced, though, was how to make all of this happen. For the answer, we looked to the market as much as we did to government powers.

## LEVERAGING MARKET FORCES FOR URBAN EXCELLENCE

The fundamental modus operandi of our generation has been the smart conversion of land rights. During the entire period of consolidation of Vancouverism, an "up market" prevailed in our city's development scene. It still does. Due to immigration but also increasingly as consumers made urban rather than suburban choices, demand commonly exceeded supply, especially for housing and related uses. Initial development allowances did not reflect either this demand or the contemporary potential of properties, particularly in the inner-city. Allowances had to be increased. With buoyant prices, great wealth has been at play – new wealth that was generated as land rights were recalibrated and buildings were constructed and sold. It was primarily through this source of wealth that we found a way to tap the self-interests of the parties that were building the new Vancouver and to bring those interests into alignment. This became apparent to us when we began to understand the relationship between development rights and land values, and then started to leverage that relationship. Let me explain.

I will say plainly that the planners in Vancouver, leading up to the years of Vancouverism, had no special understanding of urban land economics. They did not take it into account when they created the traditional development regulatory framework of the city. Many people on the civic scene just do not seem to want to talk about land economics. Even today, it is a blind spot in most local governments, and it was surely a blind spot for most of our generation as we took on our contemporary urban challenge. I remember one of the leaders of planning in Vancouver, who shall remain nameless, actually saying that he did not want to understand the business consequences of planning, because an ethical government does not concern itself with whether or not people make profits. Most private developers don't really want to get into the financial discussion either, because they see their business deals as proprietary, and truth be told, they really do not want the public to know how much money they actually make. Well, when, in the early years, we started playing with incentives, a number of civic staff became increasingly curious about what was being offered to the private sector and what was being secured by the public sector in exchange. People at city hall, such as Cameron Gray, started getting specific about the numbers. Here is what we came to understand.

First, we came to see the basic facts. In an up market, the value of urban land is generally determined by what is legally allowed to be built on that land – what it can be used for. This is spelled out in the local zoning. It was enlightening to realize that we, at city hall, actually set the land value because we set the zoning. Because development starts with a site, a careful developer will calculate what is called a "proforma" to determine what can be paid for a property in order to build anything. This is simply a formula to compute the total costs of putting up the building (plus a somewhat standard profit for the production of the building) against the estimated price that will be received by selling the building. By subtracting the construction cost from the sales price, you arrive at the amount that is available to buy the property. By the way, that base level of profit I just mentioned is included in the formula right up front because, without it, the developer would have no motivation to build, and nothing would happen – other investments would simply be more attractive. The base profit is always there, period. Now, there are times when this reality is distorted, such as when a precinct shifts into a larger-than-local market and opportunistic speculators from anywhere and everywhere start to invest in property for what they feel will undoubtedly be higher future rights. But that occasional circumstance does not alter what basically and usually goes on – legal allowances today set today's value.

Then, we began to see the opportunity. If zoning is changed to allow a more intensive or more valuable use of the land, it is easy to see that extra money will enter the equation – this extra money is often called a "land-value lift." It was doubly enlightening to realize that we at city hall created that extra wealth, like magic. The lights really went on for us when we started to speculate who might enjoy this windfall value when the City allows extra building rights, and, more importantly, that we could actually channel that value by controlling when and how the new rights are conferred. It transpires that whoever controls the land at the time of the regulatory change will expect to be the recipient of most of the land-value lift. The reality of land transactions, of course, is a little more complicated. The fact is that everyone knows or expects what might be possible, so the land-value lift is shared, based on what everyone generally expects to be allowed in the future. But if those development rights are made available in a strategic way that is cognizant of land-value implications, then most of the land-value lift can be more or less directed. This is fundamentally true as development rights change – through rezoning – but it can also be true if differing levels of allowed development within a regulation are tied to different levels of public responsibility. If rights are conferred too early or without expectation of performance, then most of the extra value will be taken by the initial landowner, who does not intend to do anything except sell the land and pocket the profits, so that extra value surely will not be available for the public. If the land-value lift is timed to fall into the hands of the developer, who thus acquires a windfall that extends beyond the base profit, then that developer will be more open to earmarking some of it to meet public needs as change occurs. Of course, it has to be acknowledged that in many urban situations the land-value lift is not shared by the developer with anybody, so it is sometimes a huge source of profits on top of the base profit that I have already posited.

Ultimately, we found our partners. Most developers began to see these arrangements as a real incentive if the value was not originally available or assumed in their proforma, thus representing genuine new wealth in their equation. If some of that money were used to pay a premium for better quality or to underwrite public goods, so be it – after all, that also made their projects more valuable. If some of that wealth was actually left with them, they became very interested indeed, even if going through the process did take a little extra time or was more complicated. In the end, the money represented a second level of profits that they had not expected. It is great to partner when each partner benefits. Then you can add "up-pricing" as an extra buffer for the developer. This is when a developer increases prices as sales are under way in a hot market. Given that prices are set by what the market will bear, not by the cost of production (which, surprisingly, most people either do not realize or seem to forget), and that Vancouver's prices are constantly trending up because of heavy demand, any risk for the developer in our more complicated system is mitigated by up-pricing as yet a third level of profit.

Managing land-value lift with offers of extra development potential at the right moment in the process, within a framework of careful assessment of all the implications, including public acceptance, became our engine. Increased land rights became the fuel. Together, these became the power of Vancouverism. It creates new wealth that serves the self-interest of participants in three ways – the developer enjoys extra profits, the public enjoys an array of public amenities and facilities, as well as higher-quality development, and the local government enjoys sponsoring a better city, without dipping into scarce tax revenues. This is one of those virtuous circles that is essentially perpetual as long as the demand side remains strong, the yields remain popular and defensible, and everybody cooperates.

**MANAGING DEVELOPMENT WITH THE CARROT, NOT THE STICK**

Managing development, in local government, is about two things. It is about the framework of regulations and requirements that lead to approval of a development proposal. It is also about the adjudication process through which the laws are applied for that approval. Because of the strategy that I have already described to facilitate positive development, Vancouver's development management system became quite unique compared to that of most local governments. The regulatory framework became very discretionary. When I say "discretionary," I mean that development approvals are not automatically granted. Instead, they are the result of judgments regarding whether a proposal is suited to the community. There are few hard rules but lots of possibilities, with indications of public preferences, some offered with incentives to lead developers to those preferred outcomes. The adjudication process became very transactional. When I say "transactional," I mean that decisions are reached via a lot of give and take through wide-ranging discussion and engagement with everybody. The City and the developer engage; the public, as individuals, interest groups, and a whole community, is involved; and all kinds of interests are brokered through intensive negotiations. Great development opportunity is offered, well beyond what might have been prima facie assumed, but great performance and contributions to the commonwealth of the city are expected. Let's now look at both the rules and process in more detail.

*The discretionary regulatory framework*

To start with the basics, you don't need to know much about zoning to know that it is simply a law that defines what land uses can occur on a property, how much can occur, and more or less how the constructions that accommodate those uses must be built. In most cities, as in Vancouver until close to the time of our story, zoning was quite straightforward. It specified which uses were allowed (most were permitted under any circumstances, and a few more were allowed under certain conditions). Uses tended to be segregated to avoid the impactful or harmful combinations that had happened in the past. A property owner had the absolute right to the allowed uses – this system is called "as-of-right" zoning. As long as the building did not exceed the specified size and met the other basic requirements for its intended use, city hall could not withhold approval for its construction. To achieve fairness, the zoning covered large areas, called districts, which included multiple properties. This system was quite direct and understandable and generally fair, but it did not lead to particularly fulfilling cities. Because there were very few mixes of uses, the diversity of the city became homogenized, creativity was constrained, and it was difficult to support organic change.

In some cities, including Vancouver as an early case in point, the desire to avoid this rather dull, boring resulting cityscape opened the door for a more complex approach, now called the "discretionary zoning system." This zoning is one where, in addition to outright uses that must be approved if done the specified way, there is a list of many other uses that might be approvable through a discretionary judgment. Getting approval rests on three things: the compatibility of the use with surrounding circumstances; the availability of an acceptable level of public supports; and how the use will be realized, first in terms of its amount or scale and then the form of its construction. You can see how this kind of system puts a lot of power into civic hands, especially if the discretionary uses are also the most popular ones in the marketplace and therefore the most valuable.

In Vancouver, once the flexible zoning door was opened through this discretionary arrangement, we realized that it was not just about more diversity and mix but also about modulating performance and leveraging public goods from private development. So, on top of a modest base of as-of-right allowances, we incrementally built a superstructure where developers can do more kinds of uses, or a combination of uses, or more of any one popular use on their property if they contribute to what we call the commonwealth of the city. A contribution can take the form of a particularly distinguished design, as judged by the community, or by the provision of specified public amenities. Improvements in performance and value are incremental, based upon clear trade options, but they are consistent and sustained. On top of this, we built an additional level for even more striking results – a higher increment of development if the developer offers a valuable and hard-to-secure public good, such as a social or cultural facility or park space. So, we created a layered, structured framework of allowances, from the most modest but easiest to expedite to the most elaborated but hardest to enjoy. Since all of this is set within an adopted by-law that has vested rights, all the flexibilities are carefully codified – including the outright allowances, the conditions for alternatives, the list of goods that are subject to special additional rights, and even which opinions are to be sought in making discretionary decisions. To avoid over-complexity within the by-law, each law itself is backed up by a set of fleshed-out possibilities and expectations in the form of what are called "guidelines" – statements that do not have the imperative effect of the law but do suggest the direction that will probably find approval. This is all still offered on an area basis to any property in a district.

Then Vancouver took this one step further, which set it apart from many cities. We realized that not all properties are created equal. Some sites become pivotal to a quality community and need special allowances and opportunities for their use, density, and form – options that we just do not want to make available to other sites or groups of properties, even directly adjacent. So, we created a zoning that can be designed for one single property and for which everything can be either tailored, using specified rules, or left for unique one-off design, going the full bore into discretion where nothing is allowed outright, but anything can be approved if it is judged good enough for the community. Just so you know, although these zoning laws are called different things in different cities, in Vancouver we call these "comprehensive development" zones. All the big megaproject sites, Coal Harbour, False Creek North, and elsewhere, ultimately were zoned for comprehensive development.

In one final dimension of the zoning regime that it is important to understand, Vancouver is similar to almost every other city, certainly in North America and the British Commonwealth, in accommodating what is called "rezoning." For some civically vital sites or for kinds of development that no one has ever thought about, a proponent who wishes to make a change submits a proposal to city hall. Then, together, the City and the proponent will work up an acceptable scheme – setting completely new building rights and public requirements through a rezoning. Alternatively, sometimes the City itself will initiate a rezoning to redefine what can happen in an area or site based on new plans or policy. Rezoning is costly, time consuming, politically fraught, and generally risky. It also wreaks havoc on land values and tax assessments, so neither developers nor local government tend to see it as attractive for most development day-to-day. However, rezoning is occasionally quite a handy way to go. It is the vehicle through which to implement a new community vision. It is the vehicle through which to apply new standards. It is the vehicle through which to do more with land. Within parameters set in long-tested common law, either or both sides can bring anything to the table, a balance will be found between public and private interests, and rights will then be conferred. Vancouver uses rezoning in a strategic way, avoiding it where possible, preferring to build options within zoning where practical, but always keeping the rezoning tool available where it best suits. The Vancouver agenda in a rezoning will normally enshrine dramatic increases in development rights, which are of extraordinary value, so citizens expect a very high yield on public goods and public interests in return. To determine this yield for the public, the values at play are very carefully calibrated. I will come back to this shortly.

So, in our system, you see simple outright zoning, complex discretionary zoning (in districts and for individual sites), and rezoning, all of which can be at play when and as needed in the city. These extraordinarily flexible zoning formats permit us to shape development at a fine level of detail, to create and direct land wealth, to realize rich public expectations, and to offer incentives so as to achieve all kinds of civic qualities and amenities that cannot be secured in any other way. Vancouver developers also use the same zoning tools to enhance the profitability of their projects, respond to changing circumstances, do new and different things that are popular among consumers, and make community investments that absolutely augment the value of their products and the prices they can achieve. Citizens also get into the centre of the action, leveraging all kinds of things they want for their neighbourhoods. As long as we are careful with compatible urban design, which, traditionally, we have fussed over in every single project, and as long as we do not allow intensive development to intrude into stable, nicely scaled communities, the public has tended to be on our side, at least as a passive beneficiary.

There is no question that the regulatory framework for this is quite complicated and vast in scale – it can be difficult to access and understand. There are tomes of zoning laws, backed up by piles of guideline documents. I have heard it said that Vancouver is one of the most regulated cities in North America. I have no doubt this is true, if you judge solely by the regulatory instruments that are in place. But we concluded early on that coping with a complex system is better than living with a bland, flat and unexciting city. We often said that the city needs to be complex, so its regulatory laws will naturally follow suit. Ironically, despite its extraordinary level of codification, the fact is that our system has fewer absolute requirements than you would see in many cities. However, the menu of options is extensive, which takes a lot more words but offers great freedom to find an alternative way to achieve the desired outcomes – a real potential for equivalencies – or even a better idea that no one has thought about before.

Perhaps the most pervasive outcome of this system has been to markedly enhance the urban design character in our city. In Chapter 7, I outlined the breadth of interests and rich agenda of urban design that have become so much a part of the personality of Vancouverism. After I left civic government, some of my colleagues from Abu Dhabi visited Vancouver. Falah Al Ahbabi, the young, energetic leader of the visiting delegation, was astounded by the detailed nature of our concern for the physical design of the place and the consistency and high quality of the results, particularly in the inner-city. I explained to them that our zoning system has enabled this.

For developers and their design teams who wanted to create great design, the system encouraged them to advance their best ideas, without the law being a barrier. In the time of Vancouverism, most designers and their sponsoring clients were experimenting with design solutions that were often well above performance elsewhere. We were able to support that.

For citizens, the system conferred the power to press for quality design because it could be covered by an enhanced development proforma. Many of our citizens have become aficionados of excellent contemporary design, so expectations have soared over the years.

For the urban designers and civic architects at city hall, such as the suave and sophisticated Ralph Segal and the erudite Scot Hein, the system empowered them to go all the way in their influence on the design of buildings and spaces to achieve the best they could envision. The regulations fully integrate the design agenda, so the urban designers were actually officially assigned to implement that agenda. To support and reinforce this, McAfee and I set up a small urban design studio in the planning department. Its task was to hone skills of urban design within the civic organization, offer quality design in-house, and engender a culture of design at city hall and out among the public. For many years, led by Scot Hein, this was a hotbed of drawing up urban design solutions in a studio format. Another measure, quite simple but amazingly effective, was that from early on, Spaxman had required all proposals to include not just drawings but also physical three-dimensional models. Models are easy to comprehend, and they quickly expose design flaws as well as highlighting good solutions.

One indicator of our design-focused discretionary system is that you see very little retro-style pastiche in Vancouver, partly because the regulatory framework and the attitudes at city hall have favoured contemporary expression but mostly because they empowered the culture of contemporary private architectural practice that has become so identifiable in Vancouver. Yes, we have had our clunkers.

We have also felt sorry, especially early on, to lose some innovative gems that would have well graced our community. I have acknowledged that in Chapter 7. But many people would testify that the general level of design has been higher than in most cities during this period, and I think the flexible system has been one of the reasons for that. The other reason has to do with how development proposals are reviewed and approved.

### The transactional adjudication process

In the traditional development management system, the process of reviewing and approving a development can be quite direct. It is essentially a policing activity. The developer submits a proposal to city hall, where someone reviews it to make sure that it meets the simple specifications of the law, and it is then approved or denied. Leading up to the late 1970s, this was the way things were handled in Vancouver, as in most other cities. The good side of this approach is that it is quite streamlined and efficient. The bad side is that it is difficult to have any real positive influence on a project to reflect public interests and concerns that are not directly dealt with in the by-law being administered but that you know are important to the people in your community. Policing simple rules is good to secure the basics, but it cannot secure excellence. It is hard to touch on more subtle matters and almost impossible to engage in a creative dialogue on the details of urban design. For the majority of straightforward developments in the less complicated parts of a city, this is all fine. So the traditional system, with modest variations, remains relevant and of great utility for much of the land-mass of any city. But in the fascinating, unpredictable, changeable, and diverse parts of a city – often the areas that matter most for people and also for the overall community – this can be frustrating if you are a public official with a sophisticated understanding of the organic needs and possibilities of those areas and people or if you are trying to make something special happen. It can also be irritating if you want to bring some coherence to these more complex settings, either across their geography or over time. And it can be downright maddening if you are try-ing to preserve a delicate and long-evolving historic or characterful place. Smart, forward-looking developers and creative citizens experience the same frustra-tion and irritation.

In these more complex and pivotal urban places, both in revitalization and new development, there is a need to do so much more. This requires the evolved regulatory framework that I have already described. But it also requires discus-sion to administer that framework. It requires brokering. It requires mutual learning, respectful debate, shared experimentation, and all the aspects of collaboration that I have already described. It requires a lot of negotiations. It requires transactions among many people on an ongoing basis. In other words, instead of just being a police officer, a public planning official needs to be a facilitator of urban ideas and design concepts. To make this happen in Vancouver, early on we put in place a well-articulated, more complex process than is typically seen in local government. It has come to be referred to as a "transactional development management system." This was just the ticket for our community as we moved into the years of Vancouverism, when expectations for the city as a great place became so pronounced and in such fine, pervasive detail. As we learned to facilitate a richer vision of our city, without insulting people, without denying their ideas, without diminishing their creative journey, we started to see better results. During the 1980s, to make the point, Ray Spaxman asked one of our best urban designers, Trish French, to catalogue these results. She produced a visually rich pamphlet titled *Eight Years After,*[1] which now can probably be discovered only in a dusty second-hand book shop somewhere. It showed the "before" and "after" images of key recent projects so that everyone could see the value added by the process. It was a convincing publication. But those were the early years, and as we became more proficient, as the design community became more central to this creative culture, as developers signed on, and as citizens joined in more fully, the city as a rich experience and appealing place became more and more compelling.

With developers, our transactions take the form of unprecedented negotiations as compared with the past, based upon the flexible legal parameters. These negotiations are intensive. For whole areas that are subject to new development through rezoning, they are wide-ranging, unconstrained, no holds barred. For projects within existing discretionary zoning, infilling into already built areas, negotiations are more focused on the specific parameters and options made available in the by-law. This is governance done in the business style. We could all see that developers wielded enormous power in civic affairs. After all, what they do is so pivotal to shaping the city and determining what it might or might not become. They also wield great resources in the political arena. They have to be agile in their business, finding their way to success in a tricky, risky endeavour, so they are always open to different ways to achieve results. We realized that we could not simply police them into submission of what the public interest required, no matter what power we might bring to bear. So, we opted instead to entice them. We decided to broker everything at stake with an eye to the success of developers as well as the city, and we added the inducements that I have already described, hoping to motivate their free delivery of public preferences. For any area or project, our conversations with developers are complicated and continuous.

One practice that helped bring a business tone to the relationships with developers has been to get real with the numbers – as they themselves must always do. So, early on, as we started to use incentives seriously, city hall moved away from a formulaic approach where something would be needed by the community and a specified increment of additional development would be offered by city hall to developers to secure that need. Instead, we started to do specific pro-forma analysis, such as I have described above, to determine just exactly how much value is being created in a project's land-value lift and how that compares with the real value of the public good to be provided by that project. This takes negotiations between the City and developers from essentially a guessing game on the financial side to one that is more like delicate acupuncture – targeting what specific aspects will be brokered and what specific actual values are at play. Now all of us know exactly what is in the quid pro quo under consideration. Of course, this process takes more time and information, but in the end, the results are calibrated more succinctly for both parties than was the case with the old-fashioned blunt formulas. This clarity has also been useful for citizens and politicians who monitor the process because they can see what values are being brokered, how they are determined, whether or not they are fair, and whether anyone is getting an accidental windfall.

With the design community, the architects, landscape architects, and other specialty designers, our transactions became more in the manner of a fascinating discussion rather than a hard negotiation. We exchange ideas, usually sketched on paper, and literally join forces to come up with better solutions. If you dissect the interests of designers, you find a natural affinity with public interests. You find a similar set of urban principles. You find creative aspirations that often go beyond profits to focus on what is just right or best for the community. The design sector is full of natural allies for public planners and urban designers. We simply had to find a way to work together as colleagues. This required two clever things at city hall – peer-to-peer engagement and independent peer review. Professional designers need to work with other professional designers, who speak their language, understand their shorthand, discuss in drawings rather than solely in words, and easily grasp three-dimensional ideas. Private architects feel resentful when the government representatives sitting across the table from them cannot match their level of design competence. So, face to face with the private architects and landscape architects making submissions, Vancouver has public architects and landscape architects, distinguished practitioners in their fields, who can inquire about any design matter at the same level of sophistication as any private designer (we call them "development planners"). With the private designers, they dream together. They draw together. They find solutions that neither could have discovered separately. Ralph Segal, the best of the best of these development planners, calls the relationship "sleeves-rolled-up collaboration." Peers talk to peers.

When public and private designers work together, the question of who has the final say can be a difficult one. Urban design is in large measure a subtle art rather than a predictable science. Private architects are irritated when public architects pull rank and make the call, merely because they are the "approval authority." However, because they are all trained through what is called a "jury system" at design school, in which their ideas are critiqued by a collegium of fellow designers, they will happily submit to a panel of peers to help make that final decision and are usually sanguine about the results. Vancouver has had an Urban Design Panel for about forty years (see Figure 9.2). It consists of independent and renowned local architects, landscape architects, urban designers, and environmental engineers, who review all significant proposals with the design teams and city staff, proffering advice and suggestions. Nominated by their professional organizations, these designers are appointed by city council and sit for two-year terms. They are not the final decision-makers, which is key because they do not try to broker issues other than design. But because they are independent and totally detached from the project and the City, they tend to be unbiased and simply give their best take on design choices. Peers review peers.

Through these arrangements, we have avoided bickering and bad blood. Instead, we have convened a rich and subtle design discussion among our best creative people, which has hit the ground in a glorious way as the contemporary city has been built.

Our transactions with the public became constant, diverse, and increasingly creative over time. This involves both a general inquiry with the public on people's preferences and needs, followed by soliciting everyone's specific critique of what is on offer. I will cover the logic and techniques of public engagement and involvement a little later, but at this point, I need to emphasize that no step of the development management process is undertaken without some format to discover and integrate public opinions about a project that is under consideration. This takes two directions. For the general community, our job is to determine how an addition to a living place will affect that place from whatever angle the locals think is important. You might describe this as a mini-planning exercise to see how the new will fit in with the existing. Then, with immediate neighbours of a project, we are interested in impacts, so we find ourselves brokering interests between those who are adjacent and the project's developer – back to hard negotiations.

The formal arrangements for decision making on applications show the ultimate result of the transactional style of the Vancouver system. As in most cities, city council makes rezoning decisions upon recommendation of the staff, with a clearly legislated process for public input at a public hearing. This is neither unusual nor innovative, although the review process does involve more public engagement than in many other places. Where Vancouver sets itself apart from other cities is in its arrangement for approvals of proposals that are allowable on a discretionary basis within current zoning. Our principle is that, though elected officials have the best handle on wide-ranging policy directions, appointed officials are better able to do a positive technical job of dispassionate adjudication of particular development proposals. So, the institution and process for development approvals have been removed from the official political process. Decisions on minor proposals are delegated to the chief planner. But for major, complex, or contentious developments, the Development Permit Board, shortened as the DP Board, performs this task (see Figure 9.3). This board is composed of four appointed officials who are leaders in the civic bureaucracy. Its voting members are the chief planner, the chief engineer, and the deputy city manager. It is chaired by the director of development services, who does not vote. None of the members is an elected politician. In fact, it is considered rude or at least bad manners for a politician even to enter the room when the DP Board is in session because this might be seen as an attempt to pressure or influence the board members. City council's sole control over the DP Board is in appointing and firing its members, though the latter is hard to do and has never happened. The DP Board sits with an advisory group of citizen representatives, including the chair of the Urban Design Panel and also a youth representative. The DP Board always sits in public (never in closed session).

Furnished with a technical report on the results of all the lead-up staff negotiations and public involvement, the board hears the applicant, the staff, any and

**9.2** For creative and mutually respectful collaboration between civic officials and the professional design community, peer review has been essential. The Urban Design Panel, shown here in action at a recent meeting, is composed of distinguished architects, landscape architects, and other environmental designers.

**9.3** Significant new development in Vancouver is adjudicated by the Development Permit Board, shown here in a recent session. The board is a professionalized and non-political body. After wide public input and peer advice, decisions are made by senior civic officials, assisted by a citizens' advisory panel. City council is not involved.

all members of the public who wish to speak, and the advisory group. It then makes its decision in full, in all its details, then and there. Everyone is on the scene. Everyone is watching as events unfold. Everyone sees the deliberations and the final decision. Nothing happens elsewhere or behind closed doors. And for most proposals, the DP Board's decisions are final, without appeal of any kind except through the courts if someone feels that an error occurred in the process. However, this almost never happens, because the process is air tight. In all the places I have ever practised, and having been a member of the DP Board for over a decade, I have not found a more intelligent, more agile, more inclusive, more timely, more defensible, more principled, or better arrangement for making these kinds of decisions. Frankly, it is a pleasure to watch the DP Board in action.

### Key features of the system

In both the regulations and the process for development approvals, there are four primary features to remember in the unfolding of Vancouverism.

First, this is a system that is very government-proactive. The public authority wants to be an integral part, maybe even an equal player, with the private sector in designing and detailing the development of the city. To put it another way, we say that "the City plans and designs the city for the whole community – not developers or special interest groups or powerful individuals or big companies." In addition, the public is a big influence, not just as consumers but also in the initial inventions.

Second, this is a system where success is motivated more with the carrot than with the stick. Its requirements are not overbearing and are usually relatively easy and economical to meet. Options with greater opportunity are wide-ranging, and though they do leverage public goods or better public performance, they also offer the possibility of wealth creation to cover the extra costs, thus making them practical.

Third, this is a system that requires sophisticated bureaucratic capacities. It needs genuine understanding of and facility with urban land economics and how the development business works. It needs strong urban design skills and talents. It needs process management expertise. It needs group facilitation knowledge and public engagement expertise. Obviously, it cannot be run by amateurs or those who lack experience.

Fourth, this is a system that moves things forward by setting clear directions and reconciling differences. It does not stall. It leads to results that reinforce one another as a basis for further results. It is strong on principles but also practical. Ultimately, it works because it is fulfilling to an array of interests. This drives the process.

It was not easy to either birth or consolidate the discretionary and transactional development management system that I have been describing. There were many knocks and bruises along the way. As I look back over a number of years, having been out of the fray, I now also realize that the system is inherently vulnerable. So much of what is achievable depends upon those principles and long-polished protocols and dedication to a philosophy of engagement. Often, these are more embedded in the consciousness of the players than in written policy or by-laws or guides. So as people like myself departed the arena – people who put the system together, believed in all of its parts, and made it work day-to-day in thousands of engagements – we saw several distortions that created some anxiety out in the community. When a system depends so strongly on a social contract of collaboration, this is always a danger. I will focus on several of the key concerns later, but let me note two things here. First, a clear understanding of how the system works is essential to its success. I lament that as we passed it on to the next generation, we left them to learn all its subtleties by themselves, on the job as they did the job. So, of course, they had growing pains. Second, if a delicate mutual respect does not exist among all the players in all the sectors, the system seems to get bogged down. Every single person has to personally build that respect, and that just takes time. The current generation is still in its shake-down, but I am confident that the system is robust enough that they will be sustained and supported moving forward. I sure hope so, because it is simply a very good system.

### HOW THE PUBLIC SETS THE PACE OF URBAN CHANGE

If the public is to play a meaningful role in local government, it needs to be empowered. To be empowered, it needs to be convened (see Figure 9.4). It is true that, when people see things they do not like, they will rise up and express themselves vigorously in a democracy, certainly at the polls but also through other forms of protest. But building a great city cannot be founded on such negativity. Positive involvement is needed. And yet, most of the public tends to be rather passive and disengaged – unlike the civic authorities or developers or a few others in the local context who have direct interests at stake. To change that, the general public needs motivation and a forum. From the early years of his reset, Ray Spaxman began to deal with this issue. He saw that people often would not

**9.4** Civic government convenes and empowers the Vancouver public to facilitate wide input. Public meetings, as seen here, are only a small part of an array of techniques for close public involvement.

be automatically clear about their own self-interests, much less the interests of others, and that, without doubt, government could not spontaneously predict private interests of either individual people or communities. Finding clarity needs good face-to-face discussion. So, he set in place a continuous process for intensive dialogue among people and between people and their government about urban problems and options for change.

Then, down through the years, we turned this process into a fine science. This involved everything from surveys and polls to community events and open houses, to public meetings and ideas fairs, to focus groups and community advisory committees, to design workshops and design-ins. Recently, all the links through social media have entered the picture. The list of techniques for engagement is endless because new formats are being invented all the time. Public engagement became a hallmark of Vancouverism, as important as technical analysis in planning and decision making. What started as a desire to inform, along with a healthy curiosity about what people wanted and needed as citizens,

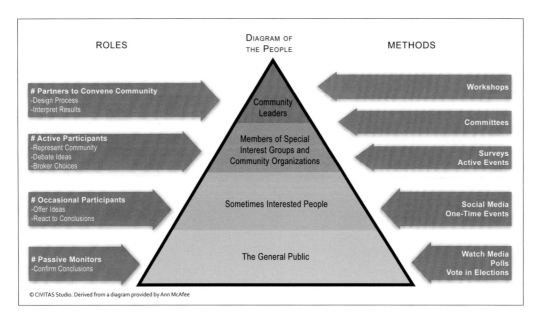

**ROLES**

**DIAGRAM OF THE PEOPLE**

**METHODS**

**# Partners to Convene Community**
-Design Process
-Interpret Results

Community Leaders

Workshops

**# Active Participants**
-Represent Community
-Debate Ideas
-Broker Choices

Members of Special Interest Groups and Community Organizations

Committees

Surveys
Active Events

**# Occasional Participants**
-Offer Ideas
-React to Conclusions

Sometimes Interested People

Social Media
One-Time Events

**# Passive Monitors**
-Confirm Conclusions

The General Public

Watch Media
Polls
Vote in Elections

© CIVITAS Studio. Derived from a diagram provided by Ann McAfee

**9.5** This diagram illustrates what is called the "triangle of citizen participation," which describes how people wish to be engaged and then targets the best methods for meeting their expectations. An overlay of advice at differing levels generally echoes common themes that decision makers can depend upon.

became a strong urge to also know about their preferences as consumers. So, we at city hall became very inquisitive about the needs and opinions of individuals, of households, of neighbours, of interest groups, and of communities. Then we developed a fascination with consumer trends and the collective perspective of the general public as a whole. What started out as public information became public input, public engagement, and then public involvement – bringing in our citizens as primary players in all the activities of planning and managing urban change.

During the CityPlan program, the planning team used a handy diagram to explain our approach to public involvement. We have not been able to get to the bottom of who invented this representation, but the CityPlan team certainly brought it to the fore in our town. They called it the "triangle of citizen participation" (see Figure 9.5). It offers a helpful characterization of both the purpose and tools of engagement and the various groupings of the public that are involved in it.

You can think of the triangle as symbolic of the totality of people who comprise the community.

At the top are a few people who see themselves as community leaders and spokespeople. Despite their small numbers, they tend to be influential if for no other reason than that they spontaneously want to tell their local government how they feel, they want to participate, and, often, if they had their way, they would want to take over the process. As a pejorative, we might call them "professional citizens." More truthfully and respectfully, they are genuine community leaders.

In the middle of the triangle are many more people. These are the good souls who make a community tick, who bring a local place its everyday life. They lead and populate the neighbourhood organizations through which a localized culture comes together – the parent-teacher committees, the childcare groups, the community centre boards, and the like – giving of their time and resources freely and thanklessly. This part of the triangle also includes all the special interest groups and spokespeople that engage in the public discourse in any city. Usually, all these people have their heads down, doing what they do as volunteers, but they have a community consciousness and are interested in the general questions of their area that go beyond their day-to-day focus. Also in this middle group are a great many people who respond to the issues they are interested in and actively participate around those issues, even though a whole program of involvement might not be their cup of tea.

At the bottom of the triangle is the great mass of the rest of the public. These are people going about their daily lives and business – busy people who don't have time, energy, or a natural inclination to link up with the local affairs around where they live. They may or may not vote in civic elections. They surely care about what happens near them and how it will affect them but usually don't try to affect it. They may also be disempowered by poverty or language barriers or disabilities or social isolation. If you ask for their opinion, they'll give it, but getting them to turn out for active discussion is difficult.

Through the years, our engagement forums became more and more shaped by this characterization of the public. We tap into the community leaders in direct, interactive ways to explore issues, perspectives, options, and solutions in detail. We call on them to help us convene the rest of the community. We use them to design and manage our outreach materials. We ask them to help interpret results. And we lean on them to become the spokespeople for results as we move toward political decisions. But we do not take their views as final or as truth. For the middle groups, we use their existing organizations as a good place for discussion – we go to them. We ask them to join in active events of engagement, such as public meetings or community fairs or roundtable discussions. We invite them to join ongoing working committees. We look to them to represent their community in brokering activities or with developers or in policy making. This group does a lot of the footwork of public involvement. But here too, we do not take these people's views as final.

Then, for the balance of the community, we do not expect continuous active involvement, but we test with them the working conclusions on the initial issues, the options, and solutions that have been generated by the more face-to-face discussions. We use surveys and polls and social media conversations and one-time events such as open houses.

My purpose is not to go into the almost limitless list of techniques but to illustrate that there are many types of forums at many levels and that we are constantly inventing more inviting and interesting ways to work with people. These are carefully tailored to suit the level of interest and inclination to engage among differing individuals and groups. Layered engagement in multiple formats reveals similar themes that echo over and over again, so the results become very dependable.

Then, to this general culture of outreach, through the years we added the special features that bring in the less spontaneous participants. Our meeting times became more sensitive to people's work and family schedules. We served refreshments and offered other features, such as childcare, to make the meetings as comfortable as possible. We became more careful about suitability and location of venues, going into the community rather than expecting people to come to us. We started thinking about the best ways to come together with really marginalized people, such as the poor and those with special needs. We added multiple languages to all our activities and materials. We tried to make all our engagement more fun and fulfilling for participants – cutting the boredom. And the civic teams learned the fine art of group facilitation and interest-based engagement, where the focus is on the diversity of interests rather than positions, so many new kinds of solutions can be explored.

Also, we always emphasized our special responsibility to solicit comments from people who are directly affected by the various vectors of change – particularly those who live directly adjacent to a proposed development project and community members whose entire area is undergoing disruption, planning, and redevelopment. Early on, Spaxman established a practice of placing an informative sign on every site that was subject to a development or rezoning application

**9.6** An early initiative to invite citizens into the civic governance process for new development proposals was placement of a sign announcing what is proposed, who proposes it, whom to contact at city hall, and how to get involved. This move showed that city hall was serious about hearing what people had to say. It remains a key feature of the process.

(see Figure 9.6). We were among the earliest in North America to do that. For each development application, there is a tailored outreach inquiry with the neighbours and those close by. I have already described the energy put into neighbourhood and area planning. Those physical three-dimensional models of projects, which I referenced earlier, make it so easy for average people to understand what is going on and how it might affect them. For people who live immediately beside sites of change, we usually have specific personal meetings to identify impacts and confirm mitigation measures for both developer and government implementation. If we feel there will be ongoing impacts that will need continuing resolution over time, such as with insinuation of a school or church hall or special needs facility within a residential setting, we often draft what we call a "good neighbour agreement" between management of the new facility and the neighbours. This agreement will specify all the agreed-upon mitigation measures, as well as who will do what. It also sets a timetable for regular review. Both the facility operator and the neighbours sign the agreement, indicating that they will abide by its terms. Although we make these documents very formal, the City lawyers through the years were often quite disdainful – they always worried because such agreements had no legal standing. But frankly, the agreements work like a charm because they create a moral imperative for everyone to cooperate, and then everyone learns how to cooperate without the need of agreements. Of course, that is what neighbourliness, that prime concept that I described in several earlier chapters, is really all about. We found many ways to instigate the outreach and collaboration that is essential for diverse uses and activities to mix up together comfortably.

The ever-changing formats and commitments of public engagement became absolutely essential to civic affairs from the beginning of the reforms in the 1970s and onward. But there have been some key parameters. We work to empower citizens through the array of forums and methods described, but we are not in the business of giving them complete control. We have always seen specific public interests as just one aspect of the equation, which has to be balanced with local government policy interests representing a broader and longer view. We have always seen the public's concerns in balance with a desire for best practices, especially in design and sustainability. We have always seen the specific interests of citizens in balance with the interests of proponents of change – private developers or agents of public infrastructure or hosts of special needs such as low-income housing. We have always seen that majority interests need to be balanced with minority concerns. The public is a key player, but it does not rule the roost. Indeed, city council has the final say, and the ultimate authority remains the law. All of the balancing and brokering of interests are framed within this context of democratic political institutions and the law. Moreover, we are always mindful of time spent and of the amount of resources that can reasonably be applied to public involvement. We do not let public outreach stall or unduly draw out the process; otherwise, the march of forward movement is too risky and unpredictable. We realize that public views can be plumbed only so deep, no matter how much time, money, and effort we expend. We have to maintain an equilibrium between the effort and the yield. But throughout, we have stayed true to the principle that every citizen has the right to participate and the right to be heard. This is a right of citizenship, and we cannot censor it in any way.

I have often said with pride that as chief planners, Ann McAfee and I had staff on the street, out in the community, every day of the year except Christmas and Boxing Day, talking about all kinds of specific and general topics and questions of urban change in Vancouver. In all of these continuous activities of public engagement and involvement, something happened that had not really been expected but that represents a valuable underpinning for Vancouver planning on an ongoing basis. A strong culture of what I call "urban connoisseurship" has been engendered among a significant segment of the community. As a result, many Vancouverites know with confidence what is good and bad about cities, what specific measures add or detract from the quality of their city, what development is positive and negative, what needs to be done for enhancements in the future, and what qualities they should treasure in the existing urban setting. They understand the concepts and language of urban design and sustainability. They know who does what in government and how to intervene. They are conversant in the rights and responsibilities of living in a community in addition to just the personal conveniences and pleasures. And with these insights, they have become a strong and powerful constituency for planning and design. This understanding and support made me, for one, very confident when I spoke to council or on a public dais about our city. It has been a pleasure to watch this consolidate and spread, and it may represent the best insurance of all that, as the world turns, the trajectory of Vancouverism will not be waylaid or denied. Ray Spaxman's public engagement focus of so many years before has come home to roost in a very helpful way.

## THE PLANNING PROCESS: BRINGING PROGRESSIVE COHERENCE OUT OF RANDOMNESS

As you might imagine, our initial planning process to create a diverse, fascinating, and fulfilling urban environment in Vancouver and to set up a sophisticated development management system was a complex undertaking. This was especially true because it entailed not only a technical activity but also wide-ranging consultation with everyone. It was iterative. It was dispersed. It did not unfold in a logical fashion through a pre-determined agenda but more as and where directions and plans were needed. And yet, it ultimately came together into a coherent presentation of the preferred arrangement, character, and image of the city that was wanted and needed by our citizens and that represented progressive principles for a livable, sustainable, and attractive place.

I have already explained that Vancouver really had no contemporary overall plan until the advent of CityPlan in 1995.[2] I have described the long tradition of community and area planning, with deep public involvement, which commenced back in the 1970s and extended right through the turn of the century. I have described the transportation plans that were finalized through the early 2000s. These plans always provided us with a general reference and even inspiration. But when the megaprojects came along, each at its own random time and location, we found ourselves with a particularly difficult challenge – we needed all the parameters to be a lot more specific. We needed tailored plans for both the megaproject lands and the areas nearby. We needed heavy public buy-in. We needed clear answers to so many questions of the public interest coming from the developers. We felt a compulsion to exemplify the best thinking of our time because we knew that these megaprojects would set the whole image of our city. So, we had to figure out a sensible way to plan these areas. We designed what became the typical planning framework in our earlier efforts, and I will always be grateful to one person who was not a public official but who helped us initially put it all together in a logical fashion. His name was Stanley Kwok. He was a wise soul, the local head of Concord Pacific Developments at the time, the first huge developer we had to deal with in what became known as False Creek North. Owning a vast stretch of downtown waterfront land, Concord Pacific proved itself to be a responsible and progressive developer, and Stanley Kwok both led his company wisely and advised us wisely as we designed a process that would meet our needs but also be acceptable to the private sector.

Our megaproject planning strategy had three elements that I want to describe in some detail.

### Iterative area planning

First, the planning process was iterative, going from the general to the specific in stages, resulting in a hierarchical framework of planning documents. Because the areas were so complicated, our government aspirations were so high, the public interests were so diverse, and the developer's interests were so strong, we could not possibly cover everything in one round of planning. It was too complex – the human brain just could not conceive it all at one time. Although each megaproject had its own particular agenda, generally the stages unfolded in the same way.

We would start with what we called the "dream document," this being a general policy statement that indicated conceptually what would and would not be included in the area. It offered targets and ideas, along with indications of character and special features, but very few actual geographical patterns or layouts. I must say, with each area, the documents became more elaborate because the public discussion became more fulsome. The key advantage of these policy statements was that they focused all our efforts right up front, motivating all of us on both the public and private side to work on what was likely to succeed rather than on tangential notions that would probably never win acceptance from either the public, the government, or the developer. If such notions are not put aside at the outset, they can highjack a great deal of time, energy, and emotion throughout the planning process.

The general policy statement was followed by an official development plan, or ODP. This area-wide scheme specified uses, densities, and heights. It laid out the particular geography of uses, buildings, streets, and spaces. It defined the exact links for contextual integration, listed public amenities to be included in the area, and cited other requirements to be leveraged through area development. A highly detailed policy and design document, the ODP covered everything that would definitely be included in the area as it developed. It also set the parameters for brokering the public goods for the development allowances.

Next, we completed the comprehensive development zonings for each discrete part of the area, usually one at a time, tying down all the allowances and requirements, getting very specific on all aspects of design, adding the guidelines to codify expected character, and securing the public goods and any financial contributions to resolve any other impacts on the public infrastructure through legal agreements registered on the title of the property. Since these specific zonings happened over time, we were able to refine and improve the schemes as we went along, make amendments to reflect changing circumstances or consumer demands, and add further embellishments that became evident as the place came together through the actual development. Once a zoning was in place, the developer could then secure actual permission to build, as well as the construction permits for those buildings. This whole iterative process allowed us to deal with a general vision and broad principles, then with more specific design concepts and targets, and finally with very particular design solutions and amenity provisions at a detailed level.

This process worked well in dealing with the complexity of the place and its players, but we had to find a way to deal with the equal complexity of diverse civic interests at play within and between the various City departments. Negotiating among these interests can be treacherous not only because civic departments are powerful and tend to struggle with one another but also because the many interests vested in laws and regulations cannot be ignored. Shopping ideas and solutions from one department to another was not a good idea and can go on forever without results. Historically, this often caused political interference as developers, if they were stuck in an impasse, would look to city councillors to intervene and find a solution. We simply could not go forward with the big megaprojects with this kind of confusion. It was too risky for them and for us. So, we put in place a handy group to broker and reconcile civic interests and to negotiate civic positions so there would be consistent messages coming out of city hall from all departments. We called it the "Major Projects Steering Committee." It included all the key civic department heads – planning, engineering, parks, social planning, and housing. While it had no official status, there was a firm agreement that authorities would be left at the door, issues would be fully aired, and results would be honoured by all parties as they took their authorities back in hand. When I became co-director, I chaired this committee for many years and it worked like a charm. We gave the developers and the public consistent and dependable one-stop shopping for services out of city hall. We offered a place to quickly resolve disputes between departments or between a department and the developer. Later, because it was so convenient and bypassed so much hassle, I convened a small sub-committee of this group to specifically broker the community amenity contributions that began to flow so that all departments enjoyed a fair share of the public goods that were leveraged through the development management process. Both staff groups were essential to the coherence and credibility of the process.

## Parallel policy planning

Second, the planning process set off a parallel analysis to determine supportive policy that would apply to the project of the moment but would also become the precedent reference for later projects. For example, we set amenity standards for all the public facilities and services so we could begin to implement a logical and equitable package in each area that would also be consistent with existing city-wide equivalents. We set a social-housing policy. We began to set environmental standards. We confirmed general urban design parameters, such as building floorplate maximums and building separations for privacy or streetwall specs that could apply to any project. The list of adopted policies is a long one, and this policy formation unfolded in an incremental and opportunistic way. I have described this in detail in Chapters 4, 6, and 7. With each major question of public requirements, we tried to spin off not just an answer for the particular area but also a policy that would apply everywhere henceforth. Fortunately, it ultimately came together as a coherent policy paradigm and direction, probably because, without realizing it, we were always working from the same guiding principles.

## Concomitant context planning

Third, as we planned each megaproject, we also launched the planning of its adjacent area and ultimately of the whole downtown. Planning the adjacent areas was essential to make sure that the new and the existing would fit together well. In earlier chapters, I have described the planning for upland areas that was set off by planning for waterfront megaproject sites. Planning for the overall central area was also essential to make sure that each megaproject scheme was playing its proper role in providing the complete package for a downtown, a progressive package for a state-of-the-art future core city, and the right overall result for the future image of Vancouver. We needed a seamless result, even though individual initiatives were somewhat random, based upon the accident of when land became available and when the economy was ready for more to happen.

What characterized all this planning is that it was continuous, it was led by the City, and it had developer and citizen involvement. There was ongoing pressure and understanding that it must all finally come together into something better than the sum of its parts.

### FINDING THE MONEY FOR PREMIUM PLACEMAKING

Canada is a country where not much money is allotted to cities from senior governments. British Columbia is a province where not much fundraising capacity is allowed for municipalities by enabling legislation. Except for property taxes and user fees, local government has few other sources of funding. Vancouver is a city where existing citizens have little tolerance for a local tax increase, especially if its purpose is to underwrite new development and to provide amenities and services for new arrivals that are better than what they themselves enjoy. We had to accept the status quo that the existing tax base would cover the annual costs of delivering existing municipal services and the debt charges on a given level of capital borrowing for new facilities that could be carried without stress on the budget. Anything new would have to be paid for some other way. Even in the face of escalating expectations for quality living and the need to entice people to higher-density living with lavish amenities, where was Vancouver to get the money for all this new and expensive infrastructure? In the years of Vancouverism, we came to depend upon five new sources of funding that allowed so much that was new and better to happen.

### Leveraged funding

I have already alluded to the most important of these new funding sources, which is the money leveraged from the rezoning process. We call this the "community amenity contribution," or CAC for short (see Figure 9.7). It is specified as a contribution rather than a tax because it is absolutely voluntary – if a proponent

**9.7** Except for the bridge in the far distance, everything in the public realm of this picture, taken in False Creek North – the seawall furnishings and finishes, the trees, and the park in the background – was paid for by the developer, Concord Pacific, as a community amenity contribution. Thank you to Terry Hui.

**9.8** The Contemporary Art Gallery, a civic non-profit arts facility shown here, was provided through bonusing, in exchange for which a developer received an extra development allowance, as laid out in the zoning for the site. Thank you to the developer.

does not wish to provide the contribution, then he or she can forgo the rezoning. It is up to the proponent. Given these circumstances, I have always felt that "contribution" was an odd word to use, but apparently it keeps everything clean in law, so who am I to judge? You will remember that the CAC is accessed from the land-value lift that comes with the approval of an increased development allowance for a site. This value can be used for anything felt necessary to serve the demand on public infrastructure of the population that comes with the new development – parks, childcare, drinking fountains, all kinds of things, large and small. Often, it is offered in kind, on-site of the contributing development, but increasingly, we also see it provided in cash that can go into a civic fund to help pay for an amenity or facility off-site that needs multiple contributions.

### Bonused funding

The second, and related, new source of funding does not actually consist of cash. I described earlier the incentives for specified public amenities that are built into the discretionary zoning applied to most areas of Vancouver outside single-family districts. Many public facilities and amenities are leveraged out of this source (see Figure 9.8). From modest embellishments, such as benches or landscaped pocket-spaces, to whole new facilities, such as the Vancouver International Film Centre and the Contemporary Art Gallery, this has become a prime source for public goods that might never make the cut in the tight capital budget cycles at city hall. These contributions to the social, cultural, and recreational infrastructure of the city are made in kind rather than in cash. So, we generally get more for the value leveraged because the public good is delivered at a wholesale price, in contrast to the retail price the City pays for the same good if it were secured through the marketplace.

### Development tax

The third source of funding is a fee on development that was allowed for Vancouver to cover the inevitable additional capital costs of social and recreational facilities and services demanded by newcomers in locations that are developing through existing zoning. We call this the "development cost levy," or DCL for short (see Figure 9.9). It was unusual for the Province to give Vancouver a new funding source, but this was one for which we argued hard. We pointed to the suburbs, which are permitted to collect a similar levy for the extension of their basic utility services, without which no development can happen. Of

**9.9** Emery Barnes Park, a green space enjoyed by everyone, was paid for by the developers who built the buildings in the area around it, as a development cost levy. The levy provided a fair share from each builder. Thank you to the Downtown South developers.

**9.10** The creation of the Athletes Village, also called Southeast False Creek was enabled by the Property Endowment Fund, a civic property portfolio whose profits underpin other civic finances and are used for special City initiatives. Then, the Millennium Group's community amenity contribution covered the cost of all public amenities in the area. Thank you to the Malek brothers. ▷

course, Vancouver already has both a full network of utility services and a smart, long-standing policy of replacement and upgrading these utilities (annually, 1 percent of capital spending is invested in utility updating). We argued that we should enjoy the same development fee as the suburbs but be allowed to use it for social infrastructure that comes under stress with growth. DCLs can be used for park space, replacement affordable housing (usually social housing), child-care centres, and engineering infrastructure.

### Funding from civic equity

The fourth source of funds is a clever one invented back in the 1970s at the beginning of the TEAM era by Mayor Art Phillips. It is value generated by using the real estate equity of City-owned land. Essentially, this is a civic-based sovereign investment fund. The vehicle to capture this is called the "Property Endowment Fund," or PEF for short. Phillips had been a wealth manager in private life, and he and his colleagues assessed all City-owned property that was not currently being used for City purposes. Unneeded land was sold, and the resulting funds were used strategically to start buying property in the city that could be expected to gain value over time. PEF real estate managers sell, buy, rent, and lease properties on an ongoing basis. They handle the land as any private

corporation might treat a real estate investment portfolio to secure profitability, but with public objectives added to the typical profit motive of such a portfolio. The PEF is effectively a land bank. The income from sales or rents for this land bank property and capital gains as the bank increases in value are used to balance the local budget, which is required by law, by topping off shortfalls so that taxes do not have to be increased too drastically. The income is also used to underwrite things needed by the City. For example, the PEF spent many years assembling properties on the southeast shore of False Creek. Some of this land was sold just after the turn of the century to provide the site for the Athletes Village for the 2010 Winter Olympic Games, which, of course, has now been further transformed into a showcase of the type of community that results from Vancouverism (see Figure 9.10). By the way, this land portfolio also helps the City achieve a high credit rating when it borrows for capital works and is even used as an in-house bank for occasional short-term borrowing for local projects.

### Cost-recovered planning service
At a much smaller scale, the fifth and final new source of funds was nonetheless important, at least to the budget of the planning department. Megaproject planning is both expensive and urgent. The City is obliged to annually balance

its operating budget. So, we had to find a way to underwrite the cost of intensive planning and the ready availability of staff to cover all the aspects of proactive involvement in the change process that I have been describing. We hit upon a very simple idea – what we called "cost-recovered" planning programs. When a developer for a major project comes to city hall requesting planning and development management services, an offer is made to either wait in line for the staff to become available or pay the complete costs for a full planning team to do all the work on a faster schedule. We project a work program and estimate the costs and then present this expedited planning service at a fixed price that the developer can take or leave. Of course, the cost-recovery payment does not give any guarantee of an outcome or of any special consideration by the City whatsoever. All aspects of the service, including staff selection, remain fully in City hands. What the service does offer, however, is very useful to developers: an agreed-upon process, timing, public process led by City staff, regular attention of city council to resolve policy conflicts, and a one-stop service that coordinates the involvement of all civic departments. Developers have found it attractive because it saves time (and time is money), and its predictability cuts risk. Every major megaproject planning process in recent memory has been completely funded outside the regular budget of city hall.

### Another funding source not exploited

Another nascent source that we experimented with but have not taken further or regularized is outreach for philanthropy. In the mid-1980s, just before the years of Vancouverism, I took a short break from planning and founded a unique civic initiative for local philanthropy hand-in-hand with a colleague, Trish French, whom I have already introduced as one of our best urban designers. It was linked with Vancouver's centennial and the Expo 86 celebration – we called it the "Vancouver Legacies Program." This city hall program offered a formal opportunity for companies and individual citizens to give gifts to the City (see Figure 9.11). Working from information provided by civic departments and service groups in the city, we systematically compiled a list of needed amenities that never seemed to get normal funding. We published a fun black-and-white newsprint catalogue of smaller gifts that we sent to every household in the city. We also published a glossy colour booklet of big gifts – that went to local companies, their boards, and executives. Many people helped us, but one person deserves special recognition, a private-sector publicist named John Plul, who really taught us how to reach out to corporate Vancouver and put together

**9.11** Constructed by Alvin Kanak of Rankin Inlet, this sculpture, called *Inukshuk,* was a gift to the City through the Vancouver Legacies Program, which was created in the mid-1980s to help fund the City's centennial celebrations. The program was successful, but outreach to philanthropists did not become a permanent funding source. It has great future potential. Thank you to Coast Hotels for the donation.

appealing sponsorship proposals. This is an art and he was an artist. For both small and big gifts, the program had significant success and garnered attention from across the country. Over about two years, we secured gifts worth several million dollars. There were thousands of gifts. Some were as small as a few hundred dollars for a tree or play equipment, and some were as large as many thousands for such big moves as the restoration of the Lost Lagoon fountain and the historic Burrard Bridge. Sadly, when the birthday party was over, the City did not continue the program. It has never been clear exactly why, except that continued operation of the program would have to be included in the normal civic budget, and that was seen as a risky use of public funds. The argument just did not seem to fly that money has to be invested if money is to be made. But one feature taken up by the park board has remained phenomenally successful. Under this following initiative, people can give a gift to the City by funding a public bench to be placed in a park or along the seawall or a sidewalk. They can dedicate their gift to whomever they wish. The bench is fitted with a bronze plaque, most of which celebrate or commemorate an individual. Now there are hundreds of benches and hundreds of personal stories captured on bronze plaques spread all over the city. Of course, many local organizations reach out for private and corporate sponsorship, but philanthropy for the City remains a significant untapped source to augment tight normal budgets. The Vancouver Legacies Program offers only a tantalizing taste of the possibilities.

## Bringing together the whole picture

In the early 2000s, Ann McAfee, Ronda Howard, and their team produced one of the most pivotal reports of the whole period of Vancouverism. It was called *Financing Growth*.[3] The analysis in this report systematically dealt with the increasing challenge of how to accommodate a growing population in the city while maintaining the level of services and amenities that people have come to enjoy as their right. It comprehensively projected growth, estimated the type, amount, and costs of City facilities to serve this new growth, and then outlined choices for how this growth could be paid for. It listed the traditional tools of taxes, user fees, and capital borrowing, as well as the various charges on new development, the newer tools I have just described. For the differing choices, the report identified which of these sources would pay and how much, and how this would hit the average taxpayer. Very helpfully, the team had local economist Jay Wollenberg weigh in on who actually pays the various development-based charges. Then, through a deliberate public and political process, involving thousands of people, the team finalized a strategy to finance growth, which city council approved in 2004. This strategy is still being more or less followed today. It was certainly in the spirit of outreach and transparency that Vancouver made decisions on this most fundamental of questions a collective effort.

## RESILIENCE OF A COMPLEX SYSTEM

As you have no doubt begun to realize, I am a great advocate for the processes and arrangements that were invented or applied to implement Vancouverism. I am not shy in saying that. But that does not mean that I have not felt worries, both through the years of my involvement and now looking into the future. I alluded to such anxieties earlier in this commentary. Let me offer just four further notes of concern.

My first concern is the complexity of our processes. I have already said that the system of planning and development control became more and more elaborate over the years, to the point that it is now complicated and time consuming. I explained why that should be acceptable in a diverse, complex city. But that does not mean that it does not remain a key anxiety and that the City should not always be finding ways to make the system work more efficiently and effectively. Many years ago, after one of many process audits, several very helpful measures were put in place. The entire activity of development management was separated from the planning function and put in its own organization, the development services department, where it might be tuned up regularly. For complex, important projects, the new department offers a service of in-house bureaucratic process managers called "facilitators." These staffers cannot cut to the chase on decisions, but they are empowered to confirm the review process and the staff participants who will input into the decisions. And, as things unfold, they also highlight bottlenecks and roadblocks. For a while, the City also made weekly announcements, in which it projected the timing for various types of applications, a move that made the process more predictable and bearable for applicants. Sadly, that practice was later discontinued, which was frustrating for many regulars to the process. Efficiencies seem to come and go, so criticisms of bureaucratic slowness and confusion still haunt city hall. There are important lessons to be learned from this experience: efficiency needs to be constantly reviewed; staff need to be regularly trained and attuned to quality and responsive service; and audits of processes and the obsolescence of regulations and procedures need to be institutionalized (in the past, I suggested that a formal, independent regulation audit department be founded within the City organization to remove outdated regulations). My biggest concern is that, if efficiencies are not constantly highlighted, then the whole system becomes sticky and therefore politically vulnerable, no matter how much it positively achieves. People have only so much patience.

My second concern is the ethics of public engagement. As we instituted more sustained public engagement over the years, we effectively gave our citizens a promise. That promise was that they would always have a central role and open access to all the processes and decisions for the future of the city and that we would listen to them. But that promise can become hollow if better and better techniques are not instituted, or if city hall becomes complacent or sloppy in its public outreach, or if outreach becomes only a step to be ticked off the list rather than used to truly evolve plans, policies, and proposals. This can happen at any time. It is vital to pay attention to the primary indicator as to whether or not the public engagement process is healthy – that is whether or not people are coming to city hall to protest how that engagement is undertaken or used. Even one such protest is a blunt indictment that city hall has dropped the ball, which should instigate an immediate reform.

My third concern is the City's over-dependence on just a few funding sources. I worry about the nature of the funding sources that have become predominant

**9.12** None of us are fond of complexity, time-consuming processes, or taxes, but if the results are extraordinary, the extra time and effort are surely justified. These women would probably agree.

in the system I have described. Leveraged funding is an excellent and defensible funding mechanism, but it can go only so far. At some point, it starts to have its own impacts, pressing the edges of both developer and citizen tolerances. The City has to remember that other funding sources are out there that might be more applicable. In the United States, for example, tax increment finance districts are widely used, where borrowing for area upgrading is financed by increased taxes from increases in land values that result from that public investment. This funding mechanism does not depend upon intensifying development, and if it is managed carefully, it can be a time-limited tool to make significant improvements to an area. Other mechanisms, which are already in use in Vancouver, might be applied more extensively, such as local improvement districts, where improvements are paid by the benefitting taxpayers over time, and business improvement districts, where a voluntary tax on businesses in an area can be used to improve the area. I don't offer these suggestions as an exhaustive list but rather to make the point that leveraged money is only one of many ways to go for the City.

My final concern, and by far the most worrisome of all, is the inclination to civic greed. As we struggled to leverage resources through the development approval process that I have so fully described, a certain factor always acted as insurance to protect the high quality of the city. That is, we always preceded any negotiation on development rights and public goods with an arm's-length analysis of whether the design and scale of a project fit the neighbourhood in which it would be built. This was completed by the civic urban designers, who had no responsibilities in the financial negotiations. It involved the urban design peer reviewers as well as public input. If the fit did not work, we scaled back the opportunity and hustled only a value of public goods that fit within that suitable scale. Over time, I have noticed that civic financial aspirations have become a higher and higher priority. City hall has become very money hungry because funding is just so tight. I see more and more situations where citizens are expressing opposition to the fit of the new with the existing, so I cannot help but worry that the urban design assessment has been dropped or marginalized. That just cannot happen, or the whole system will simply implode. Public goods cannot come at the cost of the quality of our city as experienced in human terms.

When it comes to getting things done and done well, the systems underlying Vancouverism are as important as the results. Like the substantive dimensions of our urban practice, the arrangements and processes came together incrementally and will no doubt continue to evolve as the City organization and leadership move forward. The joint venturing that became typical was discovered in relationship after relationship, as people and institutions came to understand and trust one another. Ideas were invented, tested, and institutionalized as they were needed and proven. Admittedly, the emerging way of doing business at city hall and with developers and the public is counter-intuitive to civic systems elsewhere and can be hard to believe in. But to quote an old adage, "The proof of the pudding is in the eating." Walk around the new Vancouver for any time and you will see results that surely justify all of the thoughtful and ethical practices that we have put in place (see Figure 9.12).

As our story moves inevitably to its conclusion, let me now ponder the lessons of Vancouver's adventure in urbanism and what the next quest might be for these urban adventurers.

It was once said that Vancouver was a setting in search of a city. Vancouverism has created a contemporary city that now meets the expectation of its magnificent setting.

# PART 3

# THE FUTURE OF

# VANCOUVERISM

**10.1** Vancouverism 1.0, illustrated perfectly here – density, diversity, amenity – is responsible and characterful. Vancouverism 2.0 will refine the paradigm. Vancouverism 3.0 will expand the model to a larger core city.

# NEW ITERATIONS AND LESSONS LEARNED

**IT HAS BEEN** said that chasing a dream is a journey. Well, my generation's quest for the vision that became known as Vancouverism has certainly been a trip, but we have yet to find the elusive destination. Vancouverism was a magnificent blossoming aspiration that made it to ground in record time, transforming and repositioning the whole city and redefining its lifestyles, but also creating its own challenges and its own imperatives for the future. For those of us who pieced together the first puzzle of a new Vancouver, bringing the story to its conclusion is really no more than looking forward to what might come next – what must come next – in the hope that the dream will continue. Of course, it is a perpetual puzzle. We will not be players on the scene, so the joy of putting it together belongs to the new generation. But we can hope. In this last chapter, I lay out the threads of that hope.

## VANCOUVERISM 1.0

This special way of building and evolving our city is now well under our belt – I'll call it Vancouverism 1.0 (see Figure 10.1). Our community can be confident in what was built but also that the framework of policy, plans, and designs will shape continuing urban change that is resilient, practical, popular, adaptable, and responsible. We have a typology for humanistic high-density development. We have flourishes of urban character that are ours alone. We have strong consumer appeal for diverse, intensive living that I do not see abating in the foreseeable future. Vancouverism is not a bubble. It is solid as a rock. We have an attitude about design, collaboration, and due process that is now second nature. And we have a city brand that is unique and pivotal to a vibrant economy. At the end of this chapter, I will suggest how these achievements might hold cues, lessons, warnings, or inspiration for other people in other places.

But we also have our vulnerabilities and problems. We were blind to certain worrisome vectors of change, such as escalating land and housing costs. We made some mistakes that must be remedied, and we took a few things for granted that now require a much more deliberate approach – I have not been shy in describing these things all along in this story, the most worrisome of which is urban affordability. We pushed some things only so far, but now they have to be taken much further. At the top of this list, of course, is the green agenda. And some progressive urban themes have emerged in the ensuing years that we just did not know about, so they have to be added to the Vancouver equation. My concern is that we have become so pleased with our success that we will be tempted to ignore future trends. Let's hope not. In this chapter, I will highlight how Vancouverism should be consolidated by the people who are now at the helm, how they might diversify it, and where they could take the city up a notch by doing several major resets beyond Vancouverism.

But, as the new generation goes about this business, I think it must face one fundamental fact that was just not relevant when we started our work and is the result of our work. Vancouver now has the status of a world city. It is not just a regional or even a national city. This new reality has implications for every single action that will be taken as we move ahead. We are going to have to embrace this and open our arms and our hearts to the people, cultures, networks, and capital that this brings. Then, with equal vigour, we are going to have to actively support and reinforce our local interests and identity. We will have to plan with this in mind.

## FURTHER CONSOLIDATIONS: VANCOUVERISM 2.0, 3.0, AND 4.0

Fleshing out, refining, and further purposing the urban model that is uniquely our own is a matter of consolidating a good thing. Let me summarize three new versions of Vancouverism – updated applications that should be loaded into the urban system.

### Vancouverism 2.0

The first of these I will call Vancouverism 2.0, refining the main paradigm. Citizens tell us that our work is not yet done. They have a long list of deficiencies that require resolution before they let us off the hook. In the preceding chapters,

I described some of these. I won't repeat them here, but let me add two important concerns that I have not already tabled.

One burgeoning issue that has received little attention, in public discussion
or technical work, is urban noise and the collapse of public tranquility. Traffic
noise, idling noise, construction noise, crowd noise, garbage pick-up noise, gardening machine noise, emergency vehicle noise – a constant din hits people
every day and is getting louder. I can see a new suite of policy coming forward
in the next few years to draw some essential lines around all this racket. I also
predict a public outcry and political movement to quiet things down.

Another issue where we were lax in our planning agenda was in our relations
with Indigenous communities, the First Nations that share this land with us.
There was very little content in our work that tied in with Indigenous culture or
current issues. We certainly did not pursue partnerships with First Nations. It
was not that we were biased against this important sector. We simply didn't reach
out, and nor did they. I regret that. Now, as these groups have found a positive
way to position their interests in land and development, and as society becomes
more sensitive, there are significant opportunities to work together. These collab-
orations will offer a fascinating elaboration of our existing urban typologies.

For these and the other unfinished business that I have listed, the civic government must find a way to loop back to address the details and loose ends that
are not working as well as we might have wished or that we just ignored or forgot. I urge the planning, social planning, and engineering departments of city
hall to embrace a well-organized program to tackle these issues, working hand in
hand with the people who have chosen the new Vancouverism as a way of life.

## Vancouverism 3.0

The epicentre of Vancouverism to date, in the heart of the city, is now close to
build-out. Yet, the market remains strong in this locale, and the benefits of
its growth are significant. Everywhere in the inner-city, land not already converted in the new image now trades in an international market rather than a local
one, with a long-term perspective. Also, the core is somewhat small by world
standards. If the core city increasingly stalls, it will be tragic. If development
pressure starts to demolish some of the treasured features and hospitable scale
that our people have come to appreciate, it will be even more tragic. If prices go
off the charts as consumers compete for a fixed offering of homes and workplaces, it will be cataclysmic. The inner-city simply must expand, opening up a
new generation of urban expression that we might call Vancouverism 3.0. I

am convinced that the trajectory of this growth must be to the east – from our differing perspectives, realtor Bob Rennie and I first said this back in the early 2000s. And this eastward wave must not endanger the Downtown Eastside communities or the other old neighbourhoods that skirt the core. Ultimately, this expansion must take advantage of the vast, lightly developed plain that is the False Creek Flats. This is inevitable. In Chapter 5, I explained that recent City plans and rezoning in the Flats are not cognizant of this imperative. They have limited objectives that I profoundly believe are neither stable nor resilient. I think we will find that these were holding actions at best.

However, once we commence a further replanning of the False Creek Flats, the dimensions of Vancouverism will take several interesting new directions with this growth opportunity. Although we will continue to see density and efficient use of scarce land, the forms will be of more modest scale, with a whole new parti of built form. Although we must continue mixed-use, the mixes will be different. We should embrace the new allowances for industry, high tech, logistics, and city-serving support functions but must also fold in intense degrees of housing, offices, and retail to carry the costs of development. A new formula will leverage all the needed uses by tying these in zoning to approval of uses the market strongly demands and for which it will pay a premium. In addition, we must add institutions, recreation facilities, and special-purpose spaces that need a core spot but cannot pay the super-core rents of the peninsula. Because rapid transit is coming to the area, we must have transit-oriented development, with intense clusters of mixed-use and services and deliberate networks for walking associated with the stations. Perhaps these stations will be signalled on the horizon with spikes of taller buildings. I am sure that the essential principles of Vancouverism will prevail, but their realization on the ground will be refreshingly new. This will be a new version of Vancouverism.

### Vancouverism 4.0

The biggest evolution of our paradigm for how to build a sustainable, livable city will be to retrofit the whole structure of principles, practices, archetypes, and systems for the suburbs – I note this as Vancouverism 4.0 (see Figure 10.2). Earlier, I said that my generation at Vancouver City Hall never gave much thought to how our ideas might manifest themselves in the Greater Vancouver suburbs. I am sorry to say that we were condescending about the suburbs. But now, their time has arrived. With the coming together of the regional town centres, the high costs of inner-city housing, the extensions of rapid transit, and the spread of

**10.2** Vancouverism 4.0 will take the principles out to the suburbs but will transform them to suit suburban residents and win their support. This suburban Vancouver perspective will be fertile ground for a new take on the old themes.

workplaces, suburbs are on a roll. The big question is how will they build out? Will they have the diversity, mix, choices, character, and facilities that we argued so hard for in the inner-city, or will they be just an incomplete assortment of whatever happens to be going on and whoever happens to build a building in each different suburban municipality? Will they be designed or accidental? Will they find a formula for an environmentally and socially sustainable community, or will they continue to degrade their eco-systems and exclude differences? Will they have a satisfying completeness so that locals are not obliged to go elsewhere for work, the things they need, and the experiences that make them happy? Well, the jury is still out. But I remain optimistic because I have discovered that though people love their suburbs, they do not see them as perfect. They care and are open-minded. They want to be environmentally responsible. They want a package of complete living but in a genuinely suburban form that protects what brought them there in the first place. That is the challenge for the upcoming generations – not at Vancouver City Hall but in the municipal halls of Delta, Coquitlam, Port Moody, North Vancouver, West Vancouver, Squamish, and all the other local governments that need to be forward-looking. Fortunately, I also see very progressive politicians coming to the fore in most of our suburbs. Each municipality must do the job in its own way, but a lot of collaboration and sharing of experience could be brought to bear, maybe through the efforts of Metro Vancouver.

I think the principles of Vancouverism will assist the suburban reinvention. Recent design variations in Vancouver's older neighbourhoods, discussed in Chapter 7, are indicative. But it must be said that the patterns, scale, character, and process will not be the same. Density and mix will be more modest. Ground-oriented housing will prevail but in diverse forms. Open spaciousness will be a big deal. Supports for families will override other concerns, though we will also see attention to aging in place. Natural balances will be easier to vest because more of nature will be expected. Domesticity will be more spontaneous in architectural styles. The car will definitely remain front and centre, even as other modes are enhanced. A special opportunity for pilot projects to raise the bar higher will come when large tracts of suburban land can be developed comprehensively. When a community and a developer can push the boundaries for a cool model of livable sustainable suburbanism, we should support them all the way. And, of course, because there are so many suburbs, we can hope to see many variations on the theme. Just as in the other elaborations I have discussed, the suburban programs will reflect the essential intensions while representing a wholesale evolution of the blueprint that we carefully drew in the past.

The refinements and consolidations of Vancouverism, up through version 4.0, remain fundamentally true to the template, but something quite beyond this is also on the way.

## DIVERSIFYING VANCOUVERISM

I have already described the Greenest City Action Plan.[1] This plan, in very short order, intends to bring Vancouver to the verge of what the advocates call "one-planet living" – putting our city in a genuine balance with its natural setting. I also emphasized that this work would be done by the smart new cohort that came to the fore as my generation retired. There is no doubt that this will be a city-shaping venture well beyond the parameters of Vancouverism. It is genuinely new. Just as we wanted to set the stage for Vancouver to join the ranks of the world's most livable cities, the new leaders declare their intention for Vancouver to join an even more elite vanguard – the world's leading green cities. This means zero carbon, zero waste, zero pollution, healthy eco-systems, and an economy that profits from the business to achieve these ends. That's a tall order. Most ratings already put Vancouver ahead of other North American cities, but that is nowhere near the one-planet goal or the world lead. We have a long way to go.

The greenest city strategy will take Vancouver well beyond where our ideas would have taken the city even if played out to their absolute fullest. But nothing in that new green program is counter to or challenging of the ethos that we advocated. As far as they went, it is rewarding to discover our principles, policies, and practices rooted in this new framework. The land-use and transportation aspects of the green strategy are the same as we espoused, but the green plan has raised the expectations and made the targets real and measurable for evaluation. I see this as an elegant diversification and extension of Vancouverism that reflects contemporary sensibilities. So, make no mistake, the agents of Vancouverism wholeheartedly endorse the greenest city strategy as a virtuous agenda that our city simply must achieve. Little more needs to be said, but that does need to be said. Livability and sustainability go hand in hand. In the future, no city will be taken seriously as an urban leader if it does not soar on both these fronts.

## URBAN RESETS: THE NEXT STEPS FORWARD
## FOR VANCOUVERISM

Sometimes in the life of a city, it is necessary to do a complete rethink of the way things have always been done. Vancouverism was such a rethink. The greenest city strategy is a rethink. These are essential to step up your city to a higher level – they are future-focused and disruptive, and they result in fundamental resets. You do a reset when a city has a tough problem that current solutions just cannot address. Or you do it because the world is moving forward and you must either get with it or get left behind. I suggest that Vancouver must aggressively pursue three major resets – two resets to save ourselves from being overwhelmed or even displaced and one further reset to take control of what dominates our public domain. We also need to conduct a fourth reset that has to do with process – to get the government and its citizens in sync on all the challenging fronts of urban change. These resets are exciting because, yet again, they will transform our city and put us right out there on the cutting edge, where we need to be.

### Reset 1: Secure access to housing

In Chapter 6, I declared that, as housing becomes increasingly unaffordable, we may be crippled by our own success. I said that, because we have created a popular setting for living in our naturally beautiful location, with the footloose reality of our times, we will see endless incoming demand for many urban uses, but especially for housing. This demand will continually push prices up and increasingly push people out. We know how to assist low-income citizens because we have a social-housing tradition and mechanisms that we can turn up or down at will. And as we move ahead, they will certainly need to be turned up, and spread more evenly all over the region, because low-income people cannot possibly compete in our frantic housing market. But we do not have a way of assisting the missing middle, the huge group of modest- and middle-income working households, mostly families with children (see Figure 10.3). Since at least the early 2000s, they have been left to fend for themselves, public money is not invested in their plight, and the private sector is so busy with the dependable demand that it has had no inclination to offer more affordable housing. When the 2010s dawned, we seemed to cross a threshold, and the problem became a crisis. I have already summarized the responses that will be necessary to deal with the affordability gap – firmer planning targets, new forms of housing, and new forms of tenure and financing. But if these unfold randomly and only at the inclination of activists at one point or another, they will be too little too late. How we deliver housing needs a fundamental reset – the most profound reset that I could possibly emphasize.

We must put in place a secure middle-price housing sector in Vancouver. The time has come to acknowledge that our dichotomous definition of the housing

**10.3** A major reset of Vancouverism will pay a lot more attention to people like those shown here – middle-income working people who need affordable housing, accessible workplaces, and practical supports for their families.

industry that we have worked with up to now must change. Currently, in our housing tradition, two types of housing are offered: non-market and market. The former is government-driven and is intended for the lowest-income people in the community. The latter is private-sector-driven, offered to anyone who can pay for it, and increasingly monopolized by higher-income consumers. To build a bridge to affordability for middle-income incoming households in the future, we will need a third sector of housing wedged in between. Let me describe what that might look like. It will require public funding and private wealth working together. It will have the qualities of both a semi-market and a semi-non-market housing offering.

On the semi-non-market side, public housing must be diversified to include the complete range of middle-income rentals, rather than solely the low-end-of-market offerings that are available to modest-income workers. Perhaps this could be partially added through densification on existing public-housing sites as they reach obsolescence and are replaced. Some public investment could be allocated to housing for essential-services workers, middle-income people such as teachers, firefighters, and tradespeople, without whom a community cannot function. Melbourne, Australia, and some expensive resorts, such as Whistler, just to the north of Greater Vancouver, have pursued this measure. We will need to see more subsidies of special-needs and seniors housing that are means-tested at a higher level, right through the middle-income range. More of this should also be included in private projects. These solutions will be facilitated by government, with forms of private involvement that the market can embrace.

On the semi-market side, the incentives and bonuses granted through the development management approval system will need to be applied more diversely. Inclusionary zoning, where secure-priced housing is integrated into all buildings, must become more widespread. We have some experience with this, but it needs to be expanded. This might apply to rental tenancies or to new tenure or household forms. We could also learn from places like Madrid and Rotterdam, which have embraced non-profit home ownership. Affordable quality housing could be delivered at good locations because the land profit on resale is removed from the equation even though the growth of equity is maintained through basic ownership. Secure-priced housing could be supported by alternative financing, perhaps delivered by non-profit developers, perhaps on non-profit lands. These solutions will be managed by the private sector, with assistance from government.

Most importantly, all of this must be deliberately and systematically managed, with a fair application all over the Greater Vancouver region, pervasively. I suggest a form of provincial Crown corporation, supported by the federal and local governments, which can work within both government and the marketplace to facilitate the joint ventures that will be the modus operandi of this middle-priced sector. If it is to succeed, government will need to provide seed investment – probably money from the federal government, money and land from the provincial government, and land from the civic governments. Other investment could come from the private sector through partnerships and even philanthropy. Vancouver's development and finance industries, with their sophisticated experience, could play a part as well, as could the formation of a group of socially aware development entities. This new way of delivering housing needs to be a wide movement. I expect the credit union sector could take the lead here, in partnership with the City and the development industry. VanCity Credit Union, a strong, stable, and well-respected local organization, could become the catalyst. In fact, this leadership is already emerging, which is commendable. With all these partners, the Crown corporation will need firm targets and performance expectations that might see as much as one-third of new housing constructed and secured for the middle-income sector, as an urgency, over a reasonable period. Governments and the private sector have made a few tentative efforts, but the trickle has to become a river. This reset must become a primary objective, with many new players, or the future will not belong to us or our progeny. It will belong to those who bought us out and pushed us out.

## Reset 2: Coming to grips once and for all with mental illness and addictions

In Chapter 6, I lamented that, despite our best efforts, those suffering mental illness and addictions are continuing to be victimized, and their harrowing experience tarnishes the image that we want to portray of Vancouver as a sustainable and embracing community. It must also be said that the terrible situation being experienced by those at risk every day also victimizes the rest of us. For most people, witnessing such misery is shocking and, when there is no practical way to respond helpfully, deeply alarming. With no real solutions in sight, it is inevitable that complacency sets in – people close their eyes just to cope. This is the worst outcome for everyone. The Downtown Eastside is both the epicentre and the symbol of this disaster. We need a profound commitment to undertake a major new effort to rescue these people and this community, while, frankly, rescuing our own credibility at the same time. Their plight is a blight on everything that is celebrated in this book. The fight will not be an easy one. To achieve the necessary reforms, all levels of governments must work together, and the rest of us must add our support. This form of reset will reveal who we are as a people. I say "reset" because, as the Vancouver Agreement of 2000 illustrated, simply applying current thinking will not be enough. A new paradigm is absolutely essential. And it will shock many people.

Like most tough urban issues of our day, this challenge comes under the jurisdiction of all three governments, so any solution must involve them all. They must allocate money, expertise, and priority attention, and must enter into partnerships with the private sector. The organizational style of the Vancouver Agreement will have to be replicated. The agreement itself expired in 2010, but perhaps it could even be resuscitated as a starting point. This crusade – and it will be a major crusade – will need powerful sponsors, so I look to the most distinguished Vancouverites to take on the challenge, just as Mayor Philip Owen and City Manager Judy Rogers selflessly did with the Vancouver Agreement, which was pivotal to success in its day.

The matter of the Downtown Eastside provokes so much debate and dissension that it will take a confident agent to make headway. I myself feel apprehensive even in suggesting possible directions, because any proposal will be attacked by somebody. But there must be a way forward. I certainly do not claim to have the answers, but as a society we simply cannot say that the solution is beyond our reach, thereby avoiding the issue. Someone, somewhere, must have some answers and we have to find those answers – through research, through experimentation, and through engagement with those living their challenges every day, as well as their caregivers, expert analysts, the academy, practitioners, and on and on until the path becomes clear. We could start from the well-established foundation of the four pillar drug strategy and then build in similar contemporary thinking on mental health practices as a parallel strategy. It seems obvious to me that safe-injection sites need more support and that clean drugs should probably be made available to replace the contaminated ones that are killing so many people right now. Illegal drugs should also become legal to administer in the safe circumstances of these facilities. We are beginning to see moves in this direction but this entails huge changes to prevailing attitudes in our community. I suspect that we need to ask some basic questions. For substance users, what is illness and what is preference? For the mentally ill, when is a person no longer competent to make decisions about his or her well being? What setting of care has the most potential for success? Beyond the obvious anchor of safe, respectful, and secure housing, what else needs to be part of the basic package to stabilize and support people at risk? How do we reconcile everyone's rights when they come into conflict? How do we best spend the funding that we have and can secure – and how much money is needed? I suspect we will need targets. These will focus, not only on eradicating homelessness but also on dramatically cutting the number of those with mental illnesses and addictions who are aimlessly and helplessly on the streets, unable to find home even if they have one. We will need performance measures and regular reporting. And we will need a long commitment of funding.

Our goal must be that not a single mentally challenged or addicted person is left to fend for himself or herself on our streets – that every single person will receive care as a right, and it will be our community right that they receive care. We have to work for a result that absolutely no consumption of illegal drugs happens on our streets, that people with addictions are not treated as criminals, that they are helped and respected as any other person would be with an illness. From all my experience, I see that addiction is a fact of life and is here to stay. The urgent question is how and where it is acted out and under what humane conditions. My suspicion is that, if we can deal at this level, the challenge of homelessness will become much easier to handle. My suspicion is that much of this homelessness is wrapped up with all these people at risk who now have no way to afford or even find a home. Homelessness, poverty, mental illness, and substance abuse are all wrapped together in an interconnected web of cause and effect – enabled by a social negligence that we just have to get beyond.

## Reset 3: Securing the public domain for people

In Chapter 5, I laid out the choices that may be upon us in the very near future to cope with the new technologies for personal mobility – the inevitability of autonomous driving and the already evident rise of car sharing. I noticed that driverless cars coupled with private ownership could well result in a huge prolif-eration of private vehicles and the nightmare of an absolutely swamped street system. Alternatively, driverless cars coupled with car sharing could result in far fewer cars on the street, opening up fascinating opportunities for other uses of public rights-of-way. I speculated that there may not be a middle ground in these choices, and I mused that Vancouver may not have a choice because we have already diversified our use of streets and cut back on the car footprint. Assuming all this logic holds true, then you begin to see that our city could do something that few other modern cities have had the guts, the vision, or the practical option to attempt – we could take back much of the public domain for a plethora of uses and activities that really bring a city to life and host a hot economy. We could dra-matically reset the dedications for use of urban public land. First, let me specu-late on how this might be done and then on what the outcomes might look like.

In the reset I have in mind, I would dare to target at least 60 percent of the public street footprint in the core city and in the regional town centres to be rededicated to activities other than mobility of conventional vehicles – this means banning cars and trucks, regardless of whether they are person-driven or automatic-driven. I set this bar disruptively high to make a point. I admit at the outset that I don't actually know how much land could be taken away from con-ventional transportation. That has to be discovered. Modern Copenhagen and Oslo have moved in this direction, and it is taken for granted in some historic urban places in Europe. These examples suggest that we can and should reclaim a very large portion of the public domain. Within this rededicated area, I see exciting functionalities that could take the place of all those cars and traffic.

Most importantly, this becomes the setting for walking and the wonderful distractions that come from being on foot – shopping, meeting, waiting, eating, lolling about, watching the world go by, lounging, flirting, exploring, napping, crowding, and the endless list of activities for people who find themselves face

**10.4** Another major reset of Vancouverism will reclaim much of the downtown from transportation and utilitarian use, turning it over to all kinds of community activities. This corner of a large public auto-free area in Southeast False Creek, now called the Village, is an inspiration. Here, a bunch of young people are learning how to kayak.

to face with other people (see Figure 10.4). Related to these goings on, this liberated space also welcomes the various forms of active mobility – cycling, rollerblading, and running. It becomes a place to explore new, lower-impact ways of getting around. We all know about Segways, the two-wheeled electric scooter unveiled in 2001, but that is just the beginning of the types of devices that we are starting to see. Personal mobility might even become a public utility, at least within these designated places. TransLink, the regional transit agency, could supply a fleet of mini-devices for individual movement that can convey people from A to B without the need for a giant overbearing machine and without the risk of private devices becoming as intrusive as the car. This fleet could be integrated with traditional transit and the custom transit services that are already in start-up. Nowhere in the world is the potential for innovative personal mobility devices being diversely exploited, with public control, mostly because they have not yet entered the public consciousness as legitimate transportation alternatives, augmenting existing modes. Lastly, reclaiming street space creates all kinds of potential for more flexible and convenient goods movement to serve consumers and materials movement to serve industry. I envision dedicated corridors for utility movement and new forms of devices for that transport. The intention of all this is simply to take back the streets for people and for movement that is compatible with people.

Once this occurs, the public domain can finally be completely reconstructed as an elegant, comfortable, beautiful, and spacious place for people and their activities. As people choose to live and work closer together in increasingly intricate mixes of functions, we can offer the compensations of public space that they can enjoy as a kind of living room to expand the home experience. I am not talking about a modest fix-up here. I am advocating a major overhaul. At the top of the list would be repaving the public environment with treatments that are suited to foot traffic and attractive when viewed close-up – and undergrounding all the solid-waste handling and other utilities while we are at it. Next, we would add the furniture, lighting, and weather protections that offer comfort and convenience. Then, we can expand the realm of universal accessibility for those with disabilities due to age or infirmity. Much more lush landscaping can be added, not to mention environmental features to enhance urban ecological systems. We can add the smart-technology features that link the area to an endless world of the web and monitor conditions for maintenance and upkeep. Then we can convene the programming and facilitate the organizations that kick-start community energy.

Some inspirational models offer a starting point for Vancouver. These include the lavishly finished public realm in downtown Portland, Oregon; segments of Broadway in New York City, which were pedestrianized; and certain streets in Barcelona, which were repurposed for people-oriented activities. We can surpass these great examples. This reset is desperately needed in downtown Vancouver, where the banality and condition of the public streetscapes and sidewalks is almost embarrassing. It is also needed in most clustered development areas throughout the city and region, where the most basic standards of finishing and furnishing are the norm. Once we significantly expand the pedestrian space, we can have a great time making it visually spectacular.

Imagine the results: whole areas as far as the eye can see where intensive urbanism is coupled with energetic street activity; areas of crowds but also areas of quiet escape; districts where noise levels are brought down so that the human voice is the most noticeable sound; higher levels of personal safety. Imagine the potential: the advances in social engagement, bringing camaraderie and fun; the growth of business that thrives on face-to-face public association; the flowering of mutual assistance and even understanding from seeing more people in the flesh more of the time; the spontaneity of human caprices on the stage of a lovely public place. Imagine the spinoffs: a further rebranding of the Vancouver experience that could draw tourism and appeal to the economic sectors that we hope to host; elaborations of culture that come from a ready audience; the ability to let our public property contribute to ecological systems.

Outside the redesignated areas, traditional circulation would continue, hopefully more efficiently and adding the contemporary bells and whistles that create a multi-modal future. Inside these redesignated areas, a new world will emerge – a world in vivid and positive contrast to anything seen anywhere else.

### Reset 4: Revitalizing the local government's accord with its people

In Chapter 9, I worried that public engagement processes can become stale or that city hall might begin to edit those processes in the interest of "getting things done" or "knowing best what is needed for the future." This can never become a state of grace. Vancouverism emerged from a principle set by the clan of planners under Ray Spaxman – that no matter how sure we were of an action or a direction, we always engaged with citizens to find the common ground that they could support. Yes, we ultimately made hard decisions that were often grounded in choices rather than consensus, but we always did so within a culture of wide public discussion that promoted understanding and allowed everyone to contribute ideas and perspectives. This approach was difficult, time consuming, and complicated, but it built constituency on the overall directions and trust when tough choices had to be made. Occasionally, we would fall short and need to be reminded of our responsibility to the public discourse. We constantly updated our techniques. Every so often, we had to take stock to make sure we were staying true to our commitment to the public.

Each generation, as the new cadre takes over the leadership, has to take stock. The new generation now at city hall in Vancouver has to take stock, and it undoubtedly will represent a major reset from recent practices. This reset must be comprehensive and systematic. It must reconfirm the ethics and principles, the techniques, and the pervasiveness of the agenda for public engagement and involvement. It will benefit from third-party advice. It must actually involve the public in the evaluation, particularly those who have been most critical over the years. The object of this reset should be a newly refreshed social contract between citizens and government. It must declare a wide commitment to public involvement, reaching deep into public perspectives, bringing everyone up to a high level of understanding, staying in discussion until reconciliations are discovered, using the most up-to-date techniques to involve not just the centre but also the margins, being totally transparent, and owning the outcomes without pulling rank.

A community fights to overcome many odds to be livable, sustainable, and resilient – to be great – and the most natural allies in this continuing struggle must be the government and citizens. The outcome of the public participation reset will be that government and people share a common vision and make common cause. They are partners and can always depend upon that.

## MESSAGES FROM LOTUS LAND

My friend and colleague Jonathan Barnett, the great American urbanist and educator, loudly laments the "isms" that infest the discourse about reforming cities that ebbs and flows around the planet. He rejects them as a formulaic inclination of city-builders. He worries that people will take something that suits a certain place and apply it to another place, where it just can't work. He is a wise man and his advice on this is absolutely sound. I have added the "ism" to Vancouver in this story to make a few basic points: that everything we did, put together, was of a piece, not merely a random collection; that our construction was based upon principles; that our work found a constituency as a movement in our local culture; and that, frankly, to be honest, I might draw attention to this very interesting story. I did not use the "ism" to proselytize or to suggest that the Vancouver template is transferable as a fixed concept. From the beginning, I emphasized that Vancouverism is a local phenomenon, a local ethic, with a powerful relevance on its home turf but no other aspiration.

But then, it has to be said that there are a few cues or lessons from our experience that might prove useful elsewhere. Our failures can certainly be a warning for others. Readers who have responsibilities in other places will adopt what they see as useful and leave the rest. The more specific the idea, the less applicable it probably is in a different petri dish. But from a broad perspective, several themes of advice come to mind. Let me air them here to ginger everybody's thinking.

*Proactive public leadership:* In the plurality of a modern democracy, with so many people and interests at play, it is essential that government leadership come to the city-building program. Civic government is usually in the best position to take on this role. After all, the city is a commonwealth.

*Collaboration:* No sector of society can build the entire rich package that comprises a successful modern city. A division of labour and responsibilities has to come together in joint ventures and mutual support. Passive lack of collaboration, or worse yet, active discord or unilateral action, creates gaps, half measures, and crippled results.

*Acting from principles:* If it is to be coherent, any movement of city building needs a clear vision. This must be based upon principles that are foundational to each individual action and help in the choices between actions. Principles provide clarity; clarity engenders confidence. Principles illuminate directions over a long period, as particular circumstances or emphases change.

*Organizing for success:* It is natural that both public and private organizations are arranged to best deliver the status quo. These arrangements are built up and consolidated over time. To change directions takes express reorganization, to do things differently and bring people and interests together differently. This requires fresh institutions and processes and assignments. Seldom will these be what they used to be.

*Building public constituency:* As the poet observes, "no man is an island," a sentiment that is profoundly true in city building. Thousands of people are involved, interests are diverse, leaders come and go, money comes and goes, times change, and people change. But building a city takes time – decades, if things go quickly, though much longer in most cases. So, to bring consistency, coherence, and best practices, and to stick with the plan, a solid public constituency is necessary. The more the effort feels like a movement, the better. The more widely held the understanding, the better. The more active people are in both support and critique, the better. The greater the support, the better.

*Watch out for complacency:* The most dangerous vulnerability of a progressive city-building program is that people eventually stop paying attention and stop caring. Sometimes, they become satisfied with success and stop pushing the boundaries. Other times, they become exhausted by the battle and lay down their arms or leave the field. Or they forget the original principles and reasons for the quest. No actors, no commitment, no memory of the intentions and methods – no action. It is that simple. That is my one and only warning.

I will state without hesitation that the basic substantive principles that have shaped Vancouver during my involvement have been important. They feel like universal principles, and as my practice has expanded over the years, I have carried them with me everywhere. I cannot let them be forgotten:

- taking the neighbourhood unit as the essential building block, with all its support infrastructure and organic balances
- putting in place diverse transportation choices, with emphasis on transit and active transportation and de-emphasis on the car
- achieving a wide social, economic, and physical diversity and inclusion, with endless mixes
- emphasizing coherent placemaking, with deliberate design of scale, character, and all aspects of the experience of a place
- engendering uniqueness to fend off the inclination to sameness in a globalizing world
- taking responsibility for environmental compatibility and repair
- embracing wide public engagement, transparency, shared action, and division of labour in the process of change.

Of course, I cannot really guarantee these principles can be exported to other places – each activist in each place will have to experiment to see what makes sense. The principles should be an inspiration, but they may or may not be suitable or complete. I will say that, as I put them to work in various local applications, they yielded very different-looking results, from one place to another and one culture to another. It is amazing and wonderful just how vividly contrasting people and places are around the world, so their interpretations, even of similar ideas, are splendidly diverse.

Father and daughter enjoy the autumn glory of George Wainborn Park, just outside their front door. Vancouverism gave everyone a park at their fingertips as another treasured dimension of their commonwealth.

# EPILOGUE

**E.1** Vancouverism is all about experience. Experience is all about walking. My walk starts at my own front door in Granville Slopes.

# A SPECIAL
# URBAN EXPERIENCE

**IN THE END,** after all is said and done, only one thing really tells the tale of what we tried to achieve in all our efforts that became known as Vancouverism. That one thing is the real, tangible, visceral experience of the place that we created.

I live on the downtown peninsula, in Granville Slopes, one of the new neighbourhoods that I helped design (see Figure E.1). My everyday territory is the north shore of False Creek and upland in Downtown South, another set of neighbourhoods I helped design. I write these last words in the glory of summer, but the story would be more or less the same in our extensive rainy season. Several days ago, in the afternoon, I took a walk to stretch my legs. It was a walk that made me smile.

I left my townhouse and stepped out onto the sidewalk. Across the street is a little coffee spot, Prego, tucked into the base of an apartment building, along with a hair salon, computer repair store, gift shop, and until recently, a laundry and a florist. The particular outlets change from time to time but Prego is a dependable constant. It always has a cluster of loungers, mostly locals who bring their dogs and want to chat with the proprietor, who is a local personality (see Figure E.2). My building has three towers, although I don't notice them because the trees and the building setbacks screen them from people like me walking along the sidewalk. It also has a lovely green courtyard, but that is another story. Of course, this being Vancouver, a pair of crows lives in the tree in front of my house – squawking as always, telling everyone what to do. I turned right and immediately passed a group of people heading down to the ferry dock just steps

**E.2** Prego is just across the street from my townhouse, serving great coffee and delightful hospitality for all the neighbours.

**E.3** The 888 Mini Market, up the street at the corner, is my favourite little convenience store, offering almost everything I need at a moment's notice. Across the street is May Brown Park, and up the way is Tartine, with the best lunch and take-out in the vicinity.

**E.4** Farther along, under the Granville Bridge and beyond, I reach George Wainborn Park, which is busy as usual with all kinds of goings-on for families and kids and dogs. ▶

away, to catch the Aquabus to Granville Island. I could see these were tourists because they were speaking another language and had cameras. As I followed their route with my eyes, I could see the water when I looked down the street – we made sure of that. Looking up, I saw my long-time neighbour and close friend, Lois, on her way for her daily grocery shopping on the island. Naturally, we stopped to gossip.

After passing a few other neighbours' townhouses and waving to yet another friend who lives across the street, I walked up the slope to the intersection where there is a storefront dentist and my favourite corner store (see Figure E.3). I wasn't going in but I waved to the merchant, an immigrant from Japan, who is always there at all hours. My local park, May Brown Park, is right across the street. Lots of people were walking their dogs, and a few folks were lounging on the art piece that looks like a banqueting table. I passed a few more townhouse doors and crossed a street to another local shop but also a storefront childcare centre and one of my favourite cafes, Tartine, where we often get our lunch. Just at that moment, a string of rowdy little people, holding hands and all dressed in bright orange vests, came out of the daycare – their morning adventure. There were at least twenty of them, with several moms and the childcare workers. Their laughter became my laughter.

Heading along the tree-lined sidewalk, I came to one of my favourite local spots, George Wainborn Park, where, that day, I saw lots of families with kids, picnicking, playing, running around, and generally having a blast (see Figure E.4). This is a designated dog park, so there were also lots of puppies on the move, including bathing in the big fountain that anchors the place. It was nice to see young couples strolling along but also many older people relaxing and reading, seeming to enjoy the action around them. They may live in small apartments or in the seniors' building up the street – or even in one of the houseboats across the creek. More children from another childcare centre, Sea Star, were on their way to the water's edge. I wondered if their visit that day was to learn about sea creatures.

Skirting the north side of the park, my route took me down the street, lined with rowhouses and apartments, through the rows of trees along the seawall, and into another green retreat, David Lam Park (see Figure E.5). This is where things were heating up again. Hundreds of kids – tykes and teens – played in the sports fields, more on the play equipment, and even more at the tennis courts. I passed more couples and more seniors but also cyclists and rollerbladers. Some might have been speeding to work, but others were just ambling along to enjoy the sun, in motion. Several older gentlemen looked homeless but not upset, just

**E.5** On through the neighbourhood, I come to David Lam Park, with its shaded walkway, waterfront seating, tennis and basketball courts, and play area.

**E.6** Through David Lam Park, I follow the waterfront walkway-bikeway, which stretches from Coal Harbour all the way to Kitsilano Beach. This shows the classic configuration, separating pedestrians and bikes. It is always busy.

lonely. To my left was the saltwater pumping station that supplies fire protection during earthquakes, with its waterfalls to cool the air. Of course, the park has so many trees that it is naturally quite cool anyway.

Parallel to my walk, I followed the designated walkway-bikeway. Looping all around False Creek, it runs back to Stanley Park and then on to Coal Harbour (see Figure E.6). On along, I cut in from the water and immediately to my right, I passed the Dorothy Lam Children's Centre (see Figure E.7) and Elsie Roy Elementary School. Whether or not school is in session, this is the place for all the school-age kids to meet up, and that day was no different. It's their favourite hangout. I thought I might see my friend Jane, who lives right here, but I had no such luck.

I crossed Drake Street, entering the play plaza at the back door of the Roundhouse community centre, which is opposite the busy boulevard on the other side of the building. It was packed with teens and would-be teens, hanging and crowing. Quite a few little ones were also there, bopping around playing their chalk games, with the community centre staff overseeing everything from the adjacent pottery studio. Continuing my walk, I passed a seniors' building on my left (see Figure E.8), where at least one member of the family must be fifty-five years old – it occurred to me that I could live there. On my right, I passed a luxury condo (see Figure E.9). A non-market building is set next door, housing low-income and modest-income residents (see Figure E.10). Visually, there is no

**E.7** Here's the Dorothy Lam Children's Centre, attached to Elsie Roy Elementary School. This is the hotspot for kids.

**E.8** Now, across Drake Street, I am approaching the children's play yard adjacent to the Roundhouse community centre. The housing on the left is for seniors. Its residents have a great view, and everything they need is handy nearby.

**E.9** To the right, just across the yard from the seniors' housing, a luxury condo also enjoys the views and close proximity to all the amenities and neighbourhood offerings.

**E.10** As I walk along the wall of the community centre to my left, the view to my right is lined with the gardens of a lovely set of rowhouses. They are part of the social-housing building, which also includes apartments, all for low- and modest-income households. I like the train tracks, remnants of the railroad marshalling yards that once covered the area.

**E.11** This brings me to Roundhouse plaza and Davie Street, the heart of the community, with the grocery store, shops, cafes, play spaces, train museum, and all the action of a happy neighbourhood centre.

**E.12** Up Davie Street, just a few steps beyond Pacific Boulevard, is the Yaletown subway station, marked by the large white "T" in the centre of the shot. Set among historic warehouse buildings now converted to restaurants, shops, offices, and housing, the station offers direct transit access to the airport.

**E.13** For this walk, my destination is the Starbucks on Davie Street, just across the street from the Roundhouse plaza. Friends are waiting.

**E.14** It is this kind of everyday living, its convenience and energy and happiness and surprise, which is the joy and splendour of Vancouverism. ▷

discernable difference between these two buildings, which I am always relieved about. My friend Roz, who lives in the market building, tells me that all the residents get along well – they happily share a lovely courtyard. Finally, I arrived at my destination, the south end of Davie Street, just beyond the Roundhouse. Before stepping onto the street, I walked through the round "square," with its coffee house and sushi bar, their outdoor seating filled with the coffee-and-snack crowd (see Figure E.11). On any other day, I could easily have nipped into Urban Fare to pick up some groceries, or picked up my wine at the government-owned liquor store around the corner, or deposited my drycleaning, or gone to any one

of dozens of shops that extend up the street into old Yaletown and beyond. If I'd been heading out to the airport, I could have stepped into the Yaletown subway station, just over Pacific Boulevard, tucked among the historic buildings with its big "T" insignia out front (see Figure E.12). But today, I was meeting my old friend Nathan at the Starbucks for our regular catch-up (see Figure E.13). Another friend, Setty, was there as well, so we all said hello. Afterward, I went on a nice long walk to tend to some errands before returning home.

During this one day, I walked more than eight kilometres, according to my watch (which keeps track of these things), not because it was good for me or because I planned to do it, but only because it was easier and more pleasant than taking my car. Yes, I have a car, but though I've owned it for more than twelve years, there are only forty thousand clicks on the odometer – I stash it in my private garage under the townhouse and seldom use it. Maybe soon, I will go share-car all the way.

There is nothing very special in this description of my casual afternoon walk, but I think any reader who is familiar with modern North American cities, particularly inner-cities, will know that there is everything special about it. This kind of fulfilling urban experience (see Figure E.14) is a profound achievement; it is our achievement. It is the true splendour that is Vancouverism.

# ACKNOWLEDGMENTS

**FIRST OF ALL,** I want to thank Frances Bula for keeping the faith during the several years that I geared up the time and attention to complete this book. She promised to write the Prologue at the very beginning, and she never wavered after that. She did a great job in setting the stage for what I had to say. But she also helped all the way through the adventure as an insightful reader. And, of course, her well-known elegant writing was an inspiration as I tried to bring out my own personal style.

Writing a tale like that in this book is a dramatic act of memory – and as my friends and colleagues well know, memory is not my strong suit. Many people kindly helped me in recalling times, initiatives, names, and even pieces of the story that had escaped my grasp. I deeply appreciate their involvement – their time, energy, and patience with my stream of questions. I want to particularly thank my city hall colleagues Ann McAfee, Judy Rogers, Ronda Howard, Cameron Gray, Trish French, Nathan Edelson, Jeannette Hlavach, Lon LaClaire, Ralph Segal, Michael Gordon, Tom Phipps, Kevin McNaney, and former city councillor Gordon Price. I also want to thank the distinguished Canadian architect Peter Busby, a close private-sector colleague and friend. All these people lived this history with me – it is their story – so I was thrilled when they agreed to be part of telling it. I am grateful for their input, but I naturally take full responsibility for any errors, omissions, or distortions that still slipped through. I am sure there are some because memories can be deceiving.

Two colleagues came to my aid in having their shop produce the maps in this book. I am grateful to Joe Hruda, Dan Daszkowski, and their team at CIVITAS Urban Design and Planning. Thank you, CIVITAS. Another colleague and friend took custom photographs of the key development management organizations at city hall. Thank you, Marina Dodis, for your candid shots. The City of Vancouver and Metro Vancouver were generous with several important photographs from their archives. I appreciate their support.

The times I write about in this book involved hundreds of people, who played their creative and unique part, offering innovations and critique that made Vancouverism full and real. I have referred to many by name in this text. To the many others who are not mentioned, I offer my sincere apologies for the oversight. It simply was not possible to include every name and contribution.

The greatest gratitude of all goes to my partner of fifty years, Sandy Logan. What endless patience it took as I droned through the hundreds of hours needed to craft this book, and what amazing support and advice was always there for me at every step along the journey in big ways and little ways. Sandy is and always has been my rock.

# NOTES

**PROLOGUE**

1 Harland Bartholomew, *A Plan for Vancouver Including Point Grey and South Vancouver* (Vancouver, 1929), 217. Cited in Deryck W. Holdsworth, "Cottages and Castles for Vancouver Home-Seekers," *BC Studies* 69-70 (1986): 12.

2 Holdsworth, "Cottages and Castles for Vancouver Home-Seekers," 11-32, 15, 21, 22.

3 Jill Wade, *Houses for All: The Struggle for Social Housing in Vancouver, 1919-50* (Vancouver: UBC Press, 1994), 9.

4 Diana James, *Shared Walls: Seattle Apartment Buildings, 1900-1939* (Jefferson, NC: McFarland, 2011).

5 Rosemary Ann Pickard McAfee, "Residence on the Margin of the Central Business District: A Case Study of Apartment Development in the West End of Vancouver, B.C." (MA thesis, University of British Columbia, 1962), 25.

6 Ibid.

7 Ibid., 7.

8 Homer Hoyt, *The Structure and Growth of Residential Areas in American Cities* (Washington, DC: US Government Printing Office, 1939).

9 T.R. Anderson, "Social and Economic Factors Affecting the Location of Residential Neighbourhoods," *Papers of the Regional Science Association* 9 (1962), 166. Cited in McAfee, "Residence on the Margin of the Central Business District," 59.

10 W.H. Whyte, Jr., "Are Cities Unamerican?" in *The Exploding Metropolis* (New York: Doubleday, 1957), 10. Cited in McAfee, "Residence on the Margin of the Central Business District," 66.

11 McAfee, "Residence on the Margin of the Central Business District," 106.

12 Harland Bartholomew, *A Preliminary Report upon Zoning* (Vancouver: Vancouver Planning Commission, 1946), 28-29, https://archive.org/details/reportzoning00vanc.

13 Robert Walsh, "The Origins of Vancouverism: A Historical Inquiry into the Architecture and Urban Form of Vancouver, British Columbia" (PhD diss., University of Michigan, 2013), 148.

14 McAfee, "Residence on the Margin of the Central Business District," 87.

15 Ibid., 91.

16 Ibid., 94.

17 "West End Future Lies in Its Heart," *Vancouver Sun*, September 23, 1968, 12.

18 Leonard Marsh, *Rebuilding a Neighbour-hood: Report on Demonstration Slum Clearance and Urban Rehabilitation Project in a Key Central Area in Vancouver* (Vancouver: University of British Columbia, 1950), iii.

19 Walsh, *The Origins of Vancouverism,* 26.

20 Author interview with Ray Spaxman, April 19, 2017.

21 Author interview with Ann McAfee, April 17, 2017.

22 Author interview with Ann McAfee, April 21, 2017.

**CHAPTER 1: SETTING THE STAGE**

1 John Punter, *The Vancouver Achievement: Urban Planning and Design* (Vancouver: UBC Press, 2003).

2 Arthur Erickson, "To Understand the City We Make," in *Vancouver Forum 1: Old Powers, New Forces,* ed. Max Wyman (Vancouver: Douglas and McIntyre, 1992), 146, 147.

3 City of Vancouver, "Central Area Plan: Goals and Land Use Policy," 1991, https://vancouver.ca/files/cov/central-area-plan-goals-and-land-use-policy-1991.pdf.

4 City of Vancouver, "CityPlan: Directions for Vancouver," 1995, http://former.vancouver.ca/commsvcs/planning/cityplan/dfvf.htm.

5 United Nations Commission on Environment and Development, *Our Common Future* (Oxford: Oxford University Press, 1987). This work is commonly referred to as the Brundtland Report, in acknowledgment of the Norwegian political leader, Gro Harlem Brundtland, who chaired the group that produced it.

**CHAPTER 2: A UNIQUE CONTEXT FOR URBAN INNOVATION**

1 Of course, the government arrangement in Quebec is modelled on the French system, and the law is based upon the Code Napoléon, neither of which apply to Vancouver.

2 The national government actually has two houses in Parliament. One house, the Commons, is elected by ridings and effectively comprises the government. The other house, the Senate, is composed of members appointed by the Queen upon nomination by the government; its role is one of "sober second thought" and advising the government.

3 See Joe Berridge, *Reinvesting in Toronto: What the Competition Is Doing* (Toronto: Canadian Urban Institute, 1999).

4 City of Vancouver, "CityPlan: Directions for Vancouver," 1995, http://former.vancouver.ca/commsvcs/planning/cityplan/dfvf.htm; City of Vancouver, "Central Area Plan: Goals and Land Use Policy," 1991, https://vancouver.ca/files/cov/central-area-plan-goals-and-land-use-policy-1991.pdf.

5 Greater Vancouver Regional District, "The Liveable Region 1976/1986: Proposals to Manage the Growth of Greater Vancouver," 1975, http://www.metrovancouver.org/about/library/LibraryPublications/Livable_Region_1976_1986_-_Proposals_to_Manage_the_Growth_of_Greater_Vancouver.pdf. Educated at McGill University, Harry Lash held important planning positions in Montreal and Alberta before joining the GVRD. For the best articulation of his philosophy, see his book, *Planning in a Human Way* (Ottawa: Ministry of State for Urban Affairs, 1976).

6 See the key update, Greater Vancouver Regional District, *Liveable Region Strategic Plan*, 1996.

**CHAPTER 3: COUNTER-INTUITIVE PERSPECTIVES FOR SHAPING A CITY**

1 Jane Jacobs, *The Death and Life of Great American Cities* (New York: Random House, 1961); Lewis Mumford, *The City in History: Its Origins, Its Transformations,*

*and Its Prospects* (New York: Harcourt, Brace and World, 1961).

2 An urban design movement, New Urbanism was propagated by an American organization called the Congress for the New Urbanism. See Chapter 7 for a summary of the founders and intentions of this movement.

### CHAPTER 4: NEIGHBOURHOODS

1 City of Vancouver, "About Vancouver: Areas of the City," https://vancouver.ca/news-calendar/areas-of-the-city.aspx.

2 City of Vancouver, "A Plan for the City of Vancouver British Columbia," 1928, https://archive.org/details/vancplan incgen00vanc. Completed by Harland Bartholomew, this work is commonly referred to as the Bartholomew Plan.

3 City of Vancouver, "A Review of Public Infrastructure and Amenity Requirements in Downtown Major Projects," 1992. Notably, specifications have shifted slightly over the years, but the suite of standards remains consistent.

4 Ibid.

5 Ray Oldenburg, *The Great Good Place: Cafes, Coffee Shops, Bookstores, Bars, Hair Salons, and Other Hangouts at the Heart of a Community* (New York: Marlowe House, 1989).

6 City of Vancouver, "A Review of Public Infrastructure and Amenity Requirements in Downtown Major Projects," 1992.

7 Lonely Planet, "Welcome to Vancouver," 2018, https://www.lonelyplanet.com/canada/vancouver.

8 The City of Vancouver in False Creek South, back in the 1970s, was able to secure a sustainable social mix of housing, as described in Chapter 6, but this was only because the City owned all the land in the neighbourhood and used its land equity to underwrite various levels of affordability.

9 The study was documented in a publication put out by the students, who were enrolled in the School of Community and Regional Planning, College for Interdisciplinary Studies, University of British Columbia. See "Living in False Creek North: From the Residents' Perspective," 2008, https://sarkissian.com.au/wp-content/uploads/2011/03/FCN-POE-Short-Report-2008_smaller.pdf. Unfortunately, circulation was not wide, and printed copies are now difficult to locate.

### CHAPTER 5: TRANSPORTATION CHOICES

1 Greater Vancouver Regional District and Province of British Columbia, "Transport 2021: A Long-Range Transportation Plan for Greater Vancouver," September 1993, http://www.metrovancouver.org/about/library/HarryLashLibraryPublications/TRANSPORT-2021-Report-A-Long-Range-Transportation-Plan-for-Greater-Vancouver.pdf; Greater Vancouver Regional District, *Livable Region Strategic Plan*, 1996, http://www.metrovancouver.org/services/regional-planning/PlanningPublications/LRSP.pdf#search=%22Liveable%20Region%20Strategic%20Plan%20%2B%201996%22.

2 Greater Vancouver Regional District, "The Liveable Region 1976/1986: Proposals to Manage the Growth of Greater Vancouver," 1975, http://www.metrovancouver.org/about/library/LibraryPublications/Livable_Region_1976_1986_-_Proposals_to_Manage_the_Growth_of_Greater_Vancouver.pdf.

3 City of Vancouver, "CityPlan: Directions for Vancouver," 1995, http://former.vancouver.ca/commsvcs/planning/cityplan/dfvf.htm; City of Vancouver, *City of Vancouver Transportation Plan* (Vancouver, 1997).

4  City of Vancouver, "Central Area Plan: Goals and Land Use Policy," 1991, https://vancouver.ca/files/cov/central-area-plan-goals-and-land-use-policy-1991.pdf; City of Vancouver, *Downtown Transportation Plan* (Vancouver, 2002).

5  City of Vancouver, *City of Vancouver Transportation Plan* (Vancouver, 1997), v.

6  I am grateful to the engineering department of the City of Vancouver for providing or confirming all the metrics given in this chapter regarding targets and performance on mode-split, population growth, and other changes in transportation functionality.

7  City of Vancouver, *City of Vancouver Transportation Plan* (Vancouver, 1997), vii.

8  City of Vancouver, *Transportation Plan Progress Report,* May 2006, https://council.vancouver.ca/20060530/documents/rr1a.pdf.

9  City of Vancouver, "A Plan for the City of Vancouver British Columbia," 1928, https://archive.org/details/vancplanincgen00vanc.

10  City of Vancouver, "Transportation 2040: Moving Forward," 2012, https://vancouver.ca/files/cov/transportation-2040-plan.pdf.

11  South Coast British Columbia Transportation Authority (TransLink), "Moving the Economy: A Regional Goods Movement Strategy for Metro Vancouver," 2017, https://www.translink.ca/Plans-and-Projects/Roads-Bridges-and-Goods-Movement-Projects/Goods-Movement-Initiatives.aspx.

## CHAPTER 6: DIVERSITY

1  City of Vancouver, "Central Area Plan: Goals and Land Use Policy," 1991, https://vancouver.ca/files/cov/central-area-plan-goals-and-land-use-policy-1991.pdf.

2  City of Vancouver Planning Department, *Housing Families at High Densities: A Resource Document Outlining Needs, Principles and Recommendations for Designing Medium and High Density Housing for Families with Young Children* (Vancouver: Planning Department), https://www.researchgate.net/publication/284698660_Housing_Families_at_High_Density/download.

3  City of Vancouver, "High-Density Housing for Families with Children Guidelines," 1992, https://guidelines.vancouver.ca/H004.pdf.

4  City of Vancouver, "Metro Core Jobs and Economy Land Use Plan: Issues and Directions," 2007, https://vancouver.ca/docs/planning/metro-core-jobs-and-economy-study.pdf.

5  City of Vancouver, *West End Community Plan,* 2013, https://vancouver.ca/files/cov/west-end-community-plan.pdf; City of Vancouver, "Rezoning Policy for the West End," 2013, https://vancouver.ca/files/cov/west-end-community-plan-rezoning-policy-2013-nov.pdf; City of Vancouver, "Appendix J: West End RM Design Guidelines for Infill Housing," 2013, https://vancouver.ca/files/cov/west-end-community-plan-design-guidelines-2013-nov.pdf.

6  See City of Vancouver, Safe Injection Site and Needle Exchange, https://vancouver.ca/people-programs/safe-injection-site-and-needle-exchange.aspx.

## CHAPTER 7: URBAN DESIGN

1  Patrick Condon, *Seven Rules for Sustainable Communities: Design Strategies for the Post-Carbon World* (Washington, DC: Island Press, 2010).

2  See Pamela Knight's translation of Le Corbusier, *The Radiant City: Elements of a Doctrine of Urbanism to Be Used as a Basis of Our Machine-Age Civilization* (New York: Orion Press, 1967). Le Corbusier, reacting to the tight pattern of European cities, which he felt was unhealthy, proposed that housing be set

within large green spaces well separated from one another. He replotted Paris to illustrate what this might look like, which today, most urbanists see as wiping out the joys of urban life.

3 An urban design movement started in the 1980s, New Urbanism was propagated by an American organization called the Congress for the New Urbanism, founded by Andrés Duany, Elizabeth Plater-Zyberk, Peter Calthorpe, Daniel Solomon, Stefanos Polyzoides, Elizabeth Moule, and others in 1993. New Urbanism advocates bringing back into modern cities the humane and interesting qualities of traditional cities, such as a range of housing and job types, transit, vital shopping streets, complete walkable neighbourhoods of pedestrian scale, beautiful and identifiable places, and evocative architectural expression. Proponents call their movement a revival of the lost art of placemaking to create cities the way they have been built for centuries around the world.

4 Gordon Cullen, *The Concise Townscape* (London: Van Nostrand Reinhold, 1961); Christopher Alexander, Sara Ishikawa, and Murray Silverstein, *A Pattern Language: Towns, Building, Construction* (Oxford: Oxford University Press, 1977); Kevin Lynch, *The Image of the City* (Cambridge, MA: MIT Press, 1960); Ian McHarg, *Design with Nature* (New York: Doubleday, 1969).

5 William H. Whyte, *The Social Life of Small Urban Spaces* (New York: Project for Public Spaces, 2001, originally published 1980).

6 Jane Jacobs, *The Death and Life of Great American Cities* (New York: Random House, 1961).

7 City of Vancouver, "A Plan for the City of Vancouver British Columbia," 1928, https://archive.org/details/vancplaninc gen00vanc.

8 City of Vancouver, "CityPlan: Directions for Vancouver," 1995, http://former. vancouver.ca/commsvcs/planning/ cityplan/dfvf.htm.

9 Ronald Mace founded the Center for Universal Design at the University of North Carolina, in Raleigh.

10 City of Vancouver, "Accessible Street Design," n.d., 3, https://vancouver.ca/ files/cov/AccessibleStreetDesign.pdf.

11 City of Vancouver, "Urban Design Principles Derived from Council Policy," 1994.

12 Jacobs, *The Death and Life,* viii.

## CHAPTER 8: ENVIRONMENTAL RESPONSIBILITY

1 City of Vancouver, "Clouds of Change," 1990, http://a100.gov.bc.ca/pub/eirs/ finishDownloadDocument.do?sub documentId=3851.

2 United Nations Commission on Environment and Development, *Our Common Future* (Oxford: Oxford University Press, 1987). This work is commonly called the Brundtland Report in acknowledgment of the Norwegian political leader, Gro Harlem Brundtland, who chaired the group that produced it.

3 Mathis Wackernagel, "Ecological Footprint and Appropriated Carrying Capacity: A Tool for Planning toward Sustainability" (PhD diss., University of British Columbia, School of Community and Regional Planning, 1994).

4 Mathis Wackernagel and William Rees, *Our Ecological Footprint: Reducing Human Impact on the Earth* (Gabriola Island, BC: New Society, 1996).

5 City of Vancouver, "Southeast False Creek Policy Statement," 1999, https:// vancouver.ca/docs/sefc/policy-statement -1999.pdf.

6 The blue box recycling system is a waste management program used by Canadian municipalities to collect source-separated

household refuse. First implemented in Ontario during the 1980s, it is now used in one form or another in hundreds of cities around the world.

7 City of Vancouver, "Greenest City: 2020 Action Plan," 2012, https://vancouver.ca/files/cov/Greenest-city-action-plan.pdf.

## CHAPTER 9: PUBLIC AND PRIVATE COLLABORATION

1 City of Vancouver, *Eight Years After* (Vancouver: City of Vancouver, n.d.). This is now out of print.

2 City of Vancouver, "CityPlan: Directions for Vancouver," 1995, http://former.vancouver.ca/commsvcs/planning/cityplan/dfvf.htm.

3 City of Vancouver, *Financing Growth: Paying for City Facilities to Serve a Growing Population: The Role of City-Wide Charges on New Development* (Vancouver: City of Vancouver, 2004).

## CHAPTER 10: NEW ITERATIONS AND LESSONS LEARNED

1 City of Vancouver, "Greenest City: 2020 Action Plan," 2012, https://vancouver.ca/files/cov/Greenest-city-action-plan.pdf; City of Vancouver, "Greenest City: 2020 Action Plan: Part Two: 2015–2020," 2015, https://vancouver.ca/files/cov/greenest-city-2020-action-plan-2015-2020.pdf; City of Vancouver, "Renewable City Strategy: 2015–2050," 2015, https://vancouver.ca/files/cov/renewable-city-strategy-booklet-2015.pdf.

# ILLUSTRATION CREDITS

All the photographs in this book are by Larry Beasley except as acknowledged below.

**PROLOGUE**

FIGURE P.1   Photograph courtesy of City of Vancouver Archives (LGN 700)

FIGURE P.2   Photograph courtesy of City of Vancouver Archives (CVA 28-07)

FIGURE P.3   Photograph courtesy of City of Vancouver Archives (M-11-22)

FIGURE P.4   Photograph courtesy of City of Vancouver Archives (CVA 1435-132)

**CHAPTER 1**

FIGURE 1.3   Photograph courtesy of Metro Vancouver

FIGURE 1.5   Map courtesy of CIVITAS Urban Design and Planning

FIGURE 1.6   Map courtesy of CIVITAS Urban Design and Planning

FIGURE 1.7   Map courtesy of CIVITAS Urban Design and Planning

FIGURE 1.8   Photograph courtesy of City of Vancouver

FIGURE 1.9   Photograph courtesy of City of Vancouver

FIGURE 1.17  Photograph courtesy of City of Vancouver

FIGURE 1.18  Photograph by and courtesy of William Logan

**CHAPTER 2**

FIGURE 2.4   Photograph by Waite Air Photos

**CHAPTER 3**

FIGURE 3.4   Photograph courtesy of City of Vancouver

**CHAPTER 5**

FIGURE 5.9    Map courtesy of CIVITAS Urban Design and Planning

**CHAPTER 7**

FIGURE 7.8    Photograph courtesy of City of Vancouver

**CHAPTER 9**

FIGURE 9.2    Photograph by and courtesy of Marina Dodis

FIGURE 9.3    Photograph by and courtesy of Marina Dodis

FIGURE 9.4    Photograph courtesy of City of Vancouver

FIGURE 9.5    Diagram courtesy of CIVITAS Urban Design and Planning, based upon an image made available by Ann McAfee

# INDEX

Note: "(i)" after a page number indicates an illustration; "(m)" indicates a map.

discretionary regulatory framework, 63, 332-37, 338, 341

diversity, 59-60, 179-233; consolidating principle of, 180-91; Downtown Eastside and, 230-33; land-use mix and, 191-93, 194(i); ongoing challenges of, 221-33; social mix and, 195-223. *See also entry below*

diversity, through social mix, 195-223; early adopters of/city responses to, 195-200; ethnicity as missing component of, 221-23; families and, 211-21; income and, 200-11

Dobell, Ken, 49, 231

Dobrovolny, Jerry, 153

dogs, 139, 140(i), 266(i), 267, 391, 392(i), 393

domestication/domesticity, 374; children's presence and, 214-15(i), 215-18; as common theme of residents' feedback, 137-39, 140(i), 141; of tower-podium rowhouse streetscape, 257, 258(i), 259, 260(i), 276; urban gardens and, 317

Dorothy Lam Children's Centre, 124, 395, 396(i)

Dory, Seann, 324

Downs, Barry, 184

Downtown Eastside, 44, 45-46(m), 190, 372; Expo 86 and, 190-91, 199; single room occupancy units in, 109, 190, 197-99, 201; social/health problems of, 230-33, 379-80

Downtown Eastside Residents Association (DERA), 189-91, 199

Downtown South, 44, 46(m), 52, 58(i), 112, 114(i), 117, 306(i), 391; accessibility in, 271; building types in, 217(i), 234(i), 257, 259, 260(i); community services in/near, 129-30, 131(i), 205(i), 263; cultural revitalization of, 126, 127(i), 128, 130, 132; density in, 277(i), 293; family-friendly features of, 125(i), 130, 217(i); housing-workplace mix in, 119, 120(i); sidewalk detailing in, 259, 262(i), 298. *See also* Emery Barnes Park; False Creek North

Downtown Transportation Plan (2002), 145, 156

Droettboom, Ted, 50

Duany, Andrés, 299-300, 406n3. *See also* New Urbanism

Duvall, Elaine, 184

East Fraser Lands, 62(i), 298, 299

Edelson, Nathan, 109, 184, 195-96, 198, 288, 399

Egan, Maurice, 188

Elsie Roy Elementary School, 122(i), 134-35, 138; childcare centre attached to, 124, 395, 396(i); park playground of, 116(i); waiting list for, 135, 139

Emery Barnes Park: as central social hub, 117, 118(i), 125(i), 178(i), 311(i), 358(i); cultural attractions facing, 126, 127(i); funding of, 357-58

engineering department, 88, 270-71, 340, 341, 354; and traffic issues, 48, 91, 144, 148, 151-53, 164

English Bay, 18, 20, 22, 42, 43-46(m), 114, 117, 263

environmental responsibility/sustainability, 55-57, 63, 303-25; Brundtland Report on, 55-56, 304, 305, 315; early Vancouver leaders in, 56, 303; *Greenest City: 2020* plan for, 164, 302(i), 303, 320-24, 375; of megaprojects, 308-13; ongoing challenges of, 324-25; smart-growth formula for, 305-7; of Southeast False Creek, 62(i), 63, 313-20; transportation plan (2012) for, 59, 164-67, 303, 322

Erickson, Arthur, 42, 236, 259, 295(i)

Eriksen, Bruce, 189-90

ethnicity: diversity and, 220(i), 221-23; of older neighbourhoods, 29

Etrog, Sorel: *King and Queen* (sculpture), 269(i)

Evergreen Line (rapid transit), 159, 160(m)

Expo 86, 47, 184; building boom after, 14, 110, 156, 196, 198-200; and Downtown Eastside, 190-91, 199; False Creek North built on site of, 46, 51-52, 113; Vancouver Legacies Program and, 360-62

Expo Line (rapid transit), 109, 157, 159, 160(m)

"eyes on the street," 199, 242, 244, 258(i), 259, 282

urban design, influences on, 236-40; geography/climate, 236; narrow fire exit staircase, 237; new urbanist thinking, 238-39; privacy distance between tall buildings, 237-38; proximity of megaprojects to city core, 238; street grid/small-lot subdivision, 236-37

urban design, ongoing challenges of, 291-301; affordability, 295-96; architectural expression, 291-93; density, 298-99; lack of flexibility for possible reuse, 299-300; overuse of towers, 293-95; poor quality/disrepair of public elements, 296, 298

Urban Design Panel, 31, 340, 341, 342(i)

Urban Fare (grocery store), 119, 121, 128-29, 130(i), 398

urban renewal, 20-21, 28-29, 109-10

urbanism: benefits of, 86(i), 89-90; "experiential," 55; sustainable, 49-50, 55-57, 100-1, 278, 320-24. *See also* inner-city; suburban life; suburbs

**V**anCity Credit Union, 378

Vancouver, 10(i); development history of, 13-33; environmental leadership of, 320-24; Erickson on, 42; geography/maps of, 41-44, 43-46(m); as "lotus land," 65, 84; setting of, 8, 26, 41(i), 41-42, 64(i), 65, 84, 104(i), 236, 248, 250(i), 280, 366(i). *See also entries below*; mountains; water

Vancouver, development of (to mid-1980s), 13-33; and early utopian ideal, 15-16; in False Creek South, 27, 32-33, 48; as shaped by planners, 23-27; in TEAM era, 27-33, 47-48; in West End, 16-27, 48. *See also* Vancouverism, *and entries following*

Vancouver, geography/maps of, 41-44; downtown peninsula, 44, 46(m); inner-city, 44, 45(m); rapid transit, 159, 160(m); region, 42-44, 43(m)

Vancouver Agreement (2000), 231-32, 379

Vancouver Charter (BC statute), 70-71, 74-75, 198, 313

Vancouver city bureaucracy, 74-75; development management by, 332-44; from early years to TEAM era, 23, 25, 28, 88-89;

engineers in, 151-53; "facilitators" in, 363; initiatives of, 231-32, 320-21; process/regulations and, 95-100. *See also* city manager; engineering department; planning department

Vancouver City Council: and city planning, 38-39, 47-50, 71-72, 74-75, 97, 172, 174, 185, 216, 248-49, 251; as elected at large, 73-74; and environmental planning, 304; and False Creek North, 113, 119; and freeway proposal, 27-30, 31, 47, 87, 90, 143-45, 159, 166, 285; and public-private collaboration, 337-43, 350-51, 353-54, 360, 362; and school board, 134; and Southeast False Creek, 313-20; and urban design, 291-301, 340. *See also* Coalition of Progressive Electors (COPE); Non-Partisan Association (NPA); TEAM (The Electors' Action Movement); *specific councillors and mayors*

Vancouver International Airport (YVR), 43(m), 83; access to, 154, 157, 160(m), 171, 398(i), 399

Vancouver International Film Centre, 126, 127(i), 357

Vancouver International Sculpture Biennale, 267, 268-69(i), 269

Vancouver Legacies Program, 360-62

Vancouver Park Board, 23, 136, 184, 261, 264, 361

Vancouver Playhouse, 132

Vancouver Public Library, central branch of, 123, 130, 132, 278

Vancouver School Board, 134-35

Vancouver Trade and Convention Centre, 45(m), 46(m); green roof of, 273, 274(i)

Vancouver Transportation Plan (1997), 59, 145, 153-62, 155(i); "green" revision of (2012), 59, 164-67, 303, 322

Vancouverism, 8-9, 37-65; beginnings of, 13-33; conceptual framework for, 38-41; counter-intuitive perspectives of, 53-58, 87-103; design influences on, 15, 236-40; design traditions of, 240-53; essential challenges of, 50-52; of future, 369-87; generation involved in, 48-49; geography

postwar rezoning of, 25, 48, 110, 180, 237; rise and fall of freeway proposal for, 24, 27-30; role of planners in developing, 23-27; in TEAM era, 27-32; traffic calming in, 147-48, 149(i), 161(i), 263-64

West End Community Plan, 227

West Point Grey/Point Grey, 18, 30, 263, 269

Whyte, William H., Jr., 22; *The Social Life of Small Urban Spaces*, 240-41

Wollenberg, Jay, 249, 362

Wotherspoon, Pat, 184

Yaletown, 44, 46(m), 52, 112; subway station in, 398(i), 399

Youngberg, Ron, 88

Zoning, 17, 30, 63, 74-75; and bonused development funding, 189, 191-92, 225, 270, 357; discretionary regulatory framework for, 63, 332-37, 338, 341; in heritage districts, 286; inclusionary, 203, 378; and land-value lift, 329-32, 339, 357; in megaprojects, 353; and mixed-use development, 191-93, 203, 208, 222, 225, 228; and "monster houses," 222; in shopping areas, 111; Spaxman's initiatives in, 47-48, 147, 191-92, 225, 240-41, 280, 336, 348-49; of streetscapes, 240-41, 254-55. *See also* rezoning